SAGE
Premium Video

BOOST COMPREHENSION. BOLSTER ANALYSIS.

- SAGE Premium Video **EXCLUSIVELY CURATED FOR THIS TEXT**
- **BRIDGES BOOK CONTENT** with application & critical thinking
- Includes short, auto-graded quizzes that **DIRECTLY FEED TO YOUR LMS GRADEBOOK**
- Premium content is **ADA COMPLIANT WITH TRANSCRIPTS**
- Comprehensive media guide to help you **QUICKLY SELECT MEANINGFUL VIDEO** tied to your course objectives

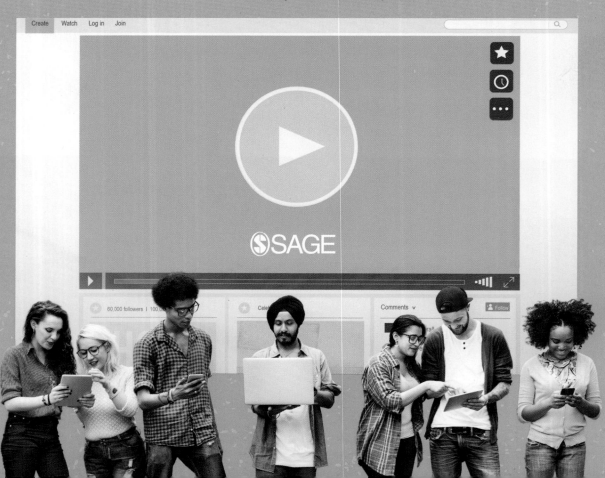

SAGE
Publishing:
Our Story

Founded in 1965 by 24-year-old entrepreneur Sara Miller McCune, SAGE continues its legacy of making research accessible and fostering **CREATIVITY** and **INNOVATION**. We believe in creating fresh, cutting-edge content to help you prepare your students to thrive in the modern communication world and be **TOMORROW'S LEADING INTERPERSONAL COMMUNICATORS**.

- By partnering with **TOP COMMUNICATION AUTHORS** with just the right balance of research, teaching, and industry experience, we bring you the most current and applied content.

- As a **STUDENT-FRIENDLY PUBLISHER**, we keep our prices affordable and provide multiple formats of our textbooks so your students can choose the option that works best for them.

- Being permanently **INDEPENDENT** means we are fiercely committed to publishing the highest-quality resources for you and your students.

interpersonal communication

Sara Miller McCune founded SAGE Publishing in 1965 to support the dissemination of usable knowledge and educate a global community. SAGE publishes more than 1000 journals and over 800 new books each year, spanning a wide range of subject areas. Our growing selection of library products includes archives, data, case studies and video. SAGE remains majority owned by our founder and after her lifetime will become owned by a charitable trust that secures the company's continued independence.

Los Angeles | London | New Delhi | Singapore | Washington DC | Melbourne

fourth
edition

interpersonal communication

Richard West
Emerson College

Lynn H. Turner
Marquette University

Los Angeles | London | New Delhi
Singapore | Washington DC | Melbourne

FOR INFORMATION:

SAGE Publications, Inc.
2455 Teller Road
Thousand Oaks, California 91320
E-mail: order@sagepub.com

SAGE Publications Ltd.
1 Oliver's Yard
55 City Road
London EC1Y 1SP
United Kingdom

SAGE Publications India Pvt. Ltd.
B 1/I 1 Mohan Cooperative Industrial Area
Mathura Road, New Delhi 110 044
India

SAGE Publications Asia-Pacific Pte. Ltd.
18 Cross Street #10-10/11/12
China Square Central
Singapore 048423

Printed in the United States of America

Library of Congress Cataloging-in-Publication Data

Names: West, Richard L., author. | Turner, Lynn H., author.

Title: Interpersonal communication / Richard West, Emerson College, Lynn H. Turner, Marquette University.

Description: Fourth edition. | Thousand Oaks : Sage, [2020] | Includes bibliographical references and index.

Identifiers: LCCN 2018040409 | ISBN 9781544336664 (pbk. : alk. paper)

Subjects: LCSH: Interpersonal communication.

Classification: LCC HM1166 .W466 2020 | DDC 302—dc23
LC record available at https://lccn.loc.gov/2018040409

Acquisitions Editor: Terri Accomazzo
Content Development Editor: Jennifer Jovin
Editorial Assistant: Sarah Wilson
Marketing Manager: Staci Wittek
Production Editor: Veronica Stapleton Hooper
Copy Editor: Diane DiMura
Typesetter: C&M Digitals (P) Ltd.
Proofreader: Barbara Coster
Indexer: Sheila Bodell
Cover Designer: Gail Buschman

This book is printed on acid-free paper.

SFI label applies to text stock

19 20 21 22 23 10 9 8 7 6 5 4 3 2 1

/// BRIEF CONTENTS

/// DETAILED CONTENTS

The theme of "preparation" continues to be our central foundation as we introduce this latest edition of *Interpersonal Communication*. As with the previous three editions, we approached the fourth revision with one overarching goal in mind: *to ensure that students are prepared to be effective communicators within and across their interpersonal relationships*. We have been quite pleased with the overwhelming positive responses we've received regarding previous editions, and this current iteration reflects the ideas, suggestions, examples, and cautions offered to us by students and faculty across the country. We are indebted to those who have made *Interpersonal Communication 4e* even more accessible, relevant, and practical!

Despite the fact that the first edition of *Interpersonal Communication* appeared more than a decade ago, many of the same motivations for writing the book remain. *We continue to view students as active agents* who are confronted with options and who must decide—sometimes in a split second—how to make their communication with others more meaningful. Yet, we do not subscribe to the common belief that students must *always* adapt to others in order to establish meaning in their interpersonal connections. Sometimes others are not particularly adept at communicating, and imitating an ineffectual communicator would be unwise. At other times, however, students may be at a loss for how to interact with a particular individual. Learning how to reduce destructive communication practices while cultivating constructive practices is critical to becoming more competent.

QUALITY INTERPERSONAL COMMUNICATION IS NEEDED—NOW, MORE THAN EVER!

Today is vastly different from even a few years ago and tomorrow will be different from a few years down the road. Throughout these times, our communication with others will require ongoing reflection, adaptation, and adjustments. Several reasons underscore our commitment to this premise:

- **The complexity of the U.S. demographic cannot be ignored.** Waves of immigrants, the increase in mixed-race families, and the surge of households with diverse family structures are just a few of the new threads comprising the fabric of a complex U.S. society. We cannot and should not ignore the wonderful diversity surrounding us. To this end, this demographic imperative should be at the forefront of our minds as we prepare to interact with others who are both similar to, and different from, us.

- **Technology demands interpersonal communication competence.** Years ago, face-to-face conversations were the norm; today, that perspective is limiting. Whether we're "Snapping" or "Facebooking," technology has ushered in different experiences and interpretations. For instance, what was once considered a "friend" is now influenced by technology. The way we present ourselves online and the images we choose to stream represent how we communicate our identities. These and a host of other issues have resonated deeply with many populations, affecting the communication taking place at home, at work, in social environments, among other contexts.

- **Our personal and professional relationships continue to evolve.** Think about a time in high school. Or, a first job. Or a past family event. There used to be a one-size-fits-all approach, for instance, to resolving conflict or to establishing intimacy with others. Popular books used to describe to people the "10 Easy Ways to Improving Relationships." Today, most of us can confidently say that there is rarely anything "easy" about improving relationships and that at times, even "one way" can be quite challenging. Whether we're working with someone or dating someone, yesterday's relationship advice must be reconfigured to accommodate our uniqueness in the 21st century. Cocreating meaning with others is anything but easy.

- **Our health may be dependent upon our interpersonal relationships.** Over 150 studies show that our relationships with others help us in our physical and psychological health. Quality, long-term relationships can aid in reducing our stress, enhancing our self-esteem, and aid in our satisfaction. Given the myriad of demands upon us, it's important to discover a path to finding quality relationships and to engage in interpersonal communication that is rewarding.

FIVE CENTRAL ASSUMPTIONS OF *INTERPERSONAL COMMUNICATION 4E*

We approach *Interpersonal Communication 4e* with several important pedagogical values. These assumptions guide our book's approach, as well as the information, examples, and concepts that we include in each chapter:

1. *We embrace a skills orientation based on a respectful application of research/ theory.* The information contained in this text is a result of a careful examination of the interpersonal communication research, theory, and scholarship. To make material readily available and understandable, we translated this information into practical ways. The result is a book that sustains a pragmatic and skill-centered approach, providing students with a consistent opportunity to apply their understanding.

2. *We remain committed to inclusion.* We can think of no alternative to providing students with stories, examples, and scholarship that reflect the diversity surrounding them. To this end, throughout *Interpersonal Communication 4e,* we are committed to presenting points of view and sharing examples that are rooted in a respect for the cultural backgrounds of communicators. Still, in order to avoid stereotyping, we temper our wording by noting that not all particular groups of people believe or behave in a certain way (e.g., "*most* Latinx" or "*many* GLBT individuals"). Out of further respect for others, we do not use the term "American" to describe those living in the United States.

3. *We recognize an expansive view of interpersonal communication.* As we alluded to earlier, our relationships with others are not always face to face. The digital world has ushered in new ways of thinking about our interpersonal communication and the innovative approaches to continuing our relationships. In each chapter, therefore, we discuss how individuals initiate, maintain, and terminate their relationships through both traditional and nontraditional means.

4. *We emphasize the timeliness of topics.* Whether we discuss the #MeToo movement, the 2016 Presidential election, the refugee crisis, celebrity relationships, or marriage equality, *Interpersonal Communication 4e* works to stay current. Topics that have received attention both in the United States and across the globe have been weaved throughout the book in order to make the material more timely and compelling.

5. *We encourage self-reflection.* We believe that students need to put their skills into action throughout their everyday lives. When students complete self-assessments, read impressions of their peers, or explore their own experiences, they begin to understand both their strengths and shortcomings as a communicator as they interact with others.

INTERPERSONAL COMMUNICATION 4E FEATURES MAKING CHOICES IN CHANGING TIMES

Regardless of the generation to which they belong, we believe that all students have choices as they relate to others. And, throughout *Interpersonal Communication 4e,* readers are introduced to various suggestions and options that will improve their relationships during times that are uncertain, complex, and often filled with frustration. This applied approach is essential for students who often grapple with how to communicate with different kinds of people with different types of backgrounds.

Retaining our widely recognized conversational writing style, we speak to the student with respect, civility, and inclusiveness. Our real-world examples are derived from teaching this course with a combined 60+ years! With the ongoing influence of media and new technology, moving students beyond the smartphone and laptop is essential if they are to have productive relationships with others. *Interpersonal Communication 4e* aims to put together a manageable set of skills that relate not only to the digital culture in which students thrive, but also the face-to-face culture which is necessary to flourish in a democracy.

We work to show students that, in many cases, they already possess the necessary skills to improve their communication partners. In most circumstances, however, *Interpersonal Communication 4e* will be especially important in discovering even more effective skills as they consider adapting to others.

Since the book's inception, we have been gratified to read student and instructor expressions of appreciation for an approach that is efficient, deliberative, and consequential. As with previous editions, *Interpersonal Communication 4e* adopts in-text learning resources that make the material come to life for students from various fields of experience. Specifically, four areas frame over a *dozen* features and pedagogies found in each chapter that reinforce the material:

I. **An Approachable Learner-Centered Style**
   In addition to an **inviting writing style**, five additional learning features include

   - *NEW IPC Voices*—Commentaries from students in interpersonal communication classes around the country regarding the chapter's focus
   - *Learning Outcomes*—Objectives that have been carefully matched with the chapters' contents and aid in helping students understand concepts and prepare for exams
   - *NEW Key Questions for Application*—End-of-chapter questions that tap both reflection and analysis
   - *Key Terms for Review/Glossary*—End-of-book collated list of terms that were introduced in each chapter
   - *NEW Wrap Up*—End-of-chapter summary of the key concepts

II. **A Bridge Between Theory and Skills**
   In addition to a widespread review of both pioneering and contemporary research, three additional theory-skill features include

   - *NEW Theory-Into-Practice* (TIP)—A theoretical snapshot that sums up a theoretical component accompanied by reflection questions
   - *Skill Set*—A composite of necessary skills that are easily retrievable for quick review
   - *REVISED Communication Assessment Test (CAT)*—End-of-chapter self-assessment quizzes that allow students to apply chapter concepts in both quantitative and qualitative ways

III. **A Clear Focus on Both Personal and Professional Applications**
   In addition to presenting examples from a variety of relational contexts and professional environments, three additional professional and personal reflection features include

   - *REVISED IPC Careers*—In-chapter summaries of professions that relate to a particular chapter topic. Reflection questions follow each career synopsis.
   - *NEW IPC Praxis*—In-chapter practical-anchored questions that relate to the content and that ask students to think about issues beyond the textbook
   - *REVISED IPC Around Us*—In-chapter reviews of how the media have portrayed or discussed a particular topic or theme found in the chapter. The Reflection questions that follow ask for an application of the information to students' lives.

IV. **An Appealing Visual Architecture**
   In addition to providing a design that will motivate students to read and review the content, two additional visual animations include

   - A comprehensive photo log in each chapter
   - Interactive tables and figures to help students understand difficult concepts

TAKING IT ONLINE

Instructors: SAGE coursepacks and SAGE edge online resources are included FREE with this text. For a brief demo, contact your sales representative at sagepub .com/findmyrep.

edge.sagepub.com/west

SAGE coursepacks for instructors makes it easy to import our quality content into your school's learning management system (LMS)*. Intuitive and simple to use, it allows you to

Say NO to . . .

- required access codes
- learning a new system

Say YES to . . .

- using only the content you want and need
- high-quality assessment and multimedia exercise

ACKNOWLEDGMENTS

We owe the previous successes of *Interpersonal Communication* to a host of people. As always, we first extend our appreciation to the thousands of students whom we've taught over the years. They have been—and continue to be—inspirational as we revised content and updated examples. Further, we are deeply indebted to the scores of students and instructors who have contacted us with various ideas and suggestions in order to make this edition even more compelling. Thank you all very much!!

We also owe our thanks to the SAGE team who took on this project with enthusiasm, confidence, and a boatload of support! There is not one publisher in the communication field that could come close to the level of engagement and encouragement that the SAGE team showed. Specifically, we are grateful to the leadership of Monica Eckman, executive publisher. We've had a long-standing affirming relationship with Monica, characterized by mutual respect and a lot of laughs! She is the epitome of charisma. In addition, we thank several new friends. First, we owe a great deal of thanks to Terri Accomazzo, acquisitions editor, for her unmatched leadership and other-centeredness. She truly served as our pedagogical docent as we moved this project to fruition. Jen Jovin, content development editor, was not only our ongoing cheerleader, but an astute colleague who clearly understood student needs. We also thank Sheryl Adams, executive development marketing manager, whose know-how provided us valuable information about how to make *Interpersonal Communication 4e* more accessible and competitive. We want to thank Sarah Wilson, editorial assistant, for her diligence in getting our manuscript ready for production and managing many of the behind-the-scenes tasks. We want to thank additional SAGE team members, including Naomi Kornhauser, photo researcher; Diane DiMura, copyeditor; Barbara Coster, proofreader; and Veronica Stapleton Hooper, production editor, for all of their work in turning the manuscript into an engaging book of which we remain proud and which we know readers will find compelling.

Ultimately, however, *Interpersonal Communication 4e* rests upon the careful reviews of scores of colleagues who took the time to offer their input. SAGE is particularly thankful to the following individuals who reviewed this edition:

Laurie Arliss, *Ithaca College*

Lisa Nelson Bamber, *Otero Junior College*

Leah E. Bryant, *DePaul University*

Anita P. Chirco, *Keuka College*

Colleen Warner Colaner, *University of Missouri*

Kathleen Czech, *San Diego State University*

L. Larry Edmonds, *Arizona State University*

Diane M. Ferrero-Paluzzi, *Iona College*

Tracy R. Frederick, *Southwestern College*

Erica J. Gannon, *Clayton State University*

Dr. Joan Gibbons-Anderson, *Riverside City College*

Daron M. McDaniel, *Panola College*

Shawn Queeney, *Bucks County Community College*

Erting Sa, *SUNY Albany*

Tony Strawn, *Henderson Community College*

Laramie D. Taylor, *UC Davis*

Ann Vogel, *University of Wisconsin-Oshkosh*

Bradley Wolfe, *Minnesota State University, Mankato*

Dr. Yanrong (Yvonne) Chang, *University of Texas–Rio Grande Valley*

Richard West is Professor in the Department of Communication Studies at Emerson College in Boston. At Emerson, he served as the department chair for several years, as the Acting Dean of the School of Liberal Arts, and as the project director of the Center for Innovation in Teaching and Learning. He is past president of the Eastern Communication Association, where he received the Past Officer's Award and was recognized as a "Distinguished Research Fellow" in the association. Rich is also the former director of NCA's Educational Policies Board. Both Illinois State University (B.A./M.A.) and Ohio University (Ph.D.) have recognized him as an Outstanding Alum in Communication Studies. He has written extensively in the area of classroom communication and has been recognized as a "Leading Scholar" in Classroom Communication by the Communication Institute for Online Scholarship. He is the co-editor of *The Handbook of Communication and Bullying* (Routledge, 2019).

Lynn H. Turner is Professor in Communication Studies at Marquette University, and former chair of the department. Lynn received her B.A. from University of Illinois, her M.A. from University of Iowa, and her Ph.D. from Northwestern University. At Marquette, she teaches interpersonal communication at both the undergraduate and graduate levels, among other courses. Additionally, she directs Marquette's interdisciplinary family studies minor. Her research areas of emphasis include interpersonal, gender, and family communication. She is the co-author or co-editor of over 10 books as well as many articles and book chapters. Her articles have appeared in several journals including *Management Communication Quarterly, Journal of Applied Communication Research, Women and Language,* and

Western Journal of Communication. Her books include *From the Margins to the Center: Contemporary Women and Political Communication* (co-authored with Patricia Sullivan; Praeger, 1996; recipient of the 1997 Best Book Award from the Organization for the Study of Communication, Language and Gender), *Gender in Applied Communication Contexts* (co-edited with Patrice Buzzanell and Helen Sterk; Sage, 2004). She has been honored by the OSCLG as one of the outstanding women in communication.

Together, Rich and Lynn have served as presidents of the National Communication Association. In addition, they have co-authored several communication books in multiple editions. The two are also co-editors of both *The SAGE Handbook of Family Communication* (2014) and *The Family Communication Sourcebook* (Sage, 2006), which won the National Communication Association's Outstanding Book Award from the Family Communication Division.

CHAPTER 1

FOUNDATIONS OF INTERPERSONAL COMMUNICATION

LEARNING OUTCOMES

After studying this chapter, you will be able to

1–1 Identify the evolution and foundation of the communication field

1–2 Define and describe the interpersonal communication process

1–3 Explain three prevailing models of human communication

1–4 Paraphrase the principles of interpersonal communication

1–5 Describe the myths related to interpersonal communication

1–6 Compare and contrast three ethical systems of communication

iStock.com/franckreporter

Master the content at
edge.sagepub.com/west

$SAGE edge™

Each day, billions of people around the globe wake up and begin one of the most basic and ancient of all human behavior: interpersonal communication. Think about it. Some people head off to school and greet people on the bus. Some leave their apartments for work and chat with colleagues in a carpool. Others drink coffee or tea in the morning at the kitchen table, needling their roommates about the overdue rent. Some Skype their friends to see if they got home safely from a previous night. And still others rush to their laptops to see if they received any replies to their online dating profiles. Although each of these situations clearly differs, they all underscore the pervasiveness of interpersonal communication in our personal and professional lives. Human communication is clearly the essence of what it means to be alive.

The following theories/models are discussed in this chapter:

Semiotics Theory

Social Information Processing Theory

Appropriate to this book and course, the word *communication* derives from two Latin words ("communis" and "communicare"), which mean "to share and to make common." Communication is a word that most people feel they understand. And, yet, when you ask a dozen people to define the term, you're going to hear a dozen different interpretations of the term! For our purposes, then, and in order for us to have a mutual foundation to draw upon, we define **communication** as the co-creation and interpretation of meaning. We are necessarily expansive in our view of the term because communication is quite layered. Throughout our conversations over the next several chapters, for example, we will examine scores of relationships, namely those that represent a cross-section of our lives, including teachers, painters, physicians, wait staff, child care providers, attorneys, college students, human resource directors, teenagers, among many others. In order to capture such a diverse list, we embrace a foundational definition that can be applied to multiple relationship types that experience a myriad of interpersonal experiences.

Despite our embrace of communication, not everyone is comfortable talking to others. In fact, some people are quite nervous about communicating. This fear or anxiety that people exhibit in the communication process is called **communication apprehension (CA)**. This sort of fear is a legitimate and a very personal experience that researchers believe negatively impacts communication effectiveness.[1] People with CA often go to great lengths to avoid certain situations because communicating can prompt embarrassment, shyness, frustration, and tension. Moreover, at times, some individuals find themselves fearful or anxious around people from different cultural groups. This **intercultural communication apprehension** not only impairs quality person-to-person conversations, but it can also affect whether or not we wish to communicate with someone *at all*.[2] We will delve much further into the intersection of culture and communication in Chapter 2 (Complete the *CAT: Interpersonal Communication Comfort Inventory* to assess your views of communicating with others).

Even if we don't experience or suffer from communication apprehension, we still may have difficulty getting our message across to others. We may feel unprepared to argue with a supervisor for a raise, to let our apartment manager know that the hot water is not hot enough, or to tell our partner "I love you." At times throughout the day, we may struggle with what to say, how to say something, or when to say something. We may also grapple with listening to certain messages because of their content or the manner in which they are presented. In some cases, for instance, someone's **microaggressions**, or the subtle insults, indignities, and denigrating messages delivered to marginalized communities, will often stump even the most articulate communicator. Such cultural challenges (several of which we detail in the next chapter) require skills that many people lack.

This book is an important beginning in addressing, understanding, and working through a great deal of the examples and episodes we just described. In each chapter and on each page, one goal remains clear: *to inspire you to work on improving your communication skills with others.* Enhancing the practices and skills related to interpersonal communication will assist you in becoming more effective in your relationships with a variety of people, including those with whom you are close (e.g., family members, friends) and those with whom you interact less frequently (e.g., contractors, baristas).

In addition to emphasizing a practical and skill-centered approach, throughout this book, you will see how interpersonal communication research and theory help us to understand everyday encounters. In the end, then, we believe that both practical and theoretical applications of interpersonal communication are intertwined to the extent that we cannot ignore the mutual influence of one upon the other. After all, theories inform practice, and practice grows out of theory.

Nonetheless, sustaining a scholarly thread is secondary to our commitment to a sensible framework of a grounded, hands-on conversation. We agree with other writers who maintain that the communication discipline can influence and enhance people's lives only by being practical.[3] So, we adhere to a pragmatic approach with this book in the hope that you will be able to use what you learn to make informed communication choices with others.

Our first task is to map out a general understanding of interpersonal communication. We begin this journey by providing a brief history of how interpersonal communication came about in the field of communication.

1–1 THE EVOLUTION AND FOUNDATION OF THE COMMUNICATION FIELD

Let's look at an overview of the communication discipline to give you a sense of its development. To understand where we are, we first must understand where we've been. In this section, we are necessarily limited. For an expansive view of the communication field, we encourage you to look at additional sources that provide a more comprehensive presentation.[4]

What we call *communication studies* today has its origins in ancient Greece and Rome, during the formation of what we now know as Western civilization. Being skilled at communication was expected of all Greek and Roman citizens. Citizens were asked to judge murder and adultery trials, travel as state emissaries, and defend their property against would-be land collectors. This sort of public communication was viewed primarily as a way to persuade other people, and writers such as Aristotle developed ways to improve a speaker's persuasive powers. In his book *Rhetoric*, Aristotle described a way of making speeches that encouraged speakers to incorporate logic, evidence, and emotions and to consider how the audience perceived the speaker's credibility and intelligence.

Aristotelian thinking dominated early approaches to communication for centuries. But as time went on, interest grew in providing speakers with practical ways to improve their communication skills in situations other than public persuasion. Being pragmatic was essential in order to reach the broadest possible audience. And, today, this pragmatism permeates much of communication studies.

 IPC Voice: Winnie

Let me be upfront here: I didn't think I needed this course. I took it as an elective and now I'm thinking it should be required! I *thought* I knew what interpersonal was all about, and after reading these chapters and doing the applications, it's like I know what I don't know. I've been in a lot of different relationships in my 20 years but never thought about all the different parts of that relationship. From listening to emotions, there is so much going on when I talk with my boyfriend . . . never thought I'd feel so dumb in a course like this!

A great deal of contemporary thinking about communication grows out of the National Communication Association (NCA). This organization is comprised of over 7,000 communication teachers, researchers, and practitioners who study dozens of different areas of communication. And, to be sure, one of the largest subfields of the communication discipline and of NCA is interpersonal communication. Still, interpersonal communication is not the only context in which communication exists. As you have experienced, we see the communication process in a number of environments. Although the following list is by no means exhaustive, it does show how the communication field has grown from a focus on speaking in front of an audience. In fact, you may notice that the communication department at your school is organized around some or all of these communication types. Many schools use these categories as an effective way to structure their curriculum and course offerings.

The following communication types build upon each other because they represent increasing numbers of people included in the process. In addition, keep in mind that although these communication categories differ from one another in some significant ways, they aren't mutually exclusive. With that in mind, let's take a closer look at the six types of communication:

- *Intrapersonal communication:* messages that are internal to communicators; communication with ourselves. For instance, intrapersonal communication takes place when you debate with yourself, mentally listing the pros and cons of a decision (e.g., choosing whether to lease or own a car) before taking action.

  Video 1.1

- *Interpersonal communication:* the strategic process of message transaction between people to create and sustain shared meaning. We will discuss this definition in more detail later in this chapter.

Video 1.2

- *Small group communication:* communication between and among members of a task group who meet for a common purpose or goal. Small group communication occurs in classrooms, the workplace, and in more social environments (e.g., sports teams or book clubs).

- *Organizational communication:* communication within and among large, extended environments with a defined hierarchy. Scheduling challenges argued between a supervisor and employee exemplify one theme in this context.

- *Mass communication:* communication to a large audience via some mediated channel, such as television, radio, the Internet (e-mail, social media, etc.), or newspapers. Using *Tinder* or *eHarmony* to find a romantic partner demonstrates the intersection of mass communication and interpersonal communication.

Video 1.3

- *Public communication:* communication in which one person presents a speech to a group of audience–listeners. Public communication is also often called public speaking. A presentation to your class, a nonprofit organization, or town council is a public speaking episode.

Each of these communication types is affected by two pervasive influences: culture and technology. As we move through the 21st century, acknowledging both of these is even more crucial to our understanding of interpersonal communication and human relationships. First, it's nearly impossible to ignore the role that culture plays as we communicate with others. Over the past several decades, scores of immigrants have arrived in the United States, bringing with them various customs, values, and practices. As a result, we now live in a country where intercultural contact is both necessary and commonplace, making effective

Technology continues both to facilitate and confound communication between and among people.

communication with others even more critical than it would be ordinarily. Despite the anxiety that some may have, we're sure to see even more cultural diversity as the years continue. This ever-increasing presence of intercultural relationships—including those between international exchange students and their host families, U.S. parents and their adopted children from other countries, working side-by-side in an office with people from different countries, among others—has prompted researchers to study the effects of these blended populations on communication effectiveness.[5] We delve much deeper into the topic of culture, community, and communication in Chapter 2.

IPC Praxis

Suppose you were asked to explain why so many people are anxious and nervous communicating with members of cultures different from their own. How would you go about discussing this issue? Does it make a difference who your conversational partner is? Why or why not?

A second influence upon the various communication types is technology. As you know from your own online experiences, for some, face-to-face (f2f) contact is no longer the default communication approach. Years ago, efforts at interpersonal communication were limited to sending letters or talking with someone personally. But today, relationships are routinely initiated, cultivated, and even terminated via electronic technology, and people derive various perceptions of others through their online interactions.[6] This phenomenon has stimulated research on technology, relationships, and interpersonal communication.[7] Technology not only has influenced people's interpretation of interpersonal communication, but also the digitalized relationship has become the norm across a large number of generations. Further, our conversations have become abbreviated, such as when we look at our caller ID and answer the phone with "And when did you get home from vacation?" instead of "Hello?" We develop close relationships with others via Instagram, even though we have probably not met all of our "followers." And, the notion of what it means to be a "friend" on Facebook has motivated social scientists to wonder about what qualities Facebookers use to define friendships. Throughout this book, we integrate technology's effect on the different topics related to interpersonal communication, providing you a chance to understand its influence in your relationships with others.

1–2 DEFINING INTERPERSONAL COMMUNICATION

Earlier, we defined communication, providing you a framework to consider as you review the topics in this book. However, because this text focuses on interpersonal communication, we begin our discussion by interpreting it for you. We define interpersonal communication as the strategic process of message transaction between two people to create and sustain shared meaning. Four critical components are embedded in this definition: strategy, process, message exchange, and shared meaning. Let's look at each in turn.

When we state that interpersonal communication is a strategy, we mean to suggest that you are deliberative in your interpersonal efforts. That is, we don't wish to have intimate communication with everyone with whom we interact; we are selective. In fact, it would be both exhausting and inappropriate to do so. Therefore, we retain an internal interpersonal barometer, exchanging personal messages with those whom we feel we need or want to communicate.

Stating that interpersonal communication is a **process** means that it is an ongoing, unending, vibrant activity that is always changing. When we enter into an interpersonal communication exchange, we are entering into an event with moments that continue to evolve. For example, consider the moments when you first meet and begin communicating with classmates during a small group activity in class. Chances are that for the first few minutes, everyone in the group feels a little awkward and uncertain. Yet, after you all introduce yourselves to one another, it's highly likely that you all feel more comfortable. This shift from feeling uncertain to feeling comfortable is the ongoing interpersonal communication process in action.

The notion of process also suggests that it is not only individuals who change, but also the cultures in which they live. For instance, today's U.S. society is very different than it was, say, in the 1960s. While there have been several important social movements taking place over the past several years (e.g., #MeToo, #BlackLivesMatter, #neveragain), most who lived in the 1960s feel that the climate was quite different back then. In one Reddit survey,[8] for example, respondents identified several differences that demonstrate the 1960s as a time of extreme tumult and clearly defined lines of authority-related demarcation. Among the conclusions noted by Redditors were the following:

- There was an open encouragement of violence against protesters.
- Racism was practiced openly and without much consequence.
- Social class was much deeper and more troubling.
- The Vietnam War ushered in serious divergent points of view on war.
- There was little "peace and prosperity" as there is today.
- Television only had three channels to report events.
- Men clearly were the decision makers—both in the family and in the workplace.

So, process is more than one short period in a conversation. Process can be expanded to include the entire cultural era as well.

IPC Praxis

Construct a brief survey that asks peers and classmates about their impressions of how they view their native country now and how they project it to be 20 years from now. Include at least two questions that ask about the good and the not-so-good changes that have occurred.

The third element of our definition of interpersonal communication highlights **message exchange**. In this regard, we mean the transaction of verbal and nonverbal *messages,* or information being sent simultaneously between people. Messages, both verbal and nonverbal, are the vehicles we use to interact with others. But messages are not enough to establish interpersonal communication. For example, consider an English-speaking communicator stating the message "I need to find the post office. Can you direct me there?" to a Spanish-speaking communicator. Although the message was stated clearly in English, no shared meaning results if the Spanish speaker is not bilingual.

Meaning is central to our definition of interpersonal communication because meaning is what people extract from a message. As we will learn in Chapter 4, words alone have no meaning; people attribute meaning to words. We (co)create the meaning of a message even as the message unfolds. Maybe it's our history with someone who ends up helping us interpret a message. Perhaps a message is unclear to us and we ask questions for clarity. Or maybe the message has personal meaning to us and no one else understands the personal expressions used. Meaning directly affects our relational life. As one team of interpersonal communication researchers state, "We suspect that 'good' and 'bad' relational experiences are sometimes a matter of personal definition and personal meaning, but always intertwined, sometimes seamlessly, in the broader human enterprise of making sense of experience."[9] In other words, when we achieve meaning, we are also achieving sense-making in our relationships with others.

When we say that people work toward creating and sustaining meaning, we are suggesting that there must be some shared meaning for interpersonal communication to take place. Because meaning is affected by culture in more ways than language differences, we have to be careful not to assume that our meaning will automatically be clear to others and result in shared meaning. For instance, note that in the United States, many people tend to ask others, "What do you do?" In the Netherlands, however, this overture is viewed as offensive since the Dutch feel that this question is rooted in classism. Or, consider the ubiquitous "TGIF" (Thank God It's Friday) in the United States. To most, this means the beginning of a weekend (of fun), and yet in Muslim countries, the first day of the week is Saturday, after Friday (the holy day). This translation, then, requires careful consideration if meaning is to be shared.

To underscore the importance of culture, we discuss various cultural groups and cultural identities throughout every chapter of this text. And we recognize that although there are many differences among various cultures, some similarities exist. In each chapter, we strive to present conclusions about cultural communities that reflect consistencies in research and work to honor the integrity of the various populations.

1–3 THREE MODELS OF HUMAN COMMUNICATION

To further comprehend the interpersonal communication process and to provide more information about the evolution of the communication field, we draw upon what theorists call models of communication. **Communication models** are visual, simplified representations of complex relationships in the communication process. They help us to see how the communication field has evolved over the years and provide a foundation you can return to throughout the book as you unpack the issues and themes we introduce. The three prevailing models we discuss will give you insight into how we frame our definition of interpersonal communication. We close this section with a projection of how technology influences model development. Let's start with the oldest model so you can discern the development of the interpersonal communication process.

Mechanistic Thinking and the Action (Linear) Model

More than 60 years ago, Claude E. Shannon, a Bell Telephone scientist, and Warren Weaver, a Sloan Cancer Research Foundation consultant, set out to understand radio and telephone technology by looking at how information passed through various channels.[10] They viewed information transmission as a linear process, and their research resulted in the creation of the action, or **Linear Model of Communication.**

The linear approach frames communication as a one-way process that transmits a message to a destination. Think about when you were a child. You may have played "the telephone game," which included punching a tiny hole in the bottoms of two plastic cups, and inserting kite string or thread through each hole. Using the cups to "talk into" and to "listen with" illustrates the one-way communication we're discussing with the Linear Model. You talk and someone hears you; that's the essence of the Linear Model. Many writers have succinctly presented the model with five questions:

Who?

Says what?

In what channel?

To whom?

With what effect?

Several components comprise the Linear Model of Communication (see Figure 1.1). The **sender** is the source of the message, which may be spoken, written, or unspoken. (If American Sign Language is your primary form of interpersonal communication, your messages will necessarily be both linguistic and nonverbal.) The sender passes the message to the receiver, the intended target of the message. The **receiver**, in turn, assigns meaning to the message. All of this communication takes place in a **channel**, which is a pathway to communication. Typically, channels represent our senses (visual/sight, tactile/touch, olfactory/ smell, and auditory/hearing). For instance, you use the tactile channel to hug a parent, and you use the auditory channel to listen to your roommate complain about a midterm exam.

Figure 1.1 /// Linear Model of Communication

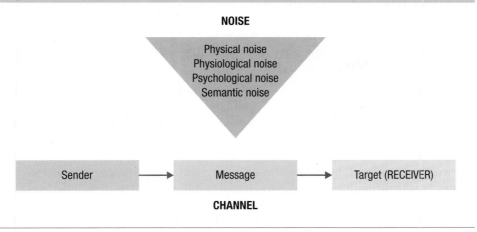

NOISE

Physical noise
Physiological noise
Psychological noise
Semantic noise

Sender → Message → Target (RECEIVER)

CHANNEL

In the Linear Model, communication also involves **noise**, which is anything that interferes with the message. Four types of noise can interrupt a message:

- **Physical noise** (also called *external noise*) involves any stimuli outside of the sender or receiver that makes the message difficult to hear. For example, it would be difficult to hear a message from your professor if someone were mowing the lawn outside the classroom. Physical noise can also take the form of something a person is wearing, such as "loud jewelry" or mirrored sunglasses, which may cause a receiver to focus on the object rather than the message.

- **Physiological noise** refers to biological influences on message reception. Examples of this type of noise are articulation problems, hearing or visual impairments, and the physical well-being of a speaker (i.e., whether they are able to deliver a message).

- **Psychological noise** (or *internal noise*) refers to a communicator's biases, prejudices, and feelings toward a person or a message. For example, you may have heard another person use derogatory language about homeless people while you reflect upon your volunteer time in a homeless shelter.

- **Semantic noise** occurs when senders and receivers apply different meanings to the same message. Semantic noise may take the form of jargon, technical language, and other words and phrases that are familiar to the sender but that are not understood by the receiver. Think about the word *dope.* It has evolved from referring to a user of drugs to something that is viewed as cool, awesome, or great (recall how the communication process can change over time).

The linear view has been studied with context and surrounding in mind. **Context** is an environment and can be physical, cultural, psychological, or historical. The **physical context** is the tangible environment in which communication occurs.

Examples of physical contexts include the hotel van on the way to the airport, the dinner table, the apartment, or the church hall. Even environmental conditions such as temperature, lighting, and space are also part of the physical context. For example, consider trying to listen to your best friend talk about her financial problems in a crowded coffee shop. The environment does not seem conducive to receiving her message clearly and accurately.

The **cultural context** refers to the rules, roles, norms, and patterns of communication that are unique to particular cultures. Culture continually influences the communication taking place between and among people, requiring us to look at the backgrounds of communicators. Consider the millions of refugees we've witnessed, over the years, who have fled their homelands, only to be confronted in other cultures with hate, fear, violence, and hunger. Compounding these challenges are the difficulties assimilating into a culture where the newcomer language is not the language of the host culture.[11] We will note later in this book that language serves as a primary factor affecting the quality of interpersonal communication. Therefore, the cultural context in which new immigrants arrive is typically fraught with anxiety, despair, and frustration.

The **social-emotional context** indicates the nature of the relationship that affects a communication encounter. For example, are the communicators in a particular interaction friendly or unfriendly, supportive or unsupportive? Or do they fall somewhere in between? These factors help explain why, for instance, you might feel completely anxious in one employment interview but very comfortable in another. At times you and an interviewer may hit it off, while at other times you may feel intimidated or awkward. The social-emotional context helps explain the nature of the interaction taking place.

In the **historical context**, messages are understood in relationship to previously sent messages. Thus, when Oliver tells Willa that he missed her while they were separated over spring break, Willa hears that as a turning point in their relationship. Oliver has never said that before; in fact, he has often mentioned that he rarely misses anyone when he is apart from them. Therefore, his comment is influenced by their history together. If Oliver regularly told Willa that he missed her, she would interpret the message differently.

We will return to the notion of context often in this book. For now, keep in mind that context has a significant influence on our relationships with others. Furthermore, context involves people and their conversations and relationships. If we don't consider context in our interactions with others, we have no way to judge our interpersonal effectiveness.

Although the Linear Model was highly regarded when it was first conceptualized, it has been criticized because it presumes that communication has a definable beginning and ending.[12] In fact, Shannon and Weaver later emphasized this aspect of their model by claiming that people receive information in organized and discrete ways. Yet, we know that communication can be messy. We have all interrupted someone or had someone interrupt us, for instance. The Linear Model also presumes that listeners are passive and that communication occurs only when speaking. But we know that listeners often affect speakers and are not simply passive receivers of a speaker's message. With these criticisms in mind, researchers developed another way to represent the human communication process: the Interactional Model.

Feedback and the Interactional Model

To emphasize the two-way nature of communication between people, researchers conceptualized the **Interactional Model of Communication**.[13] This model shows that communication goes in two directions: from sender to receiver and from receiver to sender. This circular, or interactional, process suggests that communication is ongoing rather than linear. In the Interactional Model, an individual in a conversation can be both sender and receiver, but not both simultaneously (see Figure 1.2).

The interactional approach is characterized primarily by **feedback**, which can be defined as responses to people, their messages, or both. Feedback may be verbal (meaning found in words) or nonverbal (meaning found in smiles, crossed arms, etc.). Feedback may also be internal or external. **Internal feedback** occurs when you assess your own communication (e.g., by thinking, "I never should have said that"). **External feedback** is the feedback you receive from other people (e.g., "Why did you say that? That was dumb!").

People can provide external feedback that results in important internal feedback for themselves. For example, let's say that Alexandra gives Dan the following advice about dealing with the death of his partner: "You feel sad as long as you need to. Don't worry about what other people think. I'm sick of people telling others how they should feel about something. These are *your* feelings." While providing Dan this external feedback, Alexandra may realize that her advice can also be applied to her own recent breakup. Although she may intend to send Dan

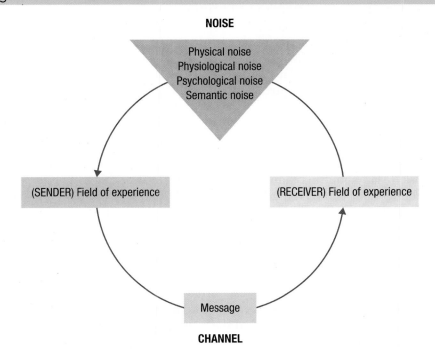

Figure 1.2 /// Interactional Model of Communication

NOISE

Physical noise
Physiological noise
Psychological noise
Semantic noise

(SENDER) Field of experience

(RECEIVER) Field of experience

Message

CHANNEL

a comforting message, she may also provide herself internal feedback as she deals with her relational circumstances.

Like the Linear Model, the Interactional Model has been criticized primarily for its view of senders and receivers—that is, one person sends a message to another person. Neither model takes into consideration what happens when nonverbal messages are sent at the same time as verbal messages. For example, when a father disciplines his child and finds the child either looking the other way or staring directly into his eyes, the father may "read" the meaning of the child's nonverbal communication as inattentive or disobedient. What happens if the child doesn't say anything during the reprimand? The father may still make some meaning out of the child's silence ("Don't just stand there with that blank stare!"). The interactional view acknowledges that human communication involves both speaking and listening, but it asserts that speaking and listening are separate events and thus does little to address the effect of nonverbal communication as the message is sent. This criticism led to the development of a third model of communication: the Transactional Model.

Shared Meaning and the Transactional Model

Whereas the Linear Model of Communication assumes that communication is an action that moves from sender to receiver, and the Interactional Model suggests that the presence of feedback makes communication an interaction between people, the **Transactional Model** incorporates a mix of many elements.[14] In this model, sending and receiving messages are simultaneous and mutual. In fact, the word *transactional* indicates that the communication process is cooperative. In other words, communicators (senders and receivers) are both responsible for the effect and effectiveness of communication. In a transactional encounter, people do not simply send meaning from one to the other and then back again; rather, they build shared meaning. Rev. Martin Luther King Jr.'s words best underscore the Transactional Model: "It really boils down to this: that all life is interrelated. We are all caught in an inescapable network of mutuality, tied into a single garment of destiny."

A unique feature of the Transactional Model is its recognition that messages build upon each other, underscoring an exchange of sorts. Furthermore, both verbal and nonverbal behaviors are necessarily part of the transactional process. For example, consider Alan's conversation with his coworker Hurit. During a break, Hurit asks Alan about his family in Los Angeles. He begins to tell her that his three siblings all live in Los Angeles and that he has no idea when they will be able to "escape the prison" there. When he mentions "prison," Hurit looks confused. Seeing Hurit's puzzled facial expression, Alan clarifies that he hated Los Angeles because it was so hot, people lived too close to each other, and he felt that he was being watched all the time. In sum, he felt like he was in a prison. This example shows how much both Alan and Hurit are actively involved in this communication interaction. Hurit's nonverbal response to Alan prompted him to clarify his original message. As this exchange shows, the nonverbal message works in conjunction with the verbal message, and the transactional process requires ongoing negotiation of meaning.

Figure 1.3 /// Transactional Model of Communication

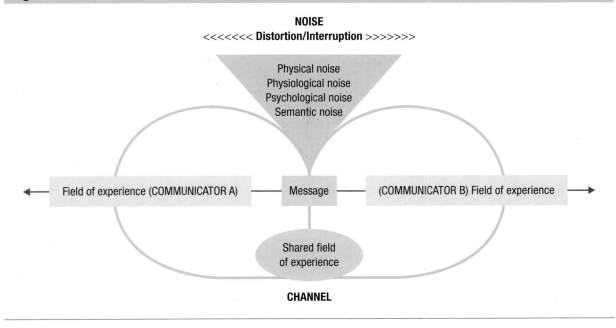

Note that the Transactional Model in Figure 1.3 is characterized by a common field of experience between communicator A and communicator B. The **field of experience** refers to a person's culture, past experiences, personal history, and heredity, and how these elements influence the communication process.

People's fields of experience overlap at times, meaning that people share things in common. Where two people's fields of experience overlap, they can communicate more effectively than if overlap was not present. And as they communicate, they create more overlap in their experiences. This process explains why initial encounters often consist of questions and answers between communicators, such as "Where are you from?" "What's your major?" "Do you ski?" The answers to these questions help establish the overlap in the communicators' experiences: "Oh, I was in Chicago over the holidays last year"; "Really, that's my major, too"; "Yeah, I don't ski, either."

Fields of experience may change over time. For instance, in class, Alicia and Marcy have little in common and have little overlap in their fields of experience. They just met this term, have never taken a course together before, and Alicia is 18 years older than Marcy. It would appear, then, that their fields of experience would be limited to being women enrolled in the same course together. However, consider the difference if we discover that both Alicia and Marcy are single parents, have difficulty finding quality child care, and have received academic scholarships. The overlap in their fields of experience would be significantly greater. In addition, as the two continue in the class together, they will develop new common experiences, which, in turn, will increase the overlap in their fields of experience. This increased overlap may affect their interactions with each other in the future.

Interpersonal communication scholars have embraced the transactional process in their research, believing that human communication "is always tied to what came before and always anticipates what may come later."[15] Many misunderstandings occur in relationships because people are either unaware of or don't attend to the transactional communication process.

In summary, early communication models showed that communication is linear and that senders and receivers have separate roles and functions. The interactional approach expanded that thinking and suggested less linearity and more involvement of feedback between communicators. The Transactional Model refined our understanding by noting the importance of a communicator's background, by demonstrating the simultaneous sending and receiving of messages, and by focusing on the communicators' mutual involvement in creating meaning.

Technology, Social Information Processing, and the _____ Model

Before we move on to the next discussion, let's keep in mind that our conceptualizations of communication models are continually evolving. New technologies, for instance, necessarily influence the communication process between communicators, as noted earlier in the chapter. To this end, the newest communication model that infuses technology has yet to be named.

Consider, for example, e-mailing a close relative asking to borrow money. Next, your relative decides to Facetime you on the phone to talk to you further about your request. After your conversation, you decide to text back and forth to make sure you both understand the final protocols related to the financial episode. You then both decide to meet face to face to talk about the situation or request. How does this infusion of technology affect the meaning? Is meaning improved because of multiple channels? Is meaning confounded because of the multiple channels?

The Transactional Model may soon become a scholarly footnote as technology boldly shapes how we view, and enact, the communication process. In fact, some research has already begun to disentangle the complexity of communication as it relates to the complexity of technology. For instance, theorists have begun to investigate the extent to which meeting someone online differs from a face-to-face meeting.[16] We call this **Social Information Processing (SIP) Theory**. This theory posits that information that is sent between communicators requires more time than traditional face-to-face (f2f). Because online communicators are motivated to develop favorable online impressions, we see a number of self-presentations that are carefully crafted on such platforms as Facebook, Google+, and Instagram. Rather than one impression as we have in a f2f encounter ("You can't make a second first impression"), SIP scholars contend that we accrue impressions from the information we review on line. And, they argue that online communicators generally think about what they post, how they post it, and for whom they are posting. According to SIP theorists, in f2f encounters, this preoccupation cannot be as thorough because we are inundated with so much stimuli surrounding us (e.g., people, noise, environmental conditions).

Let's think of this theory this way: Let's say you're using WhatsApp or WeChat and you're ready to text someone. Before sending the text, you generally reread the words and punctuation marks and may even insert emoticons. You may also "auto check spelling" in your message. Before texting, however, you decide to hold the text for any

Our fields of experience are instrumental in the cocreation of meaning.

number of reasons. In our face-to-face communication, however, most of us don't take the time to hold a message before delivering it, particularly if we're asked for a response or if we find ourselves emotionally charged. Consequently, we frequently stumble toward clarity and meaning, prompting all sorts of reactions (See the TIP below).

Theory-Into-Practice (TIP)

Social Information Processing

A primary assumption of Social Information Processing Theory is that interpersonal communication can move to higher levels of engagement between people because of how individuals manage their online images. Think about your own social media presence. What personal pieces of information have you presented that prompt others to draw conclusions about you? If you have more than one platform that you're using, is your personal information ("About Me") the same, slightly different, or completely different across platforms?

Communication scholars will likely continue to adjust and/or reconsider the Transactional Model as they take into account a number of important issues, namely technology, when they begin to rally around a new communication model. In the end, we need to recognize that the communication behaviors and roles described by the models are not absolute and can vary depending on the situation. With this foundation, let's now discuss the nature of interpersonal communication and describe what it is and what it is not.

The Interpersonal Communication Continuum

With these models in place, we need to address one additional area that will help you understand the interpersonal communication process. More than four decades ago, researchers proposed looking at communication along a

Figure 1.4 /// The Continuum of Interpersonal Communication

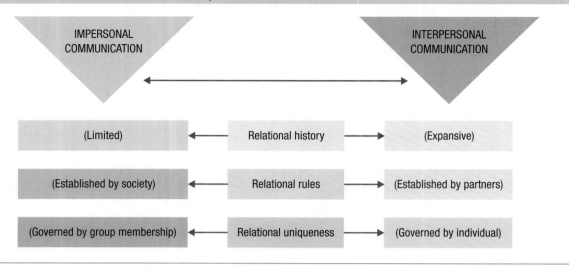

continuum.[17] It was a unique view at the time and remains significant today. Not all human communication is interpersonal (an issue we take up a bit later in this chapter). Our interactions with others can be placed on a continuum from impersonal to interpersonal (see Figure 1.4).

Think about the various conversations you have that could be considered impersonal or closer to the impersonal end of the continuum. You sit next to a person in the waiting room of your dentist and ask whether he watched *Fox News* the night before. You tell a woman hawking tickets to a sold-out basketball game that you're not interested. You tell the teenager sitting next to you at a wedding that you're a friend of the groom. Typically, these linear episodes remain on the impersonal end of the continuum because the conversations remain superficial. You do not acknowledge the people in these examples as unique individuals who are important in your life, despite the fact that they may be compelling in some ways.

Now, consider the many times you talk to people on a much deeper level. You share health-related confidences with a close friend with whom you have tea. You laugh with your grandfather about a treasured family story. You commiserate with a classmate who is disappointed about a grade. In these cases, your communication is not superficial. You share yourself and respond to the other person as a unique individual.

If you haven't already, one very real episode that you all (will) experience is the job interview. At first glance, you may be inclined to place this conversation on the impersonal end; indeed, many job interviews begin superficially, with questions related to your major, your hometown, or even your favorite hobby. Yet, most interviews dig much deeper, asking job candidates about their motivation for applying for a particular job, views on workplace ethics, and other matters that require a personal interpretation of the information. So, in a brief job interview, the interaction can evolve from impersonal to interpersonal in a matter of minutes.

These two ends of the continuum—impersonal and interpersonal—are the extremes. But, we believe that most of our communication encounters with others aren't so binary. Rather, most fall in between or along various points on the continuum. Your talks with a professor, coworker, or car mechanic may not be particularly emotionally fulfilling, but likely have a personal dimension to them. Your professor sometimes delicately asks what personal challenges might have caused a failing grade on an exam. A coworker may share family stories. And a car mechanic may ask if you have enough money for a new transmission. Each of these interactions entails some degree of closeness, but not a lot of emotional depth.

What will determine the extent to which an encounter is impersonal, interpersonal, or in between? Three issues are particularly important: relational history, relational rules, and relational uniqueness.

First, **relational history** pertains to the prior relationship experiences that two people share. For example, Rolanda and Maria have worked as servers in a restaurant for several years. Their relational history is apparent when you consider the amount of time they have spent together. This history may include working the same hours, sharing with each other their personal feelings about their boss, or having social times with each other's friends. Their relational history, then, spans both their professional and personal lives. This rich history enables their conversations to be interpersonal rather than impersonal.

Relational rules indicate what the people in a relationship expect and allow when they talk to each other. Relational rules, often unstated, differ from social rules in that the two relational partners negotiate the rules themselves as opposed to having them set by an outside source. It is true that others may influence the interpersonal rules (e.g., a supervisor's rules may have an impact on workplace relationships). Nonetheless, most relational rules are constructed by the relational partners, and at times, the two may have to consider external influences on those rules. Rules help relational partners negotiate how information is managed and stored.[18] For example, one relational rule that Rolanda and Maria may share is the belief that all restaurant gossip should remain private. Another one of their relational rules may communicate the need to be professional while on the job and to avoid tasteless jokes about one another or other coworkers.

A final influence on the relationship continuum is **relational uniqueness**, which pertains to how communicators frame their relationship and compare it to others. In other words, how is their relationship unique? In the relationship between Rolanda and Maria, they know and treat each other as unique individuals, not as generic coworkers. Thus, Rolanda asks Maria for help in making a financial decision because she knows that Maria has a good head for business. And Maria refrains from teasing Rolanda when she drops a tray because she knows Rolanda is sensitive about being clumsy. Their relational history and rules help develop their sense of relational uniqueness.

Again, much of our communication isn't purely impersonal or interpersonal; rather, it falls somewhere between the two ends of the continuum. Moreover, the relationship you have with someone doesn't always indicate whether your communication is personal or not. At times, personal communication occurs in our impersonal relationships. For example, you may consider telling your dry cleaner about your divorce or confiding to a fellow passenger that you are deathly afraid of flying. At other times, we may have impersonal communication in our close relationships. For instance, a couple with five children may be too exhausted to worry about being sensitive, loving, and compassionate with each other. Feeding the kids, bathing them, preparing their lunches, and getting them to the bus present enough challenges.

We have, thus far, given you a foundation to consider as you think about your communication with others. In order to differentiate this type of communication from other types, we now turn to a discussion of the principles of interpersonal communication in our lives.

IPC Praxis

Defend, criticize, and/or modify the following statement: "Technology is the most important issue facing relationships today." Use examples to explain your viewpoint.

IPC Careers

The "People-Centered" Professions

iStock.com/JohnnyGreig

Whether we want to call them jobs that require "social skills" or "people skills," they are in high demand. Each professional pursuit requires both knowledge and skill in interpersonal communication. Analyzing results from a jobs outlook resource, one study finds that social/interpersonal communication skills rank as the No. 1 job skill in highest demand. In data from the U.S. Department of Labor's Occupational Information Network (O*NET), research indicates some compelling information regarding professions that required skills in persuasion, mediation, negotiation, instruction/task management, and project coordination.[19] O*NET found that information from occupations that necessitate interpersonal communication skills provided a relatively high salary and high earnings growth potential. Managers round out the top jobs involving quality interpersonal communication skills. Marketing, construction, administrative services, and social/community services managers were among the highest paid and highest in demand. Yet, they require a high degree of interpersonal adeptness because these positions deal directly with individuals daily. Furthermore, O*NET concludes that while technical skills frequently become outdated, interpersonal communication skills will resonate for years to come.

Reflection: Can you think of any occupation that does not require adeptness at interpersonal communication? If so, which one(s)? Forecast what kinds of job opportunities you believe will place an emphasis on interpersonal communication skills.

1–4 THE PRINCIPLES OF INTERPERSONAL COMMUNICATION

To better understand interpersonal communication, let's explore some major principles that shape it. As you review each, keep in mind that we address these themes within a Westernized context because most of the research has adopted this view. Yet, as we will discuss in much more detail in the next chapter, we need to be culturally sensitive regarding being absolute in our conclusions. Nonetheless, we believe that interpersonal communication is unavoidable, symbolic, rule governed, learned, has both content and relationship levels, leads to self-actualization, and involves ethical choices. We now address each universal.

Interpersonal Communication Is Unavoidable

Interpersonal communication scholars repeatedly remind us that "one cannot *not* communicate."[20] Read that phrase again. Whether online or offline, this means that as hard as we try, we cannot prevent someone else from making meaning out of our behavior—it is inevitable and unavoidable. No matter what poker face we try to establish and no matter how we try to explain a text, we are still sending a message to others. Even our silence and avoidance of eye contact are communicative. It is this quality that makes interpersonal communication transactional. For instance, imagine that Kate and her wife, Chloe, are talking about the balance in their checking account. In this scenario, the two engage in a rather heated discussion because Kate has discovered that $300 cannot be accounted for in the balance.

Kate: "So, hon, I can't figure out where the 300 bucks went. I didn't take it. We didn't use it on bills. So, there's really only you left."

Chloe: (sits in silence, looking at her nails)

Kate: "Hmm. Well, let's see. You're saying nothing. You're not looking at me. You're even clearing your throat. I think we've figured out where that $300 went!"

In this brief conversation, Chloe has said nothing and yet Kate drew conclusions from her behavior. We return to the impact that nonverbal communication has on creating meaning in Chapter 5.

Interpersonal Communication Is Symbolic

The study of the use of symbols and their form and content is part of **Semiotics Theory**.[21] One important reason interpersonal communication occurs is because symbols are mutually agreed upon by the participants in the process. **Symbols** are arbitrary labels or representations for feelings, concepts, objects, or events. Words are symbols. For instance, the word *table* can represent a place to sit. Similarly, the word *hate* represents the idea of hate, which means strong negative feelings for someone or something.

The word *fear* suggests that symbols may be somewhat abstract, and with this abstraction, comes the potential for miscommunication. For instance, consider how hard it would be for someone who has never attended college to understand the following:

> *I have no idea what the prereqs are. I know that the midterm is pretty much objective. And the prof doesn't follow the syllabus too much. I wish that stuff was in the undergrad catalog. I'm sure I'd rather do an independent study than take that class.*

In the semiotic tradition, "communication is easiest when we share a common language, that words can mean different things to different people so miscommunication is a constant danger."[22] Ultimately, people are the interpreters of what constitutes meaning in language.

Interpersonal Communication Is Rule Governed

Consider the following examples of communication rules:

- As long as you live under my roof, you'll do what I say.
- Always tell the truth.
- Don't talk back.
- Always say "thank you" when someone gives you a present.
- Don't interrupt while someone is talking.

We're sure that you've probably heard at least one of these while growing up. We noted earlier that rules are important ingredients in our relationships. They help guide and structure our interpersonal communication. **Rules** essentially say that individuals in a relationship agree that there are appropriate ways to interact in their relationship. Like the rules in our childhood, most of the rules in our relationships today tell us what we can or can't do. We define a rule as "a followable prescription that indicates what behavior is obligated, preferred, or prohibited in certain contexts."[23] As this definition implies, we can choose whether or not we wish to follow a rule. Ultimately, we must decide whether the rule must be adhered to or can be ignored in our interpersonal exchanges.

To understand this principle, consider the Chandler family—a family of three who finds themselves homeless. The Chandlers live day to day in homeless shelters in a large city in the Southwest. The family members agree on a communication rule explicitly stating that they will not discuss their economic situation in public. This rule requires all family members to refrain from talking about what led to their homelessness. Each member of the family is obligated to keep this information private, an intrafamily secret of sorts. Whether or not people outside the Chandler family agree on the usefulness of such a rule is not important. Yet, one test of the rule's effectiveness is whether family members can refrain from discussing their circumstances with others. If the rule is not followed, what will the consequences be? Rules, therefore, imply choice, and participants in a relationship may choose to ignore a particular rule.

 IPC Praxis

Think of a time when you felt that your interpersonal communication failed. What surrounded this episode? What did you do, if anything, because of this transaction? How did it affect you or relationships with others?

Interpersonal Communication Is Learned

People obviously believe that interpersonal communication is a learned process. Otherwise, why would we be writing this book, and why would you be taking this course? Yet, as we mentioned at the beginning of this chapter, we often take for granted our ability to communicate interpersonally. Still, we all need to refine and cultivate our skills to communicate with a wide assortment of people. You must be able to make informed communication choices in changing times.

You're in this course to learn more about interpersonal communication. Yet, you've also been acquiring this information throughout your life. We learn how to communicate with one another from television, the Internet, our peer group, and our partners. Early in our lives, most of us learn from our family. Consider this dialogue between Amy Reid and her 9-year-old son, Luke, about his obsession with video games:

Luke: "So, better that I'm playing these games. You can see where I am. Why do I have to put it away?"

Amy: "Why? Because you're playing video games almost three hours a day. And, because you're not even 10. And because I'm your mom. And because these games teach you nothing important. And because I'm your mom."

Luke: "You already told me that you're my mom two times."

Amy: "And, I'll keep saying it."

Clearly, Amy is teaching her child a communication rule that she believes leads to interpersonal effectiveness. She tells her son that he should listen to adults. She is also reinforcing the fact that she is the authority and that as his mom, she's entitled to establish her own rules. Whether or not Luke likes it, he is learning that he cannot make his own decisions and he's learning that adults control his life.

Interpersonal Communication Has Both Content and Relational Meaning

Each message that you communicate to another contains information on two levels—content and relationship. The **content level** refers to the literal information contained in the message. The words you speak to another person and how you say those words constitute the content of the message. Content, then, includes both verbal and nonverbal components. A message also contains a **relationship level**, which can be defined as how you want the receiver of a message to interpret your message. The relational dimension of a message gives us some idea how the speaker and the listener feel about each other. Content and relationship levels work simultaneously in a message, and it is difficult to think about sending a message that doesn't, in some way, comment on the relationship between the sender

Nearly all of our conversations are guided by a code of ethics.

and receiver. In other words, we can't really separate the two. We always express an idea or thought (content), but that thought is always presented within a relational framework. Consider the following example:

> Father Felix is a Catholic priest who is the pastor of a large parish in the Rocky Mountains. Corrine Murphy is the parish administrative assistant. Both have been at the parish for more than 10 years and have been good friends throughout that time. One of the most stressful times in the church is during the Christmas season. The pastor is busy visiting homebound parishioners, while Corrine is busy overseeing the annual holiday pageant. With this stress comes a lot of shouting between the two. On one occasion, several parishioners hear Father Felix yell, "Corrine, you forgot to tell me about the Lopez family! When do they need me to visit? Where is your mind these days? Get it together!" Corrine shoots back, "I've got it under control. Just quit your nagging and focus on your work!" The parishioners listening to the two are taken aback by the way they yell at each other.

In this example, the parishioners who heard the conversation were simply attuned to the content dimension and failed to understand that the 10-year relationship between Father Felix and Corrine was unique to the two of them. Such direct interpersonal exchanges during stressful times were not out of the ordinary. Father Felix and Corrine frequently raised their voices to each other, and neither gave it a second thought. In a case like this, the content should be understood with the relationship in mind.

Interpersonal Communication Involves Ethical Choices

Although we will address this topic in more detail a bit later in the chapter, we wish to point out that ethics remains instrumental in your interpersonal communication. **Ethics** is the perceived rightness or wrongness of an action or behavior. Researchers have identified ethics as a type of moral decision-making, determined in large part by society.[24] In our conversations with those with whom we have a close relationship, nearly every encounter is guided by ethics. What you say, how you say it, the expectations you have of others' communication abilities, the conversational topic, among others, can all function prominently in our interpersonal communication with our friends, families, coworkers, and others. If we apply a technological lens, the ethical effects do not diminish. For instance, if you're on an electronic mailing list, what consequences exist for the communicator who chooses to use inflammatory language to insult you? Do you jump into the thread or do you choose to move on? Ethical choices confront all of us in a number of important and different ways.

Interpersonal Communication Can Lead to Self-Actualization

Learning about interpersonal communication can improve your life in that it can help you gain information about yourself, a process called **self-actualization**.

When we are self-actualized, we become the best person we can be. We are tapping our full potential in terms of our creativity, our spontaneity, and our talents. When we self-actualize, we try to cultivate our strengths and reduce our shortcomings. At times, others help us to self-actualize. For instance, in the movie *As Good As It Gets,* Melvin suffers from an obsessive-compulsive disorder. His love interest, Carol, has her own family problems but tries to help Melvin overcome some of his idiosyncrasies. In a poignant exchange that occurs during their first date, Carol becomes distressed and pleads, "Pay me a compliment, Melvin. I need one quick." Melvin responds by saying, "You make me want to be a better man." Although Melvin clearly frames the compliment from his vantage point, he still, nonetheless, manages to help Carol see her value through his eyes.

In this chapter so far, we have explored the definition of interpersonal communication in some detail and have described several principles associated with interpersonal communication. Now that you know what interpersonal communication is, let's focus on some of the misconceptions about interpersonal communication.

1–5 DISPELLING MYTHS ABOUT INTERPERSONAL COMMUNICATION

Dr. Phil's advice. The Internet. Old tales that never were proven true. Whatever the source, for one reason or another, people operate under several misconceptions about interpersonal communication. These five myths impede our understanding and enactment of effective interpersonal communication.

Interpersonal Communication Solves All Problems

We cannot stress enough that simply being skilled in interpersonal communication does not mean that you are prepared to work out all of your relational challenges and problems. Surely, as we noted earlier, communication will not work sometimes. You may communicate clearly about a problem but not necessarily be able to solve it. Also, keep in mind that communication involves both speaking and listening. In advising appointments, for instance, many students have revealed to us that they try to "talk out a problem" with their roommates. Although this may seem to be a great strategy, we hope that this talking is accompanied by listening. We are confident that you will leave this course with an understanding of how to communicate thoughtfully and skillfully with others in a variety of relationships. We also hope you realize that simply because you are talking does not mean that you will solve all of your relationship problems.

Interpersonal Communication Is Always a Good Thing

National best-selling self-help books and famous motivational gurus have made huge amounts of money promoting the idea that communication is the magic potion for all of life's ailments. Most often, communication is a good thing in our relationships with others. We wouldn't be writing this book if we didn't think that! Yet, there are times when communication results in less-than-satisfying relationship experiences. To this end, researchers have investigated a more provocative, yet useful, area of research in interpersonal communication called "the dark side."[25] We prefer to term this difficult communication as "destructive" communication.

Destructive interpersonal communication generally refers to negative communication exchanges between people. People can communicate in ways that are manipulative, deceitful, exploitive, homophobic, transphobic, racist, and emotionally abusive. In other words, we need to be aware that communication can be downright nasty at times and that interpersonal communication is not always satisfying and rewarding. Although most people approach interpersonal communication thoughtfully and with an open mind, others are less sincere. To contrast destructive communication, we also discuss constructive (or, the "bright side") interpersonal communication, which focuses on the altruistic, supportive, and affirming reasons that people communicate with others. Look for discussions of destructive and constructive interpersonal communication throughout the chapters of this book.

Interpersonal Communication Is Common Sense

Consider the following question: If interpersonal communication is just a matter of common sense, why do we have so many problems communicating with others? We need to abandon the notion that communication is simply intuitive. Interpersonal communication is not "common" by any means and it clearly doesn't make "sense" to adopt this belief.

It is true that we should be sure to use whatever common sense we have in our personal interactions, but this strategy will get us only so far. In some cases, a skilled interpersonal communicator may effectively rely on their common sense, but there are many situations where our common sense simply fails to "kick in" (think, for example, of those heated arguments, the euphoria we feel when we first start dating someone, and other highly emotional moments). In these and other cases, we need to make use of an extensive repertoire of skills to make informed choices in our relationships.

One problem with believing that interpersonal communication is merely common sense relates to the diversity of our population. As we discuss in Chapter 2, cultural variation continues to characterize U.S. society and places around the globe. Making the assumption that all people intuitively know how to communicate with everyone ignores the significant cultural differences in communication norms. Even males and females tend to look at the same event differently. To rid ourselves of the myth of common sense, take into account the complexity of culture and gender, for example.

Interpersonal Communication Is Always Face to Face

Although much of our discussion has centered on face-to-face encounters between people, we know that this is an outdated view. While it's true that f2f communication remains the primary way to cultivate interpersonal skills with another, we also have noted that technology can and often necessarily influences that process. Massive numbers of people utilize the Internet in their communication with others and people are finding life partners online. This mediated interpersonal communication requires us to expand our discussion of interpersonal communication beyond personal encounters. Discussing the intersection of technology and interpersonal communication is necessary to capture the complexity of our various relationships. Throughout this book, we have made a concerted effort to apply a technological lens to conclusions that may have their roots in face-to-face encounters. Failing to do so renders much of our information rather impractical.

More Interpersonal Communication Is Better

Everyone claims to be an expert in communication. In fact, a survey conducted by the National Communication Association notes that over 90% of people believe that their communication skills are "above average."[26] Is it any wonder, then, that when disagreements occur or when people don't know what to say, the "experts" advise to *communicate!*

And yet, more interpersonal communication is not always the best strategy. In fact, determining when to talk and when to remain quiet is fast becoming commonplace in several professions. For example, some doctors and medical teams at various hospitals are beginning to employ "the Pause," which is a 15- to 30-second period of silence to respect the death of a patient. This silence is intended to honor the life and efforts of both the human life and the effort of the team.[27] It's not the *amount* of interpersonal communication that matters. Rather, it's learning how to be judicious, two experiences that require ongoing attention throughout our lifetimes.

The choices we make in our relationships are rooted in our ability to determine what is right and wrong. This carries even more importance as we think about those relationships that can have lasting consequences for us, whether they relate to our closest friend or our worst adversary. One framework should always guide us as we make our difficult decision. Therefore, we close our discussion by examining a feature of the interpersonal communication process that is not easily taught and is often difficult to comprehend: ethics.

1–6 INTERPERSONAL COMMUNICATION ETHICS

Communication ethicists have concluded that "ethical issues may arise in human behavior whenever that behavior could have significant impact on other persons, when the behavior involves conscious choice of means and ends, and when the behavior can be judged by standards of right and wrong."[28] In other words, ethics is the cornerstone of interpersonal communication.

Earlier, we noted that interpersonal communication involves ethical choices. And, a primary goal of ethics is to (re)gain constraints on our own behavior. Ethical decisions involve value judgments, and not everyone will agree with those values. For instance, do you tell racist jokes in front of others and think that they are harmless ways to make people laugh? What sort of value judgment is part of the decision to tell or not to tell a joke? In interpersonal communication, acting ethically is critical. When we act ethically, we are respecting the dignity of another, embracing their individuality, working to avoid hurtful messages, and treating others in ways we wish to be treated. If we're not prepared to act in this way, one can conclude that we don't consider ethics important. Overall, being ethical means having respect

Table 1.1 /// Ethics on the Job: Views of the Most Ethical Occupations[29]

	Very High	High	Average	Low	Very Low
	%	%	%	%	%
Nurses	27	55	16	1	1
Military officers	22	49	24	2	1
Grade school teachers	20	46	27	4	1
Medical doctors	16	49	31	4	1
Pharmacists	13	49	32	5	1
Police officers	16	40	32	8	4
Day care providers	8	38	43	5	2
Judges	7	36	41	12	3
Clergy	11	31	41	10	3
Auto mechanics	5	27	53	12	2
Nursing home operators	5	21	48	18	4
Newspaper reporters	5	20	39	21	14
Bankers	4	21	54	16	5
Local officeholders	3	21	53	16	4
TV reporters	5	18	39	23	14
State officeholders	1	18	47	25	8
Lawyers	4	14	53	19	9
Business executives	2	14	54	20	8
Advertising practitioners	2	10	49	26	8
Members of Congress	2	9	29	36	24
Car salespeople	2	8	48	29	10
Lobbyists	2	6	31	33	25

Source: Brenan, M. *Gallup,* "Nurses Keep Healthy Lead as Most Honest, Ethical Profession." Adapted from https://news.gallup.com/poll/224639/nurses-keep-healthy-lead-honest-ethical-profession.aspx

Table 1.2 /// Ethical Systems of Interpersonal Communication

Ethical System	Responsibility	Action
Categorical imperative	To adhere to a moral absolute	Tell the truth
Golden mean	To achieve rationality and balance	Create harmony and balance for the community and the individual
Ethic of care	To establish connection	Establish caring relationships

for others, shouldering responsibility, acting thoughtfully with others, and being honest. The following section fleshes out these ethical behaviors more thoroughly.

Ethics is necessarily part of not only our personal relationships, but our work relationships as well. To get a sense of the interplay among ethics and various jobs, consider Table 1.1, which shows what the U.S. public views as being the most and least ethical occupations. See if you agree with how the country views ethical occupations and if your career choice is found among those listed. Try challenging others with their impressions of this list. What or who do you think influences someone's view of an ethical career?

We make value judgments in interpersonal communication in many ways. Researchers have discussed a number of different ethical systems of communication relevant to our interpersonal encounters. Here, we discuss three popular ones. In addition, because the field of communication has agreed on a code of ethical behavior, we have provided you ethical values as they relate to communicating with others (see Table 1.2). As we briefly overview each system, keep in mind that these systems attempt to let us know what it means to act morally.

IPC Praxis

Discuss what typically happens when someone is not an ethical communicator in various situations (e.g., at school, on the job). Explore situations and consequences and how an ethical approach might have rectified those ethical lapses.

Categorical Imperative

The first ethical system, the categorical imperative, is based on the work of philosopher Immanuel Kant.[30] Kant's **categorical imperative** refers to individuals following moral absolutes. This ethical system suggests that we should act as though we are an example to others. According to this system, the key question when making a moral decision is "What would happen if everyone did this?" Thus, you should not do something that you wouldn't feel is fine for everyone to do all the time. Kant also believed that the consequences of actions are not important; what matters is the ethical principle behind those actions.

IPC Around Us

To illustrate the relationship between communication ethics and corporate social responsibility, *Forbes* magazine[31] published the insights of Don Knauss, former CEO of Clorox, on the role of ethics in business–customer relationships. Knauss clearly embraces ethical business practices as he concludes: "We know that in order to build and maintain trust with our customers we have to first develop a company-wide reputation for integrity." To accomplish this, Knauss

Bloomberg/Contributor/Getty Images

claims that all employees must take part in an online training course on ethics as well as enroll in "refresher" courses that cover different ethical practices. Furthermore, Clorox employees, vendors, and subsidiaries must also abide by a company code of conduct that covers a variety of subjects—from human rights to labor and safety. Knauss contends that when a company models ethical behavior, business relationships improve, allowing for, of course, an improvement in the "bottom line."

Reflection: Comment on why you believe so many corporate cultures are both fearful and resistant to establishing a climate of ethical decision-making and trust. Explore the economic and demographic consequences when a company decides to dedicate itself to an ethical approach, as articulated by Clorox.

For example, suppose that Mark confides to Karla, a coworker, that he has the early stages of leukemia. Although the company has health benefits and although the type of leukemia is treatable, Karla, despite her belief that the supervisor should know so her coworker may benefit from further company assistance, decides to tell no one else. Elizabeth, the supervisor, asks Karla if she knows what's happening with Mark because he misses work and is always tired. The categorical imperative suggests that Karla tell her boss the truth, despite the fact that telling the truth may affect Mark's job, his future with the company, and his relationship with Karla. The categorical imperative requires us to tell the truth because Kant believed that enforcing the principle of truth-telling is more important than worrying about the short-term consequences of telling the truth.

The Golden Mean

The **golden mean**, a second ethical system, proposes that we should aim for harmony and balance in our lives.[32] This principle, articulated more than 2,500 years ago by Aristotle, suggests that a person's moral virtue stands between two vices, with the middle, or the mean, being the foundation for a rational society. The application

As a Western philosopher-teacher, Aristotle was extraordinarily influential in our ethical choices.

of the golden mean to communication is rooted in the ability to find a "middle ground" so that communicators are less inclined to honor the extremes of a discussion. Aristotle felt that thoughts or behaviors—when taken to excess—are neither productive nor especially valuable.

Let's say that Cora, Jackie, and Lester are three employees who work for a small social media company. During a break one afternoon, someone asks what kind of childhood each had. Cora goes into specific detail, talking about her abusive father: "He really let me have it, and it all started when I was five," she begins before launching into a long description. In contrast, Jackie only says, "My childhood was okay." Lester tells the group that his was a pretty rough childhood: "It was tough financially. We didn't have a lot of money. But we really all got along well." In this example, Cora was on one extreme, revealing too much information. Jackie was at the other extreme, revealing very little, if anything. Lester's decision to reveal a reasonable amount of information about his childhood was an ethical one; he practiced the golden mean by providing a sufficient amount of information but not too much. In other words, he presented a rational and balanced perspective. In this case, note that revealing too much and revealing too little may make another awkward or uncomfortable. Finding the "balance" in self-disclosure is especially difficult—a topic we discuss in greater detail in Chapter 8.

Ethic of Care

An **ethic of care**, a third ethical system, means being concerned with connection.[33] When this ethical system was first conceptualized, it centered on looking at women's ways of moral decision-making. It was assumed that because men have been the dominant voices in society, women's commitment toward connection has gone unnoticed. Initially, an ethic of care was a result of how women were raised. Yet, the ethical premise applies to men as well. Clearly, some men adopt the ethic and some women do not adopt the ethic. In contrast to the categorical imperative, for instance, the ethic of care is concerned with consequences of decisions. Let's exemplify this system with a cultural example.

Ben and Anthony are having a conversation about whether it's right to go behind a person's back and disclose that another guy is gay. Ben makes an argument that it's a shame that guys won't own up to being gay; they are who they are. If someone hides his sexuality, Ben believes that it's fine to "out" that person. Anthony, expressing an ethic of care, tells his friend that no one should reveal another person's sexual identity. That information should remain private unless an individual wishes to reveal it. Anthony explains that outing someone would have serious negative repercussions for the relationships of the person being outed and as a result, shouldn't be done. In this example, Anthony exemplifies a symbolic connection to those who don't want to discuss their sexual identity with others.

Understanding Ethics and Our Own Values

Ethics permeates interpersonal communication. We make ongoing ethical decisions in all of our interpersonal encounters, and these ethical choices are especially important in our very close relationships. Questions of ethics are all around us: Should someone's past sexual experiences be completely revealed to a partner? How do you treat an ex-friend or ex-partner in future encounters? Is it ever okay to lie to protect your friend? These kinds of questions challenge millions of interpersonal relationships.

When ethical issues confront us, we need to keep in mind society's various traditions as rooted in culture, religion, literature, philosophy, among others. Values have emerged from and are deeply enmeshed in these traditions and they often teach important lessons about life's challenging moments.

The three ethical systems can prompt you to develop strategies for making ethical decisions. However, making sense of the world and of our interpersonal relationships requires us to understand our own values. And, these values are apparent not only in our face-to-face conversations, but in our online conversations as well. Ethical behavior is particularly essential when we communicate with people whom we don't see or with whom we have no shared physical space. We return to this topic throughout the book as we discuss the various themes and skills related to interpersonal communication. A sense of ethics should guide us on a daily basis. Being aware of and sensitive to our decisions and their consequences will help us make the right choices.

/// CHAPTER WRAP-UP

We began our conversation about interpersonal communication by providing you an important foundation. In this opening chapter, we provided you a brief snapshot of the evolution of the communication field, including an overview of the various contexts in which communication occurs. We also included a definition of interpersonal communication and employed a model approach by identifying three prevailing models and a fourth that is yet to be determined. The chapter also included a discussion of why interpersonal communication matters, the primary principles related to interpersonal communication, and various myths related to the interpersonal communication process. We closed the chapter by identifying three ethical systems to consider when communicating with others.

Now, more than ever, and especially because of the integration of technology in our lives, we live in changing times. Communication skills that were once viewed as appropriate now have to be revisited. Adapting to the cultures and individuals around us is paramount in a country where race, ethnicity, gender, age, sexual identity, economic status, religion, and belief systems pervade contemporary conversations. As you learned earlier in this chapter, interacting effectively with others is a complex and unpredictable process, but one that is essential if we are to acquire understanding.

/// COMMUNICATION ASSESSMENT TEST (CAT): INTERPERSONAL COMMUNICATION COMFORT

Throughout this book, we make no assumptions about the extent to which you're comfortable communicating with another person. In fact, people can vary tremendously in their interpersonal communication comfort levels, depending upon a number of issues (e.g., field of experience, apprehension).

Complete the following 10 statements honestly and without self-judgment. Use more than one or two words to complete the thought. Be prepared to return to these questions and responses as you move through the book to assess the extent to which your comfort level has changed.

1. When someone I've never met starts to communicate with me, I _____.

2. When a romantic partner asks me to borrow money, I _____.

3. Emotionally charged interpersonal situations make me _____.

4. If I'm confused by the words of another in a conversation, I _____.

5. If I'm introduced to topics that are touchy or controversial in a conversation, I _____.

6. If I'm having a dialogue with someone who is not clear or often confusing, I find myself _____.

7. If someone confronts me because they disagree with my views, I will _____.

8. People from cultural backgrounds other than my own make me _____.

9. If I had a choice to communicate with a close friend either through social media or face-to-face, I choose _____.

10. Among the many personal challenges I have communicating with another person are _____.

/// KEY QUESTIONS FOR APPLICATION

1. **CQ/CultureQuest:** Explore the following claim: "Not all interpersonal conversations are influenced by culture." Do you agree or disagree? Defend your view with examples.

2. **TQ/TechQuest:** Explore the following claim: "Social media platforms such as Twitter and Tumblr are often viewed as a more desirable way to communicate than face-to-face." Do you agree or disagree? Defend your view with examples.

3. Let's say you and Aristotle were having lunch together. What sort of conversation would you both have? What topics would you introduce that would be relevant to the evolution of the communication field?

4. We've reiterated that interpersonal communication is a valuable skill in your personal and professional lives. But, we've also noted that not all communication is necessarily a good thing. Identify and explain those times when being silent is more desirable than being talkative.

5. If you were talking to a group of tourists—all of whom are from countries outside of the United States—what three assumptions about interpersonal communication in the United States would you propose? Be sure to clarify each assumption with an example.

6. Being ethical in your communication with others is viewed as both necessary and critical in order to co-create meaning between you and another. Yet, being ethical may be one of those behaviors that is more difficult in practice. Identify at least three ethical challenges that communicators face when having conversations with a friend, family member, coworker, or roommate.

Access practice quizzes, eFlashcards, video, and multimedia at **edge.sagepub.com/west**.

Visit **edge.sagepub.com/west** to help you accomplish your coursework goals in an easy-to-use learning environment.

CHAPTER 2

COMMUNICATION, CULTURE, AND IDENTITY

LEARNING OUTCOMES

After studying this chapter, you will be able to

2–1 Recognize and understand the interpretation and complexity of culture

2–2 Understand the importance of cultural diversity in the United States and beyond

2–3 Identify reasons for the importance of intercultural communication

2–4 Describe the dimensions of cultural variability

2–5 Explain the obstacles to achieving intercultural effectiveness

2–6 Employ strategies to improve intercultural communication

Jeff Greenberg/Universal Images Group/Getty Images

Master the content at
edge.sagepub.com/west

⑤SAGE edge™

Most people communicate with the mistaken belief that others will understand them. For instance, some people use personal expressions or inside jokes when, in reality, these words, phrases, and stories are not universally understood. And, especially in the United States, most people don't think twice about using the English language to make their point. This is rather provocative, given that many people who live in the United States speak different languages and are members of various cultural groups where English is not the primary vehicle for communication.

The following theories/models are discussed in this chapter:

Context Orientation Theory

Cultural Variability Theory

In addition, most English speakers employ their own nonspeaking codes without thinking about how nonverbal communication differs across cultures. For example, looking someone directly in the eyes during a conversation is considered a valued norm in the United States, but is typically viewed as disrespectful or a sign of aggression in other parts of the world. In addition, many people in the United States value emotional expressiveness, yet research shows that in some cultural groups, especially those in Eastern cultures, feelings are often suppressed.[1] Today more than ever, much of the meaning in our interactions with others depends on the cultural backgrounds of the communicators.

Our discussion in this book, thus far, has focused on the interpersonal communication process. This chapter homes in on one important and decisive influence upon that process: culture. Culture pervades every component of interpersonal communication, and cultural diversity is a fact of life. By thinking about and understanding culture, we can learn a great deal about the ways that we and others communicate in a multicultural society. Important too, as we conclude later, we will gain a great deal of understanding about our own communicative strengths and shortcomings.

As you can determine, the emphasis of this chapter is on intercultural communication. For our purposes, **intercultural communication** refers to communication between and among individuals and groups whose cultural backgrounds may be different from our own. Some researchers distinguish between communication across national cultures (e.g., people from Japan and from the United States) or communication between groups within one national culture (e.g., African Americans and Asian Americans). In this text, we refer to all such encounters as *intercultural* encounters. In many U.S. communities, these intercultural encounters were once very rare because most communities were comprised primarily of one race (typically Caucasians) who were fully assimilated into the dominant culture. But, clearly times are changing as nonwhite babies born now comprise the majority of births and U.S. Census estimates indicate that the "White majority" will dissipate by 2043.[2]

We live in a society that is more culturally diverse than ever. We describe this cultural complexity in this chapter and look at the significant issues associated with culture and interpersonal communication. Indeed, these words resonate as a primary rationale for this chapter: "What members of a particular culture value and how they perceive the universe are usually far more important than whether they eat with chopsticks, their hands, or metal utensils."[3] In other words, knowledge and practice of others' cultural values and behaviors enhance intercultural communication understanding.

The material I'm reading in this course makes me constantly think about how lucky (privileged?) I am being born in the United States. I can't imagine how tough it is for people to travel thousands of miles on boats, in trucks, even on foot to get to this country for a better life. I cry sometimes when I look at the pictures of the kids and how some people just don't care. If everyone thought about it, everybody's family migrated and we are all immigrants in some way!

▶ **IPC Around Us**

China remains the largest and one of the most misunderstood countries in the world. More and more people are traveling to China; in fact, many U.S. businesses continue their economic engagement with this country of nearly 1.5 billion people. China's business market and booming tourism has prompted many newcomers to travel to places like Hong Kong with little, or no, understanding of the cultural expectations. One important element in this cultural economy is something called *cultural etiquette.* This sort of etiquette is necessary in order to win business and sustain credibility. Many rules and appropriate cultural expectations exist. For instance, punctuality is key in China, and being late is a sign of disrespect. Other Chinese customs should be considered and adhered to, particularly as they pertain to eating and drinking.

Peter Dazeley/Photographer's Choice/Getty Images

Reflection: *Apply the principle of cultural etiquette to several cultural groups on your campus. Be sure to employ the chapter's discussion of the components of culture as you determine the organizations that you assess.*

For intercultural communication to occur, individuals don't have to be from different countries. In a diverse society such as the United States, we can experience intercultural communication within one state, one town, or even one neighborhood. You may live in an urban center where it's likely that people from various cultural backgrounds live together. As authors, we find ourselves immersed in this exciting cultural stew. In the South End of Boston, for instance, it is common to see people with Caribbean, Cambodian, and Latinx backgrounds all living on the same street. In Milwaukee, one would be able to find both Polish and Mexican communities on the south side of the city.

Trying to understand people who may think, talk, look, and act differently from us will be challenging at times. Just think about the words people use to describe those who may be culturally different from them: *odd, weird, strange, unusual,* and *unpredictable.* These associations have existed for centuries. Consider the words of 5th-century Greek playwright Aeschylus: "Everyone is quick to blame the alien." Today the "alien" takes many shapes and forms, with many of us embracing the diversity and heterogeneity in the population and others simply rejecting it.

Intercultural communication theorists argue that humans cannot exist without culture.[4] Our individuality is constructed around culture. As we will learn in Chapter 3, our identities are shaped by our conversations and relationships with others. Our cultural background enters into this mix by shaping our identity, our communication practices, and our responses to others. We tend to use other people as guideposts for what we consider to be "normal." And, in doing so, we can focus on how others from diverse cultures differ from us. For instance, when Paige from the United States meets Cheng from China in her philosophy class, she might notice how he smiles more frequently than his U.S. counterparts. Paige might also observe that Cheng is much more deferential to the professor than are she and her U.S. classmates. Yet this comparison is incomplete. Intercultural scholars and practitioners believe that although this classroom difference exists, a host of cultural similarities—some observable, others not—exist between Cheng and his U.S. student peers (e.g., economic background, family of origin). We note this point because this chapter explores both what factors culturally bind us as well as what elements divide us.

2–1 DEFINING CULTURE

Culture is a very difficult concept to define, partly because it's complex, multi-dimensional, and abstract. Some researchers[5] have discovered over 300 different definitions for the word! For our purposes, we believe that **culture** is the shared, personal, and learned life experiences of a group of individuals who have a common set of values, norms, and traditions. These standards, patterns of communication, and cultural customs are important to consider in our communication with others. They affect our interpersonal relationships within a culture, and the three are nearly impossible to detach from our understanding of intercultural communication.

As we define the term *culture,* keep in mind that we embrace a "global" interpretation. That is, we acknowledge culture to include these commonly held components:

- **Age** (e.g., adolescents, senior citizens)
- **Gender** (e.g., masculine, feminine)
- **Sex** (e.g., male, female)
- **Race/ethnicity** (e.g., African American, Cherokee)
- **Sexual identity** (e.g., lesbian, bisexual)
- **Spiritual identity** (e.g., Catholic, Muslim)
- **Geographic region** (e.g., New Englanders, Midwesterners)
- **Family background** (e.g., single parent, cohabiting couples)
- **Ability** (e.g., visual impairments, physical challenges)

Our examples throughout this book reflect this expansive view of culture. Let's now look at three underlying principles associated with our definition of culture: Culture is passed from one generation to another; culture both promotes and divides community; and culture is multileveled.

Culture Is Passed From One Generation to Another

We aren't born with knowledge of the practices and behaviors of our culture. People learn about a culture through the communication of symbols for meaning and we do this learning both consciously and unconsciously. Culture is a lived experience and it's passed on from one generation to another. And, we can learn about culture directly, such as when someone actually teaches us ("Here is how we celebrate Hanukkah"), or indirectly, such as when we observe cultural practices from afar, say learning about "The Festival of Lights" on *YouTube*. In the United States, our family, friends, schools, and the media are the primary teachers of our culture. Yet, we caution against accepting everything that we read or see. For instance, if you read a blog about a cultural community, keep in mind that one person does not necessarily "speak" for that community. Later in the chapter, we address a related skill set that aims to improve your intercultural competency.

PNC/Stockbyte/Getty Images

Cultural understanding is usually passed on from generation to generation.

Let's look at an example of a learned ritual that varies depending on culture: dating. In New Zealand, it is uncommon for someone to exclusively date another unless they have gone out with that person in a group of friends first. Even television shows in New Zealand suggest that romantic relationships begin in groups.[6] Furthermore, exclusive dating in New Zealand occurs only after the couple makes long-term relationship plans. And as most of you already know, in the United States, exclusive dating generally does not have to be preceded by group interactions, and many people in exclusive dating relationships haven't made long-term plans.

When you have acquired the knowledge, skills, attitudes, and values that allow you to become fully functioning in your culture, you are said to be enculturated. **Enculturation** occurs when a person learns to identify with a particular culture and a culture's thinking, way of relating, and worldview. Enculturation allows for successful participation in a particular society and makes a person more accepted by that society. Learning about a cultural society usually first takes place within a family or close relationships. For instance, in many mixed-race families, children learn about the many unforeseen consequences of being a member of a multiracial family from the parents and extended relatives.[7] With respect to gender enculturation, think about 13-year-old Jillian and her mom, Emma:

Emma: "Look, honey. I want you to go back to your room and change your clothes. You have a lot of cute skirts and dresses in your closet. Those jeans make you look like a tomboy."

Jillian: "I don't want to wear what you think I should wear! I'm sick of your damn . . ."

Emma: Don't you *ever* use that language, Jillian Suzanne! I took it from your brother, but I will not have my only daughter talking like that. And . . ."

Jillian: And what? Tell me how to walk?! Tell me who to be friends with? Yes, Mother. You have so many plans for your *only* daughter!"

In this scene, Jillian is slowly becoming enculturated, despite her overt rejection of the female script her mother is presenting her. She may be resistant to listening, but Jillian is learning rules about how to speak to her mom, the rule against profanity, the differential treatment between her and her brother, and how to dress appropriately for a girl, among others. Although she is young, Jillian is slowly being enculturated into her culture, and this process will likely continue—both directly and indirectly—throughout her lifetime.

Whereas enculturation occurs when you are immersed in your own culture, **acculturation** exists when you learn, adapt to, and adopt the appropriate behaviors and rules of a host culture. Acculturated individuals have effectively absorbed themselves into another society. However, you don't have to sacrifice your personal set of principles simply because you've found yourself in another culture. For example, some immigrants to the United States may attend school in a large city such as Phoenix or Miami. These individuals typically adapt to the city by using its services, understanding the laws of the city, or participating in social gatherings on campus. But, they may return to many of their cultural practices while in their homes, such as participating in spiritual healings or eating a family meal with multiple family generations present. To sum up, enculturation is first-culture learning, and acculturation is second-culture learning.

Culture Both Promotes and Divides Community

Central to our definition of culture is the assumption that it helps to create a sense of community. We view **community** as the common understandings among people who are committed to coexisting. In the United States, communities are filled with a number of cultures within cultures, sometimes referred to as **co-cultures**.[8] For example, a Cuban American community, a Lebanese American community, and a community of people with disabilities are all co-cultures within one larger culture (the United States). Each community has unique communication behaviors and practices, but each also subscribes to behaviors and practices (e.g., city laws, voting requirements) embraced by the larger U.S. culture. Membership in a co-culture provides individuals with opportunity and **social identity**—the part of one's self that is based upon membership in a particular group. Still, such membership may be problematic. For instance, some research[9] shows that if you are a member of an unrepresented or marginalized co-culture, you are disadvantaged in job interviews because "interview protocols" are determined by dominant groups.

Many times, the two cultures mesh effortlessly; however, sometimes a **culture clash**, or a conflict over cultural expectations, occurs. For example, consider what the reaction might be of a new immigrant from Mexico who is learning English as he tries to assimilate into a small group with three students who have lived in the United States their entire lives. Imagine the challenge of understanding slang ("dog and pony show," "jerry-rigged," etc.). Or, consider the reaction of a recently immigrated Islamic woman, who is accustomed to wearing a hijab (a headscarf or veil that covers the head and chest). In many Western countries, there are now federal laws prohibiting the wearing of the hijab in public. Many people do not embrace such modesty in dress and therefore may ridicule or express fear of the head covering. Each of the preceding scenarios is opportunistic for culture clashes.

Finally, although a much less profound example than those above, a mediated culture clash occurred when in 2018, MTV reintroduced the show *Jersey Shore*. In one episode, the show relocated to Florence, Italy, and instead of the cast and crew soaking in the Italian setting, they were targeted for cultural offenses. To the citizens of Florence, being Italian required respect for Italy's customs and reputation—the land of Michelangelo and Gucci, for instance. And so, when cast members, including Nicole "Snooki" Polizzi and Mike "The Situation" Sorrentino, publicly claimed to be Italian—combined with their public displays of drunkenness and profanity—the native Italians were not amused. Soon, "No Grazie, Jersey Shore" signs began appearing all over the city.

Still, cultural conflicts are not necessarily bad; in fact, having the opportunity to view a situation from a different cultural point of view can be productive. For instance, a writer for *Construction News* indicates that across the globe, culture clashes have resulted in increased productivity.[10] She writes that when a new hospital was being built in Sweden, the contractor (who worked in both the United Kingdom and Sweden) integrated various managerial styles and viewed it less as a difficulty and more as a step in a positive direction. And indeed, "culture clashes can produce a dynamic give-and-take, generating a solution that may have eluded a group of people with more similar backgrounds and approaches."[11]

Culture Is Multileveled

On the national level of culture, we assume that people of the same national background share many things that bind them in a common culture: language and traditions, for instance. Thus, we expect Germans to differ from the Hmong based on differing national cultures. However, as discussed in the previous section, cultures can be formed on other levels, such as generation, sexual identity, gender, race, and region, among others. For example, in many parts of a country, regionalisms exist. People who live in the middle of the United States (in states such as Kansas, Illinois, Iowa, Nebraska, Indiana, and Wisconsin), for instance, are often referred to as Midwesterners. People who live in Vermont, New Hampshire, Maine, Massachusetts, Rhode Island, and Connecticut are called New Englanders. Both Midwesterners and New Englanders often have their own unique way of looking at things, but the two regions also share something in common—namely, pragmatic thinking and an independent spirit.

A second example of the multileveled nature of a co-culture is a culture that develops around a certain age cohort. People who grew up in different time frames grew up in different cultural eras, as the labels we attach to various generations suggest—for example, Depression Babies of the 1930s or Flower Children of the 1960s. The culture of the Great Depression in the 1930s reflected the efforts of people trying to survive during troubling financial times. Thus, values of frugality and family unity dominated. In contrast, the 1960s was a prosperous era in which individualism and protest against the government flourished. As people age, they often find it difficult to abandon many of the values they learned during childhood. Now, consider the Millennials and the various responsibilities many of them represent and uphold. To be sure, this group is saddled with college debt, and individuals in this generation often take on multiple jobs to pay the bills. Are their struggles to "survive" any different from, say, the Depression Babies of the past?

Our discussion about culture thus far has focused on a general framework for understanding culture. We continue our cultural journey by addressing U.S. diversity and its value.

2–2 DIVERSITY AROUND THE GLOBE AND IN THE UNITED STATES

Intercultural contact is pervasive around the globe (see Figure 2.1) and in the United States. This diversity affects family structure, corporations, religious institutions, schools, and the media. Over 7.5 billion people live on Planet Earth and there are 255 births globally per minute or 4.3 births every second.[12] Your view of the world may be influenced by where you live, but there are astonishing differences among the continents. In particular, Asia comprises the largest percentage of the world's population (60%), followed by Africa (17%), Europe (10%), North America (8%), South America (6%), Oceania (.05%), and Antarctica (.0002%). In even starker terms, China and India comprise about 37% of the world's population.[13]

The United States, with more than 330 million citizens, is a country that has quickly become a microcosm of the global population. In other words, our nation is a heterogeneous mix of various cultural communities. The increase in diversity over the past several years is not without consequence. And U.S. diversity can be challenging, for as one essayist observes: "All across the country, people of different races, ethnicities, and nationalities, are being thrown together and torn apart. . . . .[I]t is a terrifying experience, this coming together, one for which we have of yet only the most awkward vocabulary."[14]

Native or indigenous peoples were the first to inhabit and reside in the United States. Since that time, scores of immigrants and refugees have ventured to this nation. Research shows that Latinx, most of whom are from Mexico, are the fastest growing cultural group in the United States, growing considerably over the past decade in particular.[15] And, while the United States traditionally supports cultural newcomers, polls show that the majority of registered voters do not support admitting large numbers of refugees who may be fleeing war or oppression. Indeed, a backlash of sorts has increased. Whether it's an "English only"

Figure 2.1 /// Ethnically Diverse Countries Across the Globe

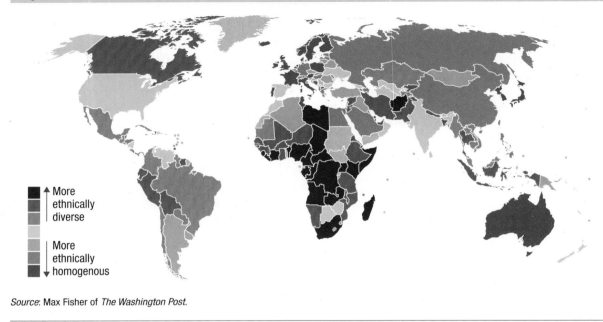

More ethnically diverse

More ethnically homogenous

Source: Max Fisher of *The Washington Post*.

movement codifying English as the official language of the country, or President Trump's 2017 efforts to slash refugee admissions to historic lows, efforts to curb new cultural voices have been unapologetically undertaken.

Over the past few decades, immigration has caused increased anxiety in the United States, prompting intercultural misunderstandings and relational challenges. The Migration Policy Institute,[16] for instance, notes that since the terrorist attacks in 2001, there have been significant immigration developments, including increased deportation, fence building along the Mexico–United States border, denying driver's licenses to those given deportation relief, and a host of other activities and laws designed to "control the immigration problem." By some estimates, there are some 11 million undocumented living and working immigrants in the United States,[17] so this topic will continue to resonate within families and across society for years to come.

Many decades ago, anthropologist Edward Hall wrote that "culture is communication and communication is culture."[18] In other words, we learn how, where, why, when, and to whom we communicate through cultural teachings. Conversely, when we communicate, we reproduce and reinforce our cultural practices. Hall's words still apply today. The United States is more diverse than ever, and everyone has been exposed to this increasing diversity in some way. The nation's growing diversity has been hotly debated, with some cultural critics believing that diversity is destroying society,[19] while others believe that understanding diversity allows for the growth of an individual.[20] Regardless of the divergent opinions on this matter, cultural variability continues to be a critical part of our country's evolution.

We are all now reminded that living with diversity is, well, a fact of life! With such diversity, learning how to communicate effectively with members of different cultures is a hallmark of a thoughtful and effective communicator. In that vein, let's explore this issue further by examining the importance of intercultural communication.

2–3 WHY STUDY INTERCULTURAL COMMUNICATION?

Adopting a cultural perspective is essential to function effectively in your lives. Intercultural communication scholars[21] note several reasons to study intercultural communication. We identify six "imperatives," or critical reasons, and provide their application to interpersonal relationships. At the heart of this discussion is our belief that intercultural communication will continue to be important well beyond the class you are currently taking.

Technological Imperative

The extent to which technology has changed the United States cannot be overstated. Computers ushered in so much more than ways to communicate online. Personal computers prompted the Information Age, which, even now, continues to move in unpredictable ways. Few will dispute the fact that the Internet remains one of the most significant influences on culture and interpersonal relationships.

Technological changes increase opportunities for intercultural communication and at times, unforeseen encounters. For example, consider Yolanda's experience with eBay. When Yolanda finds out that she holds the high bid on an antique handkerchief she wants to buy, she discovers that the seller is from a small town in Colombia. Yolanda e-mails the seller and tells him that her grandmother has relatives in the town of Tunja. He e-mails back to tell her that he, too, has relatives in that same town. As the two continue to e-mail each other, they realize that both sets of relatives in Colombia know each other! Later that year, they all *Skype* together—an event they decide to repeat each year. Stories such as these underscore the fact that technology remains vital in our cultural landscape as new relationships are established and interpersonal communication is attained.

IPC Praxis

Imagine that you were asked to sit on your campus Diversity Committee, responsible for crafting an external mission statement about your campus policy toward cultural understanding. Write up a draft statement that you plan to share with the group of administrators, faculty, students, and staff.

Demographic Imperative

Earlier in this chapter, we noted that cultural diversity continues to shape and reshape the United States, and we provided information about the demographic changes in the United States. Yet, the statistical trends frequently neglect to acknowledge the variation within a demographic group. For instance, many

Video 2.1

Table 2.1 /// Metaphors of/for Culture

Metaphor	Assumption
River	Culture flows through various peaks and valleys, and is often carved or restricted (e.g., laws, traditions) by its embankments.
City Map	Culture provides its members some direction of where to go and how to do things.
Organism	Culture uses the environment to grow, but uses boundaries to maintain uniqueness.
Jelly Bean	Each jelly bean is a color but a different color, underscoring the uniqueness of members of cultures.
Onion	To understand culture, we need to pull back the layers. Outermost layers are the most observable, and as each layer is removed, we get to the "core" of the culture.

Source: Adapted from AFS World Café, https://woca.afs.org/afs-announcements/b/icl-blog/posts/understanding-culture-using-metaphors.

co-cultures within a country reject the notion that "blending" into a national culture is ideal. Since dialogues about diversity began, writers and scholars have referred to the United States as a "melting pot," a metaphor that evokes a unified national character formed as a result of immigration. In the past, immigrants frequently changed their names, clothes, language, and customs to "fit in." Some of this behavior can be attributed to *E pluribus unum*"—out of many, one—which we can see on the back of the $1 bill.

In contrast, to accommodate the variety of cultural groups existing in the United States, more contemporary metaphors for diversity in the United States have emerged. They include a symphony, mosaic, kaleidoscope, or salad, suggesting that diversity provides for unique textures, tastes, and prisms. In these metaphors, different cultures retain their unique characteristics even while simultaneously becoming a part of the U.S. demographic. For a review of several other metaphors of culture, look at Table 2.1.[22] What other metaphors can you think of that may help others to understand culture?

Demographic metaphors suggest that the larger culture can accommodate and appreciate the contributions of co-cultures and co-cultural values. For example, in the United States, it's not uncommon for our food, dress, religion, and street signs to identify individual cultural groups. We eat at Korean restaurants, witness Saudi men wearing a *thawb* (an ankle-length white shirt), and read greeting cards celebrating Kwanzaa (an African American holiday affirming African culture). In addition, despite the efforts of the English-only movement we mentioned earlier, signs and labels in some parts of the country are written in two languages—for example, Spanish and English in the Southwest, and French and English in northern New England.

As a country, the United States will always be populated with individuals whose backgrounds are multicultural. Popular figures such as Vin Diesel, Alicia Keys, Vince Vaughn, Nicki Minaj, and Dwayne "The Rock" Johnson all have a rich multicultural ancestry. Such unique cultural configurations will continue, affecting not only the cultural fabric of the country, but also the nature of the communication taking place.

Various co-cultures remain important sources of information on how people communicate.

Economic Imperative

Today, only a handful of places on Earth are completely out of touch with the rest of the world. This phenomenon is referred to as the **global village**, which means that all societies—regardless of size—are connected in some way.[23] No country is economically isolated any longer. For instance, in 2017, with the exception of Canada and the United Kingdom, 8 of the top 10 U.S. economic exports go to countries where English is not the dominant language.[24] Therefore, the United States depends on other countries for its economic sustainability. Today, because of the availability of cheap labor, U.S. firms continue to send work and workers overseas, a practice called **outsourcing**. People in business and industry, education, media, and politics communicate with others of different cultures, if for no other reason than that it's cost efficient to do so. All of these exchanges of human resources represent one piece of the process known as globalization.

Workers from other countries who come to the United States often receive no training in intercultural similarities and differences. The result can be problematic, as one writer observes: "[International workers] can't be expected to learn our [United States] customs through osmosis."[25]

We would add that citizens of the United States can't be expected to learn about others through osmosis, either.

Peace Imperative

The Lakota Indians have a saying: "With all beings and all things we shall be as relatives." Yet, is it really possible for cultures to work together and get along on one planet? Our current state of world affairs makes it difficult to answer this question. In 2018, according to the Institute for Economics and Peace, only 10 countries in the world were determined to be conflict-free (Botswana, Chile, Costa Rica, Japan, Mauritius, Panama, Qatar, Switzerland, Uruguay, and Vietnam).[26] On one hand, the Berlin Wall has been torn down; on the other hand, other types of walls have been put up. Centuries of violence in the Middle East and Africa, tensions between China and Taiwan, and other global conflicts make this a challenging time for cultural understanding. We're not suggesting that if cultures understood each other, cultural warfare would end. Rather, we believe that learning about other cultures aids in understanding conflicting points of view, perhaps resulting in a more peaceful world. Looking at an issue from another's perspective is critical to interpersonal relationships and communication.

Self-Awareness Imperative

As we will discuss in Chapter 3, each of us has a **worldview**, which is a unique way of seeing the world through our own lens of understanding. Worldviews can help us understand our "place and space" (e.g., privilege, level of comfort talking with others) in society. Although these perspectives are often instinctive, they are directly derived from our cultural identity. When we have a reasonable understanding of who we are and what influences and forces brought us to our current state, we can begin to understand others' worldviews. For example, some of you may remember what it was like when you first discovered your sexual identity. You may have experienced an attraction to someone who is the same sex as you, a different sex from you, or even someone who identifies as non-binary. A same-sex attraction likely affects you differently if you adhere to a religion that considers same-sex attraction unnatural or immoral than if you come from a spiritual background that accepts GLBT individuals. Becoming personally aware of your own worldview and the worldviews of others will inevitably help you manage the cultural variation in your relationships and allow you to reflect on your own cultural assumptions.

Ethical Imperative

Recall from Chapter 1 that ethics pertains to what is perceived as right and wrong. Culturally speaking, ethics can vary tremendously.[27] That is, different fields of cultural experience dictate different opinions of what constitutes ethical behavior. For example, let's consider behavior associated with the family that may be viewed differently in the United States versus in China. Historically, in China, boys were valued more than girls; and until 2013, parents were required by Chinese policy to have only one child.[28] As a result, when a mother gives birth to a girl in China, the child may be abandoned or given up for adoption to allow the parents to try again to have a boy. As noted, however, Chinese officials have "loosened" this policy because of an "elderly boom," whereby seniors cannot work and need support from younger generations. That responsibility generally falls to the female, and thus, the policy has been revisited. Still, a multiple-child household is only possible if one of the parents is a single child.[29]

You may agree or disagree with this practice based upon your ethical perspective(s). Regardless of our personal opinions, each of us has an ethical obligation to ensure that cultural behaviors are depicted in the context of cultural values. We also have an ethical obligation to ensure that we fully understand cultural practices rather than imposing our own cultural will on others.

We summarize the six imperatives in Table 2.2. Each imperative is accompanied by examples of how that imperative applies to the study of intercultural communication.

Table 2.2 /// Reasons for Studying Intercultural Communication

Imperative Type	Example
Technological imperative	*Skype* is facilitating communication between and among cultures. The Internet, overall, has brought cultures closer together than ever before.
Demographic imperative	The influx of immigrants from Mexico, Russia, and Vietnam has changed the workforce and cultural profile in the United States.
Economic imperative	The global market has prompted overseas expansion of U.S. companies. Business transactions and negotiation practices require intercultural understanding.
Peace imperative	Resolution of world conflicts, such as those in the Middle East, requires cultural understanding.
Self-awareness imperative	Self-reflection of cultural biases aids in cultural sensitivity. Understanding personal worldviews promotes cultural awareness.
Ethical imperative	Cultural values are frequently difficult to understand and accept. We have an ethical obligation, for instance, to appreciate the cultural variations in dating, marriage, and intimacy.

2–4 DIMENSIONS OF CULTURE

For decades, Dutch management scholar Geert Hofstede examined work attitudes across 40 cultures.[30] His work showed that four dimensions of cultural values were held by more than 100,000 corporate managers and employees in multinational corporations: uncertainty avoidance, distribution of power, masculinity–femininity, and individualism–collectivism. These four areas comprise **Cultural Variability Theory**, and we address each dimension below.

Uncertainty Avoidance

Reducing uncertainty is a quality that defines various regions of the world. The notion of **uncertainty avoidance** can be tricky to understand. Overall, the concept refers to how tolerant (or intolerant) you are of uncertainty. Those cultures that resist change and have high levels of anxiety associated with change are said to have a high degree of uncertainty avoidance. Because cultures with a *high* degree of uncertainty avoidance desire predictability, they need specific laws to guide behavior and personal conduct. The cultures of Greece, Chile, Portugal, Japan, and France are among those that tolerate little uncertainty. Risky decisions are discouraged in these cultures because they increase uncertainty.

Video 2.2

Those cultures that are unthreatened by change have a *low* degree of uncertainty avoidance. The cultures of the United States, Sweden, Britain, Denmark, and Ireland tend to accept uncertainty. They are comfortable taking risks and are less aggressive and less emotional than cultures with a high degree of uncertainty avoidance.

Intercultural communication problems can surface when a person raised in a culture that tolerates ambiguity encounters another who has little tolerance. For instance, if a student from a culture with high uncertainty avoidance is invited to a party in the United States, they will probably ask many questions about how

to dress, what to bring, exactly what time to arrive, and so forth. These questions might perplex a U.S. host, who would typically have a high tolerance for uncertainty, including a laid-back attitude toward the party—"Just get here whenever." Recall that cultures with high uncertainty avoidance prefer to have rules and clear protocol more than cultures with low uncertainty avoidance.

Distribution of Power

How a culture deals with power is called **power distance**. Citizens of nations that are *high* in power distance (e.g., the Philippines, Mexico, India, Singapore, and Brazil) tend to show respect to people with higher status. They revere authoritarianism, and the difference between the powerful and the powerless is clear. Differences in age, sex, and income are exaggerated in these cultures, and people accept these differences.

India is an example of a culture that is high in power distance, exemplified by the caste system subscribed to by many of the Hindu people. The caste system is a social classification that organizes people into four castes or categories: *brahmins* (priests), *kashtryas* (administrators/rulers), *vaisyas*

Across the globe, societies vary in how much they accept an equal or unequal distribution of power.

(businesspeople or farmers), and *sudras* (laborers).[31] Each caste has various duties and rights. This caste hierarchy inhibits communication among caste groups. In fact, only one group (the priests), which historically has been afforded full respect, has the prerogative to communicate with all other social groups.

The cultures that are *low* in power distance include the United States, Austria, Israel, Denmark, and Ireland. People in these cultures believe that power should be equally distributed regardless of a person's age, sex, or status. Cultures with low degrees of power distance minimize differences among the classes and accept challenges to power in interpersonal relationships. Although included on the list of cultures low in power distance, the United States is becoming higher in power distance because of the growing disparity between rich and poor.

Intercultural encounters between people from high and low power distance cultures can be challenging. For instance, a supervisor from a high-power distance culture may have difficulty communicating with employees who come from lower power distance cultures. Although the supervisor may be expecting complete respect and follow through on directives, the employees may be questioning the legitimacy of such directives.

IPC Praxis

Construct a list of at least three excuses people have related to their reluctance to being culturally aware. Next, provide a response to those excuses, underscoring your cultural sensitivity.

Masculinity–Femininity

The *masculinity-femininity* dimension depicts the extent to which cultures represent masculine and feminine traits in their society. As Hofstede notes, masculinity is not the same as "male," and femininity is not the same as "female," although the use of these terms still reinforces fixed notions of how men and women should behave. **Masculine cultures** focus on achievement, competitiveness, strength, and material success—that is, characteristics typically associated with masculine people. Money is important in masculine cultures. Masculine cultures are also those in which the division of labor is based on sex. **Feminine cultures** emphasize sexual equality, nurturance, quality of life, supportiveness, and affection—that is, characteristics traditionally associated with feminine people. Compassion for the less fortunate also characterizes feminine cultures.

Hofstede's research showed that countries such as Mexico, Italy, Venezuela, Japan, and Austria are masculine-centered cultures where the division of labor is based on sex. Countries such as Thailand, Norway, the Netherlands, Denmark, and Finland are feminine-centered cultures where a promotion of sexual equality exists. The United States falls closer to masculinity.

What happens when a person from a culture that honors such masculine traits as power and competition intersects with a person from a culture that honors such feminine traits as interdependence and quality of life? For example, suppose that a woman is asked to lead a group of men. In Scandinavian countries, such as Denmark and Finland, such a task would not be problematic. Many political leaders in these countries are feminine (and female), and gender roles are more flexible. Yet, in a masculine culture, a female leader might be viewed with skepticism, and her leadership might be challenged.

Individualism–Collectivism

When a culture values **individualism**, it prefers competition over cooperation, the individual over the group, and the private over the public. Individualistic cultures have an "I" communication orientation, emphasizing self-concept, autonomy, and personal achievement. Individualistic cultures—including the United States, Canada, Britain, Australia, and Italy—tend to reject authoritarianism (think, for instance, how many rallies have occurred in the United States denouncing U.S. presidents and their policies) and typically support the belief that people should "pull themselves up by their own bootstraps."

Collectivism suggests that the self is secondary to the group and its norms, values, and beliefs. Group orientation takes priority over self-orientation. Collectivistic cultures teach their members about duty, tradition, conformity, and hierarchy. A "we" communication orientation prevails. Collectivistic cultures such as Colombia, Peru, Pakistan, Chile, and Singapore lean toward working together in groups to achieve goals. Families are particularly important, and people have higher expectations of loyalty to family, including taking care of extended family members.

Interestingly, the collectivistic and individualistic intersect at times. For instance, in the Puerto Rican community, a collectivistic sense of family coexists with the individualistic need for community members to become personally successful. In fact, as one researcher noted, "A Puerto Rican is only fully a person insofar as he

Table 2.3 /// Hofstede's Cultural Dimensions

Dimension	Description
Uncertainty Avoidance	Cultures high in uncertainty avoidance desire predictability (e.g., Greece, Japan). Cultures low in uncertainty avoidance are unthreatened by change (e.g., United States, Great Britain).
Power Distance	Cultures high in power distance show respect for status (e.g., Mexico, India). Cultures low in power distance believe that power should be equally distributed (e.g., United States, Israel).
Masculinity–Femininity	Masculine cultures value competitiveness, material success, and assertiveness (e.g., Italy, Austria). Feminine cultures value quality of life, affection, and caring for the less fortunate (e.g., Sweden, Denmark).
Individualism–Collectivism	Individualistic cultures value individual accomplishments (e.g., Australia, United States). Collectivistic cultures value group collaboration (e.g., Chile, Columbia).

or she is a member of a family."[32] Still, younger Puerto Ricans have adopted more independence and have accepted and adapted to the individualistic ways of the U.S. culture. We see, therefore, that even within one culture, the individualism–collectivism dimension is not static.

Look at the summary of Hofstede's four dimensions of culture provided in Table 2.3. As we did in the previous sections, we provide representative cultures as identified by Hofstede. Keep in mind that because his results are based on averages, you will most likely be able to think of individuals you know who are exceptions to the categorization of nations.

 Theory-Into-Practice (TIP)

Cultural Variability Theory

One intriguing and complex component of Cultural Variability Theory is the masculine-feminine dimension. This portion of the theory advances that generally, males are masculine and females are feminine. Still, we all know that feminine males and masculine females are also part of many global societies. Comment on the potential problems and opportunities of using terms like *masculine* and *feminine* to describe men and women around the globe.

One additional notion related to the discussion of cultural dimensions merits consideration: context. Recall from Chapter 1 that context is the surrounding in which communication takes place. Intercultural communication theorists find that people of different cultures use context to varying degrees to determine the meaning of a message. Scholars have referred to this as **Context Orientation Theory**.[33] Context Orientation Theory answers the following question: Is meaning derived from cues outside of the message or from the words in the message?

The cultures of the world differ in the extent to which they rely on context. Researchers have divided context into two areas: high context and low context. In **high-context** cultures, the meaning of a message is primarily drawn from the surroundings. People in such cultures do not need to say much when communicating because there is a high degree of similarity among members of such cultures. That is, people typically read nonverbal cues with a high degree of accuracy because they share the same structure of meaning. Native American, Indian, Japanese, Chinese, and Korean cultures are all high-context cultures. On a more fundamental level, high-context communities are less formal, and the relational harmony is valued and maintained as decisions are made.

In low-context cultures, communicators find meaning primarily in the words in messages, not the surroundings. In such cultures, meanings are communicated explicitly; very little of the conversation is left open to interpretation. As a result, nonverbal communication is not easily comprehended. Self-expression, then, becomes a relational value. Examples of low-context cultures include Germany, Switzerland, United States, Canada, and France.

Think about how cultural differences in context might affect interaction during conflict episodes, job interviews, or dating. If one person relies mainly on the spoken word and the other communicates largely through nonverbal messages, what might be the result? Or, if one person's communication is direct and expressive, what are the consequences and implications if the other communicator employs silence and indirect forms of communication?

So far in this chapter, we have discussed why you need to understand intercultural communication. We're confident that you are beginning to appreciate the cultural diversity in your lives and that you are prepared to work on improving your intercultural communication skills. A critical step toward understanding your culture and the cultures of others is to understand the problems inherent in intercultural communication, a subject we outline below.

 **IPC Careers**

Cultural Awareness and Human Resource Management

iStock.com/Rawpixel

(Continued)

(Continued)

A robust and productive working environment requires a "culturally and linguistically diverse workforce." So says an intellectual center that focuses on aging and cultural diversity. Human resource (HR) professionals are key to achieving such a work climate. The center advances that HR professionals should strive to ensure that cultural diversity remains paramount in both the employment and training of employees. Because of the job duties required of HR personnel, cultural awareness is multidimensional: *recruitment* ("Consider the demographics of your local community when recruiting new staff"), *staff education and development* ("Include a cultural diversity component in all staff orientation"), and *organizational support* ("Address cultural diversity in all organizational policies and practices"). The center calls for a number of other key considerations for HR professionals: working on securing bilingual staff, encouraging staff to learn a second language, providing facilities for a variety of religious and spiritual observances, reviewing assessment programs and practices for cultural bias, advertising job vacancies in "ethnic media," among other recommendations.

Reflection: *Suppose you were asked to advise an HR director regarding the role of culture in social media. What recommendations would you provide to show the consequences of ignoring culturally offensive posts?*

2–5 CHALLENGES OF INTERCULTURAL COMMUNICATION

Although intercultural communication is important and pervasive, becoming an effective intercultural communicator is easier said than done. In this section, we explain five obstacles to intercultural understanding: ethnocentrism, stereotyping, anxiety and uncertainty, misinterpretation of nonverbal and verbal behaviors, and the assumption of similarity or difference.

 **IPC Praxis**

Simply because we're members of a cultural community does not mean we have to embrace all of the community's values. What are some of your culture's customs and practices that you disagree with or outright reject? What criteria do you use to justify your decision?

Ethnocentrism

The process of judging another culture using the standards of your own culture is termed **ethnocentrism**. The term is derived from two Greek words, *ethnos,* or "nation," and *kentron,* or "center." When combined, the meaning becomes clear: nation at the center. Ethnocentrism is a belief in the superiority of your own culture in such areas as customs, traditions, and political systems. The term's application to populations and communities has its roots tracing back to the 1800s with the rise of U.S. nativism (the protection of native-born interests). Normally, ethnocentric tendencies exaggerate differences and usually prevent intercultural understanding.

At first glance, being ethnocentric may appear harmless. Few people even realize the extent to which they prioritize their culture over another. For instance, you will note that throughout this book, we avoid the use of the single term *American*. Like many researchers and practitioners, we believe that *American* can refer to people in North America, Central America, and South America. Although we understand the everyday usage of the term is normally attributed to those in the United States, we also acknowledge that the word can have a broader application. In fact, many in Latin America believe that when people in the United States refer to themselves as "Americans," such a behavior reinforces "imperialistic tendencies."[34]

We tend to notice when people from other cultures prioritize their cultural customs. For example, although many people in the United States value open communication, not all cultures do. Many Asian cultures such as China revere silence. In fact, the Chinese philosopher Confucius said, "Silence is a friend who will never betray." Consider what happens in conversations when the Western and Eastern worlds meet. Let's say that Ed, a young business executive from the United States, travels to China to talk to Yao, another executive, regarding a business deal. Ed is taken aback when, after he makes the offer, Yao remains silent for a few minutes. Ed repeats the specifics of the offer, and Yao acknowledges his understanding. This standstill in their discussion leads Ed to believe that Yao is going to reject the offer. However, if Ed had studied Chinese culture sufficiently before his trip, he would know that to the Chinese, silence generally means agreement. One speaks only if they have something of value to add. Ed's cultural ignorance may cost the company both money and respect. And the inability to look beyond his own Western view of silence represents ethnocentrism.

Stereotyping

Consider the following statements:

- Girls are not as good as boys in sports.

- Russians don't show emotions.

- Asians are good at math.

- Senior citizens don't understand technology.

These statements are **stereotypes**—the "pictures in our heads"[35]—or the fixed mental images of a particular group and communicating with an individual as if he or she is a member of that group. Stereotypes assume that "they're all alike." We have all stereotyped at one point or another in our lives. Stereotypes are everywhere in U.S. society, including politics ("All politicians are crooked"), medicine ("Doctors know best"), entertainment ("Hollywood celebrities use Botox"), journalism ("The media are so liberal"), and sports ("They're just dumb jocks"). Such statements generalize the perceived characteristics of some members of a group to the group as a whole.

Video 2.3

You may not have thought about this before, but as we illustrate above, stereotypes can be good or bad. Think about the positive stereotypes of firefighters, police officers, emergency personnel, and other rescue workers after the terrorist attacks on the United States on September 11, 2001. Words like *heroic, compassionate, daring,* and *fearless* have all been attributed to these groups of individuals, regardless of the cultural identification of the members of these groups. However, right after the attacks, many Arabs living in the United States were accused of being terrorists simply because of their Middle Eastern identity, and people used hurtful and hateful speech while interacting with Arab Americans. The point is that we must be willing to look beyond the generalizations about a particular group and communicate with people as individuals.

IPC Praxis

Describe a time when you witnessed discrimination. What was your response, if any, to the event? Do you regret your response or do you remain proud of your response? What changes, if any, would you have considered now that you're reflecting on your response?

Anxiety and Uncertainty

You may feel anxiety and uncertainty when you are introduced to people who speak, look, and act differently from you. Most societies have few guidelines to help people through some of the early awkward intercultural moments. People commonly question what words or phrases to use while discussing various cultural groups. Most of us want to be culturally aware and use language that doesn't offend, yet we frequently don't know what words might be offensive to members of cultures other than our own. For example, you might wonder whether you should refer to someone as American Indian or Native American or another as African American or black. These cultural references can be challenging, and even in the communities that are affected by the terminology, there are profound disagreements on appropriate and sensitive word usage.

Our family and friends remain influential on our perceptions. In particular, their observations and reactions to cultural differences are often passed on to us. And they can prompt us to either feel that we are members of what social scientists call an in-group or an out-group. **In-groups** are groups to which a person feels he or she belongs, and **out-groups** are those groups to which a person feels he or she does not belong.

Perceptions of belonging are directly proportional to the level of connection an individual feels toward a group. Let's say that Lianna and Nate, a devoutly Christian married couple, meet Nate's best friend, Rose. Although Rose is Jewish, she feels that she has in-group affiliation with the couple and communicates with them comfortably. Now suppose that Lianna and Nate meet Rose's mom, an atheist who believes that the couple spends too much time talking about "being saved." Her mom will likely view Lianna and Nate as an out-group member because she does not feel a sense of belonging with the husband and wife. Being a member of either an in-group or an out-group can influence our degree of comfort in intercultural communication.

Misinterpretation of Nonverbal and Verbal Behaviors

Speakers expect to receive nonverbal cues that are familiar. However, nonverbal behaviors differ dramatically across and within cultures. An Asian proverb states that "those who know, do not speak; those who speak, do not know." If Paola is a person who believes that communication must be constant to be effective, she may struggle with interpersonal exchanges with the Western Apache or the Asian Indian who value silence. However, as is true of other facets of culture, nonverbal communication varies within cultures as well as between cultures. For instance, although Italians might gesture more than people from the United States in general, not all Italians use expansive gestures. We could certainly find someone from Italy who gestures less than someone we pick from the United States. We return to the topic of culture and nonverbal communication in Chapter 5.

In addition to nonverbal differences, verbal communication differences exist between and among cultures and co-cultures. For example, generational diversity can exist with word usage. Words such as *smooching* and *necking* once referred to an act most people today refer to as *kissing*. Yet, today, some generations use the phrase "make out" or "NCMO" to cover a wide array of emotional and physical activities (we cover the use of language extensively in Chapter 4). We must understand nonverbal and verbal differences among (co)-cultures if we are to achieve meaning in our intercultural relationships.

The Assumption of Similarity or Difference

This assumption suggests that intercultural communication is possible because it simply requires homing in on people's inherent similarities. At the other end of the continuum is the belief that people from different cultures are vastly different from one another, and therefore communication between them is difficult if not impossible. Assuming similarity fails to appreciate difference, and assuming difference fails to appreciate cultural commonalities.

In the United States, we need to be careful when we place a premium on what some may call the "American way." We are ethnocentric if we believe that other cultures should do things the way that we do things here or if we hold cultures in higher esteem if they imitate or practice our cultural customs. In many cases, people who are unfamiliar with U.S. traditions often question these practices. Further, simply because something is practiced or revered in the United States does not mean that it is similarly practiced or revered in other cultures. Assuming similarity across cultures, then, is problematic.

We have given you a number of issues to consider in this chapter so far. First, we defined culture and co-culture and discussed the dimensions of culture. We then proceeded to outline several reasons for studying intercultural communication. Next, we address some of the most common challenges to intercultural communication. We now offer you some suggestions for improving your intercultural effectiveness in relationships.

2–6 SKILL SET FOR INTERCULTURAL UNDERSTANDING

In this section, we present several ways to improve your communication with people from different cultures. Because most cultures and co-cultures have unique ways of communicating, our suggestions are necessarily broad. As we have emphasized in this chapter, communicating with friends, classmates, coworkers, and others from different cultural backgrounds requires a sense of other-centeredness

Table 2.4 /// Skill Set for Enhancing Intercultural Understanding	
a. Know your biases and stereotypes.	
b. Tolerate the unknown.	
c. Practice cultural respect.	
d. Educate yourself.	
e. Be prepared for consequences.	
f. Relate to the individual, not the culture.	
g. Your skill suggestion	

as well as understanding your own feelings and abilities. In the end, knowing your intercultural sensitivity is a good first step. We have summarized the skill set (see Table 2.4) and encourage you to add your suggestions to this list based on your own cultural experiences.

Know Your Biases and Stereotypes

Despite our best efforts, we enter conversations with biases and stereotypes. How do we know we have biases and stereotypes? Listening carefully to others' responses to our ideas, words, and phrases is an excellent first step. Have you ever told a story about a cultural group that resulted in a friend saying, "I can't believe you just said that!" That friend may be pointing out that you should rethink some culturally offensive language or risk facing challenges from others during conversations. As your authors/teachers tell their students: If you wouldn't say it in front of the particular cultural group, you shouldn't say it at all!

We need to avoid imposing our predispositions and prejudices on others. Perceptions of different cultural groups are frequently outdated or otherwise inaccurate and require a constant personal assessment. Facing your biases and even your fears or anxieties is an essential first step toward intercultural effectiveness.

Recall that ethnocentrism is seeing the world through your own culture's lens. We may like to think that our particular culture is best, but as you have seen through our many examples, no culture can nor should claim preeminence. We first need to admit that to some extent, we all are biased and ethnocentric. Next, we need to honestly assess how we react to other cultures. As we mentioned previously, you can listen to others for their reactions. Looking inward is also helpful; ask yourself the following questions:

- What have I done to prepare myself for intercultural conversations?

- Do I use language that is biased or potentially offensive to people from different cultures?

- What is my reaction to people who use offensive words or phrases while describing cultural groups—am I silent? If so, do I consider my silence problematic?

- How have my perceptions and biases been shaped? By the media? By school? By talking to others?

These are among the questions you should consider as you begin to know yourself, your perceptions, and how you may act on those perceptions. We all need to understand our outdated and misguided views of others that have falsely shaped our impressions of other cultures. Recognizing that your family, friends, coworkers, school, and the media influence your prejudices is critical. Getting rid of the unwanted or misguided biases is essential if we are to begin to forge intercultural relationships with others.

Tolerate the Unknown

Earlier in the chapter, we noted that some cultures tolerate uncertainty more easily than others. Although we noted that the United States is one such culture, tolerating things of which you are unaware does not always come naturally. We may wish to *think* we are tolerant, but the truth is that differences can bother us at times.

You may be unfamiliar with various cultural practices of coworkers, craftspeople you hire for home repair, and others whose backgrounds and fields of experience differ from yours. For instance, consider the Romanian who is accustomed to greeting people by kissing the sides of both cheeks. Think about the colleague who greets you in another language other than your own. Or, perhaps as an able-bodied person you are unable to identify with someone who relies on a wheelchair or walker for mobility. Some cultural behaviors are simply different from yours and it may take time to understand the differences. Be patient with yourself and with others. If you encounter a cultural unknown, think about asking questions. For some of us, being tolerant is not a challenge at all; others of us, however, need to work at it. Regardless of competency level, being unaware or uncomfortable in an intercultural encounter will likely prevent you from experiencing a satisfying intercultural relationship.

Gaertner / Alamy Stock Photo

The extent to which we tolerate and respect cultural practices varies around the world.

Practice Cultural Respect

Various traditions, customs, and practices allow cultures and co-cultures to function effectively. Skilled intercultural communicators respect those cultural conventions. No one culture knows "the right way" to solve work problems, raise children, and manage interpersonal relationships. **Cultural imperialism** is a process whereby individuals, companies, or the media impose their way of thinking and behaving upon another culture. With cultural imperialism, a belittling of another culture occurs. We can avoid this practice by using cultural respect. This requires us to show that we accept another culture's way of thinking and relating, even though we may disagree with or disapprove of it. Different societies have different moral codes, and judging a culture using only one moral yardstick can be considered both arrogant and self-serving.

When you practice cultural respect, you empathize with another culture. **Cultural empathy** refers to the learned ability to accurately understand the experiences of people from diverse cultures and to convey that understanding responsively. When you are empathic, you are on your way to appreciating the life experiences of another person or social group. In other words, try to reach beyond the words to the feelings that the communicator is trying to show. You become other-oriented and engage in civil communication.

Developing cultural respect involves trying to look at a culture from the inside. What is it like to be a member of another culture? Avoid reading verbal and non-verbal communication solely from your own cultural point of view. Work on refraining from becoming easily frustrated or insulted if another person is not using your language or is having a hard time communicating.

Educate Yourself

Aside from taking this course in interpersonal communication, you can take advantage of numerous opportunities to educate yourself about other cultures. First, read. That's right: Read all that is available to you about other cultures. Browse magazines and books that are dedicated to culture, intercultural communication, and intercultural relationships. And, search the web. Many websites allow you to travel virtually across cultures. Some links provide you information about cultures all over the world, and in particular, some discuss business practices and protocols of dozens of global communities (e.g., www.worldbiz.com). If you're interested in, say, religion or spirituality or the various tribal nations, many online resources are valuable (e.g., www.adherents.com). These are just a few of the active websites that students have chosen as important intercultural opportunities. This information will provide you a backdrop for future reference and will allow you to discover more about your own culture as well.

Second, educating yourself requires that you learn about cultures through others. Participate in community lectures and discussions about cultural groups. Don't be afraid to chat with people who represent another race, religion, nationality, or other cultural group. Be interested in their experiences but avoid patronizing them. Further, although you should educate yourself, don't accept everything written about culture and communication as truth. Be rigorous and critical in your reading and tentative in your acceptance. Be willing to seek out information that is based on both research and personal experience.

Be Prepared for Consequences

Although we may make a serious effort to be thoughtful and considerate, having a conversation with an individual from a different (co-)culture can be challenging. So many issues operate simultaneously in a conversation—verbal and nonverbal differences, nervousness, cultural customs, rules, symbols, and norms. We may try to attend to all of these aspects of our conversation, but things still may go awry. There is no way to completely control all the things that can go astray in our cultural dialogues and cultural stumbling may happen. What we can work toward, however, is preempting potential problems.

Relate to the Individual, Not the Culture

Although we know that we have drawn on some generalizations to make some of the points in this chapter, we remain concerned about painting broad cultural strokes to define individuals. Identifying with the person and not the cultural group is paramount in intercultural communication.

Accepting individual cultural uniqueness is important. First, as we learned earlier, there are variations within cultures and co-cultures. For instance, not all Christians have the same beliefs about abortion rights, nor do all senior citizens sit around playing Scrabble. Second, people's communication behaviors and skills can vary tremendously within cultures. Some people use significant personal space in conversations, whereas others use little. Some people are direct and forthright in their dialogues, but others are more reserved and timid. Some individuals may be reluctant to share personal tragedies; however, others may have no qualms about such disclosure. Constantly reminding yourself that not all members of a certain cultural group think alike, act alike, and talk alike allows you to focus on the person instead of the group to which he or she belongs.

/// CHAPTER WRAP-UP

This chapter explored the most decisive influence on our interpersonal communication: culture. We defined and interpreted the notion of culture and three of its underlying assumptions. We also described several reasons for studying intercultural communication followed by an examination of four dimensions of culture. Numerous obstacles preventing effective cultural understanding were also introduced. We concluded the chapter by elucidating a number of different skills you might consider as you work toward achieving higher levels of excellence in your cultural communication with others.

In Chapter 1, we identified the transactional process as a communication effort involving two people simultaneously sending and receiving messages from each other. After reading and reflecting on this chapter, we hope you can see that to achieve transactional communication, we need to have an understanding of culture. Cultural similarities and differences exist across the interpersonal communication span—from the way we use our eye contact to the word choices we employ to the way we establish, maintain, or terminate a relationship. Culture is unequivocally an essential ingredient to shared meaning and it will remain an instrumental influence in our lives.

/// COMMUNICATION ASSESSMENT TEST (CAT): INTERCULTURAL SENSITIVITY SCALE

Sometimes, we may believe that we're culturally sensitive and yet we may not be able to measure this belief. Below is a series of statements concerning intercultural communication. There are no right or wrong answers. Please work quickly and record your first impression by indicating the degree to which you agree or disagree with the statement.

5 = strongly agree, 4 = agree, 3 = uncertain, 2 = disagree, 1 = strongly disagree

Please put the number corresponding to your answer in the blank before the statement.

____1. I enjoy interacting with people from different cultures.

____2. I think people from other cultures are narrow-minded.

____3. I am pretty sure of myself in interacting with people from different cultures.

____4. I find it very hard to talk in front of people from different cultures.

____5. I always know what to say when interacting with people from different cultures.

____6. I can be as sociable as I want to be when interacting with people from different cultures.

____7. I don't like to be with people from different cultures.

____8. I respect the values of people from different cultures.

____9. I get upset easily when interacting with people from different cultures.

____10. I feel confident when interacting with people from different cultures.

____11. I tend to wait before forming an impression of culturally distinct counterparts.

____12. I often get discouraged when I am with people from different cultures.

____13. I am open-minded to people from different cultures.

____14. I am very observant when interacting with people from different cultures.

____15. I often feel useless when interacting with people from different cultures.

____16. I respect the ways people from different cultures behave.

____17. I try to obtain as much information as I can when interacting with people from different cultures.

____18. I would not accept the opinions of people from different cultures.

____19. I am sensitive to my culturally distinct counterpart's subtle meanings during our interaction.

____20. I think my culture is better than other cultures.

____21. I often give positive responses to my culturally different counterpart during our interaction.

____22. I avoid those situations where I will have to deal with culturally distinct persons.

____23. I often show my culturally distinct counterpart my understanding through verbal or nonverbal cues.

____24. I have a feeling of enjoyment toward differences between my culturally distinct counterpart and me.

Interaction Engagement (your feelings of participation in intercultural communication)

(Items 1, 11, 13, 21, 22, 23, and 24).

Respect for Cultural Differences (your perception of how you orient to or tolerate another's culture or cultural opinions)

(Items 2, 7, 8, 16, 18, and 20)

Interaction Confidence (how confident you are in an intercultural setting)

(Items 3, 4, 5, 6, and 10)

Interaction Enjoyment (your positive or negative reactions toward communicating with people from other cultures)

(Items 9, 12, and 15)

Interaction Attentiveness (your effort to understand what is taking place in an intercultural encounter)

(Items 14, 17, and 19)

Source: Adapted from Lippman, W. (1922). *Public opinion*. New York: MacMillan.

/// KEY TERMS

intercultural communication   37

culture   39

enculturation   40

acculturation   41

community   41

co-culture   41

social identity   41

culture clash   42

global village   47

outsourcing   47

worldview   48

Cultural Variability Theory   49

uncertainty avoidance   49

power distance   50

masculine cultures   51

feminine cultures   51

individualism   51

collectivism   51

Context Orientation Theory   52

high-context cultures   52

low-context cultures   53

ethnocentrism   54

stereotypes   55

in-groups   56

out-groups   56

cultural imperialism   60

cultural empathy   60

/// KEY QUESTIONS FOR APPLICATION

1. *CQ/CultureQuest*: Explore the following claim: "When visiting another country and culture, people should make an effort to use the native language and practice local customs." Do you agree or disagree? Defend your view with examples.

2. *TQ/TechQuest:* Explore the following claim: "Too often, we forget that not everyone desires, or has access to, social media." Do you agree or disagree? Defend your view with examples.

3. Why is workforce diversity important for productivity in the business world?

4. What rewards or challenges exist for individuals as they reconcile their personal cultural customs and beliefs with those who have dissimilar customs and beliefs?

5. Identify and explain how you can recognize and celebrate the differences within a cultural community at school, at work, among other contexts.

6. Explore and describe various culturally sensitive values you have articulated via social media (e.g., Facebook, Instagram, Snapchat) and how they have enhanced your understanding of individuals who are different from you.

Access practice quizzes, eFlashcards, video, and multimedia at **edge.sagepub.com/west**.

Visit **edge.sagepub.com/west** to help you accomplish your coursework goals in an easy-to-use learning environment.

CHAPTER 3

COMMUNICATION, PERCEPTION, IDENTITY, AND THE SELF

LEARNING OUTCOMES

After studying this chapter, you will be able to

3–1 Identify the components in the perception process

3–2 Explain the influences on the perception process

3–3 Discuss the dimensions of the self

3–4 Identify the relationship between identity management and facework

3–5 Delineate online identity markers

3–6 Select skills for enhancing perception checking and self-actualization

iStock.com/franckreporter

Master the content at
edge.sagepub.com/west

$SAGE edge™

Look around you right now, whether you're in your dorm room, office, apartment, workplace, the train, or other location. Are people standing or moving about? Is music playing? Is the television on? Are people looking at their cell phones? Is your computer logged on to a particular website? Is your cell phone ringing? What are you wearing? Do you hear noises outside? Are you sick or healthy?

Now think about how you felt the last time you had a heated argument with another person. What did you find particularly aggravating about the argument? How did you feel about yourself as you engaged in the conflict? What reactions did you receive from the person you were arguing with during the exchange? Did anyone "win" the argument? If so, how did that happen? How do you think you will handle the next conflict with this person?

You answered these 15 questions based on two important topics in interpersonal communication: perception and the self. As you stopped to consider what was around you, you perceived your immediate surroundings. Some things you may have noticed before we prompted you to do so. However, you may not have thought about other things until we mentioned them. In both cases, you were engaged in the perception process.

As you thought about the last argument you had, you inevitably reflected on another critical component of interpersonal communication: the self. We asked you to think about your personal reactions to the conflict and how the conflict affected you. Even in a split second, you may have thought about the effect of the conflict on your relationship with the other person. You also may have reflected on how your identity influenced the type of conflict and the way the conflict developed. These considerations are part of your "self."

We discuss the perception process and an understanding of the self together in this chapter for a few reasons. First, we perceive the world around us with a personal lens.[1] That lens is necessarily part of our perceptions. Second, we can't talk about perception unless we talk about how those perceptions influence and affect all aspects of our self.

Third, perceiving requires an understanding of the self. In other words, we can't begin to unravel why we recognize some things and ignore others without simultaneously figuring out how our individual identity functions (sometimes unconsciously) within those realizations. Ultimately, perception and individual identity are inextricably linked; that is, you can't talk about one without referencing the other. So much of communication is not what is real or true, but what is perceived by you and others.

IPC Voice: Michaela

When I first met my new stepmother at my sister's birthday, I was not overly impressed. I thought she was full of herself and she barely said two words to me. She was all "made up" with too much foundation and her clothes were definitely not vintage! But, my first impression of her changed after a few other meetings. I found out that like me, she was nervous, too. She wanted to make a good impression and wanted to dress up. She also didn't want to interfere with family conversations at the party and that's why she was so quiet. I felt so bad about the first perceptions I had of her. I now know to wait before judging and evaluating someone.

The significance of these claims cannot be overstated, particularly as it affects the well-being of individuals. For instance, in research examining children with epilepsy,[2] those diagnosed with this neurological disorder frequently perceived themselves as clumsy, lacking a lot of friends, and experiencing feelings of unhappiness. In other research examining senior citizens, additional research also shows the *perception–self* dynamic. For instance, the notion of "successful aging" is, among other features, characterized by the extent to which a person is (a) self-determined, (b) motivated to be more positive, and (c) able to cope with various unexpected stressors.[3] As evidenced in these two different studies, your sense of perception and your sense of self are inextricably related and the focus of this chapter.

To get a common foundation of understanding, we begin by explaining the perception process in face-to-face (f2f) communication.

3–1 UNDERSTANDING INTERPERSONAL PERCEPTION

Video 3.1

In most of our interpersonal encounters, we form an impression of the other person. These impressions, or perceptions, are critical to achieving meaning. The process of looking at people, things, activities, and events can involve many factors. For instance, in a f2f meeting with a teacher to challenge a low grade on a paper, you would probably notice not only your instructor's facial reactions and body position, but also your own. You might also be attentive to the general feeling you get as you enter the instructor's office. And you would probably prepare for the encounter by asking other students what their experiences with the instructor had been with respect to grade challenges.

Perceiving an interpersonal encounter, then, involves much more than paying attention to the words of another person. Perception is an active and challenging process that involves all five senses: touch, sight, taste, smell, and hearing. Through perception, we gain important information about the interpersonal communication skills of others and of ourselves. Our perceptions are also derived from our needs and wants, preferences, passions, dislikes, and personal experiences. For our purposes, then, we define **perception** as a process of using our

Perception involves all of our senses.

iStock.com/Malekas85

Table 3.1 /// Stages of the Interpersonal Perception Process

Stage	Description	Example
1. **Attending and selecting**	Sorting out stimuli We choose to attend to some stimuli and to ignore others.	At the campus library, Kendrick notices his friend talking to a woman he had wanted to meet and date.
2. **Organizing**	Categorizing stimuli to make sense of them	Kendrick creates the belief that his friend and the woman are close.
3. **Interpreting**	Assigning meaning to stimuli	Kendrick decides not to ask his classmate out for a date because she is already dating his friend.
4. **Memorizing**	Storing interpretations for subsequent retrieval	Kendrick stores this situation in his mind for (possible) future "use."
5. **Retrieving**	Recalling information we have stored in our memories	Kendrick remembers that the two were together at a concert on campus a few weeks earlier.

senses to respond to stimuli. To a large extent, perception is an amalgam of several subareas, each coalescing into one interpersonal dynamic. Let's further explore this vital component of interpersonal communication by describing the perception process and its five stages: attending and selecting, organizing, interpreting, memorizing, and retrieving. (see Table 3.1).

Attending and Selecting

The **attending and selecting stage** requires us to use our visual, auditory, tactile, and olfactory senses to respond to stimuli in our interpersonal environment. When we are attentive and selective, we are mindful. Mindful communicators pay close attention to detail. Being **mindful** means being observant and aware of your surroundings. Some researchers look at it more specifically as a "conscious awareness of the present moments."[4]

 **IPC Praxis**

Think about how mindfulness can reduce some communication challenges, such as a fear of approaching an unfamiliar person or talking to a small group of people whom you've never met. What mindful strategies would you consider undertaking?

Mindfulness has been studied in a variety of settings, resulting in some important discoveries. One of the most compelling areas of mindfulness research is in medicine. In particular, it has been applied to the healing arts. In some cases, an intensive mindfulness approach whereby individuals stay in the moment without judgment can assist those with rheumatoid arthritis, side effects of HIV medications, breast cancer, and chronic lower back pain.[5] Imagine for a minute, then, the effects of this mindful communication upon one's interpersonal relationships.

We are constantly bombarded with stimuli and our sense organs are on overdrive—whether it's from the sound of music, the smell of someone's cologne, the feel of someone's breath, or other stimuli. Consequently, it's impossible to focus on every detail of a behavior, event, or encounter. As a result, we use **selective perception**. When we selectively perceive, we decide to attend to things that fulfill our own needs, capture our own interests, or meet our own expectations. We pay attention to some things while ignoring others.

In our relationships with others, we use selective perception all the time. For example, let's say that Aiden has decided to end his relationship with Maddie. He explains that he thinks it is in their collective best interests for them to break up because he's not prepared to give her the time she deserves. However, he says that he has learned a lot while in the relationship. Aiden continues talking, telling Maddie several of the things he feels he learned from being with her and reveals that he is eternally grateful to have spent time with her.

As Maddie selectively perceives this unexpected conversation, she attends to the reason that Aiden is breaking up with her ("not enough time"). Regardless of everything else Aiden says, Maddie attends to this one particular piece of information. As a result, she filters out and ignores other information, such as what Aiden learned while being in the relationship. As would most people in such a situation, Maddie will want to know more about what motivated Aiden's decision to break up. In addition to selectively perceiving his words, she may also parse out some of Aiden's nonverbal signals, such as whether or not he has averted his eye contact or whether his vocal tone varies while delivering the news.

In this example, Maddie could consider a number of different stimuli—Aiden's behaviors, the time of day, the noises in the room, and so on. But, she remains focused on fulfilling her need to hear why the relationship no longer works for Aiden.

Organizing

After we are done selecting and attending to stimuli in our environment, we need to organize them in such a way that we can make sense of them. The **organizing stage** in the perception process requires us to place what are often a number of confusing pieces of information into an understandable, accessible, and orderly fashion. We frequently categorize when we organize. For example, patients organize information they receive from physicians to reduce their uncertainty about their illness. Because doctors tend to use language that is highly abstract and usually technical, patients must organize the doctors' confusing information into specific and understandable bits of information. In a diagnosis of Alzheimer's disease, for example, a patient (and the family) may receive an inordinate amount of information, ranging from costs to medications to treatments to the emotional toll on family members. As with all families in these situations, the volume of information will have to be recognized, prioritized, and ultimately organized. In one study, for instance, patients who organized and managed their illness (breast cancer) reduced their uncertainty and ended up with a clearer understanding of their disease.[6]

When we organize, we usually use a **relational schema**, which is a mental framework or memory structure that people rely on to understand experience and to guide their future behavior. We rely on these frames or schema to support the inferences we make about the communication we have with others. Each of us requires a recognized way of understanding something or someone. Therefore, we employ schema to help sort out the perception process. Each time we communicate, we use a relational schema to facilitate that communication. For example, you may classify your boss according to *leadership style* (autocratic, diplomatic, yielding, etc.), *work ethic* (hard working, lazy, etc.), or *personality characteristic* (rude, compassionate, insincere, etc.). These schemata help you to recognize aspects of your boss's communication effectiveness without having to do a lot of thinking. Workers frequently use these types of classifications to help them organize the numerous messages given by a supervisor. For example, if the only types of messages that Jenny gets from her boss are insensitive and rude, she will likely categorize all of her boss's comments in that manner, regardless of whether the messages are framed that way.

When organizing, we look for consistencies rather than inconsistencies. Most of us would have a difficult time trying to communicate with each person in an individual manner as we meet in the subway, in the elevator, on the street, and in the grocery store. We, therefore, seek out familiar patterns of classifications: children, men, women, and others. Our decision of which classification to use is a selective process, because when we choose to include one category, we necessarily ignore, eliminate, or devalue another.

Organizing is essential because it expedites the perception process. However, as convenient as it may be, the impulse to lump people into recognizable categories can be problematic. Using broad generalizations to describe groups of people is considered **stereotyping**. Recall from Chapter 2 that stereotyping includes having fixed mental images of a particular group and subsequently communicating with an individual as if he or she is a member of that group. In many cases, stereotypes get in the way of effective perception. When we stereotype others, we use schema without being concerned with individual differences, and such categorization is problematic when we begin to adopt a fixed impression of a group of people.

Consider the following dialogue between JJ and Ryan, two students who happen to be on the school's baseball team, as they talk about their first day of class. In this scene, JJ obviously uses a unique schema to communicate about nontraditional-age learners in his class. He stereotypes this group of people as having free time, not wanting to help other students, and being uninvolved in campus activities. Ryan attempts to dispel JJ's perceptions by focusing on the value of nontraditional students in class and reminding JJ that he wouldn't want to be treated like a stereotype:

JJ: "What's with all the old people in this class?"

Ryan: "What do you mean, 'old'?"

JJ: "I mean, they don't have to take all these classes. They're in like one or two classes? It's crazy—they only have to worry about one thing."

Ryan: "Whadya mean? I had a few of what you say are 'old' students in my group in psychology, and to be honest, they really make a difference. One helped me get through the stats part of the class."

JJ: "And they ruined the curve, right?"

Ryan: "Ah . . . no. I think the professor listened to them when it came to curving the midterm. And, what is with you? Do you like it when everyone assumes you're a dumb jock just because you play baseball? I. Don't. Think. So."

We encounter problems when we act upon our stereotypes in the perception process. When we perceive people to possess a particular characteristic because they belong to a particular group, we risk communication problems. Perceiving men as lacking emotion, immigrants as recipients of public assistance, or car dealers as slick and dishonest makes honest and ethical communication difficult. People who stereotype in this way oversimplify the complex process of perception. It's a delicate balance—we need some shortcuts so that all the stimuli bombarding us doesn't overwhelm us, but not so many shortcuts that we treat people unfairly.

Interpreting

Consider the following two sets of words and phrases:

A. *beer, lake, taxes, student ID, rifle, cell phone*

B. *Canada, cheddar cheese, Mercedes-Benz, wheelchair, the Pope*

As you looked at both sets of words and phrases, chances are you tried to find some commonality or difference among them. And, despite the fact that the lists were simply random words we chose with no intention, you may have begun to find some ways in which the words are related. This process is at the core of interpretation.

After attention and selection and organization are complete, we are then ready to interpret. At the **interpreting stage**, we assign meaning to what we perceive and eventually evaluate the perception. Interpreting is required in every interpersonal

Attaching meaning to various stimuli is essential in the interpersonal perception process.

iStock.com/martin-dm

encounter. And, despite our best efforts, we usually fail to bring everything we know about something to the interpretation stage, resulting in a bias or a misinterpretation. For instance, think about the fact that our ethnocentrism (a concept we addressed in Chapter 2) often influences our perceptions. You may feel uncomfortable around someone who doesn't speak your primary language and perceive that person as a "foreigner" who doesn't understand the native land.

The process of interpreting something is not simple; it is influenced by relational history, personal expectations, and knowledge of the self and other. First, your *relational history,* a term we addressed in Chapter 1, affects your perception. Consider how you would perceive a statement by a close friend with whom you have had a relationship for more than 11 years versus a coworker with whom you have had a professional relationship for about a year. Because of your previous relationship experiences, perhaps your friend can get away with being sarcastic or pushy. However, your past experiences with the coworker are limited, and you may not be so open to sarcasm or pushiness.

Second, your personal expectations of an individual or situation can also affect how you interpret behavior. Let's say that you work in an office in which the department supervisor, Jonathan, is grouchy and intimidating. Consequently, whenever department meetings are held, workers avoid expressing their views openly, fearing verbal backlash from Jonathan. At one of these meetings, how would you talk about ways to improve efficiency in the office, fearing that Jonathan would react harshly?

In addition to relational history and personal expectations, your knowledge of yourself and others can greatly affect your interpretation of behavior. For instance, are you aware of your personal insecurities and uncertainties? Do they influence how you receive off-the-cuff or insensitive comments? What do you know about your own communication with others? Do you recognize your strengths and shortcomings in an interpersonal encounter? Further, what do you know about the other person? What shared fields of experience can be identified in your encounter? What assumptions about human behavior do you and others bring into a communication exchange? Such questions can help you assess how much knowledge you have about yourself and about the other communicator.

Memorizing

Storing meaning into your memory is what happens at the **memorizing stage**. In particular, at the memory step, we store the interpretations and evaluations from the previous stage so that we can later retrieve them. And, we maintain this memorization over time. Memory storage pertains to several areas, including how long the memory lasts (duration), how much can be stored (capacity), and the kind of information held by a communicator.[7]

Memory can be divided into short-term or long-term. **Short-term memory** (STM) is memory that is stored sequentially, meaning that something is linked up to a previously recognized memory. So, for example, if Josh introduces his best friend, Dana, to you, you will use STM when you determine that Dana and you once enrolled in a sociology class together. Your memory prompted you to "sequence" a previous Dana-related experience, specifically, one in class. Research shows that we are able to store only seven items at a time and that this storage is fragile because of various distractions or interruptions.[8] **Long-term memory** (LTM) refers to memory storage over an extended period of time. Theoretically, the capacity of LTM is unlimited and indefinite and it can range from a few minutes to a lifetime. Further, LTM can include such diverse memories as remembering your wedding day, state capitals, or requisite skills needed to ride a bicycle.

Memory is critical in our perception process because without it, we have no opportunity to have a conversation with many important people in our lives. Without storing information, for instance, it's fairly impossible to have an interpersonal encounter with anyone other than individuals whom you've not met. With a roommate, for example, you use both STM and LTM to understand things like paying the cable bill, cleaning the kitchen, or trying to figure out when you can have some downtime. Imagine not being able to talk about any previous issues with your roommate. How would that affect your perception of your roommate or challenges surrounding the relationship you have with them?

Retrieving

So far, we have attended to and selected stimuli, organized them, interpreted them, and memorized them to achieve meaning in the encounter. The **retrieving stage** of perception asks us to recall or access the information stored in our memories.

At first glance, retrieving appears to be pretty straightforward. Yet, as you think about it further, you'll see that the retrieval process involves selection and memory as well. At times, we use **selective retention**, a behavior that recalls information that agrees with our perceptions and selectively forgets information that does not. Here is an example that highlights the retrieval process and some potential problems associated with it.

Crystal sits with her friends as they talk about Professor Wendall. She doesn't really like what she hears. They talk about how boring the professor is and how hard his tests are. They also make fun of his southern drawl as they imitate his teaching. Crystal remembers that she had Professor Wendall for a class more than two years ago, but she doesn't recall him being such a bad professor. In fact, she remembers the biology course she took from him as challenging and interesting. It doesn't make sense that her friends don't like Wendall.

So, why do Crystal's friends and Crystal perceive Wendall differently? Crystal has retrieved information about her professor differently. He may have ridiculed students, but Crystal doesn't recall that. She remembers his accent, but she does not remember it causing any problems. She also recollects Wendall's exams to be fair. Thus, Crystal's retrieval process has influenced her perception of Professor Wendall in the classroom.

The selective perception process such as that of Crystal's begins as infants. In fact, babies begin processing and weeding out emotions as young as one year.[9] That is, although newborns look at faces and listen to voices, it is the retrieval of the familiar mother's voice that they prefer. This affirming retrieval can be traced back to prenatal experience insofar as the infant is continually exposed to the familiarity (and comfort) of the voice of their mother.

So far, we have examined the perception process and its components. As we know, interpersonal communication can be difficult at times. Understanding how perception functions in those encounters helps clarify potential problems. We now turn our attention to several influences on our perception process. As you will learn, a number of factors affect the accuracy of our perceptions.

3–2 INFLUENCES ON PERCEPTION

When we perceive activities, events, or other people, our perceptions are a result of many variables. In other words, we don't all perceive our environment in the same way because individual perceptions are shaped by individual differences. We now discuss five factors that shape our perceptions: culture, sex and gender, physical influences, technology, and our sense of self.

Culture

Culture is an important teacher of perception and provides the meaning we give to our perceptions. In Chapter 2, you learned how culture pervades our lives and affects communication. With regard to perception, culture dictates how something should be organized and interpreted. For instance, Bantu refugees from Somalia perceive time differently after they arrive in the United States. In Somalia, clocks and watches are rare. In the United States, we learn to be punctual and watch the clock or our cell phones regularly. In addition,

> Bantu parents learn that hitting their children is discouraged, though that was how they were disciplined in Africa. . . . They learn that Fourth of July fireworks are exploded to entertain not kill, and that being hit by a water balloon, as Bantu children were in one incident at school, is a game and not a hateful fight.[10]

In another example, in the United States, most people expect others to maintain direct eye contact during conversation. This conversational expectation is influenced by a European-American cultural value. However, traditional Japanese culture does not dictate direct eye contact during conversation.[11] So, you may erroneously feel that a classmate from Japan is not listening to you during a conversation when they don't maintain eye contact. As a final illustration, the teachings of Islam and Christianity guide many Lebanese American families in virtually every decision of life, including birth, death, education, courtship, marriage, divorce, and contraception.[12] This adherence to religious principles may be difficult for someone without any religious connection to understand.

Recall that each time you communicate with another person, you're drawing upon relational schema, a topic we discussed earlier. It may be difficult for two people with differing cultural backgrounds to sustain meaning if they are using two different schemata.

You can see, then, that cultural heritage affects how people perceive the world. In turn, that same cultural heritage affects how people communicate with and receive communication from others. Cultural variation is sometimes the reason we can't understand why someone does something or the reason why others question our behavior. Although it's natural to believe that others look at things the same way you do, remember that cultures can vary tremendously in their practices, and these differences affect perception.

Sex and Gender

Sex refers to the biological makeup of an individual (male or female). **Gender** refers to the learned behaviors a culture associates with being a male or female. As we noted in Chapter 2, we have a masculine or feminine gender. If we possess both masculine and feminine traits in equally large amounts, we are called *androgynous*. Possessing relatively low amounts of masculinity and femininity is termed *undifferentiated* (see Figure 3.1). It is possible to be a masculine female or a feminine male.

Researchers have investigated the relationship between perception and sex. Looking at perceptions of body type, researchers found that boys and girls in kindergarten and second grade differed in preferences for body types. Girls preferred a thinner figure than boys, and girls perceived thinness as both attractive and feminine. Boys preferred more athletic builds by kindergarten and were indirectly communicating "preferences for being smart, moderately strong, and somewhat prone to fighting."[13] Other researchers[14] have noted that when asked to compare themselves with others, college-age women—more than men—were inclined to compare themselves with professional models when evaluating their sexual attractiveness and weight. In fact, a website exists, www.mybodygallery.com, that allows women (but not men) to compare their bodies to other women!

Perceptual differences such as those above are a result of the way men and women have been raised. **Gender role socialization** is the process by which women and men learn the gender roles appropriate to their sex (e.g., being masculine if you are biologically a male). This socialization usually affects the way the sexes perceive the world. Messages about masculinity and femininity are communicated to children early in life, and these messages stick with us into adulthood. When we understand and organize our world around masculinity and femininity, we are using a **gender schema**.[15] Specifically, through a schema, we process and

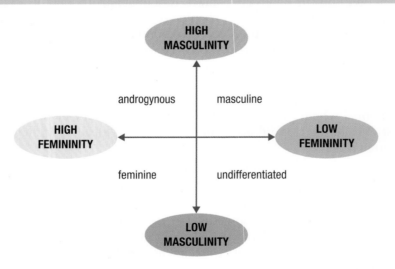

Figure 3.1 /// Gender Roles in Communication

categorize beliefs, ideas, and events as either masculine or feminine. If new information doesn't fit our gender schema, we tend to discard it.

 IPC Praxis

Discuss those times in which you imposed schemata upon others. Include at least two examples of how culture influenced your schemata.

Think about your perceptions of the following situations:

- A 5-year-old boy playing house with a 6-year-old neighbor girl
- A retired elderly male dancing with another male at a New Year's Eve party
- A newborn girl wearing a pink dress with flowers
- An adolescent female helping her father change the oil in his car

Do any of these situations contradict how you normally view male and female behavior? Does the age of the person make a difference? If so, why? What contributes to these perceptions? Parents? Media? Toys and games? Teachers? Peers? In all likelihood, each of these—in some way—has helped shape your current perceptions.

IPC Around Us

Few terms resonate more with technophiles than *selfie*.[16] The selfie has afforded people the means to perceive the world and themselves in personal ways. The selfie is a "self-portraiture" that allows people to present themselves in strategic ways. Selfies allow for a presentation of the self that transcends snapshots of accuracy. People can flex, pose, and Photoshop pictures, making the selfie less authentic. We rely on selfies because selfies tell others that we are important people, and despite pictures that may communicate otherwise, selfies often provide a lens into an individual's sense of self.

Reflection: Think about the sorts of selfies you have seen or even those of your own. Were they authentic representations of situations or did you manipulate the pictures in any way? What does that say, if anything, about your sense of self?

iStock.com/franckreporter

Men and women frequently look at things differently, depending on what gender schema they bring to a circumstance. As people sort out the various stimuli in their environment, gender cannot be ignored or devalued. Certainly, men and women can reject gender prescriptions and help society expand its perceptual expectations. However, most people continue to look at their worlds with some preconceived interpretations of the sexes, resulting in perceptions that may be distorted or inaccurate. In fact, in one study examining college student evaluations of their professors, female faculty were consistently ranked lower than their male counterparts. The researchers note that an "implicit bias" exists, suggesting that if female professors didn't conform to stereotyped notions of being "warm and supportive," then they were ranked lower than male professors. Men who were not rated as "warm" were not concurrently rated lower.[17]

Physical Influences

Our physical makeup is another element that contributes to variations in perceptions. *Age* is one example. We seem to perceive things differently as we age because of our life experiences. Being single and in debt at age 19 is different than being in debt as a single parent of three young children at age 45. No one is relying on a single teenager for sustenance, whereas a parent needs to consider their three children at home. The aging process allows us to frame our life experiences. Our *health,* too, helps shape perceptions. We broadly interpret health to mean such things as fatigue, stress, biorhythms, and physical ability. For example, consider the perceptual challenges of those who have significant health issues such as chronic migraine headaches or arthritis. Perceptions of work and home relationships will likely be influenced if an individual is in constant pain. Additionally, some people simply do not have the physical *ability* to see another person's behaviors or to listen attentively to their words. Others need some accommodation to be able to attend to stimuli in their surroundings. Our senses vary, often according to our physical limitations. Imagine the difficulty a physically challenged individual experiences trying to navigate nonaccessible curbs compared with someone who does not require motorized accommodation such as a wheelchair. If you don't use a wheelchair, you won't perceive the curbs as potential obstacles.

Social Media

Now more than ever, technology affects our perceptions. Social media, in particular—which has little oversight and relatively little accountability—requires us to be critical in our perceptions. Yet, let's establish that Facebook and Instagram, however, differ from more professionally oriented platforms such as LinkedIn. Consider, for instance, how you present yourself online (a topic we'll return to later in the chapter). For some of you, your Facebook page is filled with personal photos and quotations that provide others with indications of who you are. In fact, we already know that users of sites such as Facebook and Instagram derive a great deal of satisfaction from having others view their social network of friends and/or followers.[18] Moreover, with Facebook, in particular, researchers have concluded that user #1 perceives user #2 as more socially attractive if both have similar numbers of friends. In other words, there is less social attractiveness if one user has, say, 400 friends, and another has, say, 900 friends.

Technology makes possible the cultivation of online relationships. If, for instance, you visit a dating website and find a match, you need to remember that you are relying on text that is written onscreen accompanied by a downloaded picture. The picture may be inauthentic or out-of-date, or you might be the target of someone who gives false information. Further, you are unable to read the facial expressions, listen to the vocal characteristics, look at the clothing, watch the body movement, and observe the eye contact of the other person, all critical parts of the perception process outlined above. In sum, the Internet can leave us relationally shortchanged because we can't perceive the whole picture—we are receiving only what the other person wants us to receive. Likewise, we communicate only what we wish to communicate to the other person.

The Internet is not the only technological development that affects our perceptions. For example, consider how our perceptions are altered when we observe various people with smartphones, handheld game consoles, or Bluetooth headsets. For instance, what do you think when you see a teenager talking on a cell phone? Now, consider your reaction to an older man in a suit talking on a cell phone while walking down the street. And, still, how do you perceive an elderly woman in an assisted living facility on a cell phone? Do you experience any differences in perception? Now, change the context. A teenager is sitting with her mother at the bus stop, the older man is driving in his BMW, and the senior is enrolled in a college class. Does the context make a difference in your perceptions?

Our Sense of Self

A final factor that shapes our perceptions is self-concept, which we discuss further in this chapter. For now, it's important to point out that our perceptions of ourselves are influential in the perception process. We define **self-concept** as a relatively stable set of perceptions held by an individual. Our self-concept is rather consistent from one situation to another. For instance, our core beliefs and values about our intellectual curiosity or charitable ways stay fairly constant. Self-concept is flexible at times: for example, our beliefs about our ability to climb a mountain may differ at age 30 and age 65.

Self-concept affects our perceptions of others' feelings about us. Generally, statements from people we trust and respect carry more weight than statements from those we don't. Consider, then, the way you would perceive the same words depending on whether they came from a close friend or from a classmate. Suppose, for instance, that you perceive yourself to be an excellent listener. If a classmate tells you that she thinks you don't listen well, you might not be as willing to consider changing your behavior as you would if a close friend made the same observation. We discuss the notion of self-concept in much more detail next.

Thus far, we have given you a sense of what perception is, noted why it's important in interpersonal communication, and identified some significant influences on the perception process. Throughout our discussion, you have seen that it's virtually impossible to separate our sense of self from our perceptions. Now, we dig further into the self and explain the importance of the self in interpersonal communication. We start by explaining the self and its dimensions.

3–3 DIMENSIONS OF THE SELF

How do you see yourself? This is the key question guiding our discussion of the self. Answering this question is not easy. Certainly, we realize that you can't answer this question in a word or two. Previously, we noted that self-concept is both fixed and flexible. It makes sense, then, that you would inevitably begin your answer to this question with "Well, it depends."

This chapter will help you formulate and clarify a response to this question. If you think "it depends," you're partially correct. However, there are ways to articulate a more complete response. We hope that you will think about this question as you read this section. We are guided by the following principle as we introduce this information: *To have a relationship with someone else, you must first have a relationship with yourself.* In other words, communication begins and ends with you. Let's explore self-concept and what it entails.

Self-Concept

Earlier, we defined the self-concept as a relatively fixed set of perceptions we hold of ourselves. Self-concept is everything we believe about ourselves. This collection of perceptions is more stable than fleeting, but that does not mean that our self-concept is permanent. One reason self-concept changes is because it emerges from our various interpersonal encounters with others. More than 80 years ago, scholars posited that communication with others shapes personal identity.[19] This theory is called the **Symbolic Interactionism Theory**.

To begin our discussion, consider two versions of the following story regarding Terrence Washington. As a self-employed painter, Terrence relies on small projects to make a living. His recent surgery to correct tendonitis has caused him to be laid up at home, unable to continue to paint homes. His inability to take on jobs has not only caused him some financial problems, but has also affected his psychological well-being. Terrence feels useless and can't seem to shake a sense of self-doubt.

Now consider Terrence's situation again. This time, though, Terrence's friends visit him, assuring him that this circumstance is only temporary. One friend suggests that Terrence help her figure out a color scheme for her living room. Another friend gets Terrence a temporary job advising customers in a local paint store. Although he is unable to paint homes, Terrence finds himself as busy as ever. His self-doubt begins to dissipate, and his feelings about himself take on a positive cast.

The two examples result in different self-concepts for Terrence. In the first example, we see a man who is beginning to doubt his own abilities, and whose self-concept will likely proceed into a negative spiral: He wants to get better, but to get better he needs to feel good about himself. Because he doesn't feel good about himself, he won't get better. The second scenario underscores the importance of others in our self-concept. Terrence's friends positively affect his career prospects, and, in turn, his self-concept.

Terrence's self-concept is influenced by both an awareness of himself and an assessment of his potential. These influences—self-awareness and self-esteem—are the two primary components of self-concept (Figure 3.2).

Self-Awareness

Self-awareness is our understanding of who we are. We begin our lives as blank slates—that is, we are born with no consciousness of who we are. We rely on

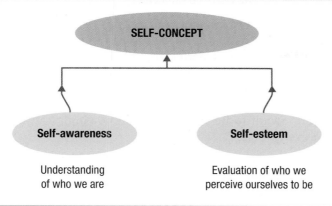

Figure 3.2 /// Components of Self-Concept

SELF-CONCEPT

Self-awareness
Understanding
of who we are

Self-esteem
Evaluation of who we
perceive ourselves to be

specialized others, or those individuals who remain central in our lives. These often include our closest friends, coworkers, or family members who help us recognize our selves. In Terrence Washington's case, his self-awareness as an adult stems from the belief that he is a painter who has successfully made a living painting other people's homes. Understanding self-awareness serves as the first step toward understanding our self-esteem.

Self-Esteem

Self-esteem is a bit more complicated than self-awareness. Our **self-esteem** is an evaluation of who we perceive ourselves to be. In a sense, our self-esteem is related to our **self-worth**, or how we feel about our talents, abilities, knowledge, expertise, and appearance. Our self-esteem comprises the images we hold—that is, our social roles (e.g., father, receptionist, electrician), the words we use to describe these social roles (e.g., doting grandparent, courteous police officer, skilled nurse), and how others see us in those roles (e.g., competent, negligible, thorough). Further, the self-esteem of a sender affects how you receive a message. This is especially important in situations where you are required to offer feedback. In an interview situation, for example, if your interviewer is awkward or uncomfortable and fumbling through the interview, then you, as the potential employee, may have a difficult time achieving meaning. Clearly, the interviewer's communication skills do not elicit an opportunity for clarity.

Video 3.2

We develop our self-esteem as a result of overcoming setbacks, achieving our goals, and helping others in their pursuits. Even when we fail, our feelings of self-worth may not be jeopardized if we think we have beaten obstacles along the way. Think, for instance, about the difficulties of divorce. For many married couples, divorce is an acrimonious process pitting one spouse against the other. Yet, some ex-spouses survive these breakups as friends. Some research, for instance, has found that ex-spouses do not remain angry forever after a divorce; indeed, some become very good friends.[20] What appears to be an insurmountable relational episode, then, can actually result in some couples being able to talk to one another on intimate terms. Some couples, overcoming obstacles, report being able to retain some of the original feelings of affirmation they once held for each other. Clearly, the self-esteem of such couples is positively affected by the ability to manage the divorce effectively.

Other people do not always enhance our feelings of self-worth. Regardless of how many family or friends surround us during difficult times, it might be the case that nothing helps us feel better about ourselves. At times, others may unwittingly contribute to our negative self-perceptions. For example, if you try to encourage someone after the loss of a relational partner by showering him with platitudes or cliché phrases (e.g., "I'm sure you'll make it" or "Hey, not all relationships were meant to be"), you may unknowingly cause your friend to feel annoyed or even worse.

Like our self-concept, self-esteem may fluctuate. One day we consider ourselves to be excellent, and the next day we are down on ourselves. This variation in self-esteem is often due to our interactions with others in our lives and the feedback we've received. As we alluded to earlier, we usually listen more carefully to those we admire or whose previous advice was worthwhile. We generally reject the opinions of those we don't know. Most of us are able to understand that one situation shouldn't necessarily affect our feelings of self-worth.

Finally, some writers have talked about the relationship between self-esteem and "selfies" (see IPC Around Us on page 75) that people take. Regardless of whether or not you believe it's technological narcissism or a "feel-good creative way" to promote yourself, this personal snapshotting is everywhere. Scholars have concluded that these selfies promote one's well-being and help in feelings of self-worth.[21] Yet, selfies can also damage one's self-esteem in that they can cause individuals to lose contact with their "authentic selves."[22] Without this authenticity, our relationship building becomes more challenging.

Self-Fulfilling Prophecy

The self is also formed, in part, by the predictions you make about yourself. When predictions about a future interaction lead you to behave in ways that make certain that the interaction occurs as you imagined, you have created a self-fulfilling prophecy. If you're in a class and do well with a professor whom you feel respects you, or conversely, do poorly in a class with a professor whom you feel disrespects you, you know what a self-fulfilling prophecy feels like.

Self-concepts frequently lead to **self-fulfilling prophecies**. These prophecies may either be *self-imposed,* which occurs when your own expectations influence your behavior, or *other imposed,* which occurs when the expectations of another person influence your behavior. Self-fulfilling prophecies can take place within a number of interpersonal situations, from the family to the workplace. Consider the following:

- Octavio is nervous about talking to someone he respects and admires, thinking that he probably is going to blunder when he speaks with that person. When he meets the person, he trips over his words.

- Diana approaches a job interview thinking that her job expertise and communication skills will get her the job, and she prepares thoroughly for the interview. The job is offered to her.

Figure 3.3 /// Stages of Self-Fulfilling Prophecies

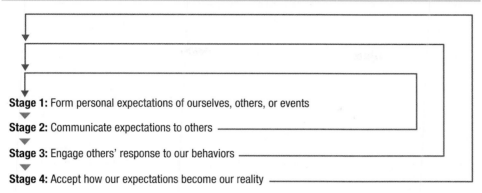

Stage 1: Form personal expectations of ourselves, others, or events

Stage 2: Communicate expectations to others

Stage 3: Engage others' response to our behaviors

Stage 4: Accept how our expectations become our reality

Although each of these prophecies is different, self-fulfilling prophecies usually follow a pattern: (a) We form expectations of ourselves, others, or particular events; (b) we communicate that expectation to others; (c) others respond to our behaviors; and (d) our expectations become reality. Ultimately, our expectations confirm and reinforce our original thinking about ourselves. However, each stage returns to the first stage, because the original perception prompted the prophecy itself (Figure 3.3).

Here is an example of how self-fulfilling prophecies function in a person's life. As a young child, Anaba felt that she was inarticulate and awkward. As a result, she wasn't particularly social and avoided talking to people face to face, especially in social settings (*Stage 1:* Form expectation of event). While attending a wedding reception, Rodney, one of the guests at her table, asked Anaba to dance. She told him that she was not a good dancer, was not interested in making a fool of herself on the dance floor, and did not want to dance with him (*Stage 2:* Communicate expectation to other). When Rodney returned to his seat, he thought to himself: "Wow, she is shy! And talk about not wanting to hang out with people" (*Stage 3:* Others respond to behavior). At the same time, Anaba thought that Rodney did not want to talk to her any further because she was not as outgoing as the other women at the reception (*Stage 4:* Confirmation of original perception).

 **IPC Praxis**

Self-fulfilling prophecies are often discussed in relationship to malevolent behaviors and practices. Yet, there are behaviors of ours that should be enhanced. Provide a few examples of a "positive" self-fulfilling prophecy and the effects of that upon your relationships with others.

As you can tell, the self doesn't simply develop without being influenced in some way. After you gain an understanding of yourself, you can begin to address how you present yourself to others. Researchers refer to this as identity management, which is the topic we explore in the next section.

3–4 IDENTITY MANAGEMENT

Video 3.3

At the heart of our discussion of the self is identity management. **Identity management** refers to the communication practices we employ to influence how others will perceive us.[23] In a general sense, our identity is associated with a category of sorts, such as sex, age, occupation, and so on. This approach suggests that people behave according to their goals and that a person's competency and identity all work together in our interactions with others. When we manage our identities, we decide on a particular communication behavior to influence how others perceive us. Another important reason to communicate our identities is to be active citizens. Voicing an identity has been frequently undertaken by activist groups, including such diverse movements as #TakeAKnee, #MeToo, #IceBucketChallenge, and #308Removed.

One of the first people to discuss identity management was sociologist Erving Goffman. Goffman believed that identity is best explained by comparing it to theatrical performances where people possess various motivations for controlling the impressions they receive from others. People are actors who "perform" for the audiences around us. And, subsequently, performers expect audiences to appreciate the veracity of their performances.

This image of a theatrical production may seem a bit odd to you. After all, who wants to admit to "acting" in an interpersonal encounter? We're not like the monarchy who "hold court" with the public or the Pope, who is often associated with "having an audience." Still, we all take on particular social roles and manage these roles to achieve meaning in our relationships with others.

Identity management does not happen without some risk and consequence. For instance, suppose Victor, a 25-year-old graduate student, decides to move back in with his parents for financial reasons, becoming one of a group of people who are called "boomerang kids" and who are part of an "accordion family." The rules that were once part of the household (e.g., "No profanity" or "Clean up your room") may now seem out of date to Victor. As he figures out how to act at home and, in turn, formulate his "new identity," he may reject the household rules because he feels that he is too old to have to abide by them. Yet, what happens if his mom or dad requires adherence to the rules? Aren't they also managing their identity as Victor manages his? How Victor handles these different identities will affect the quality of the interpersonal communication he has with his parents. We explore the notion of families and communication in Chapter 11.

Because identity management requires some risk, we may find ourselves in situations that compromise our sense of self. We become preoccupied with protecting the image we decide to present to others. In doing so, we are engaged in facework, a topic we now explore in more detail.

Identity Management and Facework

In interpersonal interactions, people shape their identities to display a particular sense of self, one fundamental theme of this chapter. When we get into conversations with others, we offer our identity and hope that others will accept it. This is critical to our self-concept overall and to our self-esteem in particular. The image of the self—the public identity—that we present to others in our interpersonal encounters is called face. Generally, face is somewhat automatic. The metaphor of face pervades U.S. society. We talk about "saving face," "in your face," and, especially in this book, "face-to-face" communication all the time. To a large extent, everyone is concerned with how others perceive them. We work toward creating an identity that is socially acceptable. To this end, we can look at **face** as how you want to be perceived by others, how you want others to treat you, and how you end up treating others. The essence of face is politeness and this politeness includes dignity and respect for others.

We take it for granted that there is a give and take in maintaining face. In other words, following the transactional nature of communication that we identified in Chapter 1, both communicators in an interaction are responsible for **facework**, the set of coordinated behaviors that help us either to reinforce or to threaten our competence. Facework is usually a two-person event in an interpersonal relationship in that relational partners typically negotiate who they are to each other.

We present two types of face in our conversations with others: positive face and negative face. **Positive face** pertains to our desire to be liked by significant people in our lives. It is the favorable image that people present to others, hoping that others validate that image. We have positive face when others confirm our beliefs, respect our abilities, and value what we value. That's not to say that individuals have to agree with everything we have to say or with everything we believe—that would be impossible! Most of us simply want to relate to people who make efforts to understand, appreciate, and respect our perceptions and competencies.

When one "loses" face (e.g., a threat to positive face), the consequences can be very real. One study, for example, found that those using social media sites similar to Facebook used retaliatory aggression such as "destroying" the face of those who experience rejection and criticism.[24] In particular, if a participant was rejected from joining particular groups ("We don't want you in our group") or criticized once in a particular group ("No offense, but when we saw your profile, we laughed"), that person was more likely to send "virtual ticking bombs" to those group members. In addition, those where a positive face was assaulted were less likely to send "virtual smiley faces." Aggressive techniques undertaken in this way were efforts in restoring positive face.

Negative face refers to our desire for others to refrain from imposing their will on us. A great number of us (especially those from the United States) desire to be independent. Negative face is maintained when people respect our individuality and avoid interfering with our actions or beliefs. Again, this is not to say that people will simply become dutiful and obedient in our conversations without challenging us. Rather, we're suggesting that people periodically need to feel autonomous and want others to be flexible enough to respect this need in interpersonal encounters.

When we receive messages that do not support either our positive or negative face, our identities become threatened. Face threats can jeopardize meaning in an interpersonal encounter. If our positive face is threatened—such as when another person challenges our skills—we have to figure out how to deal with the threat to our identity. For instance, let's say that Pat is a hairstylist and that Nola, a client of 19 years, threatens Pat's positive face by asking Pat, "Where *did* you find this color? In your basement cabinet?" Because Pat takes pride in her abilities, this insult may be difficult to overcome. Pat will have to figure out a way to preserve her positive face with Nola. Indeed, this process happens frequently in our lives, and we have to learn how to handle these face threats. In the United States, we are normally not conditioned to help others "save" their face, although people in other cultures (e.g., Japan, Vietnam) are attuned to maintaining everyone's face in an interaction.

As we discuss the topic of identity management, recognize that managing our identities is important because so much of our interpersonal meaning is based on our competency, identity, and face. Thinking of a job interview again, when you work on your identity management, three issues come into play: First, *timing* (saying "I hate meaningless jobs; this sounds like one") and second, *focusing on the present* ("I like the fact that you are encouraging innovation").

In addition, a third behavior relates to a private assessment of your own comments and behaviors in the interview. We call this self-monitoring. The term **self-monitoring** refers to the extent to which people actively think about and control their public behaviors and actions.[25] Self-monitoring is important in identity management because people who are aware of their behaviors and the effects of their behaviors in a conversation are viewed as more competent communicators. Be careful, however. Practicing self-monitoring too much will result in being preoccupied with details that may be unimportant. On the other hand, being ignorant of your strengths and shortcomings in a conversation is just as problematic. Finding a reasonable middle ground in self-monitoring is critical in identity management (see the CAT at the end of the chapter for an assessment of self-monitoring).

3–5 ONLINE IDENTITY MANAGEMENT

On the Internet, individuals typically communicate and manage their identities through identity markers. An **identity marker** is an electronic extension of who someone is. In other words, an identity marker is an expansion of the self. Two primary identity markers exist on the Internet: screen names and personal home pages.

Our need to showcase our online identity via social media continues to escalate.

As in face-to-face relationships, online relationships inevitably require introductions. Yet, unlike in interpersonal relationships, we can introduce ourselves online by using names that are odd, silly, fun, editorial, or outright offensive. Whether you're on Instagram, Tumblr, Twitter, or Skype, the screen names you choose serve to communicate the uniqueness of you—the sender of a message. For some, screen names function as a way for communicators to protect their identities from others until more familiarity and comfort develops.

You likely have never thought about this before, but people use screen names for all sorts of purposes. Maybe you just use your first and/or last name. Most, however, remain more creative. Some names may be shaped by fiction (e.g., MadMadHatter or hobbitfeets), others by popular culture (e.g., KimmelFan) and still others by a desire to reinforce personal values (e.g., veganvixen420 or xNODISHONORx). And, generally, unless some sort of online harassment occurs or a platform upgrade is required, people don't change their screen name. Think about the number of times you've changed your name for one of your social media accounts. Rarely? Never? Often? Your response to this alone suggests the extent to which you manage your online identity.

In addition to your screen name, you may also have your own personal homepage or personal diary that you decided to make public. Or, perhaps you subscribe to a series of personal homepages which are called webrings. These rings provide you even more information about an individual's identity, since they include features such as a resume or portfolio, information on personal hobbies and genealogy, photographs of the person and their family members, friends, pets, architectural preferences, sibling conflict information, preferences for local restaurants, and links to advocacy groups, among many other indicators of one's sense of self. Webring advocates are clear in how identities can be gleaned online: "With a Webring, you're not limited to one social realm. You could jump from the nightmare of a divorced attorney in New York to a teen's ramblings about going to the mall."[26]

IPC Praxis

What advice would you give to a preteen if they were interested in developing a homepage? Does this advice differ from suggestions you'd give to a parent? A senior citizen? Yourself? Use examples to illustrate your views.

Communicating one's embodied identity via webrings and homepages is often enlightening to others. First, as is the case with personal interactions, people may strategically present themselves in a certain way on their personal web pages. Digital photos, slick graphics, funky fonts, interesting links, and creative screen names may communicate a sense of organization, creativity, insight, and invitation. These sorts of intentional markers may be consciously presented on web pages so that others have a comprehensive understanding of who the person is and can find out a bit about their attitudes, beliefs, and values.

While most of these messages are aimed to communicate a personal identity about being an open and inviting individual, not everyone uses a homepage for that reason. Some research, for instance, studied identity markers of those with post-stroke aphasia (language impairment following a stroke).[27] The study investigated how these aphasia participants viewed screenshots of over 1,500 online posts related to aphasia. Results showed that stigmas related to this population were managed by posting information that was undertaken to raise awareness and to communicate whether or not they were willing to reveal their aphasia.

Throughout this chapter, we have emphasized the link between our perceptions, our sense of self, and our communication with others. The following four conclusions regarding perception, the self, and interpersonal communication illustrate how the three are closely related.

One conclusion regarding the intersection of perception, self, and interpersonal communication suggests that *each person operates with a personal set of perceptions.* An **implicit personality approach** suggests that we fill in the blanks when identifying characteristics of people, using a few characteristics to draw inferences about others. We believe that certain traits go together and communicate with people on this basis. For example, consider how you fill in the following sentences (choose from the words in parentheses):

- Dr. Hess is warm, sensitive, and (intelligent, dumb).
- Dr. Aldine is rude, distant, and (compassionate, unreliable).

Choosing *intelligent* in the first sentence and *unreliable* in the second sentence illustrates the **halo effect**, which states that you will match like qualities with each other. A **positive halo** occurs when you place positive qualities (warm, sensitive, and intelligent) together. A **negative halo** exists when you place negative qualities (unintelligent, rude, and temperamental) together. Once we form an impression (positive or negative) of another, we may begin to interact with the other person in a way that supports the impression. Yet, again, caution yourself against presuming that an impression is always accurate.

Implicit personality enables us to manage effectively a lot of information about another person. However, be careful of overusing implicit personality behaviors when communicating with others. Don't perceive characteristics in a person that don't exist. Responding to people according to such predispositions can lead to problems in interpersonal communication.

A second conclusion on the symbiotic nature of perception, self, and interpersonal communication relates to perceptual problems. In general, *perceptual errors can cause problems in our communication with others.* For example, most often we create explanations or attach meaning to someone's behavior. It has been said that we are all "naive psychologists" in that we try to uncover reasons for people's actions, yet we may have no real understanding of the person or the circumstances surrounding the actions.

Our attributions are often influenced by our feelings for another person. For instance, have you ever arranged to meet someone for coffee and that person showed up late? What were your thoughts while waiting? If the person was someone you liked, you may have attributed the lateness to something out of their control, such as car trouble, congested traffic, disobedient children, and so forth.

If the person was someone you didn't know well or didn't like, you may have attributed the delay to something within the person's control. Perhaps you viewed the person's behavior as intentional. Yet, the person might have been late because of unforeseen circumstances. We may be "naive," then, to the number of different influences on behavior. In Chapter 7, we look further into how feelings and emotions affect our relationships with others.

 IPC Praxis

There is some evidence that we make various assumptions about others based on their accents. Do you agree? Why or why not? Identify some examples to support your thoughts.

In addition to the preceding two conclusions, we also believe that *the self undergoes a continual process of modification.* Our sense of who we are changes as our relationships change. In other words, our identity—like communication—is a process, not a constant. This conclusion implies that we, and our relationships, are changing. Consequently, our interpersonal communication should reflect these changes. Think about the way you were as a sophomore in high school and look at who you are now. Your perceptions of your own strengths and shortcomings have inevitably changed over the years. Imagine what it would be like if you didn't change or if others didn't change.

Finally, our fourth conclusion is unambiguous: *The self responds to a variety of stimuli.* To understand this conclusion, consider the fact that we respond to people (e.g., father or grandparent), surroundings (e.g., noise level or lighting), and technology (e.g., an Internet site or a television program). Each has the capacity to affect the self.

Before we close this chapter, we wish to identify the interplay among the perception process, the self, and our online conversations and relationships. Communication theorists have advanced the notion that our online relationships are important and that it's possible, and even likely, that we can have highly satisfying and quality online relationships.[28] We can establish and maintain relationships online (we adapt to the medium), and although nonverbal cues are at a minimum, our perceptions and presentations of our various selves provide for a mutually satisfying relationship.

In Chapter 1, we identified Social Information Processing as a theory primarily concerned with our online relationship development. Expanding that thinking, let's briefly examine the role that perception and self-presentation play as we further elaborate upon the theory. One relevant component of that model (as it relates to the current discussion) is **impression management**, which is the unconscious or strategic effort to influence another's perceptions. Research has found that communicators will try to "fill in the blanks" with respect to incomplete perceptions (think about implicit personality processes). Subsequently, we may make assessments of another's behavior. Online, we use a "perceptual personality" framework ("You sound just like my uncle Martin; he's my favorite relative"), and this framing influences the direction of the relationship.

The online relationship between two communicators does not require both to be at their computers, laptops, or smartphones at the same time. This "asynchronous communication" provides for further perception checking. That is, when we send a text or an online message, before pressing Send, we have time to reflect on the message, edit it, and review it. The difference in elapsed time affords for both online interactants to cultivate a certain type of communication approach. Suppose, for instance, that Michael and Ben have been communicating back and forth since meeting on a dating website. Although they haven't met, they have sent texts and e-mails with personal disclosures and words that suggest a future together. In sum, the couple believes, in their eyes, that they not only have a relationship, but that it's moving to an intimate relationship, and their perception of such a relationship is illustrated by the content sequencing of messages. We know many of you have had similar experiences in your relational life that began online (see our TIP on Social Information Processing Theory).

 Theory-Into-Practice (TIP)

Social Information Processing Theory

One fundamental claim in this theory relates to the possibility of establishing equally intimate relationships online as f2f. Do you agree with this premise? Point to examples that both support and differ from your belief. What do you see as the most challenging experience getting in the way of online intimacy? How would you work to correct these challenges? What kinds of experiences do you find most rewarding—online, f2f, or does it matter to you?

Perceptions, however, remain insufficient in online relationship development. The self also manifests itself in a number of curious, yet important ways. Social networking sites (SNS) such as Facebook are filled with people who wish to provide a number of different self-presentations. As we know, many SNS allow users to use a number of different behaviors to establish and maintain a particular online identity/self-image (e.g., displaying relational status such as divorced or single, using pictures). This identity is based on how senders and receivers present themselves to others. Some, for instance, may desire to show that they are animal lovers and participate in chat rooms dedicated to pets or display pictures of their pets. Others may wish to show that they are open about their past and discuss alcoholic episodes. Still others may wish to demonstrate their intellectual curiosity by quoting philosophers or providing links to published works. Clearly, there is a strategic effort to present one's self online, and individuals are tacitly aware of these efforts.

Finally, three selves exist in online environments: the **actual self** (attributes of an individual), the **ideal self** (attributes an individual ideally possesses), and the **ought self** (attributes the individual should possess).[29] These various selves are frequently employed strategically, and they are often managed online in real time (while someone is communicating with the other). Furthermore, we gather and accrue the impressions we receive from online presentations, providing a more comprehensive understanding of our online partners.

IPC Careers

Perception and Self-Esteem for a Salesperson

iStock.com/praetorianphoto

Being a salesperson today requires skills in perception and ongoing accommodations to self-esteem. At times, salespeople need to make quick assessments of another's behavior and preferences. Other times, a strategic approach to sales is needed. Both situations require adeptness at tuning in to relevant stimuli and tuning out the irrelevant and unnecessary. Selective perception, then, becomes critical. In addition, salespeople need to be prepared for rejection and even outright rudeness. Maintaining one's self-esteem—as it relates to self-worth—is imperative to ensure ongoing success. An expert in sales recognizes that things will go both wrong and right; being able to adapt to this uncertainty is essential.

Reflection: Provide some specific examples of how self-esteem is affected for a person selling (a) T-shirts at a school fundraiser, (b) pre-owned cars, and (c) newspaper subscriptions.

By now, you should have a clear idea about the importance of perception and the self in communicating with others. How can you work toward checking your perceptions so that you don't make erroneous assumptions about others or their behavior? What can you do to improve your self-concept? How do our perceptions and self-concepts function in our interpersonal communication? Let's look at a number of skills to consider as you respond to these questions.

3–6 SKILL SET FOR IMPROVING PERCEPTION CHECKING AND SELF-ACTUALIZATION

We divide our skill set into the different areas discussed in this chapter: perception and identity. First, when we check our perceptions, we attempt to rid ourselves of our predisposed biases and images of people. Checking our perceptions also helps build meaning in our relationships. Since we believe that perception and identity are interrelated, we provide two different skill sets to consider.

Enhancing Perceptual Accuracy

As we learned, perceptions can be clouded, inaccurate, and full of misfires. Yet, we know in order to have transactional meaning, we need to be fully aware of our own habits and behaviors as well as be prepared to modify them as necessary.

Understand Your Personal Worldview

Each of us enters a communication situation with a unique worldview, a theme we introduced in Chapter 2, which is, in part, a personal framework to view the events surrounding us. Your worldview is your conception and perception of the environment around you—both near and far. Your worldview, for instance,

Table 3.2 /// Skill Set for Enhancing Perception Checking		
a. Understand your personal worldview.		
b. Realize that perceptions are incomplete.		
c. Seek explanation and clarification.		
d. Distinguish facts from inferences.		
e. Guard against the "tech trap."		
f. Your skill suggestion		

differs from that of your classmate. You may believe that humans are basically good creatures, while your classmate may have a more cynical view of humanity, citing war, famine, and greed. We all enter interpersonal encounters with various worldviews, and we need to recognize the influence that these views have on our communication.

Realize That Perceptions Are Incomplete

There is no possible way for us to perceive our environment completely. By its nature, perception is an incomplete process. When we attend to certain aspects of our surroundings, as you learned earlier, we necessarily fail to attend to something else. If you are working on a group project and think a group member is lazy, you should caution against a quick judgment. Perhaps there is some other issue, such as working a late-night job or caring for a sick relative, that is contributing to the group member's behavior. And don't forget that people, objects, and situations typically change (consider the dynamic nature of the self), thereby making it important to update your perceptions periodically.

Seek Explanation and Clarification

We need to double-check with others to make sure that we are accurately perceiving a person, situation, or event. Seeking out others regarding our perception is important because it moves two people closer to mutual understanding. Begin by offering your personal input of what you noticed and then solicit or wait for the other's perception ("Let me see if my thinking is correct here . . ."). If necessary, seek out explanation and clarification.

Consider the following encounter between 51-year-old Glenn and 36-year-old Marnita. The two have been happily dating for a month, but their 15-year age difference has prompted Glenn to reconsider his future with Marnita. Glenn calls Marnita at 10 p.m. to let her know that they had better stop dating. She is puzzled by the call because the last time the two were together, three nights earlier, Glenn talked about how much he enjoyed being with her. Marnita wonders how things could have changed so quickly. Immediately, Marnita feels defensive and recalls a few weeks ago when the two of them were in a fight over Glenn's previous partner. She knows she criticizes a lot, and her previous boyfriends didn't like that. She is convinced that's why Glenn wants out. Yet, Marnita doesn't realize that their age difference is really what is troubling Glenn.

Most likely, Marnita could have reconciled her feelings of confusion and frustration if she had sought out clarification and explanation of Glenn's perceptions. If she had, they could have arrived at a more amicable end to their relationship or perhaps even reconciled.

Distinguish Facts From Inferences

One way to explain and to clarify is to distinguish facts from inferences. **Facts** are statements based on observations; **inferences** are personal interpretations of facts. Looking at her frequent head shifts and penetrating stare of a woman at the baggage claim at an airport may prompt you to draw the conclusion that she is unhappy that the airline lost her luggage. But this is your inference, not a fact.

A reliance on technology has resulted in people becoming less patient and less accurate in their perceptions.

During the perception process, we need to be careful not to confuse facts and inferences. Remember the implicit personality dynamic which we explained earlier? Take extra care and avoid filling in the blanks or extending a perception beyond the facts. At the very least, recognize when you are using an inference.

Guard Against the "Tech Trap"

We cannot overemphasize the importance of being patient and tolerant in your perceptions. Because we live in an "instant society," we expect things to happen quickly. It's no surprise that the site Instagram is called that for a reason! However, unlike texting, our perceptions require some degree of patience. Think of this as if you had started a fitness regimen. You certainly won't walk away from the first week of classes and achieve a buffed body! The same is true with perceptions. Often, you need to check out the accuracy of your perceptions and that's a behavior that takes some time.

Enhancing Your Self-Actualization

Understanding how you function and what you bring to an interaction is paramount. In fact, we all need to work toward improving self-actualization, a concept we explained in Chapter 1. To this end, you need to understand the dynamic interplay between the self and the conversations you have with others. We explain several below.

Table 3.3 /// Skills to Enhance Self-Actualization		
a. Seek the desire to change.		
b. Set reasonable personal goals.		
c. Review and revise.		
d. Surround yourself with relational uppers.		
e. Your skill suggestion		

Seek the Desire to Change

As we mentioned earlier in the chapter, our self-concept changes as we grow. Therefore, we should be willing to change our self-concepts throughout our lifetimes. If you want to be more sensitive to others, make that commitment. If you'd like to be more assertive, take the initiative to change. Having the desire or will to change your self-concept is not always easy. We grow comfortable with ourselves even when we recognize ways we'd like to change. We need to realize that a changing self-concept can help us grow just as much as it can help our relationships grow.

Set Reasonable Personal Goals

Always strive to have reasonable goals and avoid setting goals that are impossible to meet. Otherwise, you may feel a sense of failure. A reasonable goal for a college student might be to do all the assigned reading in each class for a semester. Studying hard, reading and rereading the classroom readings and textbook, participating in class when appropriate, and being a good listener seem like reasonable and attainable goals. Setting a goal of getting a perfect grade point average, writing error-free papers, and understanding the course content without asking questions seems unreasonable. And don't expect to be someone you are not.

Review and Revise

At times, you may make changes to your self-concept that are not entirely beneficial. Think about the implication of these changes and consider revising them if necessary. For instance, you may have tried to be more accommodating to your family members, but the result was that your integrity was trampled. Perhaps you made some changes at work, trying to engage people who annoy you daily, and now you're having trouble getting your work finished on time because these people stop to talk throughout the day. Perhaps some of your past behaviors are less than ideal and it's now time to "press the refresh button," working toward a more other-centered person.

Consider Hillary, who, at age 18, described herself as a "really boring person." To bolster her self-esteem and to assert her independence, Hillary decided to get a tattoo, much to the surprise and shock of her parents. As an 18-year-old, she felt that she was an adult and didn't have to abide by her parents' rules. Now, as a 30-year-old, Hillary is rethinking her image-boosting behavior. She thinks that the tattoo, located on her right forearm, communicates an image that is contrary to the one she wants to convey as a middle school teacher in a rather conservative area. Now, it seems, demonstrating independence is not as important to her self-concept as it used to be.

Occasions in which you revise past changes may force you to think about whether changes to your self-concept were justified in the first place or whether they are appropriate for you now. For Hillary, her reflections on whether or not the tattoo was important at age 18 no doubt occupy her mind from time to time. At age 30, she probably regrets being so impulsive in her behavior without thinking about the consequences.

Surround Yourself With Relational Uppers

Think, for a moment, about the amount of stress in your life right now. You may be working full-time, raising children, taking a full course load, coping with a health issue, feeling overwhelmed by bills, or having a hard time with a particular course. Now think about hanging around people who do nothing but tell you that you need to change. Or consider interpersonal relationships with people who constantly tell you that you are deficient in one way or another. We believe that you need to avoid these types of people in favor of **relational uppers**, those people who support and trust you as you improve your self-concept. Take care to surround yourself with relational uppers, because these individuals will be instrumental for you to achieve your potential.

/// CHAPTER WRAP-UP

This chapter's focus was on the interplay between perception and identity. We established a foundation related to the perception process, explaining the elements of perception as well as various influences upon perception. In addition, we examined the dimensions of self-concept and illustrated the dynamic between impression management and facework. From self-awareness to self-esteem, you now understand that the self is multifaceted. Finally, you were also introduced to two theories that relate to the perception and the self, namely Symbolic Interactionism Theory and Social Information Processing Theory.

We are living in an era that requires each of us to recognize and understand our own worldview and the worldviews of others in our classroom, our neighborhood, and around the globe. Further, we necessarily need to understand that we may enter an interpersonal exchange with various fields of experiences and they will inevitably affect how meaning is acquired. It's impossible to divide the topics of perception and the self because each influences both how we interpret another's message and how another individual will interpret our message. Before people establish relationships with others, they first must have a relationship with themselves. This entails a realization that perception, identity, and the self all function together with each contributing to the creation and interpretation of messages.

/// COMMUNICATION ASSESSMENT TEST (CAT): SELF-MONITORING SCALE

The statements below concern your personal reactions to a number of situations. No two statements are exactly alike, so consider each statement carefully before answering. If a statement is true or mostly true as applied to you, mark T as your answer. If a statement is false or not usually true as applied to you, mark F as your answer. It's important that you answer as frankly and as honestly as you can.

1. I find it hard to imitate the behavior of other people. _____

2. My behavior is usually an expression of my true inner feelings, attitudes, and beliefs. _____

3. At parties and social gatherings, I do not attempt to do or say things that others will like. _____

4. I can only argue for ideas I already believe. _____

5. I can make impromptu speeches even on topics about which I have almost no information. _____

6. I guess I put on a show to impress or entertain people. _____

7. When I am uncertain how to act in a social situation, I look to the behavior of others for cues. _____

8. I would probably make a good actor. _____

9. I rarely need the advice of my friends to choose movies, books, or music. _____

10. I sometimes appear to others to be experiencing deeper emotions than I actually am. _____

11. I laugh more when I watch a comedy with others than when alone. _____

12. In a group of people, I am rarely the center of attention. _____

13. In different situations and with different people, I often act like very different persons. _____

14. I am not particularly good at making other people like me. _____

15. Even if I am not enjoying myself, I often pretend to be having a good time. _____

16. I'm not always the person I appear to be. _____

17. I would not change my opinions (or the way I do things) in order to please someone else or win their favor. _____

18. I have considered being an entertainer. _____

19. In order to get along and be liked, I tend to be what people expect me to be rather than anything else. _____

20. I have never been good at games like charades or improvisational acting. _____

21. I have trouble changing my behavior to suit different people and different situations. _____

22. At a party, I let others keep the jokes and stories going. _____

23. I feel a bit awkward in company and do not show up quite so well as I should. _____

24. I can look anyone in the eye and tell a lie with a straight face. _____

25. I may deceive people by being friendly when I really dislike them. _____

Scoring the Scale

The scoring key is reproduced below. You should circle your response of true or false each time it corresponds to the keyed response below. Add up the number of responses you circle. This total is your score on the Self-Monitoring Scale. Record your score below:

1. False 6. True 10. True 14. False 18. True 22. False

2. False 7. True 11. True 15. True 19. True 23. False

3. False 8. True 12. False 16. True 20. False 24. True

4. False 9. False 13. True 17. False 21. False 25. True

My Score _____

High score: 15–25; Intermediate score: 9–14; Low score: 0–8

If you are a high self-monitor,

- you are flexible in multiple contexts.
- you are adaptable.
- you have different public and private selves.
- you do better in jobs that allow you to influence others (e.g., sales, marketing, politics).

If you are a low self-monitor,

- you tend to use internal beliefs to determine how to behave in various contexts.
- you act the same across various social circles.
- you can be relied upon for opinions since you tend to be authentic.
- you tend to be better in research-based projects.

Source: Snyder, M. (1974). Self-monitoring of expressive behavior. *Journal of Personality and Social Psychology*, 30(4), 526–537.

/// KEY TERMS

/// KEY QUESTIONS FOR APPLICATION

1. **CQ/CultureQuest**: Explore the following claim: "Our perceptions are incomplete unless we understand the role of culture." Do you agree or disagree? Defend your view with examples.

2. **TQ/TechQuest**: Explore the following claim: "Social media sites such as Instagram and Snapchat do little to enhance the perception process." Do you agree or disagree? Defend your view with examples.

3. Identify and explain each stage of the perception process and then apply it to the first time you met a roommate.

4. Explore a time when you "lost face" while a student at your school.

5. Apply principles of a self-fulfilling prophecy to an Olympic athlete.

6. Differentiate the different "selves" that are possible while communicating both online and face-to-face.

⑤SAGE edge™

Access practice quizzes, eFlashcards, video, and multimedia at **edge.sagepub.com/west**.

Visit **edge.sagepub.com/west** to help you accomplish your coursework goals in an easy-to-use learning environment.

CHAPTER 4

COMMUNICATING VERBALLY

LEARNING OUTCOMES

After studying this chapter, you will be able to

4–1 Describe the attributes of verbal symbols and explain their relationship to language and meaning

4–2 Identify how factors such as culture, sex, generation, and context affect verbal symbols

4–3 Explain the ways in which verbal symbols may be used destructively and constructively

4–4 Demonstrate skill and sensitivity in using verbal communication

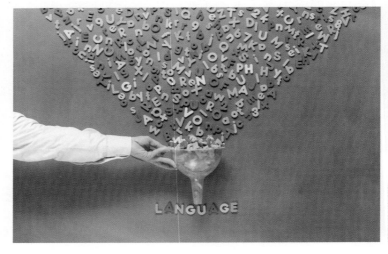

iStock.com/selimaksan

Master the content at
edge.sagepub.com/west

⑤SAGE edge™

Humans depend on verbal symbols for two related reasons. First of all, verbal language *connects us to others*. Language initiates and maintains social relationships. This means interpersonal relationships are constructed and reconstructed through conversation. When Justin asks Leila to borrow her notes from the intercultural communication lecture he missed, or Alissa talks to her mother about problems with her college roommate, they establish and reestablish their connections to each other.

Secondly, verbal language *differentiates members of an in-group from those of an out-group*. Some researchers argue that this was the main reason humans developed verbal language in the first place.[1] In thinking about verbal language as a means for connecting and separating people, we're approaching it as a tool for social interaction rather than simply as a means for expressing ideas.

> **The following theories/models are discussed in this chapter:**
>
> Communication Accommodation Theory
>
> Linguistic Determinism/Relativity
>
> Two-Culture Theory
>
> Muted Group Theory

Communication Accommodation Theory (CAT) by researcher Howard Giles[2] explains how verbal language operates both to connect and to separate people. In this theory, Giles discusses how two speakers from different backgrounds (generation, ethnicity, sex, or other differences) may adjust their style of speaking relative to each other. The theory says speakers may either **converge**, or make their speech style like the other's or **diverge**, highlighting the differences in their two styles. Consider the following example of *convergence:*

Baker: "Wassup, dude? Wanna hang tonight? Need to talk about how Tim threw some serious shade at me."

Robin: "Sure, dude. Hanging sounds good. Wassup with Tim, anyway? He's so basic."

Contrast that dialogue with this example of *divergence:*

Baker: "Wassup, dude? Wanna hang tonight? Need to talk about how Tim threw some serious shade at me."

Robin: "Maybe, Baker. I do have a lot of work, but I can try. I'm surprised to hear that Tim gave you a hard time."

CAT advances that when people want to show affiliation with one another, they are likely to converge so their speaking styles sound similar in terms of word choice, rate, accent, and so forth. When people use divergence, it may be because they are trying to teach the other speaker "correct" language or they wish to highlight their differing backgrounds, identities, or statuses. However, convergence isn't always good and divergence bad. Sometimes convergence may be seen as patronizing or condescending. Have you ever had an older person speak to you in ways that were more common to those of your own generation? How did you evaluate the speaker? Did you think it was condescending to hear someone not of your generation speak that way to you? Further, divergence can illustrate respect for different cultural backgrounds and power differences. For instance, when Liz speaks to her professor, she doesn't use all the jargon that Dr. Carlisle does, deferring to the professor's superior knowledge of her field of study, and accentuating the power difference between them.

In this chapter, we discuss verbal symbols and describe their unique attributes. Although we've separated our presentation of verbal and nonverbal communication into two chapters in this text, remember the two are inextricably intertwined, and it's often the interplay between them that makes meaning. Imagine someone close to you telling you they hate you with a laugh and a friendly push on your shoulder, compared to them saying the same thing while scowling and turning their back on you.

IPC Praxis

Think about instances when words have connected you to others and developed a sense of group identity among you. Give at least one example of how words did this. Then reflect on times when words divided you from others. Give at least one example of how this occurred. Do you agree that these are the two main functions of verbal symbols in interpersonal communication? Why or why not?

4–1 UNDERSTANDING VERBAL SYMBOLS

First, we distinguish among the related terms *language, verbal symbols,* and *grammar.* **Language** consists of both verbal symbols and grammar; it enables us to engage in meaning making with others. **Verbal symbols** are the words or the vocabulary that make up a language. **Grammar** refers to the set of rules in a specific language dictating how words should be organized.

Verbal symbols are foundational to a language system, but they must be accompanied by grammatical rules telling us how to use them. If you heard someone say, "Look on sky balloon is hanging," you would assume they didn't know how to speak English or that something was wrong with them. The words in the sentence are all recognizable as English vocabulary, but their arrangement doesn't make sense in English. The processes of **encoding** (putting our thoughts into meaningful language) and **decoding** (developing an understanding of the speaker's meaning based on hearing language) require a shared vocabulary *and* a shared understanding of grammar.

Discussing the rules of grammar is beyond the scope of this book, but we will address verbal symbols here. Verbal symbols have five specific attributes:

- They are symbolic.
- Their meanings evolve.
- They are powerful.
- Their meanings are denotative and connotative.
- They vary in specificity.

We discuss each of these attributes below.

Words Are Symbolic

Symbols are arbitrary, mutually agreed-on labels or representations for feelings, concepts, objects, or events. Because words are arbitrary symbols, there's no direct relationship between the word and the thing. For instance, the letters *c-a-t* form an agreed-on symbol for the actual furry animal English speakers call a cat. The Spanish word *gato* and the German word *katze* are equally arbitrary symbols used to represent the same animal. Figure 4.1 illustrates this concept by representing the thought, the thing, and the word that stands for the thing on three points of a triangle, an idea called the semantic triangle.[3] Each element is separate, and speakers of a given language connect them because they've been taught to do so.

The Meaning for Words Evolves Over Time

As time passes, our vocabulary changes in part because we need new words to describe new trends, inventions, and ideas. People coin terms such as *FOMO, fiscal cliff,* and *flash mob* that give labels to innovations and capture current experiences. Technological changes prompt the invention of many new words. We talk about *defriending, selfies, Bitcoin,* and *binge-watching* because new technologies have enabled these activities.

Further, some words go out of date and aren't used any longer. For example, the words *petticoat, girdle, dowry,* and *typewriter* are virtually gone from our current

Figure 4.1 /// The Semantic Triangle

thing

thought
(furry feline house pet)

word
(cat)

iStock.com/cynoclub

vocabulary. And some expressions that were popular in earlier times aren't used now. If you are younger than 80 years old, you probably haven't ever used the phrase *the bee's knees,* 1920s slang that meant something was wonderful or "hot." In the 1950s and 1960s, it was common for people to say *toodle-loo* instead of *good-bye;* and when couples wanted to go find a romantic spot, they'd tell others that they were *going to the submarine races* although there was no evidence of any water nearby! Today, we rarely hear that slang anymore unless we're watching an old movie.

 **IPC Voice: Darya**

I remember listening to my Nana and her friends talking when I was over at her house after school waiting for my mom. It was funny—kind of like they were talking in another language! They used a lot of slang that I had never heard before; I can't even remember it. But I recall thinking that this must be what it feels like for Nana when she listens to me and my friends. My generation uses a lot of tech-slang and other words that she probably doesn't get completely. I knew Nana and I were from different generations, but I never thought about us speaking different languages!

Sometimes old words remain in our vocabulary, but their meanings change. For instance, the phrase *calling card* used to mean an engraved card that you left at the home of someone whom you had just visited. Today, we still use the term *calling card,* but now it refers to prepaid cards for making phone calls. The word *awful* used to mean full of awe, rather than something bad. Now *awesome* means what *awful* used to, and the meaning for *awful* has changed. The word *nice* used to mean silly, foolish, and simple rather than the more positive meaning it has now. In the past, the word *gay* referred to being happy and lighthearted, as in "we'll have a gay old time." Incidentally, the term *gay* was chosen intentionally by people in gay communities because of the positive associations it carried from its former meaning.

Two words may be combined to make a new word (this is called a *portmanteau,* after a French suitcase with two sections). Examples of portmanteaus include

- *adorkable* (someone who's adorable and dorky)

- *hangry* (when hunger causes you to be angry)

- *procrastibaking* (procrastinating by baking cookies or other treats)

- *testilying* (police officers falsifying evidence or lying in court when they believe they have the correct person in custody, but don't have conclusive proof)

You can probably think of other portmanteaus that you and your friends use.

Economic changes may be an impetus for vocabulary revision. Amy Chozick commented that the term *middle class* faded from U.S. politicians' vocabularies in 2016. Chozick notes that the term, which used to connote the American Dream, now represents "anxiety, an uncertain future and a lifestyle that is increasingly out of reach" (para. 2). She observes that as a result, in the run-up to the 2016 U.S. presidential primaries, Hillary Clinton (D) mentions "everyday Americans," Scott Walker (R) talks about "hardworking taxpayers," Bernie Sanders (D) refers to "ordinary Americans," Ted Cruz (R) focuses on "hardworking men and women across America," and Rand Paul (R) says he speaks for the "people who work for the people who own businesses." None of these presidential hopefuls used the term *middle class*. Time will tell if *middle class* will fade from common usage and some new phrase will replace it, but Chozick states that most people think *middle class* is an inaccurate term, and are looking for a way to describe themselves as being slightly below the middle.[4]

Our vocabulary also reflects social changes. For example, the words *colored, Negro, Afro-American, African American,* and *person of color* reflect changes in the social position of black people in the United States. The words are not synonyms but actually have different meanings. *African American* communicates an emphasis on ethnicity rather than race, and *person of color* puts equal emphasis on the person and their ethnicity.

We've also observed an evolution in verbal symbols around issues of gender identity. The website for GLAAD (Gay & Lesbian Alliance Against Defamation; www.glaad.org) includes guidance for journalists in writing about transgender people. For instance, the site offers the following advice about terms that are problematic and terms that are preferred by members of the transgender community:

> Problematic: "sex change," "pre-operative," "post-operative"
>
> Preferred: "transition"
>
> Referring to a sex change operation, or using terms such as pre- or post-operative, inaccurately suggests that one must have surgery in order to transition. Avoid overemphasizing surgery when discussing transgender people or the process of transition.[5]

These sorts of language changes are sometimes ridiculed as political correctness. But language reform isn't about being politically correct. Changing language to give people respect and to be accurate is an important goal. Furthermore, using language that is appropriate to a culture's evolution strengthens a speaker's credibility.

 IPC Praxis

Take some time to listen to people who are older than you, and then to those who are younger. See if you notice differences in their vocabulary and ways that each of their vocabularies differs from your own. If possible, try to talk to some of those you listened to and ask them what some of the words they've used mean, and when they learned them. Does this tell you anything about the evolution of words?

When people are forced to apologize or even lose their jobs for what they've said, no one can deny that words are powerful.

Myles Aronowitz / ©TBS / courtesy Everett Collection

Words Are Powerful

Certain words have the power to affect people dramatically. As we've said, words are arbitrary symbols, so their power is not intrinsic; their power is a result of speakers agreeing that they're powerful. And, as we've mentioned, these agreements change over time. For example, in the 17th century, the word *blackguard* was a potent insult. Today, if you're mad at someone, you'd be unlikely to show it by calling them a *blackguard*. Other words, however (such as *ass*), have taken on power they didn't have in the 17th century.

In the United States in 2018, the power of words was demonstrated when Roseanne Barr, who was starring in ABC's highly rated sitcom *Roseanne,* was abruptly fired and her show canceled hours after she posted a tweet using the words "Muslim brotherhood" and "ape" about Valerie Jarrett, an African American woman who'd been a senior adviser to President Barack Obama. Shortly after Barr lost her job, Samantha Bee, a comedian, used a coarse expletive on her late-night TV show, *Full Frontal,* to describe Ivanka Trump. Although Bee did not lose her show in the way Barr did, she was immediately moved to apologize, saying she regretted using the expletive and that it was "inappropriate and inexcusable." TBS, Bee's network, also issued an apology immediately. In both these cases, crossing a line verbally proved highly consequential.

The power of words in the English language is further illustrated by a study examining how the phrase "think positive" affected breast cancer patients.[6] The study found that in general, that phrase sent a message that if you don't get better after being diagnosed with breast cancer, it's because you're not being positive enough. This phrase, then, had a great deal of power, often making patients feel inadequate or responsible for their own illness.

Meanings for Verbal Symbols May Be Denotative or Connotative

Denotative meaning refers to the literal, conventional meaning that most people in a culture have agreed is the meaning of a symbol. Denotation is the type of meaning found in a dictionary definition. For instance, Merriam-Webster Online defines the word *gun* as follows:

GUN:

1. a: *a piece of ordnance usually with high muzzle velocity and comparatively flat trajectory*

   b: *a portable firearm (as a rifle or handgun)*

   c: *a device that throws a projectile*

2. a: *a discharge of a gun especially as a salute or signal*

   b: *a signal marking a beginning or ending*

3. a: *HUNTER*

   b: *GUNMAN*

4. *something suggesting a gun in shape or function*

5. *THROTTLE*

6. slang: *a person's arm; specifically: an arm that has well-defined muscles— usually plural*

   Conor was spotted rowing away from The Loeb Boathouse in Central Park Saturday with his girlfriend, Dee Devlin, and their cute son, Conor Jr. The famous fighter showed off his guns while handling the oars for his crew.

   —TMZ.com

   The Heisman Trophy-winning and former NFL quarterback worked the stage the way he probably jabs through the weight room—whilst checking out his guns in the mirror.

   —Tory Barron[7]

Denotative meanings can be confusing; because the dictionary provides more than one meaning for *gun,* a listener hearing someone use the word *gun* must decide if the speaker is using definition 1a, 1b, 1c, 2a, 2b, and so forth.

The connotative meaning of a term can be even more confusing because the meaning varies from person to person. **Connotative meaning** derives from people's personal and subjective experience with a verbal symbol. For example, someone who'd been a student at Stoneman Douglas High School in Parkland, Florida, during the shooting there in 2018 would have a different emotional or connotative meaning for *gun* than would a hunter or a police officer. Stoneman Douglas students would probably have different connotations for the word *gun* than even students at Santa Fe High School in Texas, where another school shooting took place in 2018. In Texas, the rural population evinced strong support for the Second Amendment, which was different from how the Florida community reacted. Although all of these people would be aware of the denotative meanings of *gun,* their definition of the word would be colored by their personal connotative meanings.

Words Vary in Specificity

Another attribute of verbal symbols is that words can be more or less specific. The more a word restricts the number of possible **referents** (the thing the word represents), the more **specific** the word is. For instance, if Sara has 45 relatives but only three brothers, then *brother* is a more specific term than *relative,* and Scott (the name of one of Sara's brothers) is even more specific than either of the two other terms. The word *relative* is the term with the fewest restrictions, so it is the most **general**. The movement from general to specific in verbal symbols is illustrated in Figure 4.2.

In addition to words varying from general to specific, the things that words represent, or the referents, also vary. Some referents are **concrete**, meaning that you are able to detect them with one of your senses. Stated another way, concrete referents are those that you can see, smell, taste, touch, or hear. When we talk to each other about a meal or furniture, we're talking about things that are concrete, and words like *beer, cheeseburger,* and *brown leather La-Z-Boy recliner* help us understand each other's meanings. Referents that cannot be detected through your senses are considered **abstract**. Ideas such as emotion, love, and justice are abstract, and we can't communicate these concepts to each other as easily as we can talk about food and furniture. Yet, we do talk about abstract ideas, and our language allows that. When talking about abstract ideas, we might work to use specific words. When Jesse wants to explain his emotions, for instance, he can say that he feels restless and anxious. *Restless* and *anxious* provide some specificity and allow a listener to understand Jesse more clearly than they would if he simply said he's *upset* or *sad*.

Because words vary in their level of specificity, and referents vary in their level of abstraction, meaning is often ambiguous. This ambiguity may be unintentional or strategic. For instance, if Rory lacks verbal skills like clarity and the ability to fit her vocabulary to her audience, her communication may seem vague, even though that's not what she intends. However, sometimes it serves a purpose to be ambiguous. Researchers have described this phenomenon in two ways: strategic ambiguity and equivocation.

Figure 4.2 /// Moving From General to Specific

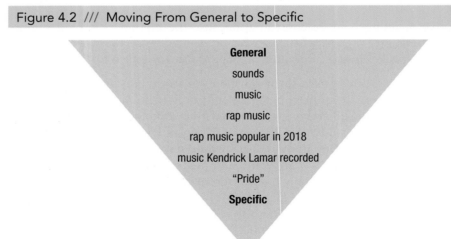

General
sounds
music
rap music
rap music popular in 2018
music Kendrick Lamar recorded
"Pride"
Specific

Strategic ambiguity refers to how people talk when they purposely do not want others to completely understand their intentions. In organizations, for instance, people (especially at the management level) may leave out cues on purpose to encourage multiple interpretations by others. It's possible that ambiguity helps people deal with tensions in an organization. To promote harmony, leaders of organizations may have to be ambiguous enough to allow for many interpretations while simultaneously encouraging agreement. This strategy can also be used in a conflict. Saying something like "That's an interesting idea" is ambiguous enough that it might end the argument.

Equivocation is a type of ambiguity that involves choosing your words carefully to give a listener a false impression without actually lying. If your grandmother sends you a birthday gift that you don't like, but you value your relationship with your grandmother and don't want to hurt her feelings, you might equivocate in your thanks. You might say "Thanks so much for the sweater, Grandma. It was so thoughtful of you to think about keeping me warm in the cold winters!"

You have not said the sweater was attractive, nor have you said you liked it, so you haven't lied overtly. However, if you are a good equivocator, you have given your grandmother the impression that you are pleased with a sweater that you, in fact, dislike. Keep in mind that such a tactic could have long-term consequences. In this case, you could receive similar unwanted sweaters for several birthdays to come.

Equivocating involves saying things that are true but misleading. It should be no surprise that the language of advertising makes use of equivocation. When an ad says that a car's seats "have the look and feel of fine leather," that means that they are *not* made of fine leather, but the use of the words *fine leather* leads an unsuspecting listener to think that they are. The word *virtually* is a good equivocal word. The phrase *virtually spotless* means that the described item has some spots on it, but the phrase leads you to believe otherwise.

Euphemisms are a kind of equivocal speech. **Euphemisms** are milder or less direct words substituted for other words that are more blunt or negative. They are used to reduce the discomfort related to an unpleasant or sensitive subject. For example, we say we're going to the *restroom* even though we're not planning to rest, we refer to a person's *passing* rather than their death, or we talk about *adult entertainment* rather than pornography.

4–2 FACTORS AFFECTING VERBAL SYMBOLS

We understand and use words differently depending on a variety of factors. In this section, we discuss the relationships between verbal symbols and

- culture and ethnicity,
- sex,
- generation, and
- context.

JASON REDMOND / Stringer/AFP/Getty Images

Culture and ethnicity affect verbal symbols in myriad ways. Perhaps the most obvious is that language codes themselves differ based on culture.

Although we discuss these factors in isolation, they can form many combinations. For example, an elderly African American man living in the United States talking to his granddaughter at home uses verbal symbols differently than a young Asian woman living in South Korea speaking to a group of business associates at their company's annual meeting.

Culture and Ethnicity

On the most basic level, culture affects verbal symbols (and vice versa) because most cultures develop their own language. Thus, the people of Kenya tend to speak Swahili, while those living in Poland usually speak Polish. This common language binds people together in many ways and can become a flashpoint for identity. There's a political movement in the United States called the English Only Movement, which argues English should be the official and only language used publicly in the United States. In 2018, a video of an attorney in a New York City restaurant yelling at an employee for speaking Spanish to a customer went viral. The attorney was captured saying, "The staff should be speaking English. . . . This is America."

Additionally, cultural values are encoded in verbal language. For instance, in a study examining eight languages around the world including English, Italian, and Lao (spoken in Laos, Cambodia, and Thailand), researchers found that many languages didn't have a word that translated to *thank you*. When the researchers listened to everyday interactions, they found that expressions of thanks were rarely used among friends and families. They attributed this to an expectation for cooperation among intimate groups. However, the study found some variations across cultures. English and Italian speakers said *thanks* more often than speakers of the other six languages. The researchers attributed this to the value of overt politeness espoused in Western cultures.[8] Other cultural traditions relating to language include the following:

- In the Lakota tradition, it is sacrilegious to say the name of a dead person in public.

- Jewish people believe that children should not be named for any living person.

- The Japanese avoid saying words in wedding toasts that refer to home or going back home.

- In traditional Native American communities, silence is an important way to communicate respect.

- In England, death is supposed to be ignored and not spoken about, even to express condolences.

- In India, people—especially your elders, relatives, or close friends—feel insulted if you thank them; saying thanks violates intimacy and creates formality and distance that shouldn't exist.

IPC Praxis

Interview a person from a culture different than your own. In your interview, try to determine what their language reveals about their outlook on the world. Compare that to your own. Speculate about how your two different native languages might impact your worldviews.

Finally, remember that culture pertains to more than just national origin. Cultures or co-cultures can form around people who share certain things in common, such as religious beliefs or professional experiences. People become **speech communities** when they share norms about how to speak; what words to use; and when, where, and why to speak. In this way, a speech community resembles a national or ethnic culture. One example of a unique speech community is people who are incarcerated in the United States. Prisoners develop a vocabulary that's quite different from the English spoken by those outside prison walls. (See Table 4.1.)

Table 4.1 /// The Language of a Particular Speech Community: Prison Vocabulary

Birds on the line	A warning that someone is listening to the conversation
Bonaroo	A prisoner's best clothes
Buck Rogers time	A parole date so far in the future that the prisoner can't imagine being released
Cat nap	A short sentence
Escape dust	Fog
T-Jones	A prisoner's mother

There are many ways that culture and ethnicity relate to language and contribute to shared meaning. Let's first look at idioms. An **idiom** is a word or a phrase that has an understood meaning within a culture, but that meaning doesn't come from exact translation. People who are learning a language have to learn the meaning of each idiom as a complete unit; they can't simply translate each of the words and put those meanings together. For example, in English the phrase "it was a breeze" means something was easy. If someone tried to translate "it was a breeze" without knowing it functions as an idiom, they would mistake the statement's meaning. However, a listener also has to pay attention to context. If "it was a breeze" is the response to the question "What messed up all the papers I had laid out under the window?" English speakers know the statement's not an idiom in this case.

Translating idioms makes communication challenging. Consider the following example: Madeline works for the International Student Center at Western State University, and some of the international students complain to her that U.S. students are unfriendly. When Madeline asks why they feel this way, they tell her the following story: They were sitting with a group of U.S. students in the Student Union two weeks ago. When they parted company, the U.S. students said, "See you later," but they have made no attempt to do so.

The international students believed that the U.S. students failed to keep their promise for future interactions. Madeline explained to the students that "see you later" is an example of a particular type of idiom called *phatic communication*. **Phatic communication** is idiomatic communication used for interpersonal contact only.

Phatic communication, like all idioms, is "content-free" because listeners are not supposed to think about literal meanings; they are expected to respond to the polite contact the speaker is making. When you see someone and say, "Hi, how are you doing?" you don't really want to know the details about how the other person is doing—you're just making contact. "How's it going?" or "How're you doing?" should elicit a response such as "Good—you?" If you said, "How's it going?" as you walked by your acquaintance Katy, and she grabbed your arm and started to tell you about her recent breakup or the big fight she just had with her brother, you would likely be very surprised and uncomfortable.

African American language is one of the most studied in terms of the effects of ethnicity on language, so we'll address some of the verbal behaviors African Americans are thought to use. Although the findings do not apply to every member of this group, African Americans are often considered to form a distinct language group. Most African Americans identify with race or ethnicity as a way of establishing personal identity. When Meghan Markle, an American biracial woman, married Prince Harry in England in 2018, a great deal of the media coverage of their wedding focused on how the ceremony introduced African American customs and speech patterns to the comparably staid, white English public. Bishop Michael Curry, who delivered the sermon at the wedding, spoke for almost 14 minutes about the power of love. The length of his sermon, the passionate delivery, and the call for the end of poverty and war prompted observers to label it as having the flavor of the Black American church. If you watched the royal wedding, do you agree? Did you hear something you'd call African American speech in Bishop Curry's sermon? How would you describe that?

African American Speech

Some research suggests that African American speech is more assertive than European American speech. According to this research, in a conversation between Renée, an African American, and Lee, a European American, Lee might say, "Is everything okay between us?" and Renée might respond, "Why are you even asking? You know I'm mad you flirted with Kim at that party!" African Americans and European Americans may truly differ in how assertive their speech is, or this finding may be complicated by perceptions. One study found that African American women think European American women are highly conflict avoidant. European American women reported their belief that African American women are assertive and confrontational. However, neither group of women characterized themselves as highly avoidant or confrontational.[9] Several studies show that European Americans hold enduring stereotypes of African American speech as more direct, emotional, profane, and less grammatical than white speech.

Video 4.1

Black speech is also seen as vibrant and exciting, and many of its words and phrases have found their way into the vocabulary of white speakers. For example, when white speakers say, "Back in the day" or "She thinks she's all that" or use words like *hip, phat,* or *testify,* they owe a debt to African American speakers. Black speech is often humorous, witty, and wise. The Linguistic Society of America supported the strengths of African American speech when they stated the following:

> The systematic and expressive nature of the grammar and pronunciation patterns of the African American vernacular has been established by numerous scientific studies over the past thirty years. Characterizations of Ebonics as "slang," "mutant," "lazy," "defective," "ungrammatical," or "broken English" are incorrect and demeaning.[10]

Some evidence suggests, perhaps unsurprisingly, that when African American children can shift between African American English and what the researchers call Mainstream American English (or *code switching*), they do better in schools, especially with regard to achievement in reading.[11] However, other research argues that the school setting is not always the most hospitable or culturally sensitive for African American youth. They note that the African American cultural preference for verve and rhythm in speech patterns, as well as in other aspects of life, is not honored in most U.S. schools.[12]

IPC Around Us

An article in *The Boston Globe*[13] notes the influence that baseball has had on the English language spoken in the United States: "Baseball lingo is more than a way to talk about what happens on the field. The sport has had an outsize influence on everyday English." Baseball has had an impact on how we talk about race and gender, as well as how we use metaphors and give people nicknames, among other linguistic practices. For example, during the government shutdown in 2013, legislators and the media used language drawing from "America's preferred metaphor for nearly

(Continued)

(Continued)

iStock.com/luvemakphoto

everything under the sun: baseball." Senator Charles Schumer exhorted House Speaker John Boehner to "Just step up to the plate and do it," and the Huffington Post accused the White House and Senate Democrats of "refusing to play ball" when the House sent back amended spending bills.

Reflection: Think about metaphors that may have affected your thinking about something. Reflect on how this may help or impede interpersonal communication.

Theorizing About Language and Culture

A framework that links culture and verbal symbols is the Sapir-Whorf hypothesis,[14] an idea put forth simultaneously by anthropologists Benjamin Whorf and Edward Sapir. In its most extreme version, the Sapir-Whorf hypothesis argues that words determine our ability to perceive and think. This form of the hypothesis is known as **Linguistic Determinism.**

Both Whorf and Sapir believed that without a word for something, a person has difficulty perceiving that thing or thinking that it's important. For example, the radio show *Radiolab* discussed the relationship between a culture's language and people's ability to perceive (or pay attention to) colors. They referred to Jules Davidoff's research testing the Himba, an indigenous people living in Northern

Nambia. The Himba have no word in their language for blue, and when Davidoff presented research participants with four cards, three colored green and one colored blue, they weren't able to tell what made the cards different. It took them a long time, and some help, to "see" that one of the cards was a different color from the others.[15]

The principle that language determines what you perceive and think about is apparent in the comments of Elizabeth Seay, who studies Native American languages in Oklahoma:

> Learning new languages can bring unnoticed ideas into focus. The Comanches have a word for the bump on the back of the neck which is thought to be a place where the body is centered. The Muscogee-Creeks single out the particular kind of love that children and their parents and grandparents feel for each other, using a word that also means "to be stingy."[16]

However, not all researchers agree with Linguistic Determinism. Even Benjamin Whorf wondered if Linguistic Determinism might be overstating the case. So, he devised another theoretical approach, **Linguistic Relativity**, which states that language influences our thinking but doesn't determine it. Sometimes researchers refer to Linguistic Determinism as the strong form of the Sapir-Whorf hypothesis and Linguistic Relativity as the weak form.

 Theory-Into-Practice (TIP)

Linguistic Determinism/Relativity

Which version of the theory do you think has the most value to you in explaining verbal symbol use in interpersonal communication: Linguistic Determinism or Linguistic Relativity? Explain your answer by giving an example. Can you think of something that you've experienced for which you don't have a specific term in your native language? If you can, how do you express that experience and what does that tell you about these theoretical approaches?

Even though compelling examples illustrate both Linguistic Determinism and Linguistic Relativity, empirical evidence hasn't completely supported either theory's assertions. One of the most famous examples illustrating the Sapir-Whorf hypothesis (the example of the number of words the Inuit have for snow) has been called into question, for instance. The Inuit example states that they have many words for snow because it is so crucial to their everyday lives. In addition, supposedly the Inuit actually see snow differently from others whose lives are not as dependent on snow. Whereas English speakers simply see monolithic white "stuff," due to having only one word, *snow,* the Inuit see all the varieties their language allows. However, the example breaks down when we realize that other languages may allow their speakers to perceive the same variety through phrases and modifiers (*fluffy, slushy, good packing,* and so forth).

The same issue exists when examining the Arabic language. In Arabic, there's no single word for *compromise*. Some have argued this is the reason that Arabs seem to be unable to reach a compromise. Yet, the Arabic language provides several ways to articulate the concept of compromise, the most common being an expression that translates in English to "we reached a middle ground."

These examples illustrate **codability**, which refers to the ease with which a language can express a thought. When a language has a convenient word for a concept, that concept is said to have high codability. Thus, the existence of the word *compromise* gives that idea high codability in English. When a concept requires more than a single word for its expression, it possesses lower codability. It's accurate, then, to say that the idea of compromise has lower codability in Arabic than in English. However, having a phrase rather than a single word to express an idea does not mean that the idea is nonexistent in a given culture, only that it is less easily put into the language code. Thus, we can see that even Linguistic Relativity has to be modified somewhat because of humans' capacity to create words and add descriptors to existing words. Still, the basic premise of the Sapir-Whorf hypothesis, that the words people use have an impact on how they perceive and process the world, has resonance for us, as well as some empirical support. For instance, some evidence suggests that bilingual speakers think differently when they speak in different languages.[17]

Sex

The impact of biological sex on language and verbal symbols has been studied extensively. However, despite decades of research examining and comparing men and women's communication behaviors, we still don't have definitive information. Early research held that women and men spoke very differently. Women were seen as using a different vocabulary from men that included, among other things, more words for colors (e.g., *mauve*), more polite words and phrases (e.g., "Would you please open the door?" rather than "Open the door"), and more modifiers (e.g., *very* and *so*).

Some researchers explained the differences between women's and men's vocabularies by advancing the idea that children play in sex-segregated groups and their different ways of interacting within the groups result in different speech behaviors. Little girls play in small groups to which it's difficult to gain entry; however, after a girl is accepted in the group, it's easy for her to be heard by her playmates. Furthermore, the preferred play activities for girls are creative interactions like house and school, which involve the players themselves setting the rules. In contrast, little boys play in large groups to which it's easy to gain access but difficult to be heard. Boys play baseball, war, and soccer—games that have preset rules. Thus, through play, girls learned negotiation and cooperation and boys learned assertive communication behaviors as well as adherence to authority.

This belief that sex operates in the same way as culture in establishing different values, norms, and language patterns for men and women is known as the **Two-Culture Theory**.[18] This theory was grounded in the notion that women and men speak differently because they essentially occupy different worlds. Although some research in the last three decades has supported the Two-Culture Theory, other studies question whether women and men actually differ much in their speech. For example, in an analysis of more than 1,200 research studies,

Sex and cultural differences may affect verbal communication choices even at an early age.

Hero Images Inc. / Alamy Stock Photo

researchers found that the differences in communication behavior attributable to sex totaled only around 1%.[19]

So, do women and men really communicate differently? That question is difficult to answer. However, keep in mind that sex makes a big difference in many cultures. In the United States, for instance, people consistently remark on sex even when sex distinctions aren't important to the situation. Grade school teachers often say, "Quiet, boys and girls!" rather than "Quiet, students!" Similarly, a performer's usual greeting to the audience is "Good evening, ladies and gentlemen." Additionally, in many cultures, women and men are treated differently; they have different job opportunities, different expectations in the home, different styles of clothing, and are presumed to have different interests in leisure activities, and so forth. Given how frequently people are divided based on sex, the fact that some sense of language community arises based on sex is not surprising. Perhaps more tellingly, men and women's language use is perceived differently even when it's essentially the same. If a man swears or speaks abruptly, do you "hear" that differently than when a woman says essentially the same things? Whether or not women and men do speak differently, sex continues to be a factor that affects expectations for how people use verbal symbols, which in turn impacts how people are heard and understood.

Generation

As we discussed earlier in this chapter, one of the functions of language is differentiating in-group members from those on the outside. One of the tasks of each generation is to distinguish itself from the generation before it. Generational differences form age cohorts that, to some extent, share experiences and beliefs. The members of any age cohort—for example, Gen Y, the Baby Boomers, Millennials, or the Greatest Generation—share a popular culture, which leads to a common language. Slang such as *cheaters* (eyeglasses), *gams* (a woman's legs), *none of your beeswax* (none of your business), and *hitting on all sixes* (giving 100% effort) peppered the talk of youth in the 1920s and 1930s but is rarely, if ever, heard today.

Technological changes affect language across generations as well. Sometimes Millennials use language forms from social media (such as LOL, laugh out loud; IDK, I don't know; SMH, shaking my head; and BTW, by the way) in their high school assignments, making their teachers uncomfortable. But their discomfort varies by age, and many of the older teachers simply don't understand what their students are submitting. The younger teachers understand the "text speak" but they are concerned about what they see as a dramatic decline in students' writing abilities. Some think that when college admission officers receive applications that are written like texts, they toss them immediately.[20]

On the other hand, Meredith Gould, who is in her sixties, wrote a book about how she found social media to be a way to transcend divisions such as generation. Gould comments that when she meets and establishes relationships with people on Twitter, for example, generation doesn't make a difference, especially when she and the other person use the same slang. When they finally find out that they're from different generations, they've already become friends and age doesn't matter to them. She quotes a friend who's 40 years younger than she as saying, "Yo, Meredith, dude, you're more Millennial than most Millennials I know."[21]

Context

Contextual cues subsume all the other elements we have discussed because the culture, ethnicity, sex, and generation of the people who are interacting factor into the context. Generally, in communication research, the context involves the setting or situation in which the encounter takes place. Thus, as we discussed in Chapter 1, *context* means all of the elements surrounding people in an interaction. Think about the same statement, "You have good legs," being said in each of the following situations:

- by construction workers to a woman walking by a construction site
- by a coach to an athlete running on a track
- by a doctor to a child in the doctor's office

Although the words remain the same, each of these situations creates a different meaning.

As we discussed previously in this chapter, the meanings of words can change over time, and historical time period forms a part of the context for communication. In the 1940s and 1950s, females over the age of 18 referred to themselves as *girls* without a negative connotation. In the 1970s, some feminists rejected the word *girl* as demeaning when applied to adult females. In the 1990s and more recently, some feminists have reclaimed that word and use the term *girl power* with positive connotations. However, many women in their 40s and 50s still reject the term *girl* and do not use it or like to hear it.

Relationships between speakers also contribute to the contextual cues that affect meaning. People who are close to you can say things that would be considered impolite if said by mere acquaintances. Teasing, joking, use of swear words, and various forms of humor known as "loving abuse" depend on a strong prior relationship between the speakers. If the relationship isn't positive, these types of interactions would probably be judged as insulting rather than friendly. Of course, even among good friends or family members, people can go too far, and a comment that was intended to be humorous can be interpreted as insulting.

As we discuss throughout this text, the channel used for a communication transaction has an impact on the meaning and experience of that transaction; channels form a part of the overall context of communication. Researchers are interested in how communicating online affects the meaning of verbal symbols, and whether or not theories of communication created before online communication can still be used to predict what happens online. For instance, some research found that for blog and Facebook users, the Spiral of Silence Theory was not predictive. Contrary to the assertions of the theory, the researchers found that those who held minority opinions about a political issue were more communicative online, not less.[22]

Other research examined online communication with an eye toward illustrating sex differences, discovering that online women used more emotion words than men (e.g., *excited*), more first-person singulars (*I*), and more words and emoticons signifying psychological and social relationships like *love*. Men swore more, used more possessive pronouns (*my* girlfriend), and made more references to objects (like Xbox) than did women. These results seemed to conform fairly closely to stereotypical sex distinctions in off-line communication.[23]

In sum, when we communicate, we are doing much more than exchanging words; we're connecting with some people and indicating to others how different we are from one another. We now address how verbal symbols operate destructively and constructively in interpersonal communication.

4–3 THE DESTRUCTIVE AND CONSTRUCTIVE SIDES OF VERBAL SYMBOLS

Verbal symbols aren't inherently positive or negative. Rather, the value of verbal symbols is determined by how people use them. Verbal symbols in the English language may be easily used for negative ends; they may be exclusionary and derisive, enable verbal abuse, provide inaccurate impressions, mislead listeners, and promote stereotypes. However, they may also be used to support, to include others, and to connect in positive ways with others.

The Destructive Side of Verbal Symbols

Here we discuss five processes: static evaluation, polarization, reification, negative contagion, and muting that illustrate how words can be inaccurate, misleading, and unhelpful. We then discuss sexist, racist, and homophobic language, all of which reveal a destructive side of verbal symbols.

Static Evaluation

Verbal symbols reflect **static evaluation** when they conceal change. When we speak and respond to people today the same way we did 10 years ago, we engage in static evaluation. To a degree, we need to think that people and things are stable. If we recognized that everything is in a constant state of flux, it'd be hard to talk or think; we'd be paralyzed by the wide variety of choices and the notion of how little control we have. However, if we ignore change, we cause other problems. Words contribute to these problems because labels aren't always updated to indicate the changes that take place over time.

For instance, *Mom* is what many people call their female parent regardless of whether they are 4, 18, or 40 years old. However, the relationship between people and their mothers, as well as the people involved, all change greatly over time. The word *Mom* doesn't help us to see these changes, and, in fact, it tends to obscure them. When parents say to their children, "No matter how old you get, you will always be my little baby," they are naming the very problem that exists with static evaluation.

Polarization

Polarization occurs when people use words that cast topics in extremes. When we refer to people as smart *or* dumb, nice *or* mean, right *or* wrong, we are polarizing. Polarization is troubling because most people, things, and events are good some of the time and bad some of the time. Labeling them as one or the other fails to recognize their totality. For example, when Kayla tells her friend Sasha about her professor, Dr. Lee, she focuses on how much she dislikes Lee. Kayla says, "He's such a sarcastic jerk! I cannot stand his class. All he ever does is make fun of students. He doesn't even realize how many stupid things he says!" Although Kayla is entitled to her opinion of Dr. Lee as a poor teacher, her use of such words as *jerk* and *stupid* is polarizing.

Polarization is also problematic because of static evaluation. If we settle on an extreme label for someone at one time and then encounter the same person later, we'll probably fail to realize that the person may have changed over time. For example, let's say that Christie briefly dated Rick in high school when they were both juniors, but she broke it off because she thought he was too immature. Two years later, they meet at a party in college. Christie remembers Rick from high school and immediately thinks of the polarizing term *immature*. Keeping this word in her mind will hinder Christie's ability to see Rick's changes and interact with him appropriately. Polarization also causes communication problems because of reification, which we address next.

Reification

Reification is the tendency to respond to words, or labels for things, rather than the things themselves. Thus, if we call people by an extreme label, reification suggests that's how we'll respond to them. Reification is often referred to as confusing the symbol with the thing. When people have a strong reaction to a symbol such as a national flag or a school mascot, they are fusing the symbol (flag or mascot) with the thing itself (their country or their school). Although symbols are potent, they are not the same as the things they represent. People who cut up the U.S. flag or burn it may be as patriotic as those who fly the flag in front of their home each day.

Negative Contagion

Negative contagion refers to a conversational ritual where one person begins with one negative comment and then that comment is matched by the next speaker's contribution. Soon the whole conversation is focused on negative statements. Research on *fat talk* exemplifies negative contagion. *Fat talk* refers to

When we confuse the idea with its symbolic representation, we are experiencing reification. Reification can be destructive to our interpersonal interactions.

iStock.com/harukaze01

conversations among friends that begin by someone stating that they feel fat. Most frequently the speakers are not fat, in objective terms, but they talk about how fat they think they are and engage in self-disparagement of their bodies. The research on this phenomenon indicates that *fat talk* is ritualistic and contagious.[24] As soon as one person begins it, others in the conversation chime in. But the most important finding in the research may be that *fat talk* isn't a harmless way for people to bond over shared complaints. Instead, the researchers found that *fat talk* relates to shame, dissatisfaction, and disordered eating behaviors.

Muting

Verbal symbols also fail users by letting some of their experiences, roles, and ideas go unnamed, creating what theorists call **lexical gaps**. Lexical gaps indicate that language does not serve all its users equally. The **Muted Group Theory**[25] explains what happens to people whose experiences or roles are not well represented by the verbal symbols in their language. The theory states that if a group has a lot of lexical gaps, they'll have trouble articulating their thoughts and feelings, will seem awkward, and may be regarded as too silent or too talkative. They may also feel that something's wrong with them because their language doesn't give them an adequate vocabulary for their unique experiences.

For example, Joanna wants to talk about her role in relation to her boyfriend's two sons, but there's no word in the English language that identifies a person's relationship with the children of their live-in partner. *Mother* or *Father* represents a biological relationship and *stepparent* represents a legal relationship, but Joanna's relationship is neither biological or legal. When she talks to her friend Austin, Joanna expresses her frustrations:

Joanna: "I'm not sure what I am to the kids. I know I love them."

Austin: "But, you're not their mother."

Joanna: "I know, but I kinda feel like I am. I do a lot of 'motherly' things with them."

Austin: "It's funny that there's no name for you."

Joanna: "Yeah, it's depressing really. I'm not a mother, but I'm nearly their mother."

Additionally, the theory suggests that groups are muted when their language draws more on others' experiences than their own. Some researchers say that expressions from sports ("hit it out of the park") and war ("he attacked all his opponents' ideas") show that English is shaped more by the experiences of men than women. Others suggest that African Americans and fathers are also muted by the English language. For instance, African Americans are muted when black speakers are said to be "aggressive" or "confrontational," because those words place black speakers in comparison to white speakers, or when Black English is marginalized and considered substandard. When parenting is assumed to be mainly a woman's experience and the words *parent* and *mother* are used interchangeably, fathers are muted.

Language is flexible, however, and people can come up with new words that fill lexical gaps. As we've discussed, people invent words all the time. However, gaining acceptance of new words isn't always easy. For example, feminists point to the trouble they had getting people to use *Ms.* instead of *Miss* and *Mrs.* In India, transgender people do have words for themselves. One group, including transgender and intersex people, is called hijras. But the power of the named categories "women" and "men" in India sometimes has made acceptance of the hijras difficult and tenuous.

Further, Muted Group Theory suggests that members of muted groups sometimes have difficulty recognizing their lexical gaps because they're distanced from their own experiences. Female speakers may not even realize when they're being judged by male standards of speaking, for instance.

Sexist Language

Video 4.2

Sexist language refers to language that is demeaning to one sex. Women running for political office in the United States report that they are often on the receiving end of sexist language and abuse sent to them via social media. Some women withdrew from their races because of the negative effects of the vulgar sexist insults directed at them. Most research examining sexist language has focused on how language can be detrimental to women, although as the previous comments about fathers suggest, men may experience sexism in language too.

Some researchers assert that the fact that English uses the generic *he* is an example of sexism in language. The **generic *he*** refers to the rule in English grammar, dating from 1553, that requires the masculine pronoun *he* to function generically when the subject of the sentence is of unknown gender, or includes both men and women. For instance, in the following sentence, *his* would be the correct word to fill in the blanks using the generic *he* rule: "A person should do ____ homework to succeed in ____ classes." Some have argued that this rule excludes women because *he* isn't truly generic; rather, it conjures up images of male people only.

Another example of sexist language is **man-linked words**. These words—such as *chairman, salesman, repairman, mailman,* and *mankind*—include the word *man* but are supposed to refer to women as well. Man-linked expressions such as *manning the phones* and *manned space flight* are also problematic. In addition, the practice of referring to a group of women and men as *guys,* as in "Hey, you guys, let's go to the movies," reinforces sexism in language. Relatively easy alternatives to these exclusionary verbal symbols are becoming more commonplace, and we may be on our way to seeing much less of this type of sexism in language. (See Table 4.2.)

Other examples of sexism in language include the practice of women taking their husband's surname after marriage, the wealth of negative terms for women, and the lack of parallel terms for the sexes. When a woman marries, she attains the honorific *Mrs.* Yet, *Mrs.* has no male counterpart; men remain *Mr.* regardless of marital status. In addition, referring to a married woman by her formal married name (e.g., Mrs. John Jones) obscures her identity and simply acknowledges her husband's identity.

Some researchers have pointed to the fact that there are more derogatory terms for women than there are for men. See how many negative terms you can think of

Table 4.2 /// Eliminating Sexism in Language

Sexist Language	Nonsexist Alternative
The scholar opened his book.	The scholar opened a book.
The pioneers headed West with their women and children.	The pioneer families headed West.
You're needed to man the table.	You're needed to staff the table.
Beth was salesman of the month.	Beth was the top seller this month.
Playing computer games cost the company a lot of man-hours.	Playing computer games cost the company a lot of productive time.
Manhole cover	Sewer access cover
Freshman	First-year student
Postman	Letter carrier
A person needs his sleep.	People need their sleep.
Mankind	Humankind, humanity

Table 4.3 /// "Parallel" Terms for Women and Men

Female	Male
mistress stewardess	master steward
governess actress	governor actor
spinster slut	bachelor stud
majorette waitress	major waiter
comedienne hostess	comedian host
songstress sculptress	singer sculptor

that label women (e.g., *slut, bitch,* etc.) and then do the same for men. Your first list is probably longer. It's also the case that parallel terms for men and women are not, in actuality, parallel. As Table 4.3 illustrates, many of the female words have a negative connotation that doesn't exist in the male version of the words. This is known as **semantic derogation**, or the use of one term (for males) with a positive connotation and its supposed parallel term (for females) with a negative connotation (e.g., *master* and *mistress*).

Racist Language

In the 21st century, most people may avoid overt racial slurs, but language can be racist in other, more subtle ways. The practice of associating negativity with black ("blackmail," "the bad guys wear black hats," "you're the black sheep of the family") perpetuates racial stereotypes on a subtle level. When Miranda, a white woman, met Lyle, a black man, she hadn't known too many black people before. She tried to speak in a way that wouldn't offend him. It didn't even occur to her that Lyle would find her use of the terms *dark side* and *blackball* troubling. Some researchers argue that racism comes from being taught language that reflects a thought system that values one race over another. For example, when whites are taught from a Eurocentric perspective and don't learn anything about African or Asian history or accomplishments, racism flourishes.

Racist language is also present in place names in the United States. Native Americans have long waged campaigns to change the names for places that include the word *squaw,* a word considered by many Indians, especially women, to be extremely offensive and derogatory. There are over 1,000 place names in the United States that include that word, and the campaign to change them has met some resistance and proved to be slow going.

Homophobic Language

When the actor Alec Baldwin used a word perceived as a slur to gay men in an altercation with a photographer in 2013, MSNBC suspended his new talk show *Up Late,* and Baldwin received a great deal of negative press. Baldwin apologized and acknowledged the power of language to wound others, saying, "I did not intend to hurt or offend anyone with my choice of words, but clearly I have—and for that I am deeply sorry. Words are important. I understand that, and will choose mine with great care going forward."[26] In 2018, MSNBC's Joy Reid also had to apologize for homophobic language she'd used 10 years previously on her blog, "The Reid Report." On the blog, she mocked then-Florida governor Charlie Crist by calling him "Miss Charlie" and suggested he married his wife to hide his sexual identity. She also made negative remarks about gay sexuality, calling it "gross." Reid, while arguing that her blog was hacked, also owned that her language had been cruel and insensitive.

While these cases are high profile, they certainly aren't isolated incidents of homophobic language use. A 2018 study reports that in a sample of almost 8,000 adolescents, 49% experienced cyberbullying involving homophobic language. Adolescents across the United States frequently use homophobic language, such as "that's so gay" to describe something that is wrong, bad, or stupid. Researchers agree that the effects of homophobic language and bullying are extremely detrimental and long lasting. People who are targets of this type of language report increased anxiety, depression, sleeping complaints, subpar school functioning, substance use, and behaviors geared toward self-harm. Recognizing the extent of the problem worldwide, UNESCO Director-General Irina Bokova said, "I am deeply concerned by the excessive trivialization of insults, sexist and homophobic remarks in the media, in everyday life, on social networks, even from political leaders."[27]

The Constructive Side of Verbal Codes

Although verbal symbols can cause all the problems we've discussed, verbal communication (coupled with nonverbal communication) can express **confirmation**, or the acknowledgment, validation, and support of another person. Through the use of confirmation, we can build supportive relationships with others. Confirming messages help other people understand that you are paying

Table 4.4 /// Disconfirming and Confirming Communication

Disconfirming	Confirming
Simply ignore and turn away.	Pay attention and lean in.
Simply maintain silence.	Provide appropriate responses to the other.
"You don't matter to me."	"You matter to me."
"You're on your own."	"We're in this together."
"You shouldn't feel that way."	"I hear how you feel."

Video 4.3

attention to them and that you recognize them as equal to you. You don't have to agree with someone to confirm them—you simply have to express that you are listening and paying attention. For example, when Dina listens intently to her sister, Char, complain about their mother, she confirms that she cares enough about Char to pay attention. Even though Dina doesn't agree with Char (Dina has a positive relationship with their mother), Char feels confirmed. There's some evidence that when parents confirm their children, it improves the children's mental health outcomes. In contrast, **disconfirmation** occurs when someone feels ignored and disregarded. Disconfirmation makes people feel that you don't see them—that they are unimportant. See Table 4.4 for examples of confirming and disconfirming behavior.

We also use language to develop inclusion rather than exclusion. Using the language of inclusion means that you are thoughtful and attentive to when others seem to be offended, and that you ask what you said to have given offense. Although we might accidentally exclude someone from time to time, through careful language use we can build supportive relationships. In addition, as we discuss in Chapter 6, we can use empathic language to connect with others. When we try to understand another's feelings, we show we care enough about that person to spend time and energy listening, and we can establish genuine relationships.

Verbal codes also help us solve problems. When we use open-ended questions (e.g., "What do you think is wrong?" or "How would you like me to respond to you?"), we can work toward problem solving in our interpersonal relationships. Verbal symbols help us explain our position while conveying that we're also interested in the other person's position.

IPC Praxis

Think about your most recent conversation when you were telling another about a problem. What were things that person did that you felt were helpful and what were behaviors that didn't seem positive to you? How did their behaviors fit the description we've given above for confirmation? Were any of their behaviors that weren't like our description still helpful to you? Why do you think that would be the case?

4–4 SKILL SET FOR IMPROVING VERBAL COMMUNICATION

To improve your verbal communication skills, we suggest cultivating an attitude of respect for others. To do so, you need to engage in **perspective taking**, which means acknowledging the viewpoints of those with whom you interact. For example, if you talk frequently with a friend who is a different ethnicity than you, perspective taking requires you to understand that ethnicity matters, and that your friend will have somewhat different experiences from yours as a result.

Marsha Houston, a communication studies scholar who is African American, writes that she doesn't like it when white women friends try to empathize with her by saying that they know exactly how she feels about racism because they have experienced sexism (or some other "ism"). Houston says that it erases her experience to state that your experience is just like hers. Listening to others without assuming that you already know about their experiences helps in perspective taking.

In addition to developing respect for others and working on perspective taking, you can practice four skills to help you be more effective in using verbal symbols: owning and using I-messages, understanding when to be specific and when to be more general, indexing, and probing the middle ground. (See Table 4.5 for a list of the skills).

Table 4.5 /// Skill Set for Enhancing Verbal Communication
a. Own and use I-messages.
b. Use specificity effectively.
c. Practice your ability to index.
d. Probe the middle ground.
e. Your skill suggestion

Own and Use I-Messages

Each of us must take responsibility for our own behaviors and feelings in communication with others. *Owning* refers to our ability to take responsibility for our own thoughts and feelings, and is often accomplished through I-messages. *I-messages* acknowledge our own position, whereas *you-messages* direct responsibility onto others, often in a blaming fashion. For example, if you are bored during a lecture, you could communicate this to the professor with a you-message ("Your lecture is boring") or an I-message ("I'm having trouble getting involved in this material"). I-messages help prevent defensiveness in the listener because they focus on the speaker's feelings and actions. See Table 4.6 for more examples of the difference between you-messages and I-messages.

Table 4.6 /// You-Messages and I-Messages

You-Messages	I-Messages
"You are insensitive."	"I want you to pay attention to me."
"You make me mad."	"I get angry when I think you're ignoring me."
"You don't understand anything."	"I don't feel understood when you interrupt me."
"You never listen to me."	"I want you to put down the paper when I talk to you."
"You are so rude."	"I was hurt when you said you thought my hair looked bad."
"You're a liar."	"I need to be able to trust you, and I feel betrayed because you didn't tell me the truth about the car accident."

Use Levels of Specificity Effectively

Earlier in the chapter, we mentioned that words operate at different levels of specificity:

- vehicle
- car
- black 2019 Chevy Camaro

The first term allows the listener to imagine a wide range of vehicles, the second term narrows the field somewhat, and the third restricts the referent much more. The more general you are, the more you allow a listener to interpret what you mean. The more specific you are, the more you direct the listener to your precise meaning.

Being skillful in this area requires you to diagnose when a situation needs specificity and when general information might suffice. A simple guideline suggests that the better you know someone, the less specific you have to be. For example, when two people have a developed relationship, they may understand each other without providing a great deal of specific description. So, when Tom tells Ella that he wants to spend some time relaxing, she knows from her 5 years of experience with him that he means he wants to go into his workshop and would appreciate not being disturbed. Tom doesn't need to tell Ella specifically what the abstract term *relaxing* means to him at this point in their relationship. However, when Tom is at work and tells a new coworker that they need to get a project finished as soon as possible, he probably should specify that *as soon as possible*, in this case, means by the end of the week. Otherwise, the coworker could spend all day working to finish the project, only to discover that Tom didn't need it so soon. And, of course, as we discussed previously, it's sometimes prudent to be ambiguous for strategic reasons.

Practice Your Ability to Index

A way to avoid static evaluation, one of the problems we mentioned earlier, involves dating your statements to indicate that you're aware that things may change over time. **Indexing** requires that you acknowledge the time frame of your judgments of others and yourself. For example, if Matt believes that Rucha is self-centered, he could index that by saying, "Yesterday, when she wouldn't stop talking about herself, Rucha acted so self-centered." Indexing reminds us that the way people act at one given time may not be the way they are all the time. Thus, it's not necessarily true that Rucha *is* self-centered, but rather simply that Matt thinks she was *acting* that way at a given point in time.

Probe the Middle Ground

Probing the middle ground is a skill that helps you avoid polarization in your verbal communication. When you are tempted to label something with an extreme judgment, try to explore the nuances that might be more descriptive of the behavior. For instance, if you are tempted to label someone as irresponsible, try to discover the areas where the person has acted responsibly so you can see that they are not completely at one extreme on the responsibility scale. Thinking about the middle ground will help restrain you from polarizing or using extreme labels that can easily become inflammatory.

/// CHAPTER WRAP-UP

In this chapter, we have explored one of the major tools we have for engaging in interpersonal communication and developing interpersonal relationships: verbal symbols. We took a social interaction approach in this chapter that acknowledges we are doing much more than exchanging words when we communicate. We noted that verbal codes are arbitrary symbols that nonetheless are invested with enormous power. Further, we illustrated how words evolve over time, have both denotative and connotative meanings, and vary in specificity. The chapter also reviewed the ways in which verbal symbols are affected by the communicants' culture, sex, generation, as well as the overall context in which the communication takes place.

We examined several theories that help us understand how verbal symbols operate; specifically, we discussed how Communication Accommodation Theory explains how language is used to both connect people and separate them. We also considered how the Sapir-Whorf hypothesis (Linguistic Determinism/Relativity) explains the relationship among perception, culture, and verbal codes. Additionally, we advanced two theories, Two-Culture Theory and Muted Group Theory, which address sex, gender, and verbal communication.

We concluded with a discussion of the constructive and destructive aspects of verbal codes and offered four skills to increase your abilities to be constructive in interpersonal encounters.

/// COMMUNICATION ASSESSMENT TEST (CAT): UTILIZING VERBAL SKILLS

1. Which of the following is positive body language to use when speaking?

   a. Fold your arms and cross your legs.

   b. Stand behind something and hide your body.

   c. Keep arms open and use open gestures.

   d. Avoid eye contact.

2. You're giving someone verbal feedback about some work they have completed that isn't up to standard. What should you do?

   a. Point out everything they did wrong.

   b. Base your feedback on what you've heard from others.

   c. Be critical.

   d. Suggest where improvements can be made and agree on a plan.

3. Which of these is the best way to ask a question?

   a. Frame it so there's only a yes or no response.

   b. Use leading words to suggest the answer you wish to hear.

   c. Ask something you wouldn't want to answer yourself.

   d. Use open-ended questions that encourage a full response.

4. You disagree with what someone has said. How should you react?

   a. Ask questions to learn more about the person's opinion.

   b. Keep talking about your own opinion.

   c. Interrupt frequently to point out where you think the person is wrong.

   d. Stop listening and concentrate on phrasing your position clearly.

5. Which of the following will NOT help you to be more persuasive in conversations with others?

   a. mirroring the other person's verbal and nonverbal communication

   b. using words the other person understands

   c. talking about your own interests and goals

   d. showing where your goals overlap with the other person's

Answers: 1.c, 2.d, 3.d, 4.a, 5.c

Source: Louise Petty at High Speed Training.

/// KEY TERMS

Communication Accommodation Theory (CAT) 99	converge 99	language 100
	diverge 99	verbal symbols 100

/// KEY QUESTIONS FOR APPLICATION

1. ***CQ/CultureQuest***: Explore the following claim: "It's not really possible to communicate effectively with someone from another culture whose first language is not the same as your own." Do you agree or disagree? Defend your views.

2. ***TQ/TechQuest***: Explore the following claim: "Technology makes it possible for different generations to communicate. Age is not an issue when people communicate online." Do you agree or disagree? Defend your views.

3. How does communication accommodation work in a workplace situation? Give an example of how employees might converge or diverge to the speaking style of their boss. Have you ever noticed yourself converging or diverging? If so, what was the situation and why did you change your language?

4. When do you think it's useful to be ambiguous in your verbal language? Why would that be the case when one of the skills advocated in the chapter is clarity?

5. Do you agree that males and females can be considered two different cultures? Give some examples to explain your position.

6. Explain Muted Group Theory. Give some examples of groups that you believe are muted in your native language.

Access practice quizzes, eFlashcards, video, and multimedia at **edge.sagepub.com/west**.

Visit **edge.sagepub.com/west** to help you accomplish your coursework goals in an easy-to-use learning environment.

CHAPTER 5

COMMUNICATING NONVERBALLY

LEARNING OUTCOMES

After studying this chapter, you will be able to

5–1 Identify the primary assumptions of nonverbal communication

5–2 Explain and exemplify the channels of nonverbal communication

5–3 Articulate the relationship between nonverbal communication and culture

5–4 Articulate the relationship between nonverbal communication and technology

5–5 Apply a variety of strategies to improve skills in nonverbal communication

iStock.com/asiseeit

Master the content at
edge.sagepub.com/west

⑤SAGE edge™

Each day, we all communicate without saying a word. This nonverbal communication has been a part of our lives since birth, and over the years, we've spent unknown hours processing, learning about, and incorporating these behaviors in all aspects of our lives. Nonverbal communication has been called the "unspoken dialogue"[1] and scholars have continually recognized its importance in conversations. Some researchers report that around 65% of overall message meaning is conveyed nonverbally[2] (see Figure 5.1), while others report up to 97% of emotional meaning in a face-to-face conversation is conveyed nonverbally.[3] From a historical perspective, employing nonverbal communication to understand others is a practice that has been with us since the beginning of civilization. For instance, thousands of years ago, the Chinese relied on the nose, eyes, and chin to judge another's character. In the ancient culture of India, since 1000 B.C.E., one could detect a liar by looking at whether the person was dragging a big toe on the ground and/or avoiding eye contact.[4] And, in early Hebrew scriptures, references to gestures as a form of language existed.[5]

When we attend to nonverbal behaviors, we draw conclusions about others and others simultaneously draw conclusions about us. This process is part of the transactional nature of communication we discussed in Chapter 1. The influence of nonverbal behavior on our perceptions, conversations, and relationships cannot be overstated. Although we are generally unaware of our use of nonverbal communication, it's always present in our interactions with others and remains a critical part of how we achieve interpersonal meaning.

 IPC Voice: Ahmed

Why would anyone not want to study how people communicate without words? My family came to this country from a place where touching and smiling and passion all come together. Whether it's in my family or in my neighborhood, we use nonverbal communication almost every minute of every day! I love that in the United States, so many guys are hung up on being called "gay." They would fall over if they visited my country! They'd think that every guy is gay. Man, I just don't get it sometimes.

This chapter explores how nonverbal behavior functions, both directly and indirectly, in our daily activities. Before we move on in our discussion about nonverbal communication, let's spend a few moments interpreting it. **Nonverbal communication** encompasses all behaviors—other than spoken words—that communicate messages and have shared meaning between people. To this end, we can define nonverbal communication as a process of sending and receiving nonlinguistic cues. This interpretation has three associated parameters. First, electronic communication is not included in our definition. Second, when we note that there is "shared meaning," we are saying that a national culture agrees on how to construe a behavior. For example, in many co-cultures in the United States, when a parent sees a child do something unsafe, the parent might wag their index finger.

Figure 5.1 /// The Communication of Interpersonal Meaning

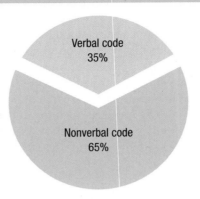

Verbal code
35%

Nonverbal code
65%

Table 5.1 /// Differences Between Verbal and Nonverbal Communication

Verbal Communication	Nonverbal Communication
Single channel (words)	Multichannel
Intermittent	Continuous
Significantly shaped by culture	Significantly shaped by biology
Can be clear or ambiguous	Inherently ambiguous
Normally content centered	Normally relational
Mostly strategic and voluntary	Frequently involuntary
Subject to verification	Instinctively credible

The child must know the meaning behind this nonverbal shaming technique to respond to the parent's reprimand. Third, as we mentioned in Chapter 4, verbal and nonverbal communication usually work together to create meaning, although clear distinctions between the two exist (Table 5.1).[6]

Nonverbal communication is central to our relational lives. Research has shown that the way people communicate nonverbally influences (1) how relationships are established, maintained, and dissolved; (2) the diagnosis of health-related problems such as autism; (3) the number of sexual partners a person has; (4) how babies show emotional distress; (5) marital satisfaction and stability; and (6) perceptions of beauty.[7] These reasons are just a snapshot of why this topic is essential to discuss in a book on interpersonal communication.

Nonverbal communication competence requires us to be able to encode and decode nonverbal messages. We also have to use nonverbal communication ourselves to achieve meaning. Further, we need to be able to adapt to people around us, paying attention to both the words they use and the behaviors accompanying those words. Suppose, for example, that Rosa and her roommate, Marta, are in a noisy place talking about the problems related to how clean their dorm room is. Marta is practicing conversation adaptation if, when Rosa leans forward to talk about the topic, Marta simultaneously leans forward to listen to the story. This "postural echo" suggests that Marta is not only mirroring Rosa's behavior, but also trying to understand Rosa's meaning.

Rosa and Marta sound like two people who are able to practice nonverbal communication with little challenge. Yet, we recognize that not everyone is afforded this level of engagement. Thus, before moving on, as with language and language use, we wish to acknowledge the distinct challenges and difficulties related to communicating nonverbally. Several learning, developmental, and physical disabilities, for instance, frequently prevent meaning from being achieved. Frankly, some people are simply incapable of being receptive to and/or practicing skillful nonverbal communication. An individual with Asperger's syndrome, for instance, may not achieve interpersonal meaning since this autistic disorder usually results in people having a hard time communicating without words.[8] In addition, individuals with various physical challenges, including vision impairment or facial paralysis, for example, will likely find the nonverbal communication process disquieting. For all sorts of important reasons, we realize that our goal of realizing and improving effective nonverbal communication may not be readily available to everyone.

IPC Praxis

Look around your surroundings right now. Identify the elements in the room that are communicating nonverbally. These elements can include both people and objects.

With this information and our definition in place, we're now ready to explore some of the assumptions pertaining to nonverbal communication.

5–1 ASSUMPTIONS OF NONVERBAL COMMUNICATION

Although it's often overlooked or downplayed, nonverbal communication is vital in all types of conversations. Consider the times when we don't say a word but manage to "say" so much. Imagine hugging a close friend at her father's funeral. And, think about holding hands with your partner during a romantic movie. Or, what about your eye rolling and teeth gritting when another tenant parks in your parking space? Further, how many times have you tried to get through a crowd, elbowing others to get to your destination? In these situations, nonverbal communication is likely more powerful than any words you could say. With this information in mind, we now turn our attention to unpacking four basic assumptions of nonverbal communication.

Nonverbal Communication Is Often Ambiguous

One reason nonverbal communication is so challenging in our relationships is that our nonverbal messages often mean different things to different people, which can lead to misunderstandings. Compared to verbal messages, nonverbal messages are usually more ambiguous. For example, suppose that Lena prolongs her eye contact with Jason and, in turn, Jason refocuses on Lena. While Lena may be showing some attraction to Jason, he may be returning the eye contact because he believes that something is wrong. Clearly, the same nonverbal behavior (eye contact) can elicit two different meanings.

Nonverbal communication is more difficult to understand because it's intangible and more abstract. A major reason for this ambiguity is that many factors influence the meaning of nonverbal behaviors, including shared fields of experience, current surroundings, and culture. Consider the following conversation between a father and son as they talk about the son staying out past his curfew:

Dad: "I told you to be home by 11! It's past midnight now. And get that smirk off your face!"

Son: "You might have told me 11, but you didn't say anything when I asked if I could stay out till 12. You didn't say for sure either way. Remember when I asked while you were changing the oil on the truck? You didn't even look at me. I couldn't hear you mumbling under the car. And, how am I . . ."

Dad: "You heard what you wanted to hear. I told you . . ."

Son: "I swear, Dad. I thought my curfew was midnight. And I've stayed out till midnight before."

This scenario between the two suggests a few things about the ambiguous nature of nonverbal communication. First, the father seems to be annoyed by his son's smirk. Is he truly smirking, or is the father misinterpreting his son's facial expression because he is angry? Second, the son took his dad's verbal message about the 11 p.m. deadline less seriously because his father neglected to make eye contact when delivering it. In addition, the son thought that his dad hesitated when he asked about a later curfew and also claimed that he couldn't clearly hear his father's response from under the car, further eroding the power of the father's verbal communication. In this example, ambiguity results from the interaction of the verbal and nonverbal behaviors of both the father and son, leading us to a second assumption.

Sometimes our nonverbal communication "speaks" volumes, although we don't have to say a word.

Nonverbal Communication May Conflict With Verbal Communication

Although nonverbal and verbal communication frequently operate interdependently, sometimes our nonverbal messages are not congruent with our verbal messages. We term this incompatibility a **mixed message**. When a friend asks you, "What's wrong?" after observing you with tears in your eyes, and you reply, "Nothing," the contradiction between your nonverbal and verbal behavior is evident. When a physician purses her lips or frowns as she reveals to her patient that the prognosis "looks good," she gives a mixed message. Or, consider a wife, who after being asked by her husband if she loves him, shouts, "Of course I love you!" Most of us would agree that angrily shouting to express our affection sends a mixed message.

When confronted with a mixed message, people have to choose whether to believe the nonverbal or the verbal cues. Because children are generally not sophisticated enough to understand the many meanings that accompany nonverbal communication, they rely on the words of a message more than the nonverbal behaviors.[9] In contrast, adults who encounter mixed messages pay the most attention to nonverbal messages and neglect much of what is being stated because we are more adept at interpreting levels and complexities of communication, including the varying nonverbal messages.[10]

Nonverbal Communication Regulates Conversation

People use nonverbal communication to manage the ebb and flow of conversations. Nonverbal regulators allow speakers to enter, exit, or maintain the conversation. The turn-taking (who talks when and to whom) is based primarily on nonverbal communication. For instance, if we want a chance to speak, we usually lean forward, toward the speaker, as Rosa and Marta did in our earlier example. If we don't want to be interrupted in a conversation, we may avoid eye contact and keep our vocal pattern consistent so that others don't have an opportunity to begin talking until we're finished. When we are ready to yield the conversation to another, we typically stop talking, look at the other person, and perhaps make a motion with our hands to indicate that it is now okay for the other person to respond.

In our online relationships, consider how regulation functions. During texting, for example, regulating can take a few forms. We may use ellipses points ("I wanted to say one more thing here . . .") to show we want to continue a sequence. Or, we may choose not to respond to an e-mail or text, frequently inciting a reaction from the receiver. In other circumstances, we may choose to use emojis to communicate our feelings at the minute, and some clearly let others know whether or not we wish to continue the dialogue (e.g., 😷 💀).

Nonverbal Communication Is More Believable Than Verbal Communication

As noted earlier, although nonverbal communication is often ambiguous, people generally believe nonverbal messages over verbal messages. You've no doubt heard the expression "Actions speak louder than words." This statement suggests that someone's nonverbal behavior can influence a conversational partner more than what is said. A job candidate being interviewed, for example, may verbally state her commitment to being professional, yet if she wears jeans and arrives late to the interview, these nonverbal cues will likely cause the interviewer to regard her statement with skepticism.

Consider how Esther reacts to the nonverbal communication of the customers at a coffee shop where she is a barista. She continues to make judgments on the likelihood of customers giving tips based upon their pleasant conversational tone and their well-dressed appearance. However, as we learned in Chapter 3, perceptions may be misleading or incomplete. One of the biggest tippers for Esther may be an old curmudgeon with a dirty jacket!

5–2 NONVERBAL COMMUNICATION CODES

Extensive study of nonverbal communication indicates that we employ several different forms of nonverbal codes in our conversations with others. Later in the chapter, we look at a number of these codes and discuss their cultural implications; thus, review this section with that lens in place. In this section, because nonverbal communication is so complex, we present a classifying system[11] which we set out in Table 5.2. This system includes visual-auditory codes, contact codes, and place and time codes.

Visual-Auditory Codes

As their name reflects, visual-auditory codes include categories of nonverbal communication that we can see and hear. These categories are kinesics (body movement), physical appearance (such as attractiveness), facial communication (such as eye contact), and paralanguage (such as pitch level and whining).

Kinesics (Body Movement)

Body communication is also called *kinesics,* a Greek word meaning "movement." **Kinesics** refers to the study of how people communicate through bodily motions. Kinesic behavior is wide ranging; it can include anything from staying put at a party after being asked to leave to gesturing during a speech.

Table 5.2 /// Categories of Nonverbal Communication

Code	Nonverbal Category
Visual-auditory	Kinesics (*body movement*) Physical appearance (*body size, body artifacts, attractiveness*) Facial communication (*eye contact, smiling*) Paralanguage (*pitch, rate, volume, speed, silence*)
Contact	Haptics (*touch*) Proxemics (*personal space, territoriality*)
Place and time	The environment (*color, lighting, room design*) Chronemics (*time*)

The primary components of kinesics are gestures and body posture or orientation. Gestures have been analyzed for almost 2,500 years. For example, Aristotle wrote that gestures are important when delivering a public speech. Gestures preceded verbal communication by tens of thousands of years.[12] What can we learn from gestures? First, gestures can be both intentional and unintentional. Second, we need to consider the context of gestures to understand them. Think about the gestures that the following individuals would use: parking lot attendant, nurse, radio disc jockey, landscaper, and auctioneer. What gestures would they have in common? What gestures are unique to these occupations? In the classroom setting, gestures such as raising a hand, writing on a board, pointing, and waving at a student to come sit in a particular seat are common. Several gesture types exist.[13] As you review each, keep in mind that cultural variations exist, a theme we revisit later in the chapter:

- **Delivery gestures** signal shared understanding between communicators. Clifton, for example, nods his head to let his friend, Kaitlin, know that he understands what she is talking about.

- **Citing gestures** acknowledge another's feedback. For instance, in a conversation with her employee, Cindy uses a citing gesture when she disagrees with what her employee is saying—she raises her hand, palm flat to the receiver, her index finger extended upward.

- **Seeking gestures** request agreement or clarification from the speaker. For instance, we may extend both our arms out, keep our palms flat, and shrug. This gesture is used when someone is communicating "I don't know what you mean."

- **Turn gestures** indicate that another person can speak or are used to request the conversation floor. We referenced this behavior earlier in the chapter when we discussed the regulating function of nonverbal messages. Turn gestures include pointing at another to indicate it is their turn, or extending your hand outward and rotating your wrist in a clockwise motion to show that the other person should continue speaking.

In addition to gestures, our body posture and orientation reveal important information. Posture has been associated with emotions, and the English language contains several expressions depicting this relationship (e.g., "Don't be so uptight," "I won't take this lying down"). Posture is generally a result of how tense or relaxed we are. For example, your body posture would likely differ depending on whether you were reading this chapter while you were alone in your room or in the waiting room of a hospital. **Body orientation** refers to how we turn our legs, shoulders, and head toward (or away) from a person. Body orientation affects conversations and the extent to which people believe what we say. Moreover, people will frequently change their body position based on their credibility. For example, typically, when people communicate with someone of higher status, they tend to stand directly facing them. Conversely, those with higher status tend to use a leaning posture when speaking to subordinates.

Our physical appearance remains one influential factor in our communication with others.

Physical Appearance

In interpersonal exchanges, physical appearance plays a role in our evaluations of others ("How could they have found him guilty?! And he's such a good-looking guy"). Physical appearance encompasses all of the **physical characteristics** of an individual, including body size, skin color, hair color and style, facial hair, and facial features (e.g., blemishes, skin texture).

How does physical appearance influence our interpersonal communication? Although we are unable to discuss every aspect of physical appearance, a few thoughts merit attention. Certainly, skin color has affected the communication process. Even today—decades after civil rights legislation and an infusion of diversity in the United States—some people won't communicate with people who are of a particular race or ethnicity. Body size, too, can influence our interpersonal relationships. Do you find yourself making judgments about people who appear overweight or too thin? What is your first assessment of a person who is more than 6 feet tall? What is your initial impression of a bodybuilder? Do you evaluate women who shave their body hair differently from women who choose not to shave? Each of these observations has the capacity to impact our perceptions of others, affecting our communication with them.

Video 5.1

Body artifacts refer to our possessions and how we decorate ourselves and our surroundings. Clothing, for example, can convey social status or group identification. Furthermore, some writers indicate that clothing can communicate quite a bit, including spending habits, emotional states, social position, economic level, and the sorts of morals and values we support.[14]

Other examples of the influence of clothing are all around us. In the corporate world, tailored clothing bolsters one's status among many peers. During Kwanzaa, a holiday celebration in African American communities, participants frequently wear traditional African clothing, which serves as a nonverbal connection among African Americans. People who wear religious symbols, such as a crucifix or the Star of David, may be exhibiting religious commitments. Military clothing is usually accompanied by medals or stripes to depict rank, which suggests military accomplishment. Many of you may have body piercings, and these can communicate many different messages. Yet, although some of you may adorn yourself with these nonverbal body symbols to show your nonconformity, some job interviewers may view them as expressions of too much independence and future unwillingness to be a team player at work. Ironically, with nearly 40% of Millennials alone who have a tattoo,[15] the notion of being a noncomformist will likely be antiquated in a few years!

Physical appearance also includes the level of attractiveness of the interpersonal communicators. Quite a bit of research exists on interpersonal attractiveness.

Two significant conclusions are particularly pertinent to our discussion.[16] First, people generally seek out others who are similar to themselves in attractiveness, just as they seek out others who are similar to themselves in other characteristics. If you are a nonsmoker, are you likely to be compatible with a smoker? If you are vegetarian, will you be attracted to a carnivore?

IPC Praxis

Discuss how physical attraction is determined in an online relationship. Identify specific examples and explain the consequences of deciding whether or not someone is physically attractive online.

Second, physically attractive people are often judged to be more intelligent and friendly than those not deemed attractive. This conclusion resonates in a number of different environments. In the classroom, in one study, professors were found to issue higher grades to students who are deemed attractive.[17] In another study, researchers discovered that students learned more in a classroom with an attractive teacher.[18] In the business setting, however, "more attractive women in executive roles are often the victims of prejudice, taken less seriously and often resented, thus feeling the pressure to come up with glasses and hairstyles that project a more severe aura."[19] It's clear, then, that although many try to avoid its influence, physical attractiveness affects perceptions and impressions of credibility.

Facial Displays

More than any other part of the body, the face gives others insight into how someone is feeling. Our facial expressions cover the gamut of emotional meaning, from eagerness to exhaustion. We often have difficulty shielding genuine feelings from others because we usually don't have much control over our facial communication. This fact further explains the point we made earlier in this chapter: People tend to believe our nonverbal codes over our verbal codes. We may try at times, but it's tough to hide our feelings. Try to conceal your reaction as you listen to a roommate talk about not getting his weekly allowance while you figure out your schedule for your third job! While looking at an infant or toddler, try suppressing a grin. When talking to a parent who has lost a child in a war, repressing a sad look on your face is pretty much impossible. It's simply too challenging to control a region of our body that is so intimately connected to our emotions.

Video 5.2

The part of the face with the most potential for communication is the eye. And, as Ralph Waldo Emerson said: "When the eyes say one thing and the tongue another, a practiced [person] relies on the language of the first." For most of us, our eyes remain instrumental in both aesthetic and practical ways. For instance, some research indicates that as we view artwork through our eyes, we establish a viewing "strategy" (e.g., linking pieces of art together) as we process the visual stimuli.[20] Still, eye behavior is complex. We can look directly into someone's eyes to communicate a number of different things, including interest, power, or anger. We may avoid eye contact when we are uninterested, nervous, or shy. Our eyes also facilitate our interactions. We look at others while they speak to get a sense of their facial and body communication. Simultaneously, others often look at us while we speak. We also make judgments about others simply by looking at their eyes, deciding if they are truthful, uninterested, tired, involved, or credible. Although our conclusions may be erroneous, most people rely on eye contact in their conversations.

Finally, with respect to the face, smiling remains one of the most recognizable nonverbal behaviors worldwide. Smiling, though, can be complex as well (smiling for a driver's license and smiling as someone tells an offensive joke). Still, smiling usually has a positive effect on an encounter. As one psychologist puts it, "Each time you smile you throw a little feel-good party in your brain."[21]

Smiling also may entice others to act as Good Samaritans. In an experiment testing the effects of smiling on helping behavior, one study found that smiling at others encourages them to assist in tasks.[22] Studying 800 passersby, the research team had eight research assistants ask others for help. One group of assistants smiled at some of the people exiting a grocery store. A few seconds later, passersby had an opportunity to help an assistant who dropped an item on the ground. Results showed that the previous smile of a stranger enhanced later helping behavior. That is, those who were smiled at earlier were more likely to help the stranger with the item.

Paralanguage (the Voice)

To introduce the concept of paralanguage, let's examine the story of Charles. A few weeks ago, Charles lost his mother, a woman whom he considered his best friend. When people around the office ask him how he's doing, he always responds, "She lived a good, long life." However, his good friend, Melissa, can hear a "voice" that is different from the one Charles normally uses. For example, sometimes when Charles says that he feels fine and that no one should be concerned about him, Melissa hears a different message. She "feels" his pain during his silence. She "listens to his pain" when Charles laughs awkwardly. Melissa is clearly drawing conclusions about the paralinguistic cues from Charles.

This story underscores a vocal characteristic called **paralanguage,** or vocalics, which is the study of a person's use of voice. Paralanguage refers not to *what* a person says, but to *how* a person says it. Included in our conversation is, as we allude to above, the use of silence, which can be both a beneficial (e.g., hugging a close friend and not saying something after a family death) and detrimental (e.g., giving someone "the silent treatment" and refusing to participate in a heated conversation).

Paralanguage covers a vast array of nonverbal behaviors that relate to the characteristics of our speaking voice, including such things as pitch and rate, and which we call **vocal qualities.** We also consider **vocal distracters** (the "ums" and "ers" of conversation) as vocal qualities. Paralanguage also encompasses such nonverbal behaviors as crying, laughing, groaning, muttering, whispering, and whining;

we call these **vocal characterizers**. Don't underestimate the usefulness of studying these paralinguistic behaviors. They provide us our uniqueness as communicators, help us differentiate among people, and influence people's perceptions of us and our perceptions of them.

IPC Praxis

Compare and contrast your use of nonverbal communication at (a) a party, (b) in a house of worship, and (c) in a job interview.

Our vocal qualities include the rate (speed), volume (loudness/softness), inflection (vocal emphasis), pitch (highness/lowness), intensity (volume), tempo (rhythm), and pronunciation associated with voices. Vocal qualities lead listeners to form impressions about a speaker's socioeconomic status, personality type, persuasiveness, and work ethic.[23] One way to tap into these vocal nuances is to practice saying the same sentence with various rates, volume, inflection, sighs, and tempo. For example, try saying the following statement to show *praise,* then *blame,* and then *exasperation:*

You really did it this time.

The next time you want to borrow a friend's car, tell your father a secret, ask your professor a question, or engage in a debate with your roommate about religion or politics, you will probably utilize a number of different vocal qualities.

The "ums" in our conversations may seem unimportant, but these vocal distractors compose an increasingly researched area of vocal qualities because they can predict whether a conversation will continue and the fluency of that conversation. How do you react when you hear a speaker use these disfluencies? You may find them appropriate for many social situations, but what happens in more professional settings, such as formal presentations at work, job interviews, or oral reports for a class? When vocal distractors are used excessively, people view them as bad habits that can jeopardize credibility.

Vocal characterizers such as laughing, moaning, or whining also communicate a great deal about how to interpret verbal messages. For example, if Lexi tells Jose, "I'm so over you," but does so with laughter, Jose probably can infer that the comment should not be taken seriously. Or suppose Ron is a member of a task group at work. Each time the group meets, his coworker complains about the time it takes to get the group together, the assignment, and the time constraints. The coworker's whining about the task will likely affect Ron's conversations with her.

Contact Codes

Contact codes include touch (haptics) and space (such as personal space). These two areas are among the most discussed and important areas in interpersonal communication. The two areas are also linked in many ways. For instance, quickly think about the last time you noticed someone touch you or you touched another person. Now, quickly think about how various space differences functioned in those interactions. The interrelationship between these two nonverbal codes merits their consideration together.

Haptics (Touch)

Touch communication, or **haptics,** is the most primitive form of human communication. Scholars have found that touch has lasting value. In particular, human touch can completely change the way the body functions. From your heart rate to your blood pressure to the efficiency of your digestive system, welcomed touch can make your body work better. Humans need touch. We crave it, we hunger for it, and we get sick and can even die from the lack of it.[24]

Touch behavior is the ultimate in privileged access to people. That is, when you touch another person, you have decided—whether intentionally or unintentionally—to invade another's physical space. When forced into circumstances where everyone is close—for example, standing in a crowded elevator, sitting next to someone on the train or bus, or standing in a cafeteria line—we normally offer an apology or an excuse if we accidentally touch someone. Interestingly, at public celebrations like Mardi Gras and New Year's Eve parties, touching another person doesn't seem as intrusive. In fact, some people enjoy it!

Touch behavior is an ambiguous form of communication, because touching has various meanings depending on the context. Touching another person takes different forms and signals multiple messages. Shaking hands upon meeting someone, making love, slapping an old friend on the back, physically abusing a partner, rubbing a partner's neck, and tickling a small child are all examples of touch behavior. There are 457 types of body contact, from the rare (e.g., kissing a hand) to the more common (stylist cutting hair).[25] Our brains are wired to interpret the various touch behaviors, and how it is received is context-dependent. Indeed, the functions of touch are many:

- Touch is employed for *status or power,* meaning that individuals engage in touch to communicate the prominence of their role in some manner. The media executive who touches an administrative associate without invitation may be exercising this type of touch.

- Touch is used for *positive affect,* which includes healing, appreciation, and affection. The nurse who touches the senior in the convalescent home is expressing tactile support to her patient.

- Touch has a *playful* function; it serves to lighten an interaction. This type of touch is apparent when two kids wrestle each other or when baseball players slap each other on the butt after a home run.

- The *healing* touch is that offered by those in the helping professions, including massage therapists.

- Touch is used to *influence* or direct behavior in an encounter. Touching another person while saying "move aside" is an example of touching to control.

- *Ritualistic* touch refers to the touches we use on an everyday basis, such as a handshake to say hello or good-bye.

- The *task* function pertains to touch that serves a professional or functional purpose. For instance, hairstylists and dentists are allowed to touch you to accomplish their tasks.

- A *hybrid touch* is a touch that greets a person and simultaneously demonstrates affection for that person. For instance, kissing a family member hello is an example of a hybrid touch.

- Touch that is *accidental* is done without apparent intent. This type of touching includes touching in close spaces, such as intimate restaurants, in elevators, at crowded restaurants, or at a religious service.

Proxemics (Space and Distance)

An episode of *Seinfeld* may come to mind as we mention the phrase "close talkers." Spatial communication is important in conversation. **Proxemics,** the study of how communication is influenced by space and distance, is historically related to how people use, manipulate, and identify their space. **Personal space** is the distance we put between ourselves and others. We carry informal personal space from one encounter to another; think of this personal space as a sort of invisible bubble that encircles us wherever we go. Our personal space provides some insight into ourselves and how we feel about other people. For instance, some research

 IPC Around Us

It was the nonverbal behavior heard around the globe: the handshake between President Obama and Cuban president Raul Castro at the funeral of former South African president Nelson Mandela. The handshake unleashed a great deal of concern from politicians, and in particular, some U.S. senators were concerned that it could be viewed as propaganda. Some thought that acknowledging the Cuban president in this way could be viewed as an effort to prop up a dictator at a time when Cuba was being looked at closely because of human rights abuses. The irony of the criticism, some others felt, was that Obama wouldn't be able to shake any hand, if he adhered to the senators' advice, given that so many countries have a record of abuse. As a result of this encounter, the handshake—a nonverbal symbol usually associated with a greeting or salutation—now carries much more significance than many anticipated.

MANDEL NGAN /AFP/Getty Images

Reflection: Have you ever greeted someone with an affirming nonverbal behavior such as a handshake, knowing that they had said or done something offensive? If so, were you hesitant to greet the person? If not, what do you think you'd do if someone asked you to shake their hand and you knew, for instance, that they told sexist or transphobic jokes?

shows that happily married couples stand closer to one another (11.4 inches) than those who have marital distress (14.8 inches).[26]

Anthropologist Edward T. Hall was the first to devise categories of personal space.[27] His system suggests that in most co-cultures in the United States, people communicate with others at a specific distance, depending on the nature of the conversation. Starting with the closest contact and the least amount of personal space, and moving to the greatest distance between communicators, the four categories of personal space are intimate distance, personal distance, social distance, and public distance (Figure 5.2). Examine Hall's categories and think about your own interpersonal encounters.

Intimate distance covers the distance that extends from you to around 18 inches. This spatial zone is normally reserved for those people with whom you are close— for example, close friends, romantic partners, and family members. Of course, in some situations, you have little choice but to allow others within an intimate distance (e.g., attending a movie or theater production, sitting on a train, watching a concert). If you let someone be a part of your intimate distance zone, you are implying that this person is meaningful to you. In fact, zero personal space—in other words, touch—suggests a very close relationship with someone because you are willing to give them part of your private space.

Video 5.3

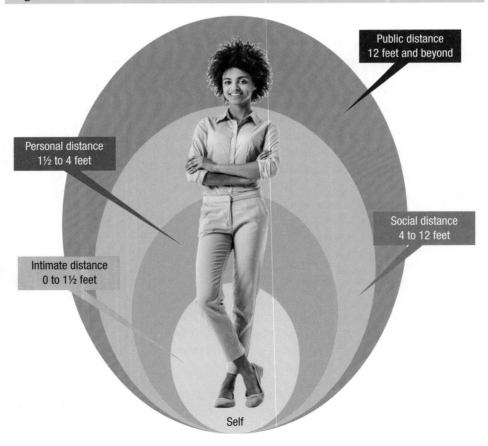

Figure 5.2 /// Hall's Proxemic Distances

Public distance
12 feet and beyond

Personal distance
1½ to 4 feet

Social distance
4 to 12 feet

Intimate distance
0 to 1½ feet

Self

iStock.com/GeorgeRudy

Personal distance, ranging from 18 inches to 4 feet, is the space most people use during conversations. This distance allows you to feel some protection from others who might wish to touch you. The range in this distance type allows those at the closest range to pick up your physical nuances (such as dry skin, body smells, etc.). However, we are still able to conduct business with those at the far range ("arm's length"), but any signs of nonverbal closeness are erased. Examples of relationships accustomed to personal distance are casual friends or business colleagues.

Social distance, which is 4 to 12 feet, is the spatial zone usually reserved for professional or formal interpersonal encounters. Some office environments are arranged specifically for social distance. Tables are aligned in a particular way, and cubicles are set up specifically to encourage social distance (rather than intimate distance or personal distance). As a result, many business transactions take place within social distance. Office kitchen chats or conversations in a break room at work also characterize the social zone. Whereas in the intimate and personal spatial zones we can use a lower vocal volume, social distance typically requires increased volume.

At the **public distance**, communication occurs at a distance of 12 or more feet. This spatial zone allows listeners to scan the entire person while they are speaking. The classroom environment exemplifies public distance. Most classrooms are arranged with a teacher in the front and rows of desks or tables facing the teacher. Of course, this setup can vary, but many classrooms are arranged with students more than 12 feet from their professor. Public distance is also used in large settings, such as when we listen to speakers, watch musicals, or attend television show tapings.

A theoretical model can help us understand the differences in distance between people. The **Expectancy Violations Theory (EVT)**[28] states that we expect people to maintain a certain distance in their conversations with us. If a person violates our expectations (if, for instance, a work colleague stands in our intimate space while talking with us), our response to the violation will be based on how much we like that person. That is, if we like a person, we're probably going to allow a distance violation. We may even reciprocate that conversational distance. If we dislike the person, we will likely be irritated by the violation and perhaps move away from the person. According to this theory, the degree to which we like someone can be based on factors that include our assessment of their credibility and physical attractiveness. Personal space violations, therefore, have consequences on our interactions. For further application of EVT, look at our TIP.

Before moving on, let's address one final point about space. Whereas personal space is that invisible bubble we carry from one interaction to another, territoriality is our sense of ownership of space that remains fixed. Humans mark their territories in various ways, usually with items or objects that are called territorial markers. For example, perhaps you go to a coffee shop each morning and stake out your table with a newspaper. Some people will often place their sunglasses or books on a table while they go to a buffet. Or, maybe you live near a house that has a fence that separates its yard from the neighbor's. Although one doesn't always own a particular territory, we nonetheless presume "ownership" by the sheer frequency with which we occupy a space or by the markers we use to communicate that the territory is "ours." In a sense, we believe that we have proprietary rights over some particular location. If, for example, you take the train each morning to work and sit in the same seat, you have claimed your territory. If someone were to occupy your seat one day, the only thing you could do about it besides merely experience displeasure would be to ask the person to leave.

Place and Time Codes

We do not often think of place and time codes when we think of nonverbal communication, but they affect us deeply. The categories of nonverbal communication included in place and time codes are environment (such as color and smell) and chronemics (time).

The Environment

Where you sit, sleep, dance, climb, jog, write, sing, play, sew, or worship are all parts of your physical environment. How we utilize the parts of the environment, how we manage them, and their influence upon us are all part of nonverbal communication. Or, as some writers put it, "Humans have always altered the environment for their purposes, interpreted meaning from it, and relied on environmental cues for guides to behavior."[29] Our physical environment entails a number of features, including the smell (e.g., restaurant), clutter (e.g., attic, dorm room, closet), and sounds (e.g., music, chatter) of our surroundings. But what do we do to the environment and what does it "do" to us? Let's explore three prominent environmental factors that affect communication between people: color, lighting, and room design.

Color is one of the most subtle environmental influences. Most researchers conclude that color affects our moods and perceptions. In other words, color has

iStock.com/GoodLifeStudio

The environment in which communication takes place can affect our interpersonal communication skills.

symbolic meaning in the environment and in our society.[30] Consider the colors in our everyday lives and their meanings. Red, for instance, embodies an interesting contradiction: It both facilitates togetherness and incites anger. Couples share their (red) hearts of candy on Valentine's Day; later, this same couple may "see red" when they get into a fight. The color blue also has several meanings. Many people associate blue with calmness (think about lakes and oceans), whereas others feel "blue" when they are sad or depressed. Yellow (joy) and purple (wisdom) are less paradoxical.

Our perceptions of color, which can be based on cultural interpretations, can affect our perception of the physical environment. Do you feel that a certain color is most conducive to learning? Next time, notice the color of your classrooms. Do you prefer bold and bright colors, or are you more of an earth-tone person? One reason that so many educational and work environments remain neutral in coloring is because these benign colors generally have a calming effect and function to enhance learning and productivity. At least that's what the color consultants believe!

In addition to color, the *lighting* of the environment can influence and modify behavior. Since the 1930s, the effect of lighting on worker productivity in particular has been investigated. Researchers have discovered that the color of environmental lighting may induce depression and alter our neural structures.[31] Lighting levels also seem to affect behavior within interpersonal interactions. Next time you're in a department store, look at how the lighting level varies in the different departments. Some departments, such as cosmetics, have soft lighting because it makes the customer look good, and she may be more inclined to buy the store's beauty products. Or, think about how lighting in dimly lit restaurants affects our behavior; it may prompt us to feel relaxed, causing us to prolong our evening (and increase our dinner tab!). Brightly lit restaurants, such as McDonald's or Wendy's, may increase people's rate of eating (thus, the term *fast food),* allowing these places to move people in and out in an efficient way.

Room design, including room size, also affects communication. For example, many retirement villages are now being designed to allow for both independence and interaction. Individual living units similar to small condominiums are built to promote privacy, but the units converge to form a meeting room where activities, events, and group functions take place.

Chronemics (Time)

Chronemics, the study of a person's perception and use of time, helps us to understand how people perceive and structure time in their dialogues and relationships with others. Time is an abstract concept that we describe using figures of speech (which we discussed in Chapter 4)—for example, "time is on your side," "time well spent," "time to kill," "time on your hands," "don't waste time," "on time," and "quality time." There is a reciprocal relationship between time and communication. That is, communication creates a person's understanding of time, and yet our sense of time restricts our communication.

Three time systems exist. *Technical time* is the scientific measurement of time. This system is associated with the precision of keeping time. *Formal time* is the time that society formally teaches. For example, in the United States, the clock and the calendar are our units of formal time. We know that when it's 1 a.m., it's usually time to sleep, and at 1 p.m., we find ourselves at work or school. Furthermore, in the United States, our arrangement of time is fixed and rather methodical. We learn to tell time based on the hour, and children are usually taught how to tell time by using the "big hand" and the "little hand" as references. *Informal time* is time that includes three concepts: duration, punctuality, and activity.

- *Duration* pertains to how long we allocate for a particular event. In our schedules, we may earmark 40 minutes for grocery shopping or an hour for a religious service. Some of our estimates are less precise. For instance, what does it mean when we respond, "Be there right away"? Does that mean we will be there in 10 minutes, an hour, or as long as it takes? And, despite its vague and odd-sounding nature, the statement "I want it done yesterday" is clear to many.

- *Punctuality* is the promptness associated with keeping time. We're said to be punctual when we arrive for an appointment at the designated time. Despite the value placed on punctuality in the United States, friends may arrive late to lunch, professors late to class, physicians late to appointments, and politicians late to rallies.

- *Activity* is related to chronemics. People in Western cultures are encouraged to "use their time wisely"—in other words, they should make sure their time is used to accomplish something, whether it's a task or a social function. Simultaneously, they should avoid being so time occupied that others view them as focused and obsessive. Our use and management of time are associated with status and power. For example, the old adage "time is money," which equates an intangible (time) with a tangible (money), suggests that we place a value on our use of time. And as a country with individualistic values (see Chapter 2), the United States is a society that supports the belief that time is intimately linked to status and power.

Suppose, for instance, that Olive arrives at an interview 10 minutes late. Unless a very persuasive reason exists, she probably won't get the job because punctuality is an important value to communicate to a future boss. However, let's say that the interviewer, Mr. Johansen, is 5 minutes late for the interview. Of course, he would not lose his job. Similarly, John's optometrist could be late for his appointment with no consequence, but if John is late for his own appointment, he might have to pay a "no show" fee.

Let's look at a few more examples. Some professors are regularly late for class, but these same professors have policies about student punctuality. And many of you have waited in long lines for school loan disbursements or to get your driver's license. If you truly had power, you wouldn't have to spend time waiting in line; you'd have someone wait in line for you! Time is clearly related to status and power differences between individuals.

We have spent a great deal of time identifying the primary types of nonverbal communication so you can better understand their comprehensive nature. We continue this chapter by considering how culture affects nonverbal messages. As we learned in Chapter 2, culture influences virtually every aspect of interpersonal communication. Understanding various cultural influences on nonverbal behavior helps you realize that not everyone shares your beliefs, values, and meanings. Particularly in the area of nonverbal communication—which, as we noted earlier in the chapter, is often ambiguous and open to interpretation—remembering cultural variations helps us become more competent communicators.

In our last two areas before articulating a skill set to consider, we address two salient areas and their influence upon our nonverbal behavior: culture and technology. We realize that we're unable to delve too deeply into these areas. But, we believe, nonetheless, that both are instrumental in the cocreation of meaning between two people. Thus, we highlight a few themes.

5–3 THE INFLUENCE OF CULTURE ON NONVERBAL COMMUNICATION

We could write an entire text about the influence of culture on nonverbal behavior. Nonverbal behaviors convey different meanings among (co-)cultures. As we note elsewhere in this book, the U.S. population is so culturally diverse that we can't always rely on our original interpretations; the meaning of nonverbal communication between and among cultures can vary and continuously change. Unless you are sensitive to this variation, you may have a tough time communicating with someone with a different cultural background from you. We've already devoted an entire chapter to culture and chose to weave cultural discussions throughout the book. Still, to provide you with a sense of how culture affects nonverbal behavior, we give you a glimpse into this area. As always, we are cautious in confidently concluding that a culture acts in only one way. Still, let's explore a few conclusions related to four different channels: body movement, facial expressions, personal space, and touch.

Kinesics and Culture

Kinesic behavior is one area where nonverbal communication and culture intersect.[32] For example, research has shown that greetings vary from one culture to another. For instance, most Westerners are accustomed to shaking hands upon meeting. In other cultures, however, the handshake is not common. In Japan, as many of you know, individuals bow when they meet to express mutual respect. What you may not know is that the person with the lower status initiates bowing and is expected to bow deeper than the individual with higher status. The person with elevated status decides when the bowing ends.

Gesturing has also been studied across cultures.[33] For instance, Mexicans, Greeks, and people from many South American countries are dramatic and animated while speaking. Mexicans tend to use lots of hand gestures in their conversations, and Italians "talk with their hands" in expressive gestures. Further, in the United States, while a thumbs-up may be viewed as a sign of support, in Thailand, some view the gesture as both a childish and obscene body movement. Some research also points out that the A-OK sign used in the United States carries different meanings around the world, including a sexual connotation in parts of Brazil and Russia. However, in a number of Asian cultures, such overt body movements are considered to be rude, and Germans generally consider hand gestures too flashy.

Eye Behavior and Culture

Since the eye is the foundation of the face, it's logical that this area has been studied extensively. The extent to which a person looks at another during a conversation is culturally based. Members of most co-cultures in the United States are socialized to look at a listener while speaking. It's common for two people from the United States to look at each other's eyes while communicating. In this country, frequent eye aversion may communicate a lack of trust. However, in other cultures, such as Japan and Jamaica, direct eye contact is perceived as communicating disrespect. Further, in Kenya, the same holds true. In fact, there's a Zulu proverb that states: "The eye is the organ of aggression."[34]

Proxemics and Culture

Spatial distances have been the focus of research in intercultural communication. And, personal space is essential to understand, since in the United States, as previously discussed, we tend to clearly demarcate our territory. There are cultural differences, however, as evidenced by research examining the territoriality of Germans and the French:

> Germans . . . barricade themselves behind heavy doors and soundproof walls to try to seal themselves from others in order to concentrate on their work. The French have a close personal distance and are not as territorial. They are tied to people and thrive on constant interaction.[35]

In addition, there are personal space differences between other cultures. In Egypt, personal space between members of the same sex is kept at a minimum. Australians expect about an arm's length in space during a conversation. Conversely, less than an arm's length is expected in Colombia. Finally, in Bangladesh, sitting close to each other signifies warmth and comfort.

Haptics and Culture

Researchers have also investigated touch behavior within a cultural context.[36] For example, adolescents from the United States touched each other less than adolescents from France. Observing friends at McDonald's restaurants in Miami and Paris, researchers found that the U.S. teenagers did less hugging, kissing, and caressing than their French counterparts. However, the U.S. adolescents engaged in more self-touching, such as primping, than the French adolescents.

As Ahmed (IPC Voice on page 131) suggests, some cultures accept more same-sex touching than others. For example, men frequently hold hands in Indonesia, and men frequently walk down the street with their arms around each other in Malaysia (interestingly, this touch may be construed as physically intimate, yet both countries remain among the least accepting of gay relationships). In addition, it's common to see men/men, women/men, and women/women touching without anxiety. Such overt touching, however, may be frowned upon in Japan, the United States, and Scandinavia (complete the CAT regarding touch avoidance to gauge your touch aversion).[37]

While we tend to focus on cultural differences, research has also uncovered similarities across cultures. Collectively, research conducted as far back as the early 1970s has shown that facial expressions are universal. In television crime shows, you may have seen micro-expressions uncovered in crime labs. Indeed, six expressions have been shown to be judged consistently across cultures: anger, disgust, fear, happiness, sadness, and surprise.[38] Today, there may be some variation because of the co-cultural backgrounds of communicators, but essentially this universality remains.

As we noted, we've only provided a brief snapshot of the cultural influences on our nonverbal communication. Still, as you can see, nonverbal behaviors should always be understood within a cultural context. Failing to do so will likely result in a loss of meaning. We cannot assume that others automatically understand our nonverbal displays, because their meanings can differ significantly within and across cultures. Further, as the U.S. population continues to grow more diverse, being sensitive to cultural communication differences and seeking clarification will help you in your interpersonal relationships.

IPC Praxis

Do you think there is too much attention paid to cultural similarities and differences as they relate to nonverbal communication? Point to specific examples to explain your viewpoint.

5-4 THE INFLUENCE OF TECHNOLOGY ON NONVERBAL COMMUNICATION

The interplay between the digital environment and nonverbal communication remains an important and growing area. It's clear that every generation has, in

Technology use across the globe has resulted in "digital natives" communicating with their cell phones without saying a word.

some way, been introduced to technology. Whether it's the printing press, telegraph, telephone, computer, fax, voice mail, e-mail, or texting, technology's evolution cannot be ignored. Yet, those generations who have relied extensively on their cell phones and the Internet have been particularly challenged with being adept at nonverbal communication effectiveness. Because of the ease of checking e-mail, Facebook, and stock quotes, digital natives might "improve their adroitness at the keyboard, but when it comes to their capacity to 'read' the behavior of others, they're all thumbs."[39] Regardless of whether or not you agree with this sentiment, one essential rings true: Technology has forever altered nonverbal communication. Consider the various nonverbal codes we identified earlier. Now think about how various technologies can, and have, affected these codes. Our "nonverbal literacy" has unquestionably been affected by the introduction of various mediated communications. When we are walking with our cell phones, many of us "forget" to look up, sometimes stumbling into another, ultimately impinging on another's personal space. When we are at dinner with a companion, we may receive a text and read it, only to look up and see our date frustrated as you averted your eye contact. Constantly looking at your tablet computer while talking to a family member may suggest that you value the technology over the conversation.

We already know that the communication process is transactional, a point we introduced in Chapter 1. But, social scientists have yet to grapple with the expansive number of topics to investigate. It seems as though each of you will have a research future once you start considering the technology–nonverbal communication interface.

So many areas are ripe for exploration. What about technology's role in the meaning-making process? Is meaning achieved, however, when one person is talking and another is responding to texts? If one is looking away and ignoring the other's words, concurrently sending a text, is there meaning? What sort of meaning is acquired as two friends simultaneously tweet each other? How do our Instagram posts prompt discussions between and among people, and what role did our posts play in the communication process? What happens, if anything, if a virtual handshake is not returned? How are unanticipated online personal disclosures received by unintended targets? These and a host of other considerations must be acknowledged as we try to unpack the challenge of sending and receiving nonverbal communication with mediated technologies.

See if you can empathize with the following insight:

> To start writing, I had to first turn off the TV (a mediated form of communication whose effects I know interfere with my ability to get work done). Then I had to exit my iTunes, put my phone in the other room (on silent so I couldn't hear the messages I was missing), exit my Skype account, log out of my e-mail, exit my favorite blog, get off all the news websites and finally the hardest part . . . log out of Facebook.[40]

These words may seem humorous, but her point should not be overshadowed. She laments the fact that we have failed in some ways to concentrate on the conversation.

5–5 SKILL SET FOR INCREASING NONVERBAL COMMUNICATION EFFECTIVENESS

As stated previously, nonverbal behavior is difficult to pin down with precision. We may think we understand what a person's hand gesture or eye behavior means, but there are often multiple ways to interpret a particular nonverbal behavior. We now turn our attention to identifying six skills for improving nonverbal communication effectiveness. As you practice these skills, keep in mind that you may have to alter your verbal communication since, as we know, nonverbal communication is closely aligned with what we say (see Table 5.3 for a summary of the skill set).

Recall the Nonverbal-Verbal Relationship

Throughout this chapter, we have reminded you that nonverbal communication is often best understood with verbal communication. That is, we need to pay attention to what is said in addition to the nonverbal behavior. Most of us blend nonverbal and verbal messages. We raise our voice to underscore something we've said. We frown when we tell a sad story. We motion with our hands when we tell others to get going. And, when young toddlers are angry, we see them jump up and down on the floor while they scream, "No!" These examples illustrate the integration of

Table 5.3 /// Skill Set for Increasing Nonverbal Communication Effectiveness
a. Recall the nonverbal-verbal relationship.
b. Be tentative when interpreting nonverbal communication.
c. Monitor your own nonverbal behavior.
d. Ask others for their impressions.
e. Avoid nonverbal distractions.
f. Place nonverbal communication in context.
g. Your skill suggestion

nonverbal and verbal messages. We need to remain aware of this relationship to achieve meaning in our conversations. In addition, we need to be aware that our nonverbal and verbal message should match. Imagine Luke, for instance, telling an interviewer, "My biggest strength as an employee is that I'm a great listener," only to follow up that statement by glancing down at a recent text coming in on his cell phone while the interviewer discusses the company's mission. There must clearly not only be alignment between what is said and done, but Luke must recognize that he cannot simply state something without knowing its nonverbal implications.

Be Tentative When Interpreting Nonverbal Behavior

In this chapter, we have reiterated the ambiguous and inconsistent nature of non-verbal communication. Because of individual differences, we can never be sure what a specific nonverbal behavior means. For example, when Ashley walks into Professor Fairfield's office, she may be confident in thinking that he is busy. After all, there are books everywhere, the phone is ringing, and the professor is seated behind a desk with many papers on it. However, these environmental artifacts and conditions may not be accurately communicating the professor's availability. Ashley needs to clarify and confirm her interpretation of this nonverbal communi-cation by asking the professor if he has time to talk to her. Also consider the cultural background of communicators. We identified how nonverbal communi-cation varies between and among co-cultures; this is an important foundation to draw upon as you interpret the meaning of a nonverbal message.

Monitor Your Nonverbal Behavior

Being a self-monitor is crucial in conversations. Becoming aware of how you say something, your proximity to the other person, the extent to which you use touch, or your use of silence are just as important as the words you use. This self-monitoring is not easy. For example, let's say that Tracy is in a heated exchange with her roommate, Hannah, who refused to pay the cable bill. When Tracy tries to make her point, it's not easy for her to think about how she is saying something or whether or not she is screaming or standing too close. Like most people, she simply wants to make her point. However, Tracy's nonverbal communication can carry significance, particularly if Hannah is focusing on it and Tracy is ignoring it. You need to look for meaning in both your behavior and the behavior of others.

Ask Others for Their Impressions

When applying for a job, we ask others for their interview strategies. When going out on a date, we ask friends how we look or smell. When choosing a class, we may ask our friends about their experiences with a particular professor. Yet, when we try to improve our communication with others, we generally neglect to ask others about our nonverbal effectiveness. Whom should we consult to ensure accuracy and clarity in our nonverbal communication?

The easy answer is that we should ask someone with whom we are close. Our close relationships can provide us valuable information, such as that our silent reactions to others' disclosures make them uncomfortable or that our constant eye rolling during a conflict is irritating. Our close relational partners are more

Body Language and Personal Space in the Nursing Profession

The ebbs and flows of the nursing profession are often based upon the relationship that nurses have with their patients. Helping patients heal is a primary goal of what it means to be an effective nurse, and the conversations that nurses have with patients are instrumental. These conversations necessarily take into consideration the importance of kinesic and proxemic behavior. Both body language and personal space should be attended to because patients can "see the mood" of a nurse. Therefore, regardless of whether a nurse is in the emergency room or in the hospital room,

practicing appropriate touch behavior will make a patient feel more relaxed and less troubled. With respect to a nurse's use of personal space, when a discussion happens, is it occurring next to the patient's bed or next to the door? In highly consequential conversations (e.g., medicine dosage, medical diagnosis), nurses will move closer to a patient to show respect and to better respond to facial expressions and unexpected body movements.

Reflection: While nurses typically show nonverbal compassion in most medical facilities, some patients abhor close proximity, prolonged eye contact, and physical touch. What advice would you give to those nurses who have patients with these underlying concerns?

inclined to inform us whether our verbal and nonverbal communication are consistent. Those who are close to us are more likely to be up front with us about any communication deficiencies. True, some may not want to be critical, but the level of comfort that is afforded to our close relationships cannot be overemphasized.

Avoid Nonverbal Distractions

The old saying "Get out of your own way!" has meaning when we communicate nonverbally. At times, our nonverbal communication can serve as noise in an interpersonal exchange. Consider, for example, playing with your hair, shifting your eyes, using vocal distractors, or texting while talking to someone. Are you having a personal conversation with someone in a noisy bar? The person is likely to focus more on your nonverbal displays than on what you are saying. In turn, it's likely that meaning would be obscured or little meaning would be exchanged in the interaction.

Place Nonverbal Communication in Context

Earlier in this chapter, we discussed the fact that we live in a society that embraces simplistic notions associated with nonverbal communication. For instance, several years ago, books were written telling others how to *Dress for Success*. Such a simplistic source informed business professionals how to dress to look "professional" and to be taken seriously in the workplace. Scores of companies embraced the basic suggestions of the book and used its conclusions to mandate changes to corporate attire.

However, when discussing human behavior, we need to avoid such superficial ideas about our nonverbal communication. We should pay attention to nonverbal cues, but we should place them in appropriate context. Be careful of assigning too much meaning to a wink, a handshake, a pair of dangling earrings, or a voice that sounds uptight. These may carry no significant meaning in a conversation. To acquire meaning, you must consider the entire communication process, not just one element of it.

/// CHAPTER WRAP-UP

We have presented a rather complete picture of the nonverbal communication process, including identifying its value in our personal and professional lives. In particular, we explained the differences between verbal and nonverbal communication. We followed up that discussion by exploring four assumptions of nonverbal communication to consider. We then devoted a great deal of the chapter to various types of nonverbal communication. These include kinesics, physical appearance, facial communication, paralanguage, haptics, proxemics, the environment, and chronemics. We then presented you information on how culture and technology function in conjunction with nonverbal communication.

We closed the chapter with several skills to practice in order to enhance your nonverbal communication with others.

As you continue to work on your interpersonal communication and your relationships with others, don't forget that what you don't say is, sometimes, more important than what you do say. We believe that nonverbal communication is often acknowledged in our conversations, but it's rarely ever fully understood. We hope this chapter provided you an important foundation to consider as you think about the complexities of the various kinds of interactions you have on a daily basis.

/// COMMUNICATION ASSESSMENT TEST (CAT): TOUCH AVOIDANCE INVENTORY

This instrument is composed of 18 statements concerning how you feel about touching other people and being touched. Please indicate the degree to which each statement applies to you by indicating whether you

1 = strongly agree, 2 = agree, 3 = are undecided, 4 = disagree, 5 = strongly disagree.

[This inventory relies upon traditional and historical identification of male and female.]

_____ 1. A hug from a same-sex friend is a true sign of friendship.

_____ 2. Opposite-sex friends enjoy it when I touch them.

_____ 3. I often put my arm around friends of the same sex.

_____ 4. When I see two friends of the same sex hugging, it revolts me.

_____ 5. I like it when members of the opposite sex touch me.

_____ 6. People shouldn't be so uptight about touching persons of the same sex.

_____ 7. I think it is vulgar when members of the opposite sex touch me.

_____ 8. When a member of the opposite sex touches me, I find it unpleasant.

_____ 9. I wish I were free to show emotions by touching members of same sex.

_____ 10. I'd enjoy giving a massage to an opposite-sex friend.

_____ 11. I enjoy kissing a person of the same sex.

_____ 12. I like to touch friends that are the same sex as I am.

_____ 13. Touching a friend of the same sex does not make me uncomfortable.

_____ 14. I find it enjoyable when my date and I embrace.

_____ 15. I enjoy getting a back rub from a member of the opposite sex.

_____ 16. I dislike kissing relatives of the same sex.

_____ 17. Intimate touching with members of the opposite sex is pleasurable.

_____ 18. I find it difficult to be touched by a member of my own sex.

How did you do? To score your Touch Avoidance Questionnaire,

Reverse your scores for items 4, 7, 8, 16, and 18. Use these reversed scores in all future calculations.

To obtain your same-sex touch avoidance score (the extent to which you avoid touching members of your sex), total the scores for items 1, 3, 4, 6, 9, 11, 12, 13, 16, and 18.

To obtain your opposite-sex touch avoidance score (the extent to which you avoid touching members of the opposite sex), total the scores for items 2, 5, 7, 8, 10, 14, 15, and 17.

To obtain your total touch avoidance score, add the subtotals from steps 2 and 3.

The higher the score, the higher the touch avoidance—that is, the greater your tendency to avoid touch. In studies the average opposite sex touch avoidance scores for males was 12.9 and for females 14.85. Average same-sex touch avoidance scores were 26.43 for males and 21.70 for females. How do your scores compare with those college students? What does your score say about you? Are you satisfied with the score? Do you wish to change anything regarding your assessments of touch?

Source: Louise Petty at High Speed Training.

/// KEY TERMS

nonverbal communication   131

mixed message   135

kinesics   136

delivery gestures   137

citing gestures   137

seeking gestures   137

turn gestures   137

body orientation   137

physical characteristics   138

body artifacts   138

paralanguage   140

vocal qualities   140

vocal distractors   140

vocal characterizers   141

haptics   142

proxemics   143

personal space   143

intimate distance   144

personal distance   145

social distance   145

public distance   145

Expectancy Violations Theory (EVT)   145

territoriality   146

territorial markers   146

physical environment   146

chronemics   148

/// KEY QUESTIONS FOR APPLICATION

1. _CQ/CultureQuest_: Explore the following claim: "The body is a language that transcends culture." Do you agree or disagree? Defend your view with examples.

2. _TQ/TechQuest:_ Explore the following claim: "It's impossible to determine motivation online because we focus too much on the nonverbal behavior." Do you agree or disagree? Defend your view with examples.

3. What advantages and disadvantages exist for those who educate themselves about the nonverbal communication of a culture prior to visiting that culture?

4. Spend two hours sitting at a coffee shop or a study area and identify as many nonverbal codes as possible. Construct a matrix that looks at the following: category

of the nonverbal behavior, the specific behavior itself, and any demographic information (e.g., age, generation) about the individual.

5. Many actors believe that a script without the words has as much value as a script with the words. What does this mean to you? Apply it to the interpersonal relationships we find ourselves in and the various "scripts" of which we may be a part.

6. Think back to the Transactional Model of Communication from Chapter 1. Now apply at least three nonverbal codes identified in this chapter to the model. Use examples to illustrate your views.

Access practice quizzes, eFlashcards, video, and multimedia at **edge.sagepub.com/west**.

Visit **edge.sagepub.com/west** to help you accomplish your coursework goals in an easy-to-use learning environment.

PRACTICE AND APPLY WHAT YOU'VE LEARNED

▶ edge.sagepub.com/west

⑤SAGE edge™

WANT A BETTER GRADE ON YOUR NEXT TEST?

Head to the study site where you'll find:

- **eFlashcards** to strengthen your understanding of key terms.

- **Practice quizzes** to test your comprehension of key concepts.

- **Videos and multimedia content** to enhance your exploration of key topics.

CHAPTER 6

LISTENING AND RESPONDING EFFECTIVELY

LEARNING OUTCOMES

After studying this chapter, you will be able to

6–1 Recognize the differences between hearing and listening

6–2 Describe the components of the listening process

6–3 Explain the value and importance of listening

6–4 Recognize obstacles to listening

6–5 Name the common poor listening habits

6–6 Identify four preferred styles of listening

6–7 Explain how culture affects listening

6–8 Utilize a variety of techniques to enhance your listening effectiveness

iStock.com/artisteer

Master the content at
edge.sagepub.com/west

⑤SAGE edge™

Listening is one of the most utilized skills in our interpersonal communication, but the skill that is attended to the least. Interestingly, most people believe that they are good listeners, and many people think all that is needed is to stay quiet and let the other person speak. But, listening is much more than that! Listening is a cooperative connection with another person, demonstrating that a receiver is equally responsible for the cocreation of meaning in a conversation. Listening can improve self-esteem,[1] is an essential part of mental health,[2] and one of the most critical of all business skills.[3] Clearly, listening is a dialogue imperative, and without quality listening, our interpersonal communication suffers.

Despite its value, so many of us experience listening deficiencies. Think about it. In the course of an average day, we don't (and can't) listen to the barrage of messages from the media, our friends, family, and coworkers. At times, our smartphones and laptops get in the way. Further, some of these messages are not altogether useful for us ("And let me tell you about my niece's new boyfriend"); others we've heard over and over again ("When I was a teenager, . . ."); others don't make sense to us ("When I cook, I usually think of Gayle's wedding dress"); and still other messages we tune out ("Wait, I do know about the blueprints of the new school"). Let's be clear: Failing to listen can have serious consequences. Consider Abby, a 21-year-old college junior who decided to go to campus counseling services because she was feeling depressed. Or, think about Dana, a 31-year-old single father who brought his toddler into the doctor's office because of an ongoing cough. Now think about Jaime, a 55-year-old construction site supervisor who meets the building inspector to talk about cutting building code money on a project that has already run over budget. Each of these scenarios requires a listener-receiver (a counselor, a physician, and a building inspector), and without effective listening, the costs can be personal, economic, physical, and emotional.

> ### 💬 IPC Voice: Vince
>
> To be honest, growing up, I took listening for granted. I just followed what was told to me. I never bothered to think for myself. Now that I'm about to graduate, it's so different. I intern at a state senator's office and, literally, people come and go all day. I have to make sure I "clear the decks" (so to speak) so that I can give everyone my attention. It's tough to listen when you have a supervisor yelling, a constituent complaining, a coworker whining, and lots of phone rings and outside traffic. Talk about focusing and listening!

This chapter discusses the importance of listening, explores reasons why we don't always listen, and suggests ways we can overcome our bad listening habits. Unlike other chapters, it's more difficult to unpack the challenges of listening on our online relationships. First, no communication research exists that helps us understand this dynamic. Second, the listening process and its relationship to the online world is rather tough to disentangle. Still, we frequently address how listening affects and is affected by such technologies as Skype, Facetime, and other technologies and platforms.

Listening is a communication behavior that we may think we all understand, but we need to explain it further to have a common foundation. We begin our discussion by first differentiating listening from hearing. Although people often interchange the two terms, *hearing* and *listening* are different processes and mean different things.

6–1 LEND ME YOUR EAR: DIFFERENCES BETWEEN HEARING AND LISTENING

Let's start by interrogating a commonly held, but erroneous myth: Listening and hearing are the same thing. They are not. Hearing occurs when you're in the range of when a sound wave hits an eardrum. The resulting vibrations, or stimuli, are sent to the brain. For our purposes, we define **hearing** as the physical process of letting in auditory stimuli without trying to understand that stimuli. We can pay attention to several stimuli and simultaneously store stimuli for future reference. When we try to organize the stimuli, we have to retrieve previous experiences and information to match it to the current stimuli. Again, all of this "processing and

Fine-tuning our listening abilities is a hallmark of effective interpersonal communication.

storage" is done at the same time, and all of it is conducted at the point in the communication process that we call hearing. For the most part, hearing is a passive process, rarely requiring us to be engaged with the stimuli.

To help understand the complex intersection between stimuli and our cognitive processes, a theory related to working memory[4] was conceptualized. **Working Memory Theory** explains why we direct our attention to relevant information and suppress irrelevant information while allowing our thinking processes to coordinate multiple tasks. The mind is usually required to perform different tasks simultaneously, and this can be quite overwhelming. Working memory temporarily holds information over a short period of time and allows you to "delegate" the things you experience to the parts of the brain that can take action. A **central executive** takes over, directing information, identifying receivers and targets, and preventing distractions. Think of the central executive as a police officer directing traffic around a car accident. What happens is that people begin to construct "mental maps" as they're introduced to various stimuli such as color, taste, shapes, space, among others. And remember this: All of this processing of stimuli happens in a split second! Now review our TIP on Working Memory Theory.

 ## Theory-Into-Practice (TIP)

Working Memory Theory

An individual's working memory allows for completing tasks and blocking out distractions so you can stay focused. College life is replete with an abundance of irrelevant and ancillary distractions, making it more difficult for you to home in on the learning process. Think about a number of these interruptions and academic noises and identify a few. How is your memory able to organize these various extraneous stimuli and provide relevance to those people and events that assist you to focus? In other words, how can you participate in activities and sustain your attention on matters related to your education?

We introduced you to the issue of stimuli in Chapter 3. With respect to its relationship to Working Memory Theory, consider the following. When Kirsten sits at The Beanpot Cafe drinking coffee and reading the morning paper online, she hears all types of noises, including people ordering coffee, couples laughing, and even the folk music coming from the ceiling speakers. However, she is not paying attention to these background noises. Instead, she is hearing the stimuli without thinking about them. Kirsten must be able to tune out these stimuli because otherwise she wouldn't be able to concentrate on reading the paper.

Like Kirsten, we find ourselves hearing a lot of stimuli throughout our day, whether it's the hum of an air conditioner, dishes breaking in a restaurant, or the sounds of fire trucks passing on the street. Most of us are able to continue our conversations without attending to these noises.

Being a good listener is much more than letting in audible stimuli. Listening is a communication activity that requires us to be thoughtful. The choices we make when we listen affect our interpersonal encounters. As we alluded to earlier, people often take listening for granted as a communication skill in interpersonal relationships. Clearly, "listening is the hardest of the 'easy' tasks; if you want to be heard, you must know how to listen."[5] Unlike hearing, listening is a learned communication skill. People often have a difficult time describing what being an effective listener is, but they seem to know when another person is not listening. And, listening is often viewed as a passive process. As one scholar put it, "The word 'just' is all too often frequently used to describe listening in the admonition 'Just listen.'"[6] This reduces listening to a simple behavior that requires little engagement.

IPC Praxis

Describe those people in your life who you find are excellent listeners. What criteria did you use to determine excellence? Is there a common denominator between and/or among these people? All family members? Friends? Coworkers? Other?

6–2 THE COMPONENTS OF THE LISTENING PROCESS

With the preceding framework in mind, we define **listening** as the dynamic, transactional process of receiving, responding to, recalling, and rating stimuli and/or messages from another. When we listen, we are making sense of the message of another communicator. Let's briefly break down this definition.

Listening is dynamic because it is an active and ongoing way of demonstrating that you are involved in an interpersonal encounter. Furthermore, listening is transactional because both the sender and the receiver are active agents in the process, as we discussed in Chapter 1. In other words, listening is a two-way street that requires both "motorists to navigate." We can't just show that we listen; we need others to show us *they know* we are listening.

The remaining four concepts of the definition require a more detailed discussion. We already know that hearing is a starting point in the listening process. Stimuli have to be present, but much more is required. The **four Rs of listening**—receiving, responding, recalling, and rating—make up the listening process (see Figure 6.1). Each of the following sections reviews a component of the listening process and the specific skill it requires. Also, because we wish to encourage you to practice your listening continuously, we include a few remarks for improving that skill. We will have broader skill recommendations later in the chapter.

Receiving

When we receive a message, we hear and attend to it. **Receiving** involves the verbal and nonverbal acknowledgment of communication. We are selective in our reception and usually screen out those messages that are least relevant to us. We also have a problem receiving all of the messages since our attention spans are

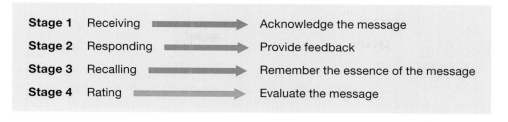

Figure 6.1 /// The Listening Process

Stage 1	Receiving	→	Acknowledge the message
Stage 2	Responding	→	Provide feedback
Stage 3	Recalling	→	Remember the essence of the message
Stage 4	Rating	→	Evaluate the message

rather short, lasting from around 2 to 20 seconds.[7] And, then there is a loss of listening abilities. Do you find yourself putting in your earbuds or headset on to listen to your music? This can cause hearing loss and, consequently, can lead to problems in receiving a message.

When we are receiving a message, we are trying to be mindful—a concept we discussed in Chapter 3. Mindfulness, you may recall, means we are paying close attention to the stimuli around us. **Mindful listening** requires us to be engaged with another person—the words, the behaviors, and the environment. Mindful listening has been employed in professional contexts, including in the treatment of adults with autism or Down syndrome and those with multiple sclerosis.[8]

The following two suggestions should improve your ability to receive messages effectively. First, eliminate unnecessary noises and physical barriers to listening. If possible, try to create surroundings that allow you to receive a message fully and accurately. That means if someone is talking to you, you have to not answer your cell phone, stop watching ESPN, or cease texting your roommate. Second, try not to interrupt the reception of a message. Although you may be tempted to cut off a speaker when they communicate a message about which you have a strong opinion, yield the conversational floor so you can receive the entire message and not simply a part of it.

Responding

Responding means giving feedback to another communicator in an interpersonal exchange. Responding suggests the transactional nature of the interpersonal communication process. That is, although we are not speaking to another person, we are communicating by listening. This suggests that responding is critical to achieve interpersonal meaning.

Responding, which lets a speaker know that the message was received, happens during and after a conversation. So, when Kenny uses both head nods and words (e.g., "I get it," "Yep, you make sense") during his conversation with his girlfriend, Keri, he's providing both nonverbal and verbal feedback. And if, after the two have stopped talking, Kenny hugs and holds her, he is still responding to his girlfriend's message.

You can enhance the way you respond in several ways. Adopting the other's point of view is important. This skill (which we talk about later in this chapter) is particularly significant when communicating with people with cultural backgrounds different from your own. Also, take ownership of your words and ideas. Don't confuse what you say with what the other person says. Finally, don't assume that your thoughts are universally accepted; not everyone will agree with your position on a topic.

Recalling

Recalling involves understanding a message, storing it for future encounters, and remembering it later. We have sloppy recall if we understand a message when it is first communicated but forget it later. When we do recall a conversation, we don't recall it word for word; rather, we remember a personal version (or essence) of what occurred.[9] Further, recall can be immediate, short term, or long term.[10]

People's recall abilities vary. For instance, in a study of rural (and urban) poverty, low-income rural children recalled tasks differently than their high-income rural counterparts. These recall differences may be attributed to poor economic and environmental conditions, an area that has often been overlooked in listening research.[11]

Let's consider another situation: Suppose another person criticizes you for recalling a conversation incorrectly. You might simply tell the other person that they are wrong. This is what happens in the following conversation between Matt and Dale. The two have been good friends for years. Matt is a homeowner who needed some painting done, and Dale verbally agreed to do it. Now that Dale has given Matt the bill, the two remember differently their conversation about how the bill was to be paid:

Dale: "Matt, you said you'd pay the bill in two installments. We didn't write it down, but I remember your words: 'I can pay half the bill immediately and then the other half 2 weeks later.' Now you're trying to tell me you didn't say that?"

Matt: "That's totally not it at all. I told you that I'd pay the bill in two installments only after I was happy that the work was finished. Look, I know this isn't what you want to hear, but the hallway wall is scratched and needs to be repainted. I see gouges on the hardwood floors by the living room, and look at the paint drips on the molding in the dining room."

Dale: "I told you that I'd come in later to do those small repairs, and you said you'd pay me."

Matt: "Sorry, bud, I don't remember it that way."

Matt and Dale clearly have different recollections of their conversation. Their situation is even more challenging because both money and friendship are involved.

A number of strategies can help you improve your ability to later recall a message. First, repeating information helps clarify terms and provide you an immediate confirmation of whether the intended message was received accurately. Second, using mnemonic devices as memory-aiding guides will likely help you recall things more easily. Abbreviations such as MADD (for Mothers Against Drunk Driving) and PETA (People for the Ethical Treatment of Animals) use acronyms as mnemonic devices. Finally, chunking can assist you in recalling. **Chunking** means placing pieces of information into manageable and retrievable sets. For example, if Matt and Dale discussed several issues and subissues—such as a payment schedule, materials, furniture protection, paint color, timetables, worker load, and so on—chunking those issues into fewer, more manageable topics (e.g., finances, paint, and labor) may have helped reduce their conflict.

Rating

Rating means evaluating or assessing a message. When we listen critically, we rate messages on three levels: (1) we decide whether or not we agree with the message, (2) we place the message in context, and (3) we evaluate whether the message has value to us.

You don't always agree with messages you receive from others. However, when you disagree with another person, you should try to do so from the other's viewpoint. Rating a message from another's field of experience allows us to distinguish among facts, inferences, and opinions,[12] and these three are critical in evaluating a message. Although we briefly explored facts and inferences in Chapter 2, let's refresh you on the subject. Facts are verifiable and can be made only after direct observation. Inferences fill in a conversation's "missing pieces" and require listeners to go beyond what was observed. Opinions can undergo changes over time and are based on a communicator's beliefs or values.

When we evaluate a message, we need to understand the differences among facts, inferences, and opinions. Let's say, for example, that Claire knows the following:

- Her best friend, Oliver, hasn't spoken to her in 3 weeks.
- Oliver is calling other people.
- Claire has called Oliver several times and has left messages on voice mail.

These are the facts. If Claire states that Oliver is angry at her, or that he doesn't care about her well-being, she is not acting on facts. Rather, she is using inferences and expressing opinions. And, her views may not be accurate at all.

Here are two suggestions that will help you improve your ability to rate messages. First, if possible, detect speaker bias. At times, messages are difficult to listen to. One reason for this may be the speaker's bias; information in a message may be distorted because a speaker may be prejudiced in some way ("Anyone with that accent sounds pretty dumb to me"). Second, listeners should be prepared to change their position. After you have rated a message, you may want to modify your opinions or beliefs on a subject because of new information or because you were quick to evaluate. Learn to become more flexible in your thinking.

 **IPC Praxis**

Imagine listening to someone who is spewing hateful and offensive language. You believe in the First Amendment of the Constitution, but you've found yourself in a conversation alone with this person. How is your listening affected by this person's words? What do/should you do, if anything, to work toward meaning?

6–3 THE VALUE AND IMPORTANCE OF LISTENING

It's probably hard to find people who will admit the following: "I'm a really bad listener." Although we like to think we are good listeners, we all need help in this area. Listening is an ongoing interpersonal activity that requires lifelong training. Active listening, a behavior we discuss in more detail later in the chapter, is particularly crucial. Because we listen for a variety of important reasons (see Figure 6.2), listening needs to be a high priority in our lives. Let's offer a few more reasons why studying this topic has lasting value.

Listening is a goal-directed behavior[13] and is essential to our relationships with others, whether they are coworkers, family members, friends, or other important people in our lives. Several conclusions merit some consideration. Listening is used at least three times as much as speaking and at least four times as much as reading and writing.[14]

Employers rank listening as the most important skill on the job.[15] Hourly employees spend 30% of their time listening; managers, 60%; and executives, 75% or more.[16] Liz Simpson, a writer for the *Harvard Management Communication Letter*, offers the following advice to those in the workplace: "To see things from another's point of view and to build trust with her [him], you have to listen closely to what she [he] says" (p. 4).[17]

Researchers and writers have called listening a 21st century skill because it's now more important than ever. Further, new technology and changes in current business practices have changed all of our listening patterns.[18] Listening errors can debilitate worker productivity.[19] And because of our preoccupation with apps, some people today have focused more on their smartphones and have failed to practice effective listening with others.

Good listening skills are valuable in other types of interpersonal relationships as well. For example, successful medical students must develop effective listening skills because, on average, a medical practitioner may conduct over 250,000

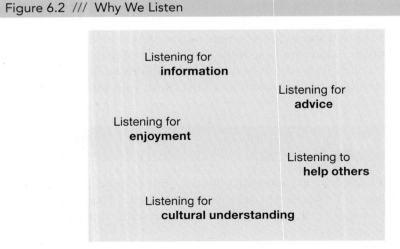

Figure 6.2 /// Why We Listen

Listening for **information**

Listening for **advice**

Listening for **enjoyment**

Listening to **help others**

Listening for **cultural understanding**

interviews during a 40-year career.[20] Additional research[21] shows that doctor–patient communication, of which listening is identified as paramount, is especially pivotal in health care. Many hospitals, responding to national surveys on patient satisfaction, are now requiring assessments of a physician's listening skills for fear of malpractice suits. Answers to questions such as "During this hospital stay, how often did doctors listen carefully to you?" will now be collated and provided to patients to use to make health care choices.

Other contexts require skill in listening. In the educational context, researchers have found that effective listening is associated with more positive teacher–parent relationships and more positive student learning.[22] On the home front, many family conflicts can be resolved by listening more effectively.[23] And, in our friendships, some research has shown that the intimacy level between two friends is directly related to the listening skills brought into the relationship.[24]

Although the topic of listening dates to the 1940s,[25] it's clearly relevant today. You would have trouble thinking of any interpersonal relationship in your life that doesn't require you to listen. Improving your listening skills will help improve your relational standing with others.

Before we discuss the listening process further, we should point out that not everyone has the physical ability to hear or listen. Although our discussion in this chapter focuses on those who are able to hear physiologically, we are aware that many individuals rely on another communication system to create and share symbols: **American Sign Language (ASL)**. ASL is among the fastest growing languages in the United States,[26] with an increase of nearly 20% since 2009. A visual rather than auditory form of communication, ASL is composed of precise hand shapes and movements. According to the World Federation of the Deaf, there are about 70 million people who use ASL. In fact, ASL is also seen as an instinctive communication method for visual learners who aren't hearing impaired. The hard-of-hearing and deaf communities have embraced ASL, and it is used to create and sustain communication within the community.

With this important recognition, we now turn our attention to various challenges people have with listening. You already know that listening is important in our personal and professional lives. Yet, for a number of reasons, people don't listen well.

6–4 THE BARRIERS: WHY WE DON'T LISTEN

As we noted earlier in the chapter, people don't want to acknowledge that they are often poor listeners. As we present the following context and personal barriers to listening, try to recall times when you have faced these problems during interpersonal encounters. We hope that making you aware of these issues will enable you to avoid them or deal with them effectively. Table 6.1 presents examples of these obstacles in action.

Noise

As we mentioned in Chapter 1, the physical environment and all of its distractions can prevent quality listening. Noise, you will remember, is anything that

Table 6.1 /// Barriers to Listening

Barrier Type	In Action
Noise (physical, semantic, physiological, psychological)	Marcy tries to listen to Nick's comments, but his racist words cause her to stop listening.
Message overload	As a receptionist for a church, Carmen's daily tasks include reading about 20 e-mails, listening to approximately 10 voice mails, opening nearly 50 pieces of mail, and answering about 40 phone calls. When the minister approaches her with advice on how to organize the church picnic, Carmen's message overload interferes with receiving the minister's words accurately.
Message complexity	Dr. Jackson tells her patient, Mark, that his "systemic diagnosis has prevented any follow-up"; Mark tunes out because he doesn't understand what she means.
Lack of training	Jamie is asked to supervise a task force at work. He has never taken a course on communication, and he does not have any formal training in listening. He struggles with wanting to listen to the group and wishes he better understood how to listen.
Preoccupation	As Sara talks with Kevin, a coworker, she tries to listen to him talk about his job, but she is thinking about what time she will need to leave work to get to her little brother's graduation that evening. Sara also continues to search the Web to find her last-minute graduation gift.
Listening gap	As Loretta tells her grandkids how she and her husband met, the 6- and 7-year-olds grow impatient and tell their grandma to hurry up.

interferes with the message. Suppose, for instance, that a deaf student is trying to understand challenging subject matter in a classroom. Attempting to communicate the professor's words, the signer begins to sign words that are incorrect because she doesn't understand the content. Or, the signs are slurred or incoherent because the signing is too fast. These distractions would certainly influence the reception of the message by the deaf student.

Distractions can include physical, semantic, physiological, and psychological noise that prevent a listener from receiving the sender's message. You may recall each from Chapter 1, but they bear repeating as we talk about this critical area. Physical noise is any external distraction that prevents meaning between communicators. We may have difficulty listening to our boss at work because a printer is running. Maybe a friend is not able to listen to you at a bar because the music is too loud. Perhaps the noisy dishwasher at home interferes with a parent–child conversation. We run into physical distractions on a daily basis.

Semantic noise results from a sender using language that is not readily understood by a receiver. Semantic noise may take the form of antiquated words or phrases, or language that is confusing or filled with jargon. If you are listening to your grandfather talk about reverse home mortgages, you may "check out" of the conversation because his language may be too technical or irrelevant to you.

Eliminating distractions and noise will enhance our interpersonal meaning with others.

The third type of noise, physiological noise, is any physical, chemical, or biological disturbance that interferes with communication. For instance, it's difficult to listen when you have a migraine headache or have stomach cramps.

Finally, psychological noise occurs when the sender and/or receiver has biases and prejudices that distort the message meaning. Think of this as mental interference in message meaning. We may enter a conversation with preconceptions or stereotypes that affect our understanding of what the other person is going to say, and our assumptions may get in the way of effective listening. For example, you may be a volunteer at Planned Parenthood, and therefore it may be difficult for you to be open-minded when a colleague talks to you about the right to protest at medical facilities that provide reproductive services.

Message Overload

Senders frequently receive more messages than they can process, which is called **message overload**. With the advent of more and more (social) media and advanced media technology, multitasking is now commonplace both at work and home. The average worker in the United States spends about 28% of a workday on e-mail.[27] We used to visit a coworker's desk just a few feet away, but now we e-mail her. Years ago, we'd visit a neighbor to borrow something; now we call him instead. We tweet out opinions on sports and steroids. We can't get pictures up fast enough on Facebook. We now find ourselves talking on the phone while downloading a document, sending an e-mail while chatting with a roommate, and text messaging while driving (*please* don't do this!). With all of this technological maneuvering, who wouldn't be tired of listening at some point during the day?

Message Complexity

Messages we receive that are filled with details, unfamiliar language, and challenging arguments are often difficult to understand. For example, at the closing of a property sale, many homebuyers are overwhelmed by the number of documents they have to sign; the complex federal, state, and local laws they are told about; and the stress of signing financial papers that will put them in debt for 30 years or more. This is a great deal to manage and listen to, and it's likely that the unfamiliar and cumbersome language will negatively affect their listening skills. This can be a serious problem, because important information is communicated at the closing. Many people in technical professions are changing their behaviors. For example, experts in science, technology, engineering, and math (STEM) are spending considerable time and resources making their messages less complex and more amenable to laypeople's understanding.[28]

IPC Praxis

Some think that it's impossible to rid ourselves of noises in a communication channel. Yet, we know that noise can distort the reception of a message, negatively affecting meaning transmission. What suggestions do you have to get rid of various types of noises?

Lack of Training

Both the academic and corporate environments include opportunities to learn about listening, but more could be done. Because listening is a learned activity, we are seeing more and more schools—including Capital Community College, the University of Northern Iowa, Nassau Community College (New York), Penn State University, and the University of Maryland—offer courses on the topic. Still, most students' preparation in listening is limited to a chapter such as the one you're reading now. And yet, consider the tens of millions of people who have never enrolled in an interpersonal communication class! Finally, more and more employers are realizing that increased productivity, positive employee morale, and a healthy organizational climate can be attributed to listening. Training makes both economic and professional sense.

Preoccupation

Even the most effective listeners become preoccupied at times. When we are preoccupied, we are thinking about our own life experiences and everyday troubles. Those who are preoccupied may be prone to **conversational narcissism**, or engaging in an extreme amount of self-focusing to the exclusion of another person.[29] Those who are narcissistic are caught up in their own thoughts and are inclined to interrupt others. Most of us have been narcissistic at one time or another; think of the many times you've had a conversation with someone while you were thinking about your rent, your upcoming test, or your vacation plans. Or, think about trying to hijack a conversation to make it personally relevant ("Oh, you think your surgery was bad! Let me tell you what I went through!"). Although such personal thoughts may be important, they can obstruct our listening. Narcissism, however, has some rather profound implications in our perception process. In one study, for instance, auditors from an accounting firm found that a client's narcissistic communication influenced auditor perceptions of a client's fraudulence.[30]

Preoccupation can also result from focusing on the technology in front of us. How many times have you been on the phone and typing at your computer at the same time? How often have you been told to "listen up" by a friend, only to simultaneously text-message another friend. This preoccupation with technology while others are communicating with us can undercut effective and engaged listening.

Listening Gap

We generally think faster than we speak. In fact, research shows that we speak an average rate of 150 to 200 words per minute, yet we can understand up to 800 words per minute.[31] That is, we can think about three or four times faster than we can talk. The **listening gap** is the time difference between your mental ability to interpret words and the speed at which they arrive to your brain. When we have a large listening gap, we may daydream, doodle on paper, or allow our minds to wander. This drifting off may cause us to miss the essence of a message from a sender. It takes a lot of effort to listen to someone. Closing the listening gap can be challenging for even the most attentive listeners.

6–5 POOR LISTENING HABITS

Poor listening is something that usually occurs over our lifespan. For one reason or another, we have picked up behaviors that do little to develop and maintain quality interpersonal relationships. Although some of these occur more frequently than others in conversations, each is serious enough to affect the reception and meaning of a message. Table 6.2 offers some tips to help you overcome the poor listening habits we discuss next.

Selective Listening

You engage in **selective listening** if you attend to some parts of a message and ignore others. Typically, you selectively listen to those parts of the message that interest you. For an example of how spot listening can be problematic, consider what happens when jurors listen to a witness's testimony. One juror may listen to only the information pertaining to *where* a witness was during a crime to assess the witness's credibility. Another juror may selectively listen to *why* a witness was

Table 6.2 /// How to Overcome Poor Listening Habits

Poor Listening Habit	Strategy for Overcoming Habit
Selective listening	Embrace entire message.
Talkaholism	Become other-oriented.
Pseudolistening	Center attention on speaker.
Gap filling	Fill gap by mentally summarizing message.
Defensive listening	Keep self-concept in check.
Ambushing	Play fair in conversations.

near the crime scene. Their selective listening prevents them from receiving all relevant information about the crime. Controlling for such selective listening first requires us to glean the entire message. Attending to only those message parts that interest you or tuning out because you believe that you know the rest of a message may prompt others to question your listening skills.

Talkaholism

Some people become consumed with their own communication. These individuals are **talkaholics**, defined as compulsive talkers who hog the conversational stage and monopolize encounters. When talkaholics take hold of a conversation, they interrupt, directing the conversational flow. And, of course, if you're talking all the time, you don't take the time to listen. For instance, consider Uncle Jimmy, the talkaholic in the Norella family. The nearly 15 members of the Norella clan who gather each Thanksgiving dread engaging Uncle Jimmy in conversation because all he does is talk. And talk. Some family members privately wonder whether Jimmy understands that many of his more than a dozen relatives would like to speak. But without fail, he comes to dinner with story after story to tell, all the while interrupting those who'd like to share their stories, too.

Not all families have an Uncle Jimmy, but you may know someone who is a talkaholic—that is, someone who won't let you get a word in edgewise. If you are a talkaholic and have the urge to interrupt others, take a deep breath and refrain from talking until your conversational partner has finished speaking. If you find yourself talking in a stream of consciousness without much concern for the other person, you are susceptible to becoming a talkaholic. Remember that other people like to talk, too.

Pseudolistening

We are all pretty good at faking attention. Many of us have been indirectly trained to **pseudolisten**, or to pretend to listen by nodding our heads, by looking at the

Talkaholics fail to consider that their communication is being perceived as self-centered.

Andrea Pittori / Alamy Stock Vector

speaker, by smiling at the appropriate times, or by practicing other kinds of attention feigning. The classroom is a classic location for faking attention. Professors have become adept at spotting students who pseudolisten; many of their nonverbal behaviors give away pseudolistening. Or, consider a less strategic fake listening experience: Imagine that you just received word that you failed an exam and you're out to dinner with your roommate and her parents. You may pseudolisten because of what's on your mind. You can correct this poor listening habit by making every effort to center your attention on the speaker.

Gap Filling

Listeners who think that they can correctly guess the rest of the story a speaker is telling and who don't need the speaker to continue are called gap fillers. Gap fillers often assume that they know how a narrative or interpersonal encounter will unfold. They also frequently interrupt; when this happens, the listener alters the message and its meaning may be lost. Although an issue may be familiar to listeners, they should give speakers the chance to finish their thoughts.

Defensive Listening

Video 6.1

Defensive listening occurs when people view innocent comments as personal attacks or hostile criticisms. Consider Jeannie's experiences. As the owner of a small jewelry shop in the mall, she is accustomed to giving directions to her small staff. Recently, one of her employees commented, "Look, Jeannie, I think you could get more young girls in here if you brought in some rainbow beads. The young ones love them." Jeannie's response was immediate: "Well, . . . here's what I recommend: Why don't you find a lot of money, get your own store, and then you can have all of the rainbow beads you want! I've been in this business for almost 10 years, and I think I know what to buy! Why is it that everybody thinks they know how to run a business?"

Jeannie's response fits the definition of defensive listening. Those who are defensive listeners often perceive threats in messages and may be defensive because of personal issues. In this example, Jeannie may not have any animosity toward her employee; she simply may have misinterpreted the comment. To ensure that you are not a defensive listener, keep your self-concept in check. Don't be afraid to ask yourself the following question: "Am I too quick to defend my thoughts?"

Ambushing

People who listen carefully to a message and then use the information later to attack the individual are ambushing. Ambushers want to retrieve information to discredit or manipulate another person. Gathering information and using it to undercut an opponent is now considered routine in politics. Divorce attorneys frequently uncover information to discredit their clients' spouses. Ambushing in this manner should be avoided; words should never be viewed as ammunition for a verbal battle.

Listening to others can be tough, and yet by now, we're sure you agree that if we aren't practicing quality listening, we are less likely to have quality relationships. We now focus on the styles of listening that you and others are likely to manifest in your conversations with others.

6–6 STYLES OF PREFERRED LISTENING

Typically, we adopt a style of listening in our interpersonal interactions. A **listening style** is a predominant listening approach to the messages we receive. We adopt a listening style to understand the sender's message. In general, listening requires us to think about the relationships we have with others and the tasks that are assigned to us. Providing a template for these listening styles, here we identify four: **p**eople-centered, **a**ction-centered, **c**ontent-centered, and **t**ime-centered.[32] We call this establishing a "P-A-C-T" between communicators (see Figure 6.3).

People-Centered Listening Style

The style associated with being concerned with other people's feelings or emotions is called the **people-centered listening style**. People-oriented listeners try to compromise and find common areas of interest. Research shows that people-centered listeners are less apprehensive in groups, meetings, and interpersonal situations than other types of listeners.[33] People-centered listeners quickly notice others' moods and provide clear verbal and nonverbal feedback, feedback that can make a tremendous difference in a person's life. For instance, in one study,[34] those who practiced person-centered listening with terminally ill patients included them in diagnostic decision-making and in their overall care.

Action-Centered Listening Style

The **action-centered listening style** pertains to listeners who want messages to be highly organized, concise, and error free. These people help speakers focus on what is important in the message. Action-centered listeners want speakers to get to the point and are often frustrated when people tell stories in a disorganized or random fashion. They also **second-guess** speakers—that is, they question the assumptions underlying a message. If second-guessers believe a message is false, they develop an alternative explanation which is viewed as more realistic.

Action-centered listeners also clearly tell others that they want unambiguous feedback. For instance, as an action-centered listener, a professor may tell her students that if they wish to challenge a grade, they should simply delineate specific reasons why they deserve a grade change and what grade they feel is appropriate.

Figure 6.3 /// Styles of Listening

People-centered

Action-centered

Content-centered

Time-centered

Content-Centered Listening Style

Individuals who engage in the **content-centered listening style** focus on the facts and details of a message. They consider all sides of an issue and welcome complex and challenging information from a sender. However, they may intimidate others by asking pointed questions or by discounting information from those the listener deems to be nonexperts. Content-centered listeners are likely to play devil's advocate in conversations. Therefore, attorneys and others in the legal profession are likely to favor this style of listening in their jobs.

Time-Centered Listening Style

When listeners adopt a **time-centered listening style**, they let others know that messages should be presented with a consideration of time constraints. That is, time-oriented listeners discourage wordy explanations from speakers and set time guidelines for conversations, such as prefacing a conversation with "I have only 5 minutes to talk." Some time-centered listeners constantly check the time or abruptly end encounters with others. One of your authors has a friend who lives on an island. Her time-centered listening is an inside joke to her friends because she keeps looking at her watch so that she doesn't miss the island ferry to her home. Whether being invited to dinner or to a movie, she is intent on letting others know that she can't go too far from the ferry terminal.

Which of the four listening styles is the best? It's not a trick question because it all depends on the situation and the purpose of the interpersonal encounter. In fact, because one conversation may require all types of listening, it's both inappropriate and impossible to answer that question.

You may need to change and adapt your listening style to meet the other person's needs. For example, you might need to be a time-centered listener for the coworker who needs information quickly, but you might need to be person centered while speaking to your best friend about his divorce. However, remember that just because you have adjusted your style of listening does not mean that the other person has adjusted their style. You will both have to be aware of each other's style. Know your preferred style of listening but be flexible in your style depending on the communication situation.

Our listening style is often based on our cultural background. So, let's now turn our attention to the role of culture in listening. When speakers and listeners come from various cultural backgrounds, message meaning can be affected.

6–7 CULTURE AND THE LISTENING PROCESS

As we learned in Chapter 2, we are all members of a culture and various co-cultures. We understand that cultural differences influence our communication with others. Because all our interactions are culturally based, culture affects the listening process. Further, it's important to know that one's culture's listening practices are not universally applied across all cultures. Much of the research in this area pertains to race, ethnicity, and ancestry.

National Culture and Listening

Recall from Chapter 2 our discussion of individualistic and collectivistic cultures. We noted that the United States is an individualistic country, meaning that it focuses on an "I" orientation rather than a "we" orientation. Individualistic cultures value direct communication, or speaking one's mind. Some collectivistic cultures, such as China, respect others' words, desire harmony, and believe in conversational politeness.

In fact, listening (*tinghua*) is one of the key principles in Chinese communication. While listening to others, communicators need to remember that differences in feedback (direct or indirect) exist. Let's explore a few examples of the interface of culture and listening.

Listening variations across cultures affect the ability to be an effective salesperson.[35] For example, for the French, listening for information is the main concern. For citizens of several Arab countries, however, listening is done for know-how or for gain. And people in some cultures, such as Germany, do not ask for clarification; asking a presenter to repeat something is seen as a sign of impoliteness and disrespect. As a practical application of this information, consider how a salesperson's recognition of these cultural differences might positively affect their company's bottom line.

Here we offer an additional example of how culture and listening work together. Looking at listening as a personal opportunity to interrelate with the environment, the Blackfeet Indians are important to consider:[36]

> Blackfeet listening is a highly reflective and revelatory mode of communication that can open one to the mysteries of unity between the physical and spiritual, to the relationships between natural and human forms, and to the intimate links between places and persons.

In fact, Native American communities have come together to form an Intertribal Monitoring Association on Indian Trust Funds with the sole purpose of having "listening conferences." Representatives from various tribal nations gather to listen to how the federal government is adhering to Trust Fund Standards, to provide tribal

Culture plays a significant role in the listening process.

forums, and to keep up to date on policies and regulations on federal initiatives, among others. These listening conferences have been taking place for over 15 years.

In addition to the preceding, a study that examined both Iranian and U.S. students looked at the perceptions of listening competency.[37] While Iran continues to transition into the digital age, the primary forms of listening that occur are related to appreciative or aesthetic listening (e.g., listening to poetry or music). Looking at both high school and college students, the results showed that while both cultures were generally similar in their perceptions of listening competency, the U.S. students perceived themselves to be better listeners than their Iranian counterparts. One interpretation relates to the fact that U.S. students are generally comfortable with self-praise, and in Iran, modesty is an important cultural value. Furthermore, several similarities were observed between both cultures in their perceptions of recalling, responding, and rating listening behaviors.

The common thread in these different types of examples is the notion that while cultures vary in their value systems, listening remains a critical part of the various cultural communities. Staying culturally aware of these variations as you consider the message of another person is important.

What strategies can you use to become a better listener with individuals from various (co-)cultures? First, don't expect everyone else to adapt to your way of communicating (recall our discussion of ethnocentrism in Chapter 2). Second, accept new ways of receiving messages and practice patience with senders who may not have a similar cultural background. Third, wait as long as possible before merging another's words into your words—don't define the world on your terms. Finally, seek clarification when possible. Asking questions in intercultural conversations reduces our processing load, and we are better equipped to translate difficult concepts as they emerge.

 **IPC Careers**

Listening Skills and a Mental Health Counselor

It has been referred to as a "grunt job" and "an endless experience of sadness." Yet, those who pursue a career as a mental health professional also identify it as richly rewarding. These counselors are dedicated, thoughtful, and always other-centered listeners. In fact, whether through diagnosis, support, or education, a mental health expert must adapt to and adopt various communication styles, most prominently the ability to listen actively. Poor listening habits, such as talkaholism and pseudolistening, will only weaken the communication taking place. Clients must feel welcomed and heard, and the four Rs must function prominently in a profession that guides others to self-fulfillment and self-sufficiency.

iStock.com/nullplus

Reflection: *Suppose you were visiting a mental health expert to offer some suggestions for being more "other-centered" in their therapy. What ideas would you identify to make sure clients feel at ease?*

Gender and Listening

Video 6.2

One final note regarding culture and listening remains important. Recall from Chapter 2 that our interpretation of culture involves many components, including gender. Let's briefly explore this dynamic to give you a glimpse into the research.

To begin, some research points to actual brain hemispheric differences between men and women, although research is inconclusive regarding which sex is the better listener. In addition, recall our conversation about the P-A-C-T that communicators have with each other. With respect to differences between men and women, research shows that men are more prone to action-oriented listening while women typically prefer people-centered listening. Women tend to understand the emotional elements of a message than do men, and yet, men listen less to women than women listen to men.[38]

Finally, in her bestseller *You Just Don't Understand: Women and Men in Conversations,* author Deborah Tannen[39] also identifies a framework to understand the differences between women and men and how they cultivate intimacy through listening. Women typically engage in building a relationship with another through their listening, a communication approach called **rapport talk**. Women establish connections through this communication. Men, on the hand, use **report talk**, which is communication related to asserting independence and to negotiate and maintain status. Men are inclined to dominate conversations.

The rapport–report challenge can be understood this way. Suppose that Brianna decides she wants to adopt a child and tells her best friend, Neil. As she tells her best friend, she may become frustrated and even angry. While she seeks empathy (establishing connection), Neil instead tells her that he thinks it will be too expensive (establishing status via knowledge). Researchers interested in this conversation would say that misunderstandings between women and men could be reduced if they each understood that the other might have a different listening style with different communication patterns.

IPC Praxis

What have your experiences been when listening to and speaking with various genders? Do you see any similarities? Differences? What sorts of criteria did you use to make your decisions?

In the rest of the chapter, we review effective listening skills you should practice. We know that improving your listening habits is a challenging and lifelong process. So, you shouldn't expect changes to your listening behaviors to happen overnight.

6–8 SKILL SET FOR EFFECTIVE LISTENING

This section outlines five primary skills for improving listening. Whether we communicate with a partner, boss, close friend, family member, coworker, or another, we all must choose whether we will develop good or bad listening habits. And yes, this is a *choice* for you. Let's explore the following guidelines in Table 6.3 for effective listening.

Table 6.3 /// Skill Set for Listening and Responding
a. Evaluate your current skills.
b. Prepare to listen.
c. Provide empathic responses when necessary.
d. Use nonjudgmental feedback.
e. Practice active listening.
f. Your skill suggestion

Evaluate Your Current Skills

A first step toward becoming a better listener is assessing and understanding your personal listening strengths and weaknesses. To begin, think about the poor listening habits you have seen others practice. Do you use any of them while communicating? Which listening behaviors do you exhibit consistently, and which do you use sporadically? Also, which of your biases, prejudices, beliefs, and opinions may interfere with receipt of a message?

In addition, we have stressors and personal problems that may affect our listening skills. For example, if you were told that your company was laying off workers, how would this affect your communication with people on a daily basis? Could you be an effective listener even though you would find yourself preoccupied with the financial and emotional toll you would experience if you were downsized? In such a situation, it would be nearly impossible to dismiss your feelings, so you should just try to accept them and be aware that they will probably affect your communication with others.

Prepare to Listen

After you assess your listening abilities, the next step is to prepare yourself to listen. Such preparation requires both physical and mental activities. If you are hearing impaired, you may have to ask for some assistance to ensure that the message is delivered to you accurately. You may have to locate yourself closer to the source of the message (of course, depending on who the speaker is, your physical proximity will vary). If you have problems concentrating on a message, try to reduce or remove as many distractions as possible, such as your laptop or TV. Have you ever had a friend or parent say, "Will you please stop texting and listen to me?" Before being confronted with this question, set your phone aside and prepare for the conversation you're about to have.

 IPC Around Us: Empathy

A teen's empathy skills continue to be important to cultivate.[40] In adolescence, empathy skills continue rising steadily in girls at age 13. Boys, however, do not begin until age 15 to show gains in what is called "perspective taking." Between ages 13 and 16, adolescent males show a decline in their ability to recognize and respond to others' feelings. When teens have empathy skills, they are less likely to argue or be confrontational both at

(Continued)

(Continued)

iStock.com/Sladic

home and at school. While all adults are critical in making sure they affirm a teen's empathy skills, fathers, in particular, can talk to their sons about the malice related to teasing others and taking part in jokes that undercut empathy.

Reflection: *Do you believe that parents and other adults are important figures in cultivating empathy at home and at school? Or, regardless of whether or not an adult is present, will an adolescent act out as many normally do: highly independent, emotionally immature, and/or preoccupied with "fitting in"?*

To prepare yourself mentally, do your homework beforehand if you are going to need information to listen effectively. For example, if you want to ask your boss for a raise, you would want to have ready a mental list of the reasons why you deserve a raise and possible responses to reasons why you do not. If you are a student, reading the material before class will make the lecture or discussion much more meaningful because you will have the background knowledge to be able to offer your thoughts on issues as they arise. In your personal relationships, you should be prepared to consider other points of view as well as your own.

Provide Empathic Responses When Necessary

Video 6.3

When we use empathy, we tell other people that we value their thoughts. **Empathy** is the process of identifying with or attempting to experience the thoughts, beliefs, and actions of another. Empathy tells people that although we can't feel their exact feelings or precisely identify with a current situation, we are trying to cocreate experiences with them. You are said to be empathic (not "empathetic") when you work toward understanding another person. You're not actually reproducing a person's experiences, but trying to cocreate the meaning (think back to our definition of *communication* in Chapter 1). We show we're responsive and empathic by giving well-timed verbal feedback throughout a conversation, not simply when it is our turn to speak. Doing so suggests a genuine interest in the sender's message and has the side benefit of keeping us attentive to the message. To show empathy, we must also demonstrate that we're engaged nonverbally in the message. This can be accomplished through sustained facial involvement (avoiding a blank look that communicates boredom), frequent eye contact (maintaining some focus on the speaker's face), and body positioning that communicates interest.

Learning to listen with empathy is sometimes difficult. We have to show support for another while making sure that we are not unnecessarily exacerbating negative feelings. For instance, examine the following dialogue between two friends, Camilla and Tony. Camilla is angry that her boss did not positively review her work plan:

Camilla: "He's self-righteous—that's all there is to it. He didn't even say that my idea made sense. I think he's just jealous because he didn't come up with it first."

Tony: "Yeah, I bet you're right. He really didn't show you any respect. And because he's the boss, I'm sure he wanted to take the credit."

Although Tony meant to show empathy, he may have unintentionally perpetuated the idea that Camilla's boss was a "bad" man. Because Tony seems to be supporting her thoughts, Camilla will have a difficult time changing her perception of her boss. This negative view won't help Camilla in future conversations with her boss. Now, consider an alternative response from Tony that doesn't reinforce Camilla's negative perception:

Camilla: "He's self-righteous—that's all there is to it. He didn't even say that my idea made sense. I think he's just jealous because he didn't come up with it first."

Tony: "Wow, you're obviously frustrated with him. You sound like you want to quit. I know that it's rough for you right now, but hang in there."

In this example, Tony not only demonstrated some empathic listening skills, but helped Camilla redirect her thinking about her boss. When Tony changed the direction of the conversation in this way, Camilla could consider less resentful impressions of the situation. Helping others alleviate their anxiety is a necessary emotional support skill for many interactions.

Use Nonjudgmental Feedback

Many of us provide feedback with little concern for how the receiver will interpret it. Particularly with those whom we have close relationships such as family members, we may not think twice about providing feedback—regardless of its content. When we give **nonjudgmental feedback**, we describe another's behavior and then explain how that behavior made us feel. As we will discuss in Chapter 7, centering a message on your own emotions without engaging in accusatory finger wagging can help reduce interpersonal conflict.

Consider the difference between the following statements:

- "You are so rude to come in late. You made me a nervous wreck! You're pretty inconsiderate to make me feel this way!"

- "When you come home so late, I really worry. I thought something had gone wrong."

In heated moments especially, taking ownership of your feelings and perceptions, as in the second statement, is difficult. Owning your feelings rather than blaming others for your own feelings results in more effective interpersonal communication.

Practice Active Listening

We define **active listening** as a transactional process in which a listener communicates reinforcing messages to a speaker. Research shows that people who receive active listening responses or advice were more satisfied with their conversations than those who were simply acknowledged.[41] When we actively listen, we show support for another person and their message. In our interpersonal relationships, active listeners *want to* listen rather than feel *obligated to* listen. Particularly in close relationships with others, demonstrating that you are actively involved in the conversation will help both your credibility as a communicator and your relationship standing with others. Additional elements of active listening are paraphrasing, dialogue enhancers, questions, and silence. We briefly discuss each of these in the following subsections.

Paraphrasing

Active listening requires **paraphrasing**, or restating the essence of another's message in our own words. Paraphrasing is a perception check in an interpersonal encounter; it allows us to clarify our interpretation of a message. When paraphrasing, try to be concise and simple in your response. For instance, you can use language such as "In other words, what you're saying is . . ." or "I think what I heard is that you . . ." or "Let me see if I get this right." Such phrases show others that you care about understanding the intended meaning of a message.

Dialogue Enhancers

Active listening requires us to show the speaker that even though we may disagree with their thoughts, we accept and are open to them. As we noted earlier, speakers need support in their conversations. **Dialogue enhancers** take the form of supporting expressions such as "I see" or "I get it" or "I'm listening." Dialogue enhancers should not interrupt a message. They should be used as indications that you are involved in the message. In other words, these statements enhance the discussion taking place.

Questions

Asking well-timed and appropriate questions in an interpersonal interaction can be a hallmark of an engaged active listener. Asking questions is not a sign of ignorance or stupidity, unless your questions are trying to trap the speaker or are meant to deceive or manipulate the sender. What question asking demonstrates is a willingness to make sure that you receive the intended meaning of the speaker's message. If you ask questions, you may receive information that is contrary to your instincts or assumptions, thereby avoiding gap filling, a problem we identified earlier. Don't be afraid to respectfully ask questions in your relationships with others. Your input will likely be met with gratitude as the other communicator realizes your desire to seek information.

Silence

Not interrupting. Sitting still. Attending to the words. Watching, when possible, the facial reactions and focusing on the vocal tones. As we noted elsewhere, keeping quiet is usually not viewed as a virtue in many Western societies. In fact, in the self-help book sections in U.S. bookstores, you will likely find no books on the importance of keeping quiet because the culture rewards talkativeness.

Silence is a complicated concept in conversations and in the listening process. Indeed, at times, we should honor **silent listening**, which requires us to stay attentive and respond nonverbally when another person is struggling with what to say. Despite the challenge, particularly with a subject area of which we know a great deal, we need to allow the entire message to be revealed before jumping in. We also need to be silent because sometimes words are not needed. For example, after a conflict has been resolved and two people are looking at each other and holding each other's hands, they don't need to speak to communicate. In this context, silence may be more effective than words in making the people in the relationship feel closer.

However, as noted in our discussion of nonverbal communication (Chapter 5), silence is not always positive. It can also be used to manipulate or coerce another person in an interpersonal exchange. This is an example of the debilitative side of communication that we discussed in Chapter 1. For instance, giving someone "the silent treatment"—that is, refusing to talk to someone—may provoke unnecessary tension. Also, imposing your own code of silence in an encounter may damage a relationship. For example, if you choose to remain silent in an interpersonal conflict, you may exacerbate the problem and cause your conversational partner to be even more conflicted.

iStock.com/Jacob Wackerhausen

We should practice more silent listening if we are to become more adept in our interpersonal communication.

/// CHAPTER WRAP-UP

We introduced one of the most important of all the interpersonal communication skills: listening. We began by providing you a glimpse into the importance of listening in our personal and professional lives and identified several reasons why we listen. We then defined *listening* and explained several challenges and obstacles to effective listening. Next, we introduced Working Memory Theory, explaining how it functions when we are bombarded with stimuli. We then examined several poor listening habits and introduced four preferred listening styles of individuals. Finally, we discussed several research conclusions of how culture—specifically national culture and gender—and listening are interrelated.

We cannot overstate the fact that listening is not an easy communication behavior, and yet, it's rarely formally taught in schools. Some people believe we need to teach young children about several of the issues we presented in this chapter, if, for any other reason, the material might help everyone to understand that listening is critical for success. As we now know, so many of us can get into poor rituals and routines as they relate to listening. Our hope is that many of these annoying and ineffective behaviors will soon dissipate as you begin to work on becoming a more active and empathic listener.

/// COMMUNICATION ASSESSMENT TEST (CAT): LISTENING TO YOUR "SELF"

For the following statements, indicate the extent to which you practice the behavior. Choose among the responses *Most of the time, Often, Rarely*, and *Never*.

Most of the time	Often	Rarely	Never
1. During face-to-face conversations with others, I find myself texting and reading e-mails.			
2. When someone uses language that I find offensive, I tend to lose concentration on the message.			
3. In a conversation with another person, when I encounter a word or phrase that I don't understand, I will ask the person to clarify what they meant.			

Most of the time	Often	Rarely	Never

4. I repeat words back to another person to clarify my understanding of their message.

5. I value silence in conversations.

6. I interrupt people when I feel the need to express an opinion.

7. I allow others to interrupt me when they feel the need to express an opinion.

8. I focus on the other person's nonverbal communication while speaking to them.

9. I give others my full attention when they are speaking to me.

10. At times, I daydream while another person is speaking to me.

11. When listening to another person, I use eye contact.

12. During conversations with others, I acknowledge that cultural background may influence how they listen to me.

13. To clarify my understanding of their message, I will ask another person appropriate questions.

14. If a person hesitates in a conversation, I encourage them to continue.

15. People tend to come to me to communicate their feelings because I am viewed as an effective listener.

How to Score

This is a self-assessment, and no comparison between or among classmates is necessary. Still, in order to further understand your listening abilities, return to your impressions. Provide an example or two to illustrate why you rated the statement in a particular way. Then, be prepared to return to this CAT from time to time as you continue to learn about the interpersonal communication process.

Some questions to consider:

1. Did time affect the rating of a particular statement?

2. How might a critical incident (e.g., a major conflict, saying "I love you," etc.) influence a response?

3. Is it possible to be an effective listener while paying attention to other things, including a cell phone text, a television program, or an email?

Source: Madelyn Burley-Allen, in *Coaching Conversations: Transforming Your School One Conversation at a Time*; Cheliotes and Reilly, 2010.

/// KEY TERMS

hearing   162

Working Memory
    Theory   163

central executive   163

listening   164

four Rs of listening   164

receiving   164

mindful listening   165

responding   165

recalling   166

chunking   166

rating   167

American Sign Language
    (ASL)   169

message overload   171

conversational narcissism   172

listening gap   173

selective listening   173

talkaholics   174

pseudolisten   174

gap fillers   175

defensive listening   175

ambushing   175

listening style   176

people-centered listening style   176

action-centered listening style   176

second-guess   176

content-centered listening
    style   177

time-centered listening style   177

/// KEY QUESTIONS FOR APPLICATION

1. **CQ/CultureQuest:** Explore the following claim: "Listening is much more challenging with people you love." Do you agree or disagree? Defend your view with examples.

2. **TQ/TechQuest:** Explore the following claim: "Reading a blog and sitting with the blog's author require two different approaches to listening." Do you agree or disagree? Defend your view with examples.

3. Identify your desired career path. How will or does listening function in that career? Use examples to demonstrate listening's importance.

4. What is your preferred style of listening? Do you have more than one? Explain with examples.

5. Some writers believe that we could never eliminate noise from the communication channel to improve our listening. Do you agree or disagree? Explain.

6. It's often easier to tell people to be better listeners. Yet, there are times when the advice simply doesn't work. What are some situations where listening has been the toughest for you?

Access practice quizzes, eFlashcards, video, and multimedia at **edge.sagepub.com/west**.

Visit **edge.sagepub.com/west** to help you accomplish your coursework goals in an easy-to-use learning environment.

PRACTICE AND APPLY WHAT YOU'VE LEARNED

▶ edge.sagepub.com/west

$SAGE edge™

WANT A BETTER GRADE ON YOUR NEXT TEST?

Head to the study site where you'll find:

- **eFlashcards** to strengthen your understanding of key terms.

- **Practice quizzes** to test your comprehension of key concepts.

- **Videos and multimedia content** to enhance your exploration of key topics.

CHAPTER 7

COMMUNICATING AND EMOTION

LEARNING OUTCOMES

After studying this chapter, you will be able to

7-1 Understand the definition of emotion

7-2 Describe the differences between Biological and Social Interaction theories

7-3 Explain the relationship between emotion and interpersonal communication

7-4 Clarify the influences on emotional expression

7-5 Recognize the way emotional blends are associated with emotional expression

7-6 Employ skills for emotional expression

iStock.com/alessandro0770

Master the content at
edge.sagepub.com/west

⑤SAGE edge™

Emotional experiences shape our lives, and are often what we remember most about interpersonal encounters. For example now that he's 30, JJ barely remembers any of his high school teachers. But his ninth-grade English teacher, Mr. Laurent, is someone he'll never forget. He remembers him because he helped him feel proud of his work, and optimistic about his future. Further, emotion often influences how we judge interpersonal interactions and relationships. When Angie thinks back to her friendship with Rosa, for instance, she's glad it's over because of all the arguments between them, which left Angie feeling angry and depressed most of the time. Thinking about those emotions led Angie to believe she and Rosa had an unhealthy relationship.

> **The following theories/models are discussed in this chapter:**
>
> Biological Theory
>
> Social Interaction Theory

In this chapter, we investigate emotion and its powerful role in the interpersonal communication process. We all know intuitively how important emotion is, but often we don't have much information about emotion—it's not a subject discussed much in school, as you've probably noticed. But if we don't pay attention to emotion, we cannot be competent communicators. As with so many aspects of interpersonal communication, we need to gain adequate knowledge before we can develop our skills, and so we'll begin by defining emotion.

 **IPC Voice: Oliver**

It's really true that we don't get any instructions in expressing, or even feeling, emotion. I've never heard any instructor even really mention emotion in class at all. In my family we try to stay pretty stoic about everything, so I definitely don't get any information about emotion from them. It's only now with my girlfriend, Fiona, that I've ever talked about emotion or been encouraged to express any emotion I've felt. Fiona is a great communicator and she acknowledges her own and my emotions.

7–1 DEFINING EMOTION

Defining the term *emotion* is complicated. Some say that emotion involves only one person's feelings (e.g., anger, fear, anxiety, happiness). Others include those emotions we feel in relationships, such as envy and love. A third approach differentiates between *real* feelings and *manufactured* feelings that are produced because some outside norm dictates that they are appropriate. For instance, if you are a server in a restaurant, your job requires you to smile and act happy around your customers even if you've had a horrible day and don't feel like smiling at all. Manufacturing a feeling that you're not actually experiencing is called *emotion labor.*

In this book, we'll define **emotion** as the feelings we have within ourselves and related to our relationships with others. Thus, for us, the term *emotion* encompasses both the internal feelings of one person (e.g., when Joe feels anxious before he meets Ana's parents) as well as feelings that can be experienced only in a relationship (e.g., when Joyce feels competitive when she hears how well Barb did on the chemistry exam).

Our definition of emotion rests on the notion of *process*. Process means that emotion, like communication itself, is experienced over time and goes through changes. Emotions are affected by your own evolution (something that excited you when you were 12 years old may not evoke much emotion for you now) as well as cultural changes over time (something considered exciting in 1950, like getting a television set in your home, would be unlikely to generate that emotion in 2019). Your emotional life is ongoing and unending, and it's always influenced by what came before and it conditions what comes after. For instance, if Javier's father has told him repeatedly that real men don't cry, then how Javier expresses sorrow is restrained by those admonitions. However, if Javier does find himself crying after hearing particularly bad news, and it actually makes him feel better to release the emotion through tears, then that will influence his expression and experience of emotion in the future.

IPC Praxis

Think about a time in the past when you were very happy or upset about something in your life. Would that same experience evoke the same feelings in you today? If you don't think they would, why do you suppose that is? If you would still feel the same way, why do you think that is? What do these reflections tell you about the role of process in the definition of emotion?

Now we'll discuss two category systems for emotion and then explore the relationships among emotion, reason, and physicality, or the body.

Two Category Systems for Emotion

Video 7.1

Some U.S. researchers have created category systems for classifying commonly experienced emotions. These systems focus on attributes of emotion, such as **valence** (whether the emotion reflects a positive or negative feeling), **activity** (whether the emotion implies action or passivity), and **intensity** (how strongly felt the emotion is).

One system[1] categorizes emotion along two dimensions at once: valence and activity. This system allows us to see how specific emotions cluster together depending on whether they are active-negative, active-positive, passive-negative, or passive-positive (see Figure 7.1). For example, when Cate feels an emotion such as excitement, we can see on Figure 7.1 that it is positive and implies some action. When she feels an emotion such as contentment, the figure shows that it's just as positive but less active than excitement.

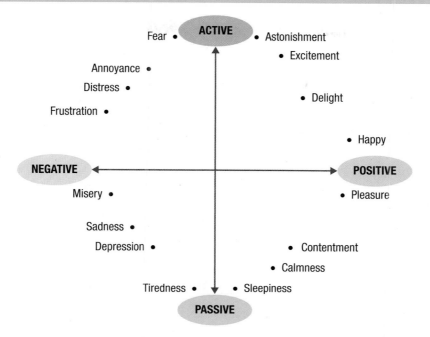

Source: Based on Guerrero, L. K., Andersen, P. A., & Trost, M. R. (1998). *Handbook of communication and emotion.* San Diego, CA: Academic Press, p. 14.

IPC Praxis

Think about an emotion you've experienced recently. How would you map it on the dimensions of valence and activity? Do you see a difference between emotions you feel based on valence and activity? How useful do you think this category system is for understanding the emotions you feel?

Video 7.2

Another system for classifying individual emotion is based on its intensity. The emotion cone[2] provides a graduated image of emotional range (see Figure 7.2). The lowest level of each vertical slice represents the mildest version of the emotion, and each successive level represents a more intense state. This system points to the impact of labeling an emotion with a particularly intense name. For example, if Anderson says he is bored in French class, that statement carries a much different meaning, and is far less intense, than if he says he loathes French. How do you think it would affect Anderson to say to himself that he's bored in the class compared to saying that he loathes it?

Figure 7.2 /// Emotion Cone

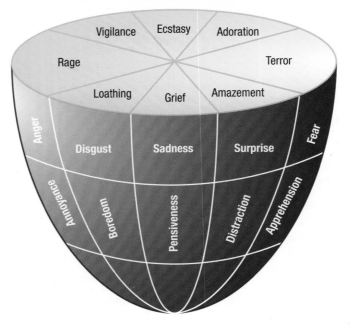

Source: Plutchik, R. (1984). Emotions: A general psychoevolutionary theory. In K. R. Scherer & P. Ekman (Eds.), *Approaches to emotion* (pp. 197–219).

Emotion, Reason, and the Body

One of the complexities of emotion is that it's often framed within the either/or framework that characterizes a great deal of Western thought. This either/or thinking, also known as *dualism,* originated in the 18th century with philosophers Immanuel Kant and René Descartes. **Dualism** is a way of thinking that constructs polar opposite categories encompassing the totality of a thing, prompting us to think about it in an either/or fashion. Dualism creates the problem of polarization that we discussed in Chapter 4. For example, dualism encourages us to think about all people as either female or male or all of any person as either good or bad. Figure 7.3 lists common dualisms that pervade the English language and the thinking of those who speak it.

When we phrase things as either/or choices, we can't see a third (or fourth) possibility. When political leaders believe that they and their political opponents do not share any goals, and they frame issues in terms of good or evil, it is difficult to negotiate and get things done for the country. Discussions in the United States in 2018 about the Iran nuclear deal reflected this type of dualistic thinking. The Iran nuclear deal, struck in 2015, reduced Iran's stockpile of uranium and their ability to enrich uranium and made Iran subject to inspections to be sure they weren't developing nuclear missiles. In return, sanctions against Iran were lifted. In 2018, some people argued that the deal was ineffective, and Iran was testing missiles anyway. Other people argued just as strongly that, while the deal wasn't perfect, it reduced global risk and helped the world move toward peace. Each side argued from an either/or position, although in 2018, the French president, Emmanuel Macron, tried a tactic that avoids this type of thinking.

Figure 7.3 /// Common Dualisms in Western Thought

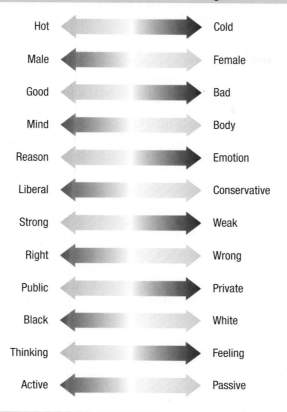

Hot	Cold
Male	Female
Good	Bad
Mind	Body
Reason	Emotion
Liberal	Conservative
Strong	Weak
Right	Wrong
Public	Private
Black	White
Thinking	Feeling
Active	Passive

The tactic Macron tried involves conceptualizing "the third side"[3] and negotiating something that helps resolve conflict among people. For instance, the third side makes an effort to find some overarching place of agreement among differing positions, such as peace and security, and begin negotiations from there. Macron attempted this approach with the U.S. president, Donald Trump, and although he was ultimately unsuccessful, he illustrated a way to think beyond dualism.

Dualism encourages us to consider a person to be split into two parts—mind and body—that operate completely independently. The historic division between mind and body is further split when the mind is seen, in another dualism, as either reason or emotion. Dualism is illustrated whenever someone says to another in a conflict, "Stop being hysterical about this! You have to be reasonable." Lisa Feldman Barrett refers to this approach to emotion as the *classical view,* or the way we're inclined to believe that emotion is a brute force that needs to be controlled by reason.[4]

Yet, this classical view prompts us to think in ways that aren't accurate. Reason and emotion depend on each other; they're not completely separate spheres. Hunches and gut reactions show emotion in service of reason. Emotion helps us to decide between competing alternatives when all else is equal—sometimes called "going with your gut." How do you choose between your brown scarf and a black scarf when both look equally good with your coat? How do you choose whether to go visit your friend Grant or stay home and watch TV, when either alternative sounds fun? We would be paralyzed by indecision if we didn't have emotional responses to help us make decisions.

Further, the process of perception, which we discussed in Chapter 3, illustrates the relationships between reason, body, and emotion. When we perceive something, we first attend to stimuli. So, let's say that several stimuli are coming toward you and you feel threatened in some way, believing that your safety is at risk. That is, you feel the emotion of fear. This insight involves reason. You must first notice that something dangerous is happening (e.g., someone approaches you looking threatening). In this step, you compare your knowledge of a non-dangerous event to what is actually happening, and you see the discrepancy (e.g., you say to yourself, "I could have no one bothering me, but that's not happening now"). You also have to determine the importance of this behavior and evaluate the context (e.g., you and this person are friends playing football, or you are walking down a dark alley and the person is a stranger). All these judgments are part of the cognitive element of emotion. Emotion also has a physiological component. For example, if someone approaches you with a scowl on their face, you are likely to experience physiological reactions such as accelerated heart rate, breathing changes, a lump in your throat, and tense muscles. Table 7.1 presents a listing of common emotions with their accompanying cognitive and physical elements.

Despite our knowledge of these connections, dualistic thinking persists in many arenas. For instance, thinking about emotion as separate from reason and the body is often reflected in medical school curricula, although there are some efforts to change this. Many courses in medical school teach students to treat physical symptoms, but relatively few address the thoughts and feelings of patients and their families. However, on some level, we understand that emotion, the body, and reason are inextricably linked. Our language helps us see the connections. Think about words we use to describe emotion: *heartache, heartsick, heartened, heartless, heartfelt, lighthearted.* All these words indicate our instinctive knowledge of the connections between emotion and the body (the heart). And, some physicians are including elements of *narrative medicine,* or encouraging patients to tell their stories, into their medical practice. This approach encourages a focus on the patient as a whole person.

Table 7.1 /// Emotions, Physical Reactions, and Cognitions

Emotions	Physical Reactions	Cognitions
Joy	Warmth suffusing face Fast heartbeat	"I am so happy, and this feels wonderful."
Anger	Fast heartbeat Tense muscles	"I feel anger, and I want to do something."
Sadness	Lump in throat Tension in body	"I am feeling sadness wash over me."
Shame	Hot flushes Fast heartbeat	"I am ashamed. What can I do?"

Experiencing emotion seems to affect people's physical functioning in ways that are not simply physical manifestations of the emotion. Many studies advance the idea that physical health is impacted by emotions. One study found that this relationship between body and emotion is mediated by culture. The researchers argue that positive health outcomes relate to the "fit" between emotion and culture. In other words, people who experience emotion in the ways advocated by their culture seem to enjoy better overall physical health.[5] Further, another study found that when people simply remembered positive emotional events, they began to feel better and happier.[6] In sum, we see that emotion can be understood in terms of its valence, activity, and intensity. Additionally, we argue that, despite a Western tendency to see things as either/or, emotion is best explicated in the context of reason (or cognitions) and physicality (or the body).

IPC Praxis

When you think about emotion, do you also think about how cognitions and physicality relate to it? Can you make a chart like Table 7.1 for an emotion you've experienced recently? How does it help you to understand the role of emotion in interpersonal communication to think of it relating to the body and mind rather than accepting the dualistic thinking that's common in Western thought?

7–2 EXPLAINING EMOTION: BIOLOGY AND SOCIAL INTERACTION

Many theories help us understand emotion. We now review two that explain how emotions originate: the Biological and Social Interaction theories.

The Biological Theory of Emotion

Proponents of the Biological Theory agree with Charles Darwin and others that emotion is mainly biological, related to instinct and energy. Because advocates of this view believe that emotions are universal across many types of people, they propose that people from a variety of cultures should experience feelings in the same manner.

This theory assumes that emotion exists separately from thought and that we need thought only to bring a preexisting emotion to our conscious awareness. For example, let's say that Maura is arguing with her friend, Rolanda, about how to plan a campus event. While they talk, Maura is thinking about advancing her ideas in the argument and is not paying any attention to the emotion she is experiencing. However, as she walks away from Rolanda, she notices that she's slightly irritated because Rolanda disagrees with her about the best way to advertise the event. Although Maura had been experiencing emotion during the argument, she needed introspection, or thought, to bring it to her attention.

Charles Darwin believed that the majority of emotional gestures are the same across cultures.

Darwin placed importance on observable emotional expressions, not the meanings associated with them. Darwin argued that these "gestures" of emotion were remnants of prehistoric behaviors that served important functions. For instance, when we bare our teeth in rage, our behavior is a remnant of the action of biting. When we hug someone in an expression of affection, our action is a remnant of the act of copulation. And when our mouths form an expression of disgust, our action is a remnant of the need to regurgitate a poisonous substance or spoiled food. Thus, in the Biological Theory, "emotion . . . is our experience of the body ready for an imaginary action."[7] Furthermore, Darwin argued that people enact these gestures as a result of experiencing emotion. However, he also asserted that the opposite is true—that is, when people enact a certain gesture, they experience the related emotion. Darwin also believed that these emotive gestures (with a few exceptions, such as weeping and kissing) are universal, meaning that they cross all cultures.

The Social Interaction Theory of Emotion

The Social Interaction Theory[8] acknowledges that biology affects emotion and emotional expression. However, proponents of this theory are also interested in how people interact with social situations before, during, and after the experience of emotion. In this way, the theory adds social factors, like interactions with others, to the biological basis for explaining emotion.

Let's say that Catherine finds out on Tuesday that her best friend, Lita, is having a party on Friday. Lita hasn't invited Catherine. The Social Interaction Theory is interested in the following questions: What elements contribute to how Catherine feels about being left off the guest list? That is, do any contextual elements affect her experience of emotion? For example, if Catherine's birthday is coming up, she might think Lita is giving her a surprise party. The Biological Theory of emotion considers these questions unimportant, but they are central to the Social Interaction Theory.

Like the Biological Theory, the Social Interaction Theory talks about gesture. However, the Social Interaction Theory focuses on how the reactions of others

Table 7.2 /// The Biological and Social Theories of Emotion

	The Biological Theory	The Social Interaction Theory
Definition of emotion	Biological processes	Feeling states resulting from social encounters and interactions
Relationship of emotions to cognitions	Separate	Interrelated
Assumption of universality	Yes	No
Concern with subjective meaning	No	Yes

to our gestures help us define what we are feeling. Let's say that Catherine tells another friend, Alex, about not being invited to the party, and she starts to cry. Alex interprets Catherine's tears as a manifestation of anger, saying to Catherine, "You must be really mad!" Catherine hears this and agrees, "Yes, I can't believe that jerk didn't invite me after all the times she's been to my parties!" Catherine's sense of her own emotional experience may have been confused before she talked to Alex, but his interpretation swayed her and influenced how she labeled her emotion. Further, because the Social Interaction Theory is focused on context and interpretation within a specific cultural milieu, this theory does not argue that emotions and emotional expressions are universal. See Table 7.2 for a comparison of the Biological and Social Interaction theories.

 **Theory-Into-Practice (TIP)**

Social Interaction Theory/Biological Theory

What kinds of questions would you ask using the Social Interaction Theory of emotion if you wanted to understand how you felt after breaking up with a significant other? How would these questions differ from those you'd ask using the Biological Theory?

Now that we have defined emotion and discussed two theories that help us understand it, we are ready to address our primary concern in this chapter: how emotion relates to interpersonal communication. As you probably guessed, this focus leads us in the direction of the Social Interaction Theory rather than the Biological Theory.

7–3 EMOTION AND COMMUNICATION

Emotion clearly affects interpersonal communication. It influences how we talk to others, how others hear what we say and vice versa, as well as how our communication affects our relational outcomes. For example, people who feel betrayed by a relational partner have many communication choices to express their feelings. Consider the following dialogue:

Aaron: (*Red-faced and yelling*): "Asha, you've been lying to me about your plans for next year! I can't believe you'd do that. You led me to believe you'd go to grad school wherever I went, and now I find out you've accepted an offer in Canada!"

Asha: "I know. I didn't tell you before because I knew you'd start yelling like this."

Aaron: (*Still yelling*): "Great. How am I supposed to react? (*Takes a step closer to Asha*) I can't think of anything else to do!! I've been planning for a life with you and you've been going a completely different way!"

Asha: "Please calm down—we can talk about this."

Aaron: (*Coming even closer*) "Don't tell me to calm down! I'm done with talking about this." (*Turns and walks away, slamming the door*)

Obviously, Aaron has chosen one way to express his disappointment and feelings of betrayal. How do you think that will affect Aaron and Asha's relationship? What other options does Aaron have?

Interpersonal communication can be influenced by the feelings of those around us through **emotional contagion**, or the process of transferring emotion from one person to another. Emotional contagion occurs when one person's feelings "infect" those around them. You have probably experienced emotional contagion yourself. Think of a time when you were with a friend who communicated in a nervous manner. Did you find yourself becoming nervous too, just watching her fidget? Or you may have become depressed yourself after spending time with a friend who expressed that they were down in the dumps. Conversely, if you are around someone who expresses positive feelings, you usually find your own mood brightening and your communication becoming more upbeat. This is called **emotional afterglow**.[9]

In examining the relationship between interpersonal communication and emotion, we need to clarify several terms. **Emotional experience** refers to feeling emotion and thus is intrapersonal in nature (Jorie felt nervous before her interview). **Emotional effects** relate to how emotional experience impacts communication behavior (when Sophie ran into her friend Laura at the mall and accidentally called her Deanna, the name of another friend, Sophie was so embarrassed and flustered that she was unable to conduct the rest of the conversation with Laura without stammering and stuttering). **Communicating emotionally** suggests that the emotion itself is a part of the way the message is delivered (Roberto yells at his wife, Tess, telling her that she is making them late for their dinner reservations). **Emotional communication** means actually talking about the experience of emotion to someone else (Dean told Patrick how he was feeling about the possibility of adopting a child as a single dad). Clarifying these terms allows us to see the myriad ways that emotion and interpersonal communication intersect. In this chapter, we consider *emotional communication* and *communicating emotionally* together and refer to them as **emotional expression**. When we engage in emotional communication, we need a vocabulary to express the emotion we are experiencing. So, the first part of this section focuses on the metaphors used in the United States to articulate feelings. The second part of this section discusses how verbal and nonverbal cues are used in emotional expression.

Metaphors for Emotion

People often employ figurative language, especially metaphors, to talk about abstract ideas such as emotion. Metaphors may help people communicate complicated emotions that are difficult to express in literal language. We use metaphoric language to distinguish among various emotions as well as to clarify "the subtle variations in a speaker's emotional state (e.g., *get hot under the collar* refers to [a] less intense state of anger than does *blow your stack*)" (p. 3).[10] Table 7.3 lists some common metaphors for emotions used in the United States.

Table 7.3 /// Common Metaphors for Emotions	
Anger	
A hot fluid in a container	"She is boiling with anger."
A fire	"He is doing a slow burn."
Mental illness	"George was insane with rage."
A burden	"Tamara carries her anger around with her."
A natural force	"It was a stormy relationship."
A physical annoyance	"He's a pain in the neck."
Fear	
A hidden enemy	"Fear crept up on him."
A tormentor	"My mother was tortured by fears."
A natural force	"Mia was engulfed by fear."
An illness	"Jeff was sick with fright."
Happiness	
Up	"We had to cheer him up."
Being in heaven	"That was heaven on earth."
Light	"Miguel brightened up at the news."
Warm	"Your thoughtfulness warmed my spirits."
An animal that lives well	"Amy looks like the cat that ate the canary."
A pleasurable physical sensation	"I was tickled pink."
Sadness	
Down	"He brought me down with what he said."
Dark	"Phil is in a dark mood."
A natural force	"Waves of depression swept over Todd."
An illness	"Lora was heartsick."
A physical force	"The realization was a terrible blow."

Source: Adapted from Kovecses, Z. (2000). *Metaphor and emotion: Language, culture, and body in human feeling.* Cambridge, England: Cambridge University Press.

Much of the figurative language for emotion in English implies that emotion has a presence independent of the person experiencing it—as in the phrase "she succumbed to depression." Emotions are frequently framed as opponents ("he struggled with his feelings") or as wild animals ("she felt unbridled passion"). We speak of guilt as something that "haunts" us, fear as something that "grips" us, and anger as something that "overtakes" us.

Although these phrases are evocative of the feelings that various emotions engender, they leave the impression that people are not responsible for their emotion—that is, that people are acted upon by emotional forces beyond their control. This way of talking about emotion fits in with our earlier discussion of the division between emotion and reason. Such language depicts emotion as something that can make us lose our minds completely as we are overwhelmed by forces beyond our rational control. But, as we've mentioned, this dualism fails to stand up to the research illustrating the many ways emotion and reason are intertwined.

 IPC Voice: Heather

It's interesting to think about metaphors for emotion, and it's true that a lot of them seem to make the person powerless over them. But, honestly, that's often how I feel when I am emotional. It is a lot like something taking over me. Sometimes when I'm arguing with my sister, I do see red flash before my eyes and I can't even remember what I said afterward. When I get angry I lose control. I've had to do a lot of apologizing because of that.

Cues for Emotional Expression

As we discussed in Chapters 4 and 5, verbal and nonverbal cues form our communication tools. In this section, we'll briefly discuss nonverbal and verbal cues that we use for emotional expression. We'll also discuss how people use combinations of these cues.

Nonverbal Cues

Facial expressions are obviously one of the most important means for communicating emotion. Perhaps the most researched facial expression is the smile. Smiles usually indicate warmth and friendliness, but, as we mentioned in Chapter 5, smiles can be interpreted to mean something other than positive emotion. For example, Brooke's boss, Melanie, often uses a smile as a mocking gesture. Therefore, when Melanie approaches Brooke's office with a smile on her face, Brooke feels nervous and braces herself for some type of unpleasant interaction. Further, nonverbal cues can mean more than one thing at the same time. So, a smile you receive from the host when you arrive at a holiday party may be an expression of genuine happiness in seeing you as well as a part of a well-learned greeting ritual.

Although it is not as well researched as the face, the voice is probably equally important in conveying emotion. How loudly people talk, how high pitched their tone is, how fast they talk, how many pauses they take, and so forth all provide

The face is one of the most emotionally expressive parts of the human body.

clues to emotion. In addition, the tone of a person's voice can offer clues to whether the emotion they are expressing is positive or negative. For example, when Jack calls his coworker Theo one morning before work, Theo can tell right away by the way Jack says "hello" that something is wrong. Before Jack explains his problem verbally, Theo is cued by the tone in Jack's voice.

Emotion is *embodied*. This means that "people scratch their heads, clench their fists, shake, gesture wildly, hug themselves, pace the floor, lean forward, fidget in their seats, walk heavily, jump up and down, slump, or freeze in their tracks"[11] when they're communicating emotion. However, there isn't a great deal of research on gestures and body movement as they relate to emotion.

One study investigated how caregivers can communicate compassion nonverbally through place and time codes. Caregivers stated that they tried to show compassion to patients by being on time to see them and by structuring the environment so that the temperature is comfortable and so forth. One obstetrician in this study said that an environmental concern was organizing appointments so that pregnant women weren't coming into the office at the same time as women struggling with fertility issues.[12]

Verbal Cues

It is often the case that people fail to state a specific emotion directly. Instead, they use indirect cues. For example, Gabe guesses that Russ is angry with him when Russ calls Gabe an idiot and tells him that he wants to be alone. Russ doesn't tell Gabe any direct information about his emotion, but calling him a name and saying that he wants to be by himself are indirect verbal indicators of Russ's emotional state. In this way, people fail to use *emotional communication* (talking to another about feelings) but rather *communicate emotionally* (demonstrate emotions in the way they communicate).

This leaves listeners in the rather tricky position of inferring others' emotional states. For instance, let's say that Isabella invites Ruth over for dinner, and Ruth shows up 20 minutes late. When Isabella greets Ruth by saying sarcastically, "Nice of you to show up on time," Ruth gets the idea that Isabella is angry, but she also has the option of interpreting Isabella's comment literally. Or Ruth could choose to believe that Isabella isn't angry at her, but just generally irritated. Ruth perhaps should know that being late could cause Isabella to be annoyed with her, but because Isabella is indirect, Ruth is free to make an inference that there's another emotion or reason involved in Isabella's greeting. Later in this chapter, we discuss using I-messages to verbalize emotions, which can prevent the confusion that might result from indirect communication.

Combinations of Cues

Verbal and nonverbal cues can be discussed separately, but in practice, people usually express emotion through a mixture of cues. People often use verbal and vocal cues while gesturing and displaying facial expressions. For example, when Dwight surprises Pat with a vacation to Acapulco, Pat tells him that she's happy in a high-pitched voice while grinning and giving him a hug. Sometimes, however, cues are conflicting or incongruent. When Sandy tells her son, Jake, that she is angry that he hasn't put away all his toys, but she laughs indulgently, her nonverbal and verbal communication conflict with each other. Especially in cases of conflicting cues, people rely on other information to try to discern meaning. We discuss some of these other influences in the following section.

IPC Praxis

Think about the ways you express emotion. How do you use verbal and nonverbal cues (or combinations) to externalize what you're feeling? Think about a particular time you felt you did an effective job of letting someone know how you felt and then think about a time when the opposite occurred. Can you recall anything you did differently in those two instances in terms of verbal and nonverbal cues? Do you think those differences made the difference between you feeling effective or ineffective?

7–4 INFLUENCES ON EMOTIONAL EXPRESSION

Emotional expression is influenced by several factors, including meta-emotion, culture, sex, and context. We will discuss each of these influences briefly in the following sections.

Meta-Emotion

How people communicate about emotion is influenced by a related topic: meta-emotion. **Meta-emotion** means emotion about emotion. People who study emotion tend to focus on specific emotions, without paying much attention to how people feel about expressing them. For example, in the case of anger, "some people are ashamed or upset about becoming angry, others feel good about their capacity to express anger, and still others think of anger as natural, neither good nor bad."[13] In other words, feeling emotion may engender another emotion.

Differences in the effects of communicating emotion may result in part because of meta-emotion. Let's compare two couples who each have been dating for a year: Andrea and José, and Marla and Leo. Andrea's expression of love for José is accompanied by the meta-emotion of pride. She is proud of her ability to engage in a committed relationship. José feels the same way. On the other hand, when Marla expresses love to Leo, she experiences the meta-emotion shame for becoming so vulnerable in a relationship. Communication transactions between Andrea and José will likely differ significantly from those between Marla and Leo because of their meta-emotion; one couple is proud of their commitment whereas one person in the other couple (i.e., Marla) feels shame.

Culture

Remember from our discussion of the Biological Theory of emotion that Darwin asserted that emotions are primarily universal—that is, people of all cultures respond to the same emotions in the same way. That assertion has been called into question, however. Although some emotional states and expressions—such as joy, anger, and fear—might be universal, the current focus of research is on differences in emotional expression across cultures. As we've discussed throughout this text, culture is an important influence on most communication behaviors. The brief review in this section gives you an overview of how different cultures think about emotion and how emotion is communicated in various cultures.

Cultures differ in how much they think and talk about emotion. One study demonstrates, for example, that while English and Arabic languages both have the ability to translate words for emotions (such as *happiness, sadness, fear, anger, embarrassment*), these translations do not provide equivalent definitions for their native speakers. Further, English and Arabic speakers identified different facial expressions for the same emotion word. The meanings of these emotions tended to vary by culture although the translation made it seem as though the two languages were talking about the same emotion. Further, the only emotion out of 12 that were tested that was equivalent across the two languages was *happiness* (English) or *farah* (Arabic).[14]

Additionally, 95% of Chinese parents say their children understand the meaning of *shame* or *xiu* by age 3, whereas only 10% of U.S. parents say their children do. Because of this difference, it would seem that shame plays a more important role in Chinese culture than it does in U.S. culture.[15] Yet, one study found that Chinese respondents suffered less from shame after engaging in deception than did U.S. respondents.[16] One explanation for this difference might be that deception is more acceptable in China than it is in the United States. Another explanation might be that U.S. and Chinese respondents defined shame differently. It may be that collectivist cultures (like China) conceptualize shame as more publicly shared and less threatening than do individualistic cultures (like the United States). It is important to consider not just the emotion but also what triggers the emotion and how the emotion is framed within the culture.

There's also some evidence that the Chinese think less about love than do people in the United States. Furthermore, when the Chinese do think of love, they have a cluster of words to describe "sad-love," or love that does not succeed; such words are absent in the vocabulary of those in the United States. In the Japanese culture love is also thought about differently than in the United States. In Japanese stories, when a conflict exists between a couple and the families of the couple, it is resolved in favor of the families, even when that means the couple has to leave each other. In Japan, stories that end with the lovers separating because of family objections are celebrated as showing the right way to resolve this problem. In contrast, in the United States and other Western European cultures, many of the stories in books, magazines, and

Culture is one of the most important influences on emotional expression because different cultures think differently about emotion, as well as have different norms for expressing it.

movies end with the couple staying together against the wishes of their families. In these cultures, listeners cheer the lovers on, enjoying the triumph of romantic love.

People of different cultures express emotion differently. For instance, people from warmer climates have been found to be more emotionally expressive than those from colder climates. In addition, people from collectivistic cultures (such as Korea, China, and Japan) are discouraged from expressing negative feelings for fear of their effect on the overall harmony of the community. Thus, people from these cultures are less inclined to express negative feelings. This does not mean that people from collectivistic cultures do not have negative feelings; it simply means that emotional restraint in communication is a shared cultural value. People from individualistic cultures like the United States have no such cultural value—in fact, emotional openness is valued—so they are more expressive of negative emotions.

Sex

Sex differences in communication (as well as other behaviors) are widely researched. In the United States as well as other countries such as India and Japan, many activities are divided according to sex, so people are interested in the ways in which men and women are presumed to differ. For example, although sex roles remain in flux in the United States, for couples with children, parenting is still seen as primarily the responsibility of women. And, in heterosexual couples, working to pay the bills still is seen as primarily men's responsibility. The two sexes are expected to do different things and have different strengths in the workplace and at home. In this section, we first review research that examines emotion and sex-role stereotypes and then we explore research on the expression of emotion and sex.

Emotion and Sex-Role Stereotypes

Of course, the stereotypical view holds that women are more emotional, more emotionally expressive, and more attuned to the emotions of others than are men.

One Dutch researcher wonders why women are thought to be the emotional sex while men are perceived to be unemotional. She asserts:

> As far back as I can remember I have encountered emotional men; indeed, I have met more emotional men than emotional women. My father could not control his nerves while watching our national sports heroes on television (which made watching hardly bearable); my uncle immediately got damp eyes on hearing the first note of the Dutch national anthem; a friend would lock himself in his room for days when angry; a teacher at school once got so furious that he dragged a pupil out of the class room and hung him up by his clothes on a coat-hook; one of the male managers at our institute was only able to prevent having a nervous breakdown by rigidly trying to exercise total control over his environment; and a male colleague's constant embarrassment in public situations forced him to avoid such settings altogether. (p. ix)[17]

Our point isn't that men are *more* emotional than women. Rather, it's that all the examples of men expressing emotion go unnoticed because they don't support the stereotype we have of men as unemotional.

This notion is further refined in a review of research on masculinity, tears, and sport in North America. Men definitely express emotion through crying, and they do so in the most masculine of arenas: athletics. The goal of the review is to explain how this can be the case when the stereotype of masculinity suggests that tears should be taboo. The conclusion is that it's not the absence of emotional expression that makes a man masculine, but rather the "correct" expression of emotion. Correct expression of emotion for men is passionate and controlled, and it can include crying as long as it is done in "the right way." What constitutes the right way is nuanced, and it depends on several factors such as whether the player was responsible for the team's loss, whether the player is retiring, and so forth. The researchers conclude that perhaps the most important factor is that the player should never cry in a way that is deemed feminine. According to this research, the former San Francisco 49ers' running back, Derek Loville, cried correctly and Tim Tebow did not.[18]

Emotional Expression and Sex

Researchers are interested in the differences between men and women in nonverbal expressions of emotion, as well as in their abilities in decoding emotional expression. Three differences are well documented and may be caused by men and women conforming to stereotyped sex roles. First, women smile more than men in social situations. Second, men and women also differ in nonverbal expressiveness, or facial animation and the liveliness of gestures. Again, women tend to demonstrate their emotional states by using more nonverbal cues than men do. Finally, women are also more accurate than men in figuring out what others' emotional states are based on nonverbal cues.

Scholars have also investigated sex differences in the verbal expression of emotional support to others. In general, men are less likely to give emotional support to a person in distress, and when they do provide it, they are less focused on emotion and less person centered than women. The results of one study suggest that men provide poorer emotional support than women because they see good emotional support as not fitting a masculine identity.[19]

Men express emotion regularly, although this may go unnoticed because of the gender role stereotype of males being unemotional.

Research indicates that women tend to demonstrate emotional states through nuanced nonverbal cues.

As people age, these stereotypes seem to exert less influence on their behaviors. Men tend to become more emotionally expressive, and women become more instrumental or task oriented. A study of 20 married couples over the age of 60 who had been married for an average of 42 years shows this change. The researchers interviewing the couples found the men to be expressive about their emotions (saying things like they fell in love with their wives at first sight and reporting how nervous they'd been to meet her parents), whereas wives were more matter-of-fact in their accounts.[20]

Some research suggests that women are associated with the expression of specific emotions (happiness, sadness, and fear), while men are seen as expressing the emotions of pride and anger. Thus, women and men may be equally emotionally expressive, but just associated with different emotions. In addition, emotional expression is moderated by at least three variables: cultural norms (i.e., what the culture says is appropriate behavior for men and women), social role (i.e., government officials, police officers, and health care providers should express emotion as their role prescribes regardless of the sex of the person occupying the role), and emotional intensity (i.e., how strongly the emotion is felt). Women may express more emotion than men, but not necessarily feel more emotion than men. Finally, the preponderance of research driving these conclusions has been performed on young, white, highly educated men and women, so the results may not generalize beyond this population.

Context

The contexts in which we express emotion are infinite: We express emotion at work, with friends, in our families, at school, over the phone, in person, and so on. We discuss two specific contexts here: historical period and electronic media.

Historical Period

The book *American Cool* traces the changes in emotional communication in the United States from the Victorian period (beginning approximately in the 1830s) to the 1960s. The main thesis is that the Victorians were much more emotionally expressive than U.S. citizens of the 1960s. North Americans in the 1960s favored "cool" over the emotional excesses of the Victorians. This is because culture is governed by **feeling rules**, or the norms a culture develops to instruct people in expressing their own emotions and reacting when others express emotions. The feeling rules of U.S. culture changed considerably from the Victorian period to the 1960s.

In the 1890s, men in the United States were instructed to express their anger. However, 70 years later, child-rearing experts warned parents not to encourage boys to express anger, arguing that an angry man is possessed by the devil. In the area of romantic love, Victorian men were also encouraged to be expressive, in contrast to the 1960s vision of males as primarily sexual and silent in love relationships. A love letter written by a man of the Victorian era illustrates the flowery emotional expression that was the cultural norm:

> I don't love you and marry you to promote my happiness. To love you, to marry you is a mighty END in itself. . . . I marry you because my own inmost being mingles with your being and is already married to it, both joined in one by God's own voice.[21]

Obviously, a man in Victorian times would be influenced by the feeling rules of his time and would express himself much differently than a man of the 1960s, who would be equally influenced by a very different set of feeling rules. Today, we have different feeling rules as well, although the influence of "cool" is still strong in contemporary U.S. society.

IPC Praxis

Describe the contemporary feeling rules of your home culture. How do these rules affect the way you express emotion? Give a few specific examples of feeling rules and their impact on interpersonal communication.

Electronic Media

As we discussed in Chapter 1, the channel for a communication transaction influences the communication. Because more and more of our communication time is spent in electronic communication or on social media, online emotional expression is a worthwhile subject of study. In the past, media like texts that are print only have been seen as somewhat impoverished forms of communication because they lack the nonverbal dimension that's so important for emotional expression. The emoticon is one way that users of social media express nonverbal communication online. **Emoticons** are icons that can be typed on the keyboard to express emotions. They are used to compensate for the lack of nonverbal cues online, and are sometimes called *quasi-nonverbal communication*. Most Western emoticons look like a face (eyes, nose, and mouth) when rotated 90 degrees clockwise. Emoticons originating in East Asia are usually interpreted without rotation and can incorporate nonstandard characters. Table 7.4 presents examples of commonly used emoticons and their translations.

Table 7.4 /// Emoticons

Common Western Emoticons	
:) :-) :] =) :D xD	Happiness, sarcasm, laughing, or a joke
: (:-(:[>: (:'(	Unhappiness, sadness, or disapproval
:| :-| :-\ :-/	Indifference, confusion, or skepticism
:-P ;-) ;-P :3	Cute, playful, or joking
Common Eastern Emoticons	
(^_^) (^-^) (^o^)	Happiness, sarcasm, laughing, or a joke
(>_<) (;_;) (._.)	Unhappiness, sadness, or disapproval
('_>') (¬_¬) O_o	Indifference, confusion, or skepticism
(~_^) (^_~) ('•ω•')	Cute, playful, or joking

Additionally, graphical emoticons (**emojis**) have been used to express emotion in texts and blogs among other online communications. Emojis can be used to differentiate similar emotions within a text. For instance, the verbal statement "The class I just left wasn't good" accompanied by two different emojis could convey two different emotional meanings. Figure 7.4 presents common emojis available on Apple phones.

Some researchers argue that when people are experienced users of social media, it is just as rich a communication process as any other, including face to face. Furthermore, communication online doesn't necessarily inhibit emotional expression; one study found that 27% of the total message content online consisted of emotion.[22] In a debate on the opinion pages in *The New York Times* online, Sherry Turkle quotes a student who observed that "technology makes emotions easy." Turkle thinks the student meant that it is easy to edit oneself online, and she observes that the opposite is true of face-to-face communication. Off-line, Turkle argues, emotions aren't easy; they are risky. She states that "without the benefit of editing, we are more likely to show ourselves as we are, not as who we want to be."[23] However, in the same forum, Alice Marwick observes that "the lack of depth in some online-only friendships . . . doesn't mean they exist outside human emotion. Instagram 'Likes' or Twitter 'Favorites' can be powerful reinforcement mechanisms for engagement." Marwick also asserts that very negative emotion is expressed in aggressive arguments represented in comments sections online. Overall, Marwick believes that when we interact with others online, those interactions invoke deep emotion and we find ways to express that.[24]

Figure 7.4 /// Emojis

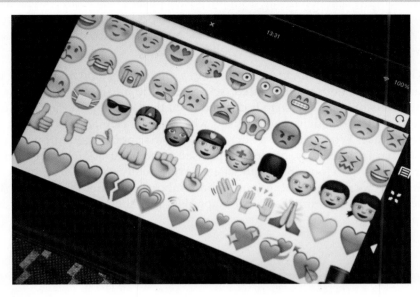

Source: Jeffrey Blackler/Alamy.

Other researchers agree, noting that emoticons and emojis are used extensively on blogs to allow for emotional "venting."[25] Further, some research finds that different online platforms are perceived to be more or less appropriate for expressing certain types of emotion. One study[26] specifically examined norms for expressing emotion on social media. Study participants (who were ages 15–25 years old) reported that Twitter was the platform least appropriate for expressing positive emotions, and Instagram was the least appropriate platform for expressing negative emotions, although there was an overall bias for positive emotions in general across platforms. These findings help to explain some of the vitriolic tweets found on Twitter as well as the commonly reported depression resulting from viewing others' perfectly filtered photos on Instagram. Overall, electronic media seem to provide a context for emotional expression.

7–5 RECOGNIZING BLENDS IN EMOTIONAL COMMUNICATION

As we discussed earlier in this chapter, our definition of emotion depends on the notion of process. Although we have names for discrete emotions such as fear, sadness, pride, ecstasy, and so forth, emotion is often experienced as a blend that involves cycling through several emotions. *Strategic embarrassment* is an example of an emotional blend. Although embarrassment is an unpleasant emotional state, people sometimes plan embarrassing situations for others, and creating an embarrassing moment for someone else is often socially acceptable. For example, it's a common practice among adolescents to use strategic embarrassment in the following way: Tom knows that his friend Jesús is interested in Jessica.

Video 7.3

He also knows that Jesús is shy and won't introduce himself to her. As Jessica and Jesús pass in the school hallway, Tom purposely pushes Jesús into Jessica. Jesús is embarrassed, but he recognizes that Tom actually has helped him connect with Jessica, producing a blend of emotion. Jesús is angry, grateful, and embarrassed all at the same time.

The German word *schadenfreude* illustrates another way of thinking of emotion as blended. Loosely translated, schadenfreude means to take pleasure in another's misfortune. The term is derived from the German words for "damage" and "joy." Often schadenfreude is used when we see rich and powerful people fall from grace. When the most successful, popular person in a group is found to be failing in some way, others are pleased to see that failure after having to admire them for so long. But even when we're actually sorry for someone else's bad fortune, we may also experience a little mixture of relief that we didn't suffer the same fate or a small sliver of happiness that they finally fell after being on top for so long.

 IPC Around Us

Spencer Platt/Getty Images News/Getty Images

In an article for *Quartz*,[27] Rebecca Schuman notes that 2017 was a year singularly lacking in humor in the United States, and throughout the world. Schuman does find some humor, however, in the feeling of schadenfreude. She argues that schadenfreude allows her to laugh while watching powerful men like Roy Moore, Louis C.K., Michael Flynn, Harvey Weinstein, and others receive their "just deserts." Taking a malicious delight in the justified comeuppance of powerful men was the only humor Schuman found in the events of 2017.

Reflection: *Have you felt schadenfreude yourself either while watching disgraced public figures or while seeing a person you knew get a comeuppance after being admired for a long time? Do you think of schadenfreude as a harmless diversion or a negative emotion?*

Emotional blends also exist when we feel sorrow but yet can see some positive aspects to our pain. One example from a support group for family members of breast cancer patients illustrates the blend of pain and positivity:

> A 20-year-old daughter was tearfully coming to terms with the sudden downhill pre-terminal course of her mother's breast cancer: "I see this black hole opening up in my life. I don't think I will want to live without my Mom. She would stay up at 2 a.m. and talk me through my misery for two hours. She won't be there, but I don't want to make her feel guilty for dying." Her father, also at the family group meeting, held her hand and tried to comfort her, but he clearly was overwhelmed by his own sadness and his lifelong fear of strong emotion and dependency on him by others. The husband of another woman whose breast cancer was progressing rapidly started to comfort her but found his voice choked with emotion: "I am sure you will get through this—there's so much love in your family." "Why are you crying?" the father asked. "I don't know," he replied, and everyone, tearful daughter included, found themselves laughing. (p. 101)[28]

Coming to terms with the pain of her mother's imminent death provides an inkling of positivity in an otherwise overwhelmingly sad situation.

In a similar vein, Jason Rosenthal wrote in *The New York Times* in 2018 about the blend of emotion evoked by his wife's death and the Modern Love essay she published in the *Times* just before she died in 2017. The essay was in the form of a personal ad inviting other women to think about marrying her husband after her death. Rosenthal observes that when he read the draft, he was overwhelmed by how his wife had combined the emotions of unbearable sadness and ironic humor in what she wrote. The essay caused Rosenthal to experience both sadness and gratitude—another blend. He writes that though he misses his wife Amy every day, her grace in writing her essay gave him permission to go on with his life and make the most of his remaining time without her.

The mix of sadness and positive emotion in those examples shows the complex tapestry of emotional expression. Another example of blending in emotional expression can be seen in the communication of forgiveness. Forgiveness, which is based in numerous religious teachings, represents positive emotional communication because it allows for peace and reconciliation. Some research suggests that forgiving provides important benefits for the forgiver as well as the forgiven. Some survivors of mass shootings in the United States have focused on how forgiveness is necessary for them to go on living after losing so much. Shay Makonde was a 16-year-old junior at Marjory Stoneman Douglas High School in Parkland, Florida, in 2018 when a teenage gunman entered and killed 17 people in the school. Makonde says he cannot hate because hatred only breeds pain and more hatred. He wants to be able to forgive for himself and to honor the friends he lost.

Nelson Mandela, the first black president of South Africa and the statesman widely credited with leading the emancipation of the country, freeing blacks from oppressive white rule, died in 2013. The many accounts of his life, written in the immediate aftermath of his death, focused on his amazing ability to forgive. Mandela had been imprisoned by the government for 27 years, had experienced and witnessed enormous brutality, yet he argued for reconciliation and enacted forgiveness in his life and leadership. Roger W. Wilkins, a civil rights activist and history professor at George Mason University, agrees with Mandela, but he recognizes the limits of forgiveness when he reflects on the bombing of the 16th Street Baptist Church in Birmingham, Alabama, in 1963, which killed four young black girls. In 2002, Bobby Frank Cherry was convicted of the bombing deaths and sentenced to life imprisonment. He did not ask for forgiveness and denied his guilt. This makes things complicated because forgiveness requires participation from both sides. In this case, Wilkins suggests that people can purge hatred from their hearts without actually forgiving.

7–6 SKILL SET FOR EMOTIONAL COMMUNICATION

Competence in expressing emotion and in listening and responding to the emotional expression of others is critical to your success as an interpersonal communicator. Lacking this competence is called *alexithymia,* and some research suggests that it's associated with high levels of depression and poor quality romantic relationships. Research finds that people high in alexithymia (i.e., those who are not competent in recognizing and communicating their emotional states) are less capable of developing meaningful relationships with others. Further, those romantic relationships they do develop seem to be of lesser quality. This may be the case because of the person's lesser abilities to communicate empathy, to express affection, and to provide and accept social support.[29] Given the association of negative outcomes with poor emotional expression, it's important to provide several skills for improving competence in emotional communication: acknowledging your feelings, analyzing the situation, owning, reframing, and empathizing. (See Table 7.5.)

Acknowledge Your Feelings

Competence in communicating an emotion begins with your ability to identify the emotion or mix of emotions you are experiencing at a particular time. This skill requires you to do several things:

1. Recognize the emotion you're feeling.

2. Establish that you are stating an emotion.

3. Create a statement that identifies why you are experiencing the emotion. (You may or may not choose to share this statement with anyone else; it is sufficient that you make the statement to yourself.)

Table 7.5 /// Skill Set for Enhancing Emotional Communication	
a. Acknowledge your feelings.	
b. Analyze the situation.	
c. Own your feelings.	
d. Challenge yourself to reframe.	
e. Focus on empathy.	
f. Your skill suggestion	

Recognize the emotion you're feeling.

This step requires you to stop for a moment and ask yourself what your emotional state is at present. In other words, you are to take a time-out from the ongoing process and take your emotional temperature. It is important not to skip this step because it involves making a link between yourself and outer reality. To name your feelings signals how you perceive them and alerts you to what your expectations are. For instance, when you recognize that you are irritable, that tells you that you have less patience than usual, and you may expect others to make allowances for you. The opposite process occurs as well. When you give a feeling a name, you respond to that label, which triggers perceptions and expectations.

This step is difficult for several reasons. First, in the heat of an emotional encounter, you may not be prepared to stop and take a time-out. Second, we are often so detached from our feelings that it's difficult to name them. And third, some people are simply less aware than others of their emotional states.

You need to practice this skill and work on methods to overcome these obstacles. For example, in a highly charged emotional interaction, you can repeat a phrase such as "It's time to take a time-out," or you can make a prior agreement with a relational partner that you will check every half hour to see if a time-out is needed. You might want to list emotions in a journal so that you can consult the list to remind yourself of the variety of emotions you might be experiencing. You can also monitor your physical changes to check for signals of emotion. As we noted in Table 7.1, emotion is often accompanied by physiological conditions such as a hot flush, a lump in the throat, and so on. And you can monitor your thoughts to see how they might relate to feelings.

Establish that you are stating an emotion.

This step in the process provides a check to see that you are really in touch with emotion language. It isn't enough to simply say, "I feel"; you must be sure that what follows really is an emotion. For instance, if you say, "I feel like seeing a ball game," you are stating something you want to do, not an emotion you are experiencing. A phrase highlighting emotion would be "I feel anxious right now. I'm jumpy and uneasy."

Create a statement that identifies why you are feeling the emotion.

This step involves thinking about the antecedent conditions that contextualize your feelings. Ask yourself, "Why do I feel this way?" and "What led to this feeling?" Try to put the reasons into words. For example, statements such as the following form reasons for emotion:

- "I'm angry because I studied hard and got the same grade on the exam that I got when I didn't study."

- "I'm feeling lonely. All my friends went to spend the weekend upstate and left me alone at home because I couldn't take time off from work."

- "I'm feeling really happy, proud, and a little anxious. I finally got the job I wanted, and I worked especially hard to make a good impression at the interview. All the prep work I did paid off. But now I have to actually make good on everything I said I could do!"

- "I'm feeling guilty. I told my boyfriend I couldn't see him tonight because I had to study, but I really just felt like having a night to myself."

Going through this exercise should help you clarify why you are experiencing a particular emotion or emotional mix. It also should point you in a direction to change something if you wish to. For instance, if you wish to reduce your guilt, tell your boyfriend that you need some time to yourself occasionally without having to give him a reason.

Analyze the Situation

After identifying your emotion, analyze the situation by asking yourself these questions:

1. **Do you wish to share your emotion with others?** Some emotional experiences are not ready for communication—that is, you may not completely understand the emotion yet or you may feel that you would quickly slide into conflict if you communicated the emotion. Or, you might decide that you are comfortable with the emotion and that you don't ever need to share it. For example, if you are looking through your high school yearbook and feel nostalgia for the time you spent there, you might enjoy your memories and not feel the need to talk about that with anyone. If you wake up early one morning and experience a beautiful sunrise, you may feel joy without needing to tell anyone about it.

2. **Is the time appropriate for sharing?** If you decide you want to communicate an emotion to someone else, an analysis of the situation helps you decide if the time is right. If your partner is under a great deal of stress at work, you may want to wait until the situation improves before talking about your unhappiness at how little time you spend together. If you just found out you are pregnant with a wanted baby and your best friend has recently suffered a miscarriage, you also might decide to wait to share your joy.

3. **How should you approach the communication?** Analyzing the situation helps you think about how to share your emotion. If you are angry with your boss, you need to consider if you should express it, and if so, how to express your anger. Obviously, anger at a boss and anger at a partner provide entirely different situational constraints. Because the workplace climate is not conducive to emotional communication, you may decide not to tell your boss how you feel even though you would like to do so.

4. **Is there anything you can do to change the situation if needed?** Your analysis allows you to think about how and whether to change the situation. In the case of a workplace issue, you might consider instituting new norms at work, accepting the way things are, or looking for a new job.

Own Your Feelings

As we discussed in Chapter 4, **owning** is the skill of verbally taking responsibility for your feelings, and is often accomplished by sending **I-messages**. These messages show that speakers understand their feelings belong to them and aren't caused by someone else. For skillful emotional communication, I-messages take the following form:

"I feel _____ when you _____, and I would like _____."

For example, let's say that Ashleigh is unhappy that her boyfriend, Charles, spends more time with his buddies than with her. Ashleigh's I-message would be something like the following:

> "I feel unhappy when you spend four nights a week with your friends, and I would like you to spend one of those nights with me."

I-messages differ from you-messages, in which I place the responsibility for my feelings on you. If Ashleigh had sent a you-message to Charles, she might have said:

> "You are so inconsiderate. All you do is hang with your friends. I can't believe I'm staying with you!"

IPC Careers

I-Messages and the Teaching Profession

As Kelly Cherwin[30] asserts, effective teaching may depend just as much on a teacher's emotional intelligence as it does on the teacher's intellectual prowess. One reason that this is the case, according to Cherwin, is because "not every student learns through the same methods, is motivated in the same manner, or acts in the same way in a classroom (live or online). So, it seems apparent that recognizing differences in teaching and learning styles, as well as being able to connect with your students, is important to produce a beneficial outcome" (para. 1).

iStock.com/monkeybusinessimages

One skill that Cherwin advocates is the use of I-messages. She acknowledges that when teaching, it's inevitable that a teacher will become frustrated or upset. Teachers need to learn to manage these emotions and not demonstrate visible anger toward their students. They also need to take responsibility for their emotions and not blame their students. Cherwin argues that one way to do this is to focus on *I* rather than *you* when making statements about the emotional situation. She states, "For example, instead of saying, 'You are not working hard enough to understand this concept,' say, 'I am confused about what is making this concept difficult to understand. Let's try together to understand what is not making sense'" (para. 4). Cherwin concludes that if teachers can master the art of managing their emotions and using I-messages, they will avoid putting their students on the defensive, which should help them open their minds and increase their learning.

Reflection: How would you react if a teacher of yours used this technique with you? Do you think you would appreciate having a teacher focus on you in this manner? Why or why not?

You can see that Charles's reaction might be more positive to the I-message than to the you-message. Using I-messages does not guarantee that you will get what you ask for, however. Charles could still tell Ashleigh that he wants to spend four nights with his friends. But I-messages help to ensure that Charles hears what Ashleigh wants and that he doesn't get sidetracked into a defensive spiral where he argues with her characterization of him as inconsiderate. The I-message focuses on Ashleigh's emotion, which is what she wants to talk about with Charles. Although sometimes it is useful to deviate from I-messages, they are a helpful skill to have in your repertoire.

Challenge Yourself to Reframe

Reframing refers to the ability to change the frame surrounding a situation to put it in a more productive light. For instance, you might think about someone who upset you with a critical comment as a person who's having a bad day rather than a totally insensitive person. When Stephen got cut off by a driver on the freeway, he tried to reframe by thinking of the other driver as on their way to some emergency instead of an inconsiderate jerk. It's easier for us to reframe our own thinking about something than it is to change the world. After you discover what makes you mad, you can reframe those irritants by changing the messages you give yourself. If you think of other people as rude, that frame may cause hostility. If you change the frame to respecting yourself for being polite, you will probably feel less anger and hostility.

Focus on Empathy

As we discussed in Chapter 6, empathy is the ability to put yourself in another's place so you are able to understand their point of view. Empathy is dependent, to a degree, on trust. In addition, people tend to empathize more easily when they agree with the other. That is, it's more likely you can be empathetic if you readily grasp the other's perspective and it makes sense to you. It's more difficult to empathize if you think the other person is completely wrong.

In interpersonal communication, empathy is often accomplished through the skill of *active listening*, which calls for you to suspend your own responses for a while so you can concentrate on the other person. In active listening, you usually allow the other person a full hearing (no interruptions), and when it's your turn, you say something like "You sound really troubled by your relationship with your dad. Tell me more about how you're feeling." Sometimes people find active listening difficult to do and comment that repeating back what you've heard sounds corny. But, you can find ways to express empathy that don't sound phony or false, and however you express it, empathy is a valuable skill. People experiencing strong emotion usually feel the benefits of empathy. When Tommy comes storming into his fraternity house, throwing his books on the table, and swearing about his problems with his girlfriend, Chloe, he would probably appreciate it if someone listened to him with empathy.

Often, our response to hearing someone's emotional outburst is to attempt to solve the problem ("Here's what you should say to her the next time you see her"), question the person ("How long has she been acting like this?"), tell a story about a similar problem that you have had ("Hey, I know just how you feel; my ex-girlfriend did the same thing! That's why I dumped her"), or evaluate the person's problem ("You know, all couples fight—it's not that big a deal"). Although some of those responses might prove useful later, empathizing is usually the best first approach because it keeps the focus on the person who is expressing the emotion and allows them to set the pace and the content of the conversation. In this way, that person can explore how they really feel while you lend a listening ear.

These skills take practice and require sensitivity to know when and how to apply them. There's no one prescription that will work in all instances. Still, it is the case that knowing your feelings, recognizing your emotion, being able to identify reasons for your emotion, phrasing an emotion statement, analyzing the situation, owning, reframing, and empathizing all contribute to your interpersonal communication competence in emotional encounters.

/// CHAPTER WRAP-UP

In this chapter, we discussed a critically important component of interpersonal communication, but one that is often ignored in teaching and scholarship: emotion. Emotion affects how people speak as well as how they interpret what others say. In this way, emotion plays a major role in the interpersonal communication process. We advanced a definition of emotion and examined two category systems that help us understand emotion. We then interrogated the classic, but erroneous, belief that emotion and reason as well as mind and body are opposites. We investigated two theories (the Biological and Social Interaction theories)

purporting to explain emotion before focusing on several specific ways emotion and interpersonal communication interact. We reviewed how meta-emotion, culture, gender and sex, and context influence emotional expression. Finally, we suggested five skills for improving your effectiveness in emotional expression and interpretation.

As you engage in interpersonal communication, and continue in this class, we hope you grasp how important emotion is to the process. Understanding emotion is a huge step toward becoming a skilled interpersonal communicator.

/// COMMUNICATION ASSESSMENT TEST (CAT): ASSESSING EMOTIONAL INTELLIGENCE

This self-assessment is composed of four sections with 10 statements in each section. Rank each of the following statements in terms of how much it applies to you using this scale:

0 = never, 1 = rarely, 2 = sometimes, 3 = often, 4 = always

There are no "right" answers. Be as honest as you can.

Emotional Awareness

1. _____ My feelings are clear to me at any given moment.

2. _____ Emotions play an important part in my life.

3. _____ My moods impact the people around me.

4. _____ I find it easy to put words to my feelings.

5. _____ My moods are easily affected by external events.

6. _____ I can easily sense when I'm going to be angry.

7. _____ I readily tell others my true feelings.

8. _____ I find it easy to describe my feelings.

9. _____ Even when I'm upset, I'm aware of what's happening to me.

10. _____ I am able to stand apart from my thoughts and feelings and examine them.

Section Total: _____

Emotional Management

1. _____ I accept responsibility for my reactions.
2. _____ I find it easy to make goals and stick with them.
3. _____ I am an emotionally balanced person.
4. _____ I am a very patient person.
5. _____ I can accept critical comments from others without becoming angry.
6. _____ I maintain my composure even during stressful times.
7. _____ If an issue doesn't affect me directly, I don't let it bother me.
8. _____ I can restrain myself when I feel anger toward someone.
9. _____ I control urges to overindulge in things that could damage my well-being.
10. _____ I direct my energy into creative work or hobbies.

Section Total: _____

Social Emotional Awareness

1. _____ I consider the impact of my decisions on other people.
2. _____ I can tell easily if the people around me are becoming annoyed.
3. _____ I sense when a person's mood changes.
4. _____ I am able to be supportive when giving bad news to others.
5. _____ I am able to understand the way others feel.
6. _____ My friends tell me intimate things about themselves.
7. _____ It genuinely bothers me to see other people suffer.
8. _____ I usually know when to speak and when to be silent.
9. _____ I care what happens to other people.
10. _____ I understand when people's plans change.

Section Total: _____

Relationship Management

1. _____ I am able to show affection.
2. _____ My relationships are safe places for me.
3. _____ I find it easy to share my deep feelings with others.
4. _____ I am good at motivating others.
5. _____ I am a fairly cheerful person.
6. _____ It's easy for me to make friends.
7. _____ People tell me I'm sociable and fun.
8. _____ I like helping people.
9. _____ Others can depend on me.
10. _____ I can talk someone down if they're very upset.

Section Total: _____

Scoring:

Compare your totals in each section to the following key:

0–24 = an area for *enrichment.* Requires attention and development.

25–34 = an area of *effective functioning.* Consider strengthening.

35–40 = an area of *enhanced skills.* Use as leverage to develop weaker areas.

Source: Adapted from a model by Paul Mohapel (paul.mohapel@ shaw.ca).

/// KEY TERMS

/// KEY QUESTIONS FOR APPLICATION

1. **CQ/CultureQuest**: Explore the following claim: "As the Social Interaction Theory argues, people of different cultures will think, experience, and communicate emotion differently. There's no such thing as a universal emotion that all cultural groups will respond to in the same way." Do you agree or disagree? Defend your views.

2. **TQ/TechQuest**: Explore the following claim: "Emotion is frequently and easily communicated online. Online communication is not a barrier for expressing emotion." Do you agree or disagree? Defend your views.

3. Emotion is somewhat difficult to define. Do you agree with the definition we've provided? Explain your answer.

4. Provide a metaphor for emotion that wasn't discussed in the chapter. Explain what that metaphor conveys about emotion and emotional expression.

5. In the chapter, we discussed the following influences on emotion: meta-emotion, culture, sex, and context. Can you think of any other influences on emotion and emotional expression? Provide some examples to support your answer.

6. We discussed how some people find that expressing owning through I-messages can sound fake or corny. Do you agree? Why or why not? If you do agree, provide an alternate way to communicate owning.

Access practice quizzes, eFlashcards, video, and multimedia at **edge.sagepub.com/west.**

Visit **edge.sagepub.com/west** to help you accomplish your coursework goals in an easy-to-use learning environment.

SHARING PERSONAL INFORMATION

LEARNING OUTCOMES

After studying this chapter, you will be able to

8–1 Understand the complexity of self-disclosure

8–2 Explain the reasons for engaging and not engaging in self-disclosures

8–3 Identify the effects of individual differences, relational issues, culture, sex and sex role, and channel on self-disclosing

8–4 Describe the principles of self-disclosure

8–5 Present explanations for self-disclosing behavior

8–6 Use a variety of techniques to enhance effectiveness in self-disclosing

iStock.com/hocus-focus

Master the content at
edge.sagepub.com/west

◎SAGE edge™

M ost interpersonal communication scholars believe self-disclosure helps relationships develop, and contributes to strengthening our self-concept, and even our physical health. Relational partners tend to like themselves and each other more after they have self-disclosed to one another. One study showed that when teachers in online classes self-disclosed, it increased their students' sense of their social presence and made the students like them more.[1] Greater disclosure is related to greater emotional involvement in a relationship, and people believe that intimate relationships require important self-disclosures.

> **The following theories/models are discussed in this chapter:**
>
> Johari Window Model
>
> Communication Privacy Management Theory
>
> Social Penetration Theory

You can probably think of a time when a relationship became more intimate after you or your partner shared something personal with each other. Because self-disclosure is so important to our interpersonal relationships, we examine it closely in this chapter. What does it mean to self-disclose? What are the risks? What are the boundaries between private information and information we're willing to make public? How can we become skillful self-disclosers? In this chapter, we'll discuss this exciting, complex interpersonal communication behavior, and provide answers to these questions.

8–1 DEFINITION OF SELF-DISCLOSURE: OPENING UP

Self-disclosure is the process of telling another person personal information, shared intentionally, that they'd have trouble finding out without being told. Statements such as "I think I really like Dan," "I only feel myself with my family," or "I'm disappointed in where I'm at in my career" all may be self-disclosures. Some of these comments reveal descriptive information (i.e., I really like Dan) while others focus on evaluative assessments (i.e., I'm disappointed in myself). Implicit in our definition is the fact that self-disclosures are verbal behaviors. We do reveal information about ourselves nonverbally—for example, by dressing in certain clothes, wearing a wedding ring, or making facial expressions—but these types of revelations don't fit our definition of self-disclosure because they don't have the same intentionality as information we reveal verbally to a specific person. Nonverbal behaviors are more generally sent—for example, everyone we come in contact with sees what we wear. Our definition highlights several important features of self-disclosing, all discussed below: process, intentionality and choice, private information and risk, and trust. In addition, our definition points to the fact that decisions about choice, risk, and trust are subjective. That means what feels like risky information to one person seems like no big deal to another. Below we discuss each of these elements in greater detail and present the Johari Window Model to illustrate the overall process of self-disclosing.

Process

Sometimes, people think of self-disclosure as an event in which one person tells another something of consequence. When Greta confesses to her sister, Belle, that she's become romantically interested in Belle's boyfriend, Jackson, that's a single event that both Greta and Belle recognize as self-disclosure. In fact, thinking of disclosures as events is the way many researchers have approached the subject. However, disclosures usually aren't just discrete, finite events; rather, they are processes that occur on a continuum. Greta may need to tell Belle other details about her growing attraction for Jackson, and these details will probably come out over time, after their first conversation. Belle's responses will impact how Greta continues her disclosures.

Contemporary research indicates that self-disclosing is an ongoing process that should be studied over time.[2] One study investigating how gay men told others about their sexual identity found that the respondents described coming out as a process. One of the participants said, "I . . . am in the process of coming out. . . . When you say, 'Hey, I'm gay,' That's the beginning. Yeah, [first you come] out to yourself and then [you] slowly [come] out to other people as well"[3] (p. 87). In 2018, the openly gay U.S. Olympic figure skater, Adam Rippon, made a similar statement about coming out. Rippon mentioned in an interview with *InStyle.com* that when he came out, it wasn't just one moment, because coming out is a never-ending process. He states that coming out involves self-discovery, and self-discovery happens in stages. Self-disclosures are unfinished business because they change as people and relationships change.

Intentionality and Choice

When you engage in self-disclosure, you choose to tell another person something about yourself. When Owen tells Elizabeth that he's afraid he isn't smart enough to make it in med school, his disclosure is a conscious, voluntary decision to confide a vulnerability to a friend. Owen isn't coerced into telling Elizabeth his concerns; rather, he freely discloses them. Although disclosures sometimes slip out unintentionally (e.g., when someone is drunk, overly tired, or otherwise impaired), these "slips" don't meet our definition for real self-disclosure.

We choose *whether* or not to tell something, and we also choose *how* to tell it. For instance, Owen tells Elizabeth about his fear of failing in medical school, but he does so in a self-deprecating manner, and laughs while he talks. Owen is in control of how he tells his story and, therefore, how vulnerable he allows himself to be with Elizabeth.

As we choose whether and how much to self-disclose in our interpersonal relationships, we negotiate the boundaries between privacy and openness. Selectively self-disclosing helps us create the balance among what we keep private, what is shared only with intimates, what is disclosed to close friends, and what is known to many others.

Private Information and Risk

Self-disclosure involves information that another would not easily find out without being told; it must be private information rather than public. **Public information** consists of facts that we make part of our public image—the parts of ourselves that we present to others. Usually, people strive to present socially approved characteristics in public information. Some researchers use the metaphor of the theater to describe life, and they refer to public information as what is seen "on stage." You might think about what you and your friends post on Instagram and Facebook as public information.

Private information reflects things we're unlikely to share indiscriminately with others. Private information consists of the assessments—both good and bad—we make about ourselves. It also includes our personal values and interests, fears, and concerns. Sometimes things posted on Snapchat may fall into the domain of private information. In the life-as-theater metaphor, private information is what is kept "backstage." When we're backstage, we can forget about some of the social niceties we use for public information. The following dialogues illustrate this. The first conversation is between Gwen and her boss at Clarke Meat Packing Plant, Ms. Greene; the second is between Gwen and her best friend, Robin, who doesn't work at the plant.

Gwen: "Ms. Greene, I need to take a personal day on Friday."

Ms. Greene: "That's a problem, Gwen. Our new plant policy is that we don't allow personal days if they'll result in having to pay other workers overtime. As I look at the work flowchart, I see that there are only two workers scheduled for that shift. So, I'm afraid I'll have to deny your request."

Gwen: "I'm kind of surprised to hear that. When did that policy go into effect?"

Ms. Greene: "It's been our policy for the past 6 months now. . . . Didn't your union rep inform you?"

Gwen: "Ah . . . no, um, I don't think he did, but I may have missed the meeting—I can check with the rep. In the meantime, what should I do about Friday?"

Ms. Greene: "I suggest you come to work, Gwen. But if you don't like the conditions here, you can always look for another job."

Gwen: "I like working here, Ms. Greene, and I don't want another job. I will be in on Friday."

In this dialogue, Gwen displays public information. She tries to show her supervisor that she is a cooperative, dedicated worker who enjoys working at the plant and who takes responsibility for her own problems (e.g., she volunteers to talk to the union rep). In the next dialogue, Gwen is free to exhibit private information with her best friend.

Gwen: "Oh, Robin, I'm so mad! Greene won't let me take a personal day on Friday. The entire plant is being run on the stupid whims of the bosses!"

Robin: "Whoa, slow down, Gwen. What happened?"

Gwen: "I asked that jerk for a personal day on Friday, and she said no because she'd have to pay someone else overtime. I hate my job. She even came out and told me if I didn't like it I could take a walk. I wish I could—I should start looking for a new job, but I hate the job hunt. Maybe I'm too lazy to make a change because it seems like so much work. But, it would serve them right if I did leave and I didn't give any notice. I can't stand that place!"

When displaying private information, Gwen is unconcerned about presenting herself as competent and responsible. Instead, she vents her emotions and reveals some of her less than positive self-assessments: She feels she might be lazy and she doesn't like change or job seeking. In short, she self-discloses.

A great deal of research on self-disclosure has left it to the researcher to define private information. But one study investigated what people themselves thought was personal. The researchers asked study participants to describe what constituted highly personal information. They received answers ranging from self-concept to death and illness (see Table 8.1 for a summary of their findings). However, changes in communication practices as a result of social media have left many people wondering if the concept of privacy itself is changing or if it's even possible to keep any information private now.

Certainly social media sites like Facebook may be changing what we consider to be private as opposed to public, and they may even be changing the nature of self-disclosure. In the scandal involving the U.K. firm Cambridge Analytica, the personal data of 50 million Facebook users were collected without their knowledge. Their personal information was used to create personalized political ads geared toward persuading them to vote for Donald Trump in the 2016 U.S. presidential election. Cambridge Analytica was also found to have used personal data from Facebook users in a variety of other political campaigns including the Brexit vote. Facebook has said it's deleted Cambridge Analytica from its platform. But, given the public nature of sharing our information on social media, people are questioning the nature of privacy in the 21st century.

Table 8.1 /// Highly Personal Topics for Self-Disclosure

Topic	Example
Self-concept	"I may not have the drive to succeed in life."
Romantic relationships	"When my boyfriend and I broke up, he wouldn't talk to me at all for a month. He ignored my e-mails and calls."
Sex	"I'm a virgin, and I am proud of that."
Psychological problems	"I am an alcoholic."
Abuse	"My father put his hands around my throat and pinned me to a wall."
Death/Illness	"My middle brother passed away right before my eyes."
Family relationships	"My father left when I was seven and never looked back."
Moral issues	"I hit a car on purpose."
Unplanned pregnancy	"I recently became pregnant, and I'm not married."
Friendships	"I hate my best friend's girlfriend."
Miscellaneous	"I had to declare bankruptcy at the age of 24."

Source: Adapted from Mathews et al., 2006, "What is highly personal information and how is it related to self-disclosure decision-making? The perspective of college students." *Communication Research Reports, 23,* 88–89.

Yet, even in the era of social media, you can see where risk comes into play when we self-disclose. Self-disclosure involves sharing who we really are with another and letting ourselves be truly known by them. The scary part is that we may be rejected after we have exposed ourselves in this fashion. Risk may also be inherent in the situation or the topic of self-disclosures. Some research takes on this notion by examining sexual self-disclosures. The researchers don't mean telling another person about sex in general but rather speaking to a partner before engaging in sex, and talking about personal preferences with regard to sexual behavior. They note that people rarely talk specifically about sex, and when they do, it is often indirect communication rather than a clear self-disclosure, but they argue that it's important to engage in sexual self-disclosures to avoid health risks and increase relational satisfaction.[4]

Trust

The concept of trust explains why we decide to take the plunge and reveal ourselves through self-disclosure. When we are in a relationship with a trusted other, we feel comfortable self-disclosing because we believe that our confidante can keep a secret, will continue to care for us, and won't get upset when we relate what we are thinking. Our perception of trust is a key factor in our decision to self-disclose, and most self-disclosures take place in the context of a trusting relationship.

Video 8.1

iStock.com/Fouque Michaël

Self-disclosures generally take place in a relationship where both partners feel a great deal of trust in one another.

Self-Disclosure Is Subjective

As we've mentioned, whether information is considered self-disclosure depends on subjective assessments made by the discloser. The degree of risk involved is a personal judgment; what one person considers risky might be information that someone else would find easy to tell. Taking this fact into consideration, we make a distinction between *history* and *story.*

History consists of information that sounds personal but really is easy for the speaker to share. Disclosures that are classified as history may be told easily because of the teller's temperament, changing times, or simply because the events happened a long time ago and have been told and retold. For instance, Nell was the driver in a serious car accident when she was 19, and a good friend of hers was badly injured. The story of the accident and its aftermath is a dramatic one, but it doesn't feel risky to tell because she has told it so many times that it's become routine, and her friend eventually completely recovered.

Melanie, who married Jeff in 1979, used to feel nervous about telling people that her husband had been married once before. She really didn't know anyone who'd been divorced, and she felt it was kind of shameful to be married to a divorced person. By 2019, when she and Jeff had been married for 40 years and the divorce rate in the United States was quite high, Melanie stopped being concerned about that disclosure.

In contrast, **story**, or true self-disclosure, exists when the teller *feels* the risk they're taking in telling the information. A disclosure should be considered story (or authentic) even if it doesn't seem personal to the average listener. For instance, when Donna told her friend Oscar that she had never known a Mexican American person before, Oscar thought that she was simply making a factual observation. However, to Donna, that admission felt very risky. She was afraid that Oscar would think less of her and judge her as unsophisticated because she was unfamiliar with people other than white European Americans such as herself. Donna was engaging in story even though Oscar heard it as history.

Another way to think about history and story relates to the topic of a disclosure. Some topics seem inherently more or less personal than others, as we've mentioned. For example, you could share a great deal of information about a topic such as sports without seeming to become very personal ("I love the Cincinnati Bengals," "I think the Saints are the most improved team in the NFL," or "I believe that professional athletes make too much money"). However, topics such as sex or money seem intrinsically more personal. Nonetheless, a person can reveal an actual disclosure (i.e., story) about what seems to be a low-intimacy topic. For instance, Jill might feel she's taking a risk to tell her feminist friends that she's a devoted Green Bay Packers fan. The reverse is also true; a person can reveal very little significantly personal information about a high-intimacy topic. For example, when Bailey tells his friend Gus that he plans to take a course in the sociology of sex, he may not think he's risking much. The distinction between real self-disclosures and simple disclosures depends on the risk the teller feels while sharing them.

Think about something you've told someone recently that you thought of as a self-disclosure. Does it contain all the features that we've discussed above (process, intentionality and choice, private information and risk, trust, and subjectivity)? Explain how it does or does not involve all these features. What does this application of the text material to your own self-disclosing behavior tell you?

The Johari Window

The Johari Window is a model illustrating the process of self-disclosure. Although *Johari* sounds like a term from a mystical language, it's simply a combination of the first names of its creators, Joseph Luft and Harry Ingham. Luft and Ingham were interested in the self, and the model they created helps us understand both self-disclosure and self-awareness.

The **Johari Window** provides a pictorial representation of how "known" you are to yourself and others. As Figure 8.1 illustrates, the model is a square with four panels. The entire square represents you as a whole. It contains everything there is to know about you. The square is divided by two axes: one representing what you know about yourself and one representing what you have revealed about yourself to others. The axes split the window into four panes: the open self, the hidden self, the blind self, and the unknown self.

Figure 8.1 /// The Johari Window

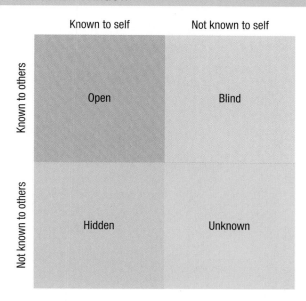

Source: Adapted from Mathews et al. (2006).

- The **open self** includes all the information about you that you know and have shared with others through disclosures. Whenever you tell someone a piece of information about yourself (e.g., your opinion or your concerns), the open self increases.

- The **hidden self** contains the information that you are aware of but have chosen not to disclose. When you decide that it's too soon to tell a friend that you used a lot of drugs in high school, that information remains in the hidden self.

- The **blind self** encompasses information that others know about you, although you're unaware of it. For example, if you have a tendency to twist the rings on your fingers or chew gum loudly when you are nervous, others watching you know this, but you aren't conscious of your habit.

- The **unknown self** consists of information about you that neither you nor others are aware of. Neither you nor any of your friends or family might know that you have a capacity for heroism. If you're never tested, that information might remain forever in the unknown self. Luft and Ingham believed that there's always something about each person that remains a mystery. So, there are always things about you to learn and discover.

In Figure 8.1, all the quadrants are the same size, but the Johari Window reflects the notion of process in self-disclosure, and it's a person-specific model, meaning that we need to draw a different window for each person with whom we interact. For instance, your Johari Window for you and your mother will differ from your Johari Window for you and your professor. Also, the sizes of the panes can change as your relationships evolve. For example, after you disclose something personal to a professor, in redrawing the window of your relationship with that professor, your open-self panel will increase and your hidden-self panel will decrease. (See Figure 8.2.)

Figure 8.2 /// The Johari Window After Self-Disclosure

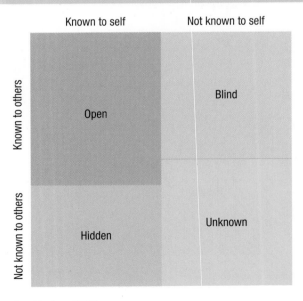

Source: Adapted from Luft and Ingham (1955).

The Johari Window helps us understand self-disclosure in many ways. First, self-disclosures come from the parts of the self that are known to us: the hidden self and the open self. Second, self-disclosures regulate the relative sizes of the open and the hidden selves. As we choose to disclose, the open self becomes larger, and the hidden self becomes smaller; when we decide to withhold disclosures, we achieve the opposite result. Third, as others provide us with feedback, we learn more about ourselves, the blind self decreases, and our ability to self-disclose increases. Finally, as we have new experiences and learn more about ourselves, the unknown self decreases, and we have more available information that we may choose to disclose to others.

IPC Praxis

Think about a relationship you have where you have self-disclosed. Draw the Johari Window that describes that relationship. Compare that to a relationship where you've not engaged in much self-disclosure. What do these pictures tell you about your relationships and about the process of self-disclosing?

Now that we understand more about the concept of self-disclosure, we'll examine several reasons why we choose to self-disclose as well as reasons why we choose not to.

8–2 REASONS FOR REVEALING AND CONCEALING PERSONAL INFORMATION

People have many reasons for both disclosing and keeping personal information private. Because our definition focuses on information that's shared intentionally, not things blurted out by accident, it's important to examine how people think about the disclosure process. First, we'll consider reasons why people choose to share personal information with another. Then, we'll examine reasons for concealing information.

Reasons for Revealing Personal Information

Several specific motivations encourage people to take a risk and reveal themselves to another. Some of the reasons represent factors specific to an individual, whereas others relate to the relationship between people. Table 8.2 presents these motivations, and this section briefly discusses each of them.

To Experience Catharsis and Improve Psychological Health

One reason psychologists are interested in self-disclosure is probably because individuals are believed to experience **catharsis**, or a therapeutic release of tensions and negative emotion, through disclosing. Although this position has moderated somewhat, in general, engaging in self-disclosure is seen as a method for

Table 8.2 /// Reasons to Self-Disclose

Individual Reasons	Relational Reasons
To achieve catharsis (therapeutic release of tensions) and to improve psychological health	To initiate a relationship To maintain or enhance a relationship
To maintain physical health	To satisfy expectations for a close relationship
To attain self-awareness	To achieve relational escalation (can be manipulative)

helping individuals achieve psychological health. The adage "A trouble shared is a trouble halved" expresses the common wisdom that self-disclosing about troubles provides some relief from those troubles. In one study testing that assumption, 243 Chinese workers in Hong Kong filled out questionnaires about occupational stress and disclosing to a best friend. The researcher found that disclosing to a best friend did reduce the workers' perception of occupational stress.[5]

Researchers have argued that in addition to sharing troubles, self-disclosures help people enjoy good news as well. This process, called **capitalization**, means that people enjoy good news more when they share it with others. This enjoyment is presumed to be characteristic of psychological health. Further, engaging in capitalization has been shown to occur frequently. People disclose their most positive experiences 60 to 80% of the time.[6]

To Improve Physical Health

Some evidence supports the belief that self-disclosure provides physical as well as psychological benefits. In a 1959 article in the *Journal of Mental Hygiene,* Sidney Jourard stated that self-disclosure promotes physical health and that failure to disclose may cause ill health. This was a controversial position in 1959, and few others followed up on Jourard's thesis. Yet, it's a viable argument today because a great deal of evidence supports the relationship between self-disclosing and physical health.

For example, a study of Holocaust survivors found that people who disclosed their experiences showed better physical health than those who concealed more.[7] Likewise, researchers found that adolescents with type 1 diabetes had better results in managing their disease when they were not secretive and self-disclosed to their parents.[8] Other researchers conducted a 9-year study of gay men with HIV-positive status. They found that men who concealed their sexual identity and their health issues had more deterioration in their immune systems, a quicker onset of AIDS, and lived a shorter time with AIDS than did men who self-disclosed.[9] In addition, a large body of research supports the contention that disclosing has a positive impact on blood pressure levels and resistance to cardiovascular disease.[10]

To Achieve Self-Awareness

Self-disclosures provide us with the means to become more self-aware. We're able to clarify our self-concepts through feedback we receive from others and by the process of hearing ourselves disclose. For example, when Kara discloses to her sister, Marti, that she feels stupid for not learning how to swim until she was an adult, Marti responds by praising Kara for having the courage to tackle a new skill later in life. Marti tells Kara that she is really proud of her and feels that she's setting a good example for their children that it's never too late to learn. Kara is pleased to hear her sister's comments. As she reflects on them, she realizes that persisting with swimming lessons was worthwhile, even though it was more difficult to learn at age 35 than it would have been at age 5. After talking to Marti and thinking about their conversation, Kara feels really good about herself.

When George discloses to his friend Julia that he is thinking about quitting his job and starting his own business, he surprises himself. Although he'd been feeling discontented with work, until he heard himself tell Julia that he wants to start his own business, he hadn't really been sure. When he puts that thought into words for Julia, he begins to clarify his feelings for himself. This process is pictured in the Johari Window, which we described earlier; as we listen to ourselves disclose and receive feedback, we increase the side of the window that is known to us.

To Initiate a Relationship

As we discussed previously, disclosers are prompted to tell private information as a way of developing a new relationship with someone who seems interesting. Several studies support the idea that self-disclosures help develop new relationships. Initial encounters usually result in liking when the partners both self-disclose throughout the conversation.[11]

To illustrate these findings, look at the case of Anita and Zoe. Anita is a working single mother attending the local community college part time and holding down a part-time job as an administrative assistant at a law firm. Because she's so busy, she hasn't made many friends at school or work. One day when she's rushing to finish a project at the firm, she bumps into Zoe. Anita had met Zoe, who's also a single mother, during orientation. Zoe works full time at the law firm and mentors new employees.

iStock.com/narvikk

Some research supports the idea that mutual self-disclosures promote liking in initial encounters.

When they met, Anita had thought that it would be nice to get to know Zoe, but she just hadn't had the time. When they bump into each other, Anita is worrying about her son, Brad, who's been getting into fights at school. Zoe says "hi" in a friendly way and asks if Anita would like to have coffee later. Although Anita really doesn't have the time, she says yes and over coffee finds herself telling Zoe some of her concerns about Brad. Zoe listens with empathy and then responds that her son had some behavior problems when he was Brad's age, and that she, like Anita, had worried that her work schedule might have been partly to blame. Zoe mentions that she and her son had benefited from some counseling sessions with the school psychologist. When Zoe and Anita part, they both think that they have begun a friendship.

To Maintain Existing Relationships

Existing relationships also benefit from self-disclosures. In an interesting study examining why people tell others about their dreams, researchers found that 100% of their participants attributed their disclosures to some type of relational goal. People said that they told a relational partner about a dream to enhance closeness, warmth, and trust. The authors quote one of their respondents, who explained why revealing dreams was important:

> My brother and I have a good sibling relationship. We tell each other everything that goes on in our dreams. Each time we reveal something, the bond between us strengthens. It seems melodramatic, but there is a strong bond between us. (p. 141)[12]

To Satisfy Expectations of What Constitutes a Good Relationship

As we mentioned earlier, people believe that good relationships depend on being open and self-disclosive. If we consciously keep secrets from intimate others, we often believe that our relationships are flawed or not as good as we want them to be. Self-disclosing allows us to see our relationships in a positive light.

In the study about dreams referred to above, some study participants said that they told a partner about their dream because the partner was already close to them, and the participants' expectation was that in a close relationship people tell each other everything, including their dreams. As one of their respondents stated, "He knows everything about me. I love him and trust him and pretty much share everything with him" (p. 141).

To Escalate a Relationship

Video 8.2

As we've discussed, self-disclosing provides a way to get to know someone and to allow that person to know you. This process escalates relationships, often moving them to a more intimate level. Casual acquaintances may become close friends after they spend some time telling each other personal information about themselves. For example, when Dario tells his friend Elena that he used to suffer from bulimia and that he still worries every day that he might slip back into his old binge-and-purge habits, Elena feels honored that Dario trusts her with this information. His self-disclosure makes her feel closer to him and advances their relationship to a deeper level.

However, as we discuss throughout the text, communication can be used for destructive purposes as well as positive goals. Indeed, self-disclosures can be used to manipulate a relational partner. For example, a person can offer an inauthentic self-disclosure (or history) to manipulate a relational partner into revealing something truly personal about themselves. In this manner, the relationship may escalate faster than it would have otherwise, which might be the devious objective of the first discloser. Or, one person may say, "I love you" early in a relationship, without necessarily meaning it, simply to advance intimacy.

IPC Praxis

Think about a time when you have self-disclosed. Did any of the reasons we've discussed above motivate your disclosure? Which ones? If none of them seemed to be operating in your own example, what did motivate your self-disclosure?

Reasons Not to Self-Disclose

Although opening up to another person provides benefits, there are also compelling reasons to keep our secrets to ourselves. Both desires are extremely important. We want to be open with our partners, but at the same time, we want to maintain our secrets. Although ethical questions arise when we keep something that is critically important from someone else, most of the time, maintaining privacy is ethical. We need to remember that it's our choice as to whether we disclose or not. People choose not to disclose for the following reasons, which we discuss below: avoiding hurt and rejection, maintaining individuality, avoiding stress and depression, and avoiding conflict. The first three of these reasons are rooted in individual desires while the fourth is a relational concern. See Table 8.3 for a summary.

To Avoid Hurt and Rejection

Perhaps the most common reason for keeping a secret is because we believe that the person we reveal it to may use the information to hurt us or may reject us when they know our inner selves. For example, Mick doesn't tell his friend Adella that he served time in a juvenile detention center for multiple drunk driving offenses because he fears that she will be angry, respect him less, or bring it up in a taunting way in an argument. All of these negative outcomes are reasons for keeping a secret private.

Table 8.3 /// Reasons Not to Self-Disclose

Individual Reasons	Relational Reason
To avoid hurt and rejection	To avoid conflict and protect a relationship
To maintain individuality	
To avoid stress and depression	

Furthermore, if we share a really critical piece of information about ourselves, even with a sympathetic friend, we have given this friend some potential power over us, and we can't be absolutely sure that our friend would never use this power against us or in a way that we would not like. When Audra confides in Allen that she thinks she's really not female and she may begin transitioning, she figures he's a trustworthy confidante because he is a longtime friend, and he's gay. However, she doesn't realize that Allen feels strongly that one's true identity is nothing to hide. Allen tells several mutual friends about Audra's disclosure. Although Audra doesn't believe that being transgender is shameful, she wasn't ready to tell their friends yet; she was still getting used to the idea herself. She was extremely hurt by what she saw as Allen's betrayal.

Finally, because you don't know exactly how your relational partner will respond, disclosing may feel like an unwise risk to your relationship. Some research indicates that if you disclose to someone who responds in a negative fashion, you are likely to feel bad about the interaction, the other person, and about your relationship with the other person. Some people may believe disclosing isn't worth that risk.

To Keep Your Image Intact and Maintain Individuality

People sometimes withhold self-disclosures because they're concerned that if they begin disclosing, they will lose control and be unable to stop. Furthermore, these people fear that disclosures will bring with them unrestrained emotionality, perhaps causing them to cry uncontrollably. In a related vein, some people worry that self-disclosing will cause them to lose their sense of mystery and individuality. For instance, Caitlin may fear that if Nolan knows all about her she won't seem interesting to him any longer. And Gary's fear is that if he tells his friend Lyle all about himself he'll disappear into the relationship and stop being a unique individual.

If someone has established a particular image in a relationship, they may fear that self-disclosure could threaten that image and cause the other to "see" them differently. Lucy and Rebecca have been friends for 5 years. In their relationship, Rebecca often turns to Lucy, who has been married for 15 years, for advice when she has problems with a boyfriend. When Lucy and her husband fight, she doesn't feel comfortable confiding in Rebecca because it seems to negate her identity as a happily married person who gives support but doesn't need to ask for it.

To Avoid Stress and Depression

Although it's possible that telling someone something personal can relieve the stress of keeping a secret, some evidence indicates that self-disclosures sometimes actually increase stress. For instance, Valerian Derlega and his colleagues give the following example:

> Bill, 20, and Mark, 21, are juniors at a state university. They are flying together to Florida for spring break. Bill is uncomfortable about flying, and he tells Mark about being nervous. Mark, in turn, describes an unpleasant experience when, on another flight, his plane had mechanical problems. As the plane takes off, neither of them is feeling very good. Somehow, talking about their fears made them feel worse rather than better. (p. 103)[13]

A growing body of evidence indicates that the more adolescents exchange disclosures about their problems with their friends (a process called co-rumination), the more likely they are to become depressed. Researchers have hypothesized that this may be the case because the more youth talk about their problems, the more they think about these problems and, thus, the more depressed they become.[14]

To Avoid Conflict and Protect a Relationship

Some secrecy may actually be helpful in a relationship. If people believe that sharing personal information would cause conflict with a relational partner, and they don't think the information is necessary for their partner to know, they may choose to conceal the information. For example, Lois thinks she doesn't need to tell her friend Raymond that she voted Republican in the last election. Lois knows Raymond is a staunch Democrat, and she believes the disclosure would cause a conflict that could harm their relationship. The study of Chinese business people, that we referred to earlier, found that disclosing to one's mother was negative for the relationship because it increased the likelihood that they would engage in conflict.

In another example, Lindsey does not like her brother's wife. When Lindsey chooses not to tell this to her brother Hal, she figures that her silence keeps the relationship between them more peaceful. Because Lindsey knows that Hal is happy with his wife, it seems irrelevant to reveal that she isn't. This secret does not affect their relationship much, because they live in different cities separated by thousands of miles, and Lindsey and Hal keep in touch mainly by text and on Facebook.

 **IPC Praxis**

Think about a time when you have decided not to self-disclose. Did any of the reasons we've discussed above motivate your decision? Which ones? If none of them seemed to be operating in your own example, what did motivate your decision?

8–3 FACTORS AFFECTING SELF-DISCLOSURE

A complete understanding of self-disclosure requires consideration of many factors, including individual differences, relational patterns, cultural values, sex and sex role, as well as channel. We explore each below.

Individual Differences

People have different needs for openness. Whereas David has no problem telling his friends all about his personal feelings, Selena saves disclosures of that nature for her family and her most intimate friends. Think about your own tendencies to share information with others in your life. Do you believe that some things are better left unsaid, or do you think that friends and family should know everything about you?

Even people who have a high need to disclose don't wish to tell everyone everything. Although Deanna might tell her partner, Cameron, about the fact that she was sexually abused by her stepfather, she may want to keep that information from her friend Trish. Some people are comfortable telling personal disclosures to every one of their close friends but one; others may only wish to confide in one close friend.

Research suggests that certain personality traits such as self-esteem, the ability to elicit disclosures from others (called *responsiveness*), self-consciousness, and social anxiety are all related to people's need for self-disclosure, as well as their abilities to be effective at self-disclosing. People with high self-esteem, high responsiveness and low self-consciousness and low social anxiety are believed likely to effectively engage in self-disclosing.[15] Another individual difference that researchers relate to self-disclosing is sex, and we'll discuss that in a separate section later, because a great deal of research attention has been directed toward that topic.

Relational Patterns

Self-disclosures wax and wane over the life of a relationship. Telling each other every secret may be important early in the relationship, but in long-term friendships, marriages, or partnerships, self-disclosures account for a much smaller amount of communication time. "Getting to know you" is an important part of developing a new relationship, but as relationships endure and stabilize, the participants need to disclose less because they already know a great deal about one another.

Researchers suggest that some general patterns of self-disclosure may be related to the life of a relationship (see Figure 8.3). The first pattern pictured represents the general scenario we've described: People meet, get to know each other, begin to tell each other more and more personal information, and then decrease their disclosures as the relationship endures. This pattern shows a gradual increase in self-disclosing that parallels the growth of the relationship until the relationship stabilizes; at that point, self-disclosures decrease without a corresponding diminishment of satisfaction.

The second pattern pictured in Figure 8.3 represents two people who know each other as casual friends for a long time before escalating the relationship with self-disclosures and increasing intimacy. Their long-term relationship is characterized by low self-disclosures and then a spike up before a leveling off of openness. This pattern is illustrated by the following example: Steven, an emergency room nurse at a local hospital, has worked for several years on the same shift as Amanda, an ER physician at the hospital. They have spoken to each other a lot about working conditions and emergency health care. Although Steven and Amanda don't know each other well, they like each other and respect each other's medical skills and steadiness in an emergency. One night, Steven's father suffers a stroke and is brought into the emergency room. When his dad dies a few hours after being admitted, Steven finds comfort in sharing his feelings with Amanda. This tragedy leads to increased disclosures between them. One year later, they refer to each other as best friends. This pattern shows that, as with the first pattern, Amanda's and Steven's disclosures will eventually decrease over time.

Figure 8.3 /// Three Patterns of Self-Disclosure in Relationships

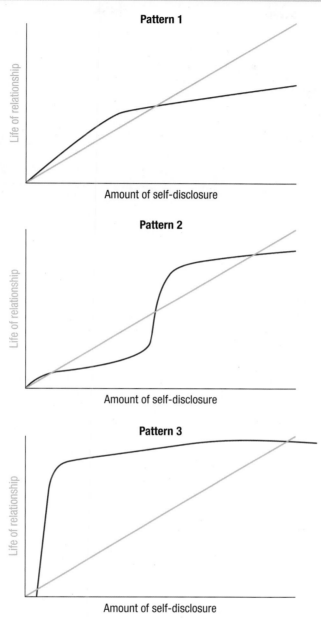

The third pattern, sometimes referred to as "clicking," shows a high incidence of self-disclosing almost immediately in the relationship. Researchers refer to these relationships as ones that just "click" from the start rather than needing a gradual build. For example, Ben and Marcus met 20 years ago as 12-year-olds at football camp. They immediately found each other easy to talk to and enjoyed being together. Now, two decades later, they still enjoy an open and deep friendship.

Clicking takes place when two people identify each other as friends immediately and begin self-disclosing right away.

Cultura Creative (RF) / Alamy Stock Photo

Researchers explain the clicking process by suggesting that people carry around relationship scripts in their heads, and when they find someone who fits the main elements of that script, they begin acting as though all the elements are there. In other words, let's say that some of the things Ben expects in a friend are to have the same interests he has, resemble him physically, be open and attractive, and have a good sense of humor. When he finds all those characteristics in Marcus, he quickly begins acting as though they have a developed friendship. If Marcus has a similar response, we should see the clicking pattern. Again, in this third pattern, there is a leveling off of self-disclosures over time.

In all three patterns in Figure 8.3, self-disclosures eventually level off—and, in many cases, they eventually decrease dramatically if relationships last a long time. However, when new issues arise, even longtime friends or couples who have been together many years will self-disclose. Self-disclosures may also increase if people feel that their relationship has fallen into a rut and they wish to bring back some of its earlier excitement and intensity. Furthermore, if self-disclosures decrease suddenly and radically between people, the decrease may signal that a relationship is in trouble.

Culture and Ethnicity

Like all the behaviors we discuss in this text, self-disclosing is moderated by cultural prescriptions and values. For example, some evidence suggests that Asian Indians' sense of appropriate self-disclosure differs from those of North Americans and Western Europeans. Asian Indians might be considered overly private by North American or Western standards, and Westerners would be seen as talking too much about personal topics when judged by Asian standards. Parents and children in Pakistan self-disclose to each other less often than parents and children who are native to the United States. Most Japanese people also self-disclose less than North Americans primarily because privacy is a Japanese cultural value. Most Asians believe that successful persons do not talk about or exhibit feelings and emotions, whereas most North Americans and Western Europeans believe that a willingness to disclose feelings is critical to relationship development.[16]

However, there is some anecdotal evidence that attitudes may be changing, at least for some Chinese people. One young Chinese woman, Mengwen Cao, a lesbian now living in New York City used FaceTime to show her parents in China a video she'd made about her lesbian identity. Ms. Cao notes that coming out is an extremely fraught disclosure for Chinese people because of the stigma of being gay in the culture as well as the emphasis in China on saving face. Yet, she perseveres and comments that she needed to tell her parents this truth about herself in order to be truly close with them. Watching the video of Ms. Cao speaking with her parents, and seeing her parents' loving reactions to her words, provides an intimate insight into how self-disclosures are handled in this Chinese family.[17]

The amount of self-disclosure deemed appropriate by a culture relates to whether it's a high-context or low-context culture. As we have discussed previously in this text, high-context cultures (such as China and Japan) derive meaning mainly from activity and overall context, not verbal explanation; the reverse is true in low-context cultures (such as the United States). Thus, explicit verbal disclosures are unnecessary in high-context cultures. For example, some research confirms that the Chinese value actions rather than talk in developing relationships. In addition, differences in how self-disclosure is valued depends on whether a culture is collectivist or individualistic. One study showed that husbands' marital satisfaction and self-disclosing behaviors were dependent on whether they came from a collectivist or individualistic culture.[18] Another study suggests that acculturation might have an impact on self-disclosing behaviors. The researchers surveyed Latinx people living in the United States and found that more acculturated Latinx disclosed more to white American friends than did less acculturated Latinx.[19]

Some researchers have observed that scholars, students, and teachers focus on the communication behavior of self-disclosure because of a Western bias that favors openness over privacy and disclosure over withholding information. These researchers criticize the cultural biases that cause Westerners to value disclosure more highly than privacy and secrecy, and suggest that cultures that value privacy should not be seen as deficient, or evaluated in comparison to a Western standard.

Sex and Sex Role

As we've mentioned, many people believe that sex is a major factor in self-disclosing behaviors. However, the research remains inconclusive on this topic. Some studies suggest that in general, women in the United States seem to self-disclose more than men, and they value self-disclosures more. This belief was confirmed in research that found when female friends talked, they usually related emotional disclosures both online and face to face.[20] Furthermore, some research shows that adult, white, heterosexual men self-disclose less to friends than women do.[21] Yet an analysis of 205 studies examining sex differences in self-disclosure found that the differences between women and men were rather small, and other researchers found no sex differences in self-disclosing behaviors.[22]

Biological sex might not be as important to differences in self-disclosure as other issues such as sex role or the sex composition of the couple. In terms of sex role, men who are **androgynous** (meaning they embody both masculine and feminine traits) believe that self-disclosure characterizes close relationships. Androgynous men desire friends who want to share themselves through talk, and they want to do the same. With reference to sex composition, male–male pairs seem to disclose the least and female–female pairs the most.

Because the way in which sex and sex role influence self-disclosing behavior is complex and uncertain, you might be tempted to fall back on stereotypes depicting disclosing women and silent men. However, most of the research doesn't support such a conclusion. The overall differences between women and men as self-disclosers, and communicators in general, are relatively small, and they are more likely to be the result of other factors, such as power, culture, and so forth, rather than simply an outcome of biological sex.

Channels

As more and more of our relationships are being formed and maintained online, this phenomenon raises questions for our conclusions about interpersonal communication. We have to test whether or not our beliefs about communication behaviors, such as self-disclosure, which were formed based on face-to-face relationships, still hold true online. Some research, for example, noted that adolescents in Bermuda experience self-disclosure and friendship in unique ways online.[23] Other researchers argue that many expectations about online self-disclosure are contested when the empirical literature is examined. When comparing online and offline communication, researchers found that online channels did not necessarily increase the amount of personal disclosure by users. Other factors such as the relationship between communicators, the specific online venue, and the context of the interaction had a moderating effect on the amount of disclosure. Additionally, the combination of online trust and offline trust interacted to result in disclosing online.[24]

Other research examined the effects of anonymous disclosing online. One study found, contrary to expectations, that anonymity did not increase self-disclosures in all cases. When bloggers shared a photo of themselves, they actually self-disclosed more than when there was no visual to identify them. But, when they shared their real names, some bloggers did tend to disclose less.[25] Another study examined anonymity in the context of disclosing sexual assault online. The researchers found that disclosers did seem to like the anonymous online forum as a place where they could talk about this sensitive and traumatic topic. Several of them indicated that they saw the online venue as one place they could disclose when they had nowhere else to turn. Yet, a small but troubling number of unsupportive and negative responses to people's disclosures by other posters caused the researchers to sound a note of caution. They suggest more monitoring of websites to prevent this.[26]

Video 8.3

Some research has moved away from comparing disclosure online and face to face, and simply investigated online disclosing. Researchers have found the following: disclosing information about your feelings about your self-concept online was the topic that elicited the most interaction and reciprocal self-disclosures; people often have strategic goals for self-disclosing on social media; disclosure online is affected by a combination of individual traits such as willingness to trust and the perceived attractiveness of the profile of the stranger to whom the disclosure is directed; and people are motived to disclose online to relieve guilt for bad behaviors they've engaged in.[27]

When reading studies about online self-disclosure, we should interpret their results based on whether they were performed in a laboratory or in a naturalistic setting because respondents tend to self-disclose more in a lab with a researcher present than in a natural online channel that they chose themselves.

In sum, this brief review of studies investigating online disclosures suggests that the channel may make a difference in how people approach self-disclosure. However, we need to look at more factors than simply whether disclosures take place online or offline in order to make good conclusions and build theory explaining this communication behavior.

8–4 PRINCIPLES OF SELF-DISCLOSURE

From our discussion so far, you should have a picture of the self-disclosure process, why or why not people choose to engage in disclosing, and how self-disclosure is affected by factors we've mentioned, such as individual differences, relational patterns, culture and ethnicity, and sex and sex role, as well as channels. To focus this picture further, we now examine four principles, or norms, of self-disclosure:

- We disclose a lot in a few encounters.
- Self-disclosures generally occur in the context of a close relationship between two people.
- Self-disclosing is reciprocal.
- Self-disclosures occur gradually over time.

Of course, these are general principles, and sometimes you may find yourself disclosing, or listening to another's disclosure, in ways that don't totally adhere to one or more of these principles. However, these norms do hold true for the most part in terms of describing self-disclosing behaviors.

We Disclose a Great Deal in Few Interactions

This principle suggests that if we examine our total communication behavior, self-disclosures are somewhat rare. Some researchers estimate that only approximately 2% of our communication can be called self-disclosure. We generally spend a lot more time in small talk than in the relatively dramatic behavior of self-disclosure.

 IPC Around Us

K. J. Dell'Antonia[28] blogs in *Motherlode* about how initially she had no intention of self-disclosing to her children while driving the three of them to school one morning. She began by mentioning to them that one time she had suffered a severe case of food poisoning and had to go to the hospital. That led to the children questioning her about the experience, and she ended up telling them that it was the time she had a stillborn daughter who would have been her second

(Continued)

(Continued)

iStock.com/LightFieldStudios

child. Dell'Antonia realized that she had never really talked to any of her children about this loss, and she felt that she might have waded into deep waters with the conversation. Thinking something like "in for a penny, in for a pound," she told the children about her feelings at the loss of the baby, and they talked about how their family would have been different if the baby had lived. Dell'Antonia honestly admitted that her youngest child might not have been born in that case. As they speculated about these issues, Dell'Antonia reflected on the results of her self-disclosures, saying, "If you had asked me at 7:30 this morning whether my children were ready to contemplate those kinds of contradictions in some way beyond the abstract, I'm not sure what I'd have said. But by 7:40, we were all the way in" (para. 12). She left the conversation hoping that her honesty and openness would be good for her children, but not really knowing for sure.

Reflection: *How do you see this example as relating to the material we're discussing about the definition, features, and principles of self-disclosure? In some ways, this story violates the notion that self-disclosure is intentional communication. Given that, do you think the story describes true self-disclosure? Why or why not?*

For instance, think about a typical day any one of us might have. We'll illustrate this day with Joe's activities. Maybe Joe gets up at 7 a.m. and mumbles a morning greeting to his roommates as he hurries to get showered and dressed. He grabs a fast-food breakfast at a drive-through and then goes to his part-time job. At work, he has to give guidance to and take instructions from a variety of people. He might spend a little bit of time complaining to his coworkers that he's tired and has a great deal to do. Joe makes some phone calls and places orders, types up a report, and files some paperwork. For lunch, he meets a friend, and the two of them chat about a movie they both saw last week. They engage in some trivial gossip about a mutual friend who might be getting divorced. Joe leaves lunch to hurry over to campus to take two classes. He doesn't speak much in class because he's busy taking notes during the lectures. After the classes, Joe heads over to the coffee shop to study. He orders a latte and sits at a table to read the week's assignment. Joe leaves the coffee shop and stops at the store on the way home to pick up the ingredients for a quick dinner. He runs into a friend at the grocery store and exchanges a few words before hurrying home. When he gets home, he turns on television and watches a basketball game while he's putting dinner together. Over dinner, the TV remains on, and then Joe cleans up the dishes and sends a few texts. Joe falls into bed around midnight.

In that scenario of a typical day, Joe probably didn't self-disclose at all, even though he talked to many people. His interactions were routine, phatic, or instrumental and didn't involve sharing much personal information. However, on another day, he might call a friend and spend an hour talking about a problem that's been bothering him. This generalized example about self-disclosure indicates that most of our interactions are short, routine, and relatively impersonal. Only a few of our interactions are truly self-disclosive. Yet, because of the emotional impact that self-disclosure has on us and our relationships, we (and researchers) pay it more attention than some other communication behaviors, which actually take up more of our time.

Self-Disclosures Occur Between Two People in a Close Relationship

Although it's possible for us to tell personal information to small groups of people (or even to large groups, such as on Facebook), generally researchers have believed that self-disclosure occurs when only two people are present. Further, how much and how frequently we self-disclose depend in great part on the nature of our relationship with another person. People disclose most in relationships that are close (e.g., in marital, cohabiting, or family relationships and close friendships). People have to think their relationships are secure to feel comfortable enough to self-disclose.

However, a principle is only true *most* of the time, and there are some exceptions to this generalization. The main exception is called "the bus rider phenomenon" or "strangers on a train." This notion refers to self-disclosures made to strangers rather than to close friends or relatives. The phenomenon derives its name because such self-disclosures often occur on public transportation such as buses, planes, or trains where two people are confined together for a period of time with not much to do but talk to each other. In such cases, the relationship between the people is temporary and transient rather than close and ongoing. We're sure that many of you have heard a stranger's life story while traveling across the country on public transportation, or perhaps you yourself have shared personal information with strangers in this context.

Self-Disclosures Are Reciprocal

The essence of this principle is the tendency to respond in kind. Most research suggests that the self-disclosures of one member of a pair will be reciprocated with self-disclosures by the other. Although, there are exceptions. A notable exception to the norm of reciprocity exists in professional relationships; therapists, for instance, are not expected to reciprocate the self-disclosures of their clients. Parent–child relationships also offer an exception. Children don't expect their parents to tell them

People are most comfortable if self-disclosures they provide are reciprocated by self-disclosures provided by the other in the relationship.

personal disclosures in response to the information they disclose. But, in most peer relationships (friends and romantic relationships), the norm of reciprocity is strong.

The **dyadic effect** describes the tendency for us to return another's self-disclosure with one that matches it in level of intimacy. For example, if Leila tells her friend Victoria that she experienced date rape when she was 18, Victoria's reciprocal disclosure would have to be about something equally serious and intimate. The dyadic effect suggests that Victoria wouldn't respond by simply telling Leila that at one time she dated a basketball player.

Reciprocity is sometimes explained by noting that it keeps people in the relationship on an equal footing. If two people reciprocate disclosures, they have equalized the rewards and the risks of disclosing. In addition, disclosure reciprocity may be governed by global conversational norms such as the requirement that a response has to be relevant to the comment that preceded it. Thus, when Leila tells Victoria her story about date rape, Victoria responds with a story about how she narrowly escaped date rape herself. In doing so, Victoria matches Leila's intimacy level and keeps the conversation on the same topic.

However, conversations involving self-disclosures do not always contain immediate reciprocal self-disclosures like the one we just described between Leila and Victoria. Victoria doesn't have to reciprocate immediately; she may simply listen with empathy while Leila tells her story. Instead of telling about her own experience after hearing about Leila's, Victoria might express empathy and encourage Leila to tell her more about what happened, how she feels about it now, and so forth. Research suggests that expressing concern for the speaker is actually a better response (because it makes a more favorable impression on the discloser) than responding with a matching self-disclosure.

Does this mean that the norm of reciprocity is wrong? Not exactly. People in close relationships don't have to engage in immediate reciprocity, but they should reciprocate within the conversation at some point, or in a later conversation in the near future. In other words, Leila would be unhappy about the conversation (and maybe her relationship with Victoria) if Victoria never reciprocated. But Victoria's self-disclosures don't have to come immediately after Leila's to satisfy the norm of reciprocity.

When people are just getting to know one another, the need for immediate reciprocity is strong and tends to result in positive outcomes for a relationship.[29] As relationships develop and mature, this need is relaxed, and reciprocal disclosures may no longer need to occur even within the same conversation. In these cases, the participants trust that disclosures will equalize over the course of their relationship. Sarah might simply listen to her sister, Miranda, as she discloses that she's thinking about divorcing her husband, without disclosing anything to Miranda at all. But Sarah has disclosed a lot to Miranda in the past and will continue to do so in the future.

Self-Disclosures Occur Over Time

Disclosures generally happen incrementally over time. We usually tell a low-level self-disclosure to a relational partner first and then increase the intimacy level of our disclosures over time as our relationship with that person continues and deepens. In our previous example of Leila and Victoria, this principle suggests that Leila would make her disclosure about date rape after she had already disclosed other, lower level personal information about herself (e.g., that she had flunked calculus and she was thinking of leaving the university to go into a training program to become a real estate agent). This principle illustrates how relationship development and self-disclosure are intertwined. Learning more about one another changes a relationship, and the nature of the self-disclosures changes as the relationship matures or deteriorates.

This principle also refers to the fact that time affects the meaning of disclosure. For example, when Bethany tells her boyfriend early in their relationship that she's afraid to assert herself around authority figures, he might respond with empathy and support. He might even think it's appealing that Bethany needs his help. But, if Bethany and her boyfriend stay together, the same disclosure 20 years later could be heard as an indication that Bethany refuses to grow up and take responsibility for herself. In this case, the disclosure would probably not be met with empathy and support.

8–5 EXPLAINING SELF-DISCLOSURE

People have suggested many ways to explain the process of self-disclosure. We discuss two theories in this section: Communication Privacy Management Theory and Social Penetration Theory.

Communication Privacy Management Theory

Communication Privacy Management Theory (CPM)[30] explains how and why people decide to reveal or conceal private information to others. Before discussing the theory itself, we need to talk about the polar oppositions of openness and privacy.

In early research on self-disclosure, theorists asserted that self-disclosures created our sense of self and contained the essence of being human. As we've mentioned, in the 1950s Sidney Jourard suggested that we must engage in self-disclosure to be psychologically and physically healthy. His position came to be known as "the ideology of intimacy" because he believed that disclosing to create intimacy with another was the most important thing a person could do.

More recently, people have rejected this idea in favor of emphasizing the benefits of privacy and even deception. Some researchers now contend that concealing information can have positive effects on relationships. For example, suppose you had a brief fling with your old lover shortly after you met the person who's now your partner. Afterward, you became serious with your current partner and never saw or spoke with your old lover again. Would it be a good thing to tell your current partner about this or might it be better for your relationship to conceal it? This is an ethical question, and issues involving concealing or revealing information always involve ethical decisions. Would it make a difference if the situation were not that you had a fling with an old partner, but simply that you daydream about this person from time to time? Should you tell a current partner about your thoughts and fantasies focused on a person other than them?

CPM takes the position that there are good reasons for both sharing and withholding private information. One of the key principles of CPM involves the rules that people create to govern when and how information is shared with others. These rules are developed based on some of the factors relating to self-disclosing that we discussed earlier in the chapter: sex and sex role, culture, individual motivations, reciprocity, and risk, for instance.

Furthermore, CPM argues that boundaries are created around private information. A person is considered to "own" information about themselves; if they tell another, the boundary around the information expands and the two people now "co-own" the information. Sometimes boundary turbulence arises because the rules about sharing private information are unclear. If Craig tells his daughter Ella that his wife, Kay, Ella's stepmother, worries about losing her job, boundary turbulence may ensue if Kay hadn't wanted to reveal that information to Ella. Kay will maintain that her expectations for privacy were violated. The theory predicts that some resolution has to occur at this point. Perhaps Kay will redraw her boundaries and include Ella as a co-owner of the information. Or perhaps Kay will redraw her boundaries to exclude Craig from future private disclosures.

 Theory-Into-Practice (TIP)

Communication Privacy Management Theory

Do you think the concept of owning private information is still viable in the age of the Internet? Is it possible for people to be in complete control of the boundaries around their private information? Do we really get to choose who co-owns information with us, or does this theory have to change to accommodate the easy access to our private information that other people have today?

Social Penetration Theory

Social Penetration Theory[31] says that people, like onions, have many layers. A person's layers correspond to all the information about them, ranging from the most obvious to the most personal. For example, when two strangers meet in person, some information—such as their clothing style, approximate height and weight, and hair color—is easily observable. This information makes up the outer layer of the person. Other information—such as gender (masculinity, femininity, androgyny), how a person feels about their height and weight, and whether their hair color is natural or dyed—is less accessible, and conversation is necessary to "peel" these layers of the onion away. Through interaction, people may choose to reveal these deeper layers of themselves to one another and, in so doing, perhaps intensify their relationship.

Figure 8.4 /// Social Penetration in Action

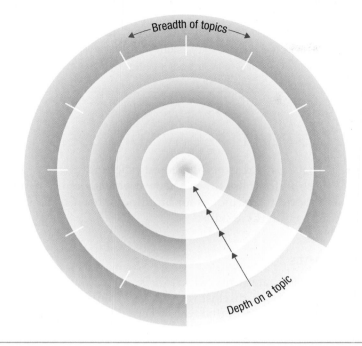

Social Penetration Theory pictures all the topics of information about a person—such as their interests, likes, dislikes, fears, religious beliefs, and so forth—along the perimeter of an onion that has been sliced in half (see Figure 8.4). We can have a relationship with a casual friend in which all our discussions are at the surface layer of the onion. For example, Alissa may know that her friend Zach is interested in mixed martial arts, likes cat videos on YouTube, listens to electronic music, is afraid of snakes, loves to travel, has four brothers, and is a member of the Catholic Church. Zach knows that Alissa loves to dance, is a business major, has a sister and two brothers, wants a pet pig, went to Spain a year ago, had an internship last semester, and can't carry a tune.

In this example, Alissa and Zach's relationship has a fair degree of **breadth** (i.e., they both know information about the other across several different topics) but not much depth. **Depth** occurs when they tell each other how they feel about the topics—for example, that Zach's experiencing a crisis in his Catholic faith or that Alissa is much closer to her youngest brother than anyone else in her family and feels estranged from her parents. Some relationships have a great deal of breadth without depth, and vice versa. Other relationships have a great deal of both—for example, an extremely close friend or partner would probably know a lot about us in a variety of areas. Yet, other relationships involve not much of either, as when a distant relative knows only a few things about us, and none of them in much depth. The degree to which you self-disclose controls the social penetration described by the model.

8–6 SKILL SET FOR EFFECTIVE DISCLOSING

Although we may have good reasons for keeping silent at times, we need to refine our self-disclosing skills for those times when we wish to open up. In this section, we outline nine important techniques for building our self-disclosing skills. See Table 8.4 for a summary of these skills.

Use I-Statements

Owning, or the use of I-statements, which we've discussed in previous chapters, is the most basic skill for self-disclosing. Saying "I think," "I feel," "I need," or "I believe" indicates that you accept that what you're saying is your own perception, based on your own experiences and affected by your value system. When you self-disclose using owning, you take responsibility for your feelings and experiences. In addition, your listener realizes that you are speaking for yourself and not trying to make a generalization. Compare these two disclosures:

1. Edward tells Travis, "I don't know if I will really be happy going to college in New York. It's so far away from my family—I think I'll be homesick."

2. Edward says to Travis, "It's important to stay near home for college. It's not good to put too much distance between family members."

Table 8.4 /// Skill Set for Self-Disclosure Effectiveness		
a. Use I-statements.		
b. Be honest.		
c. Be consistent and focused with your verbal and nonverbal communication.		
d. Choose the appropriate context.		
e. Be sure your disclosure is relevant.		
f. Estimate the risks and benefits of disclosing.		
g. Predict how your listener will respond.		
h. Be sure the amount and type of disclosure are appropriate.		
i. Estimate the effect of the disclosure on your relationship.		
j. Your skill suggestion		

Marek Uliasz / Alamy Stock Photo

If we're not honest in our disclosures, we defeat the purpose of self-disclosure.

When Edward uses the latter phrasing, he doesn't own his feelings; instead, he presents them as a general rule that all people should consider when deciding where to go to college. The first statement Edward makes illustrates owning as he focuses on disclosing his unique feelings.

Be Honest

Honesty in self-disclosure refers to being both clear and accurate. If you are too ambiguous and unclear, your self-disclosures may not be "heard" as real disclosures. Yet, if you and your partner know each other very well, you may be able to offer disclosures more indirectly. For instance, if you know that your partner is struggling with several deadlines at work, you will be able to hear a disclosure in your partner's sarcastic comment: "I had a great day at work today. What a pleasure palace that job is!" Generally speaking, however, you need to be clear and accurate in your disclosures. If you are dishonest or inaccurate while disclosing, you are defeating the purpose of self-disclosure.

Be Consistent and Focused With Your Verbal and Nonverbal Communication

Consistency means that your nonverbal communication should reinforce, not contradict, your verbal communication. For example, if Shannon tells Josie that she's really upset about her grades this semester but smiles while saying it, Josie may be confused about whether Shannon is upset or not. Focusing means that your nonverbal communication adds meaning to and doesn't distract from your message. For instance, if Maya continually taps her pencil against a table while telling her mother that she wants to quit school, her mother may be distracted by the gesture and have trouble concentrating on Maya's disclosure.

💬 IPC Voice: Jamila

Whenever I talk to my friend Mason, he confuses me so much. He's always smiling when he says the most serious stuff. His brother got shot last year, and when Mason opened up to me about how he felt about it, he smiled a little. I finally called him on it and asked what the heck was going on with the smiling, given that his brother almost died and he was saying how scared and uncertain it made him. Mason ducked his head, and then he told me that he didn't even realize he was smiling, but he thought it was a nervous reflex. I think that was the real self-disclosure there.

Choose the Appropriate Context

This refers to an assessment of the appropriateness of the disclosure to the situation itself. When Ron and his partner attend the annual company picnic, for instance, Ron concludes that it's not the time or place to tell his partner that he's unhappy at work, and wants more responsibility. Even though Ron is motivated to get his feelings out in the open, he knows this isn't the best spot for a self-disclosure of that type. He will wait to disclose his feelings until the occasion is more appropriate, such as when he and his partner have returned home to their apartment.

Be Sure Your Disclosure Is Relevant

Relevancy means that you are able to weave your disclosure naturally into the conversation. When Jeff and Noel go out bowling together for the first time, for instance, they begin talking about their involvement in sports in the past. The situation and the topic seem to invite Jeff to tell Noel that he's insecure about his athletic abilities. If Jeff and Noel were at a restaurant talking about a movie they'd both recently seen, that topic wouldn't have been so inviting for Jeff's disclosure.

Estimate the Risks and Benefits of Disclosing

To be competent in self-disclosure, you need to be able to estimate and balance its risks and benefits. As we've mentioned previously, there are compelling reasons to reveal and to withhold disclosures, many of which pertain to issues of self-identity. To be effective at self-disclosing, you need to practice judging when the benefits outweigh the risks, and vice versa.

IPC Careers

Self-Disclosure in the Workplace

Ira Berger / Alamy Stock Photo

One example of blurring the lines between public and private information may occur in the workplace when employees need to decide whether to come out to coworkers and clients as lesbian or gay. Although you might believe that a person's sexual identity shouldn't come up at work, there are many situations where heterosexual people reveal their sexuality without issue. Heterosexual people may have pictures of their families on their work desk, may mention their husbands or wives in passing, may discuss wedding plans briefly, or may reveal that their newest boyfriend or girlfriend is picking them up after work. These types of self-disclosures are more complex for gay and lesbian people. One study examined strategies that women used in the workplace to reveal or conceal their lesbian identity.[32] Women reported the following strategies: (1) gender performances such as hairstyles, clothing worn, wearing rainbow pins, and so forth; (2) analyzing others' acceptance level and adjusting as needed—that is, mentioning a girlfriend to clients who seemed open, and calling her a boyfriend if they felt a client was hostile to lesbians; and (3) being ambiguous—that is, talking about their girlfriend without using specific pronouns.

Reflection: How do you think disclosures about sexual identity should be handled in the workplace?

Predict How Your Listener Will Respond

Your ability to decode messages of warmth, concern, and empathy on the part of the other person helps you make judgments about when to tell and when to be silent. Mark knows that his partner, Sean, is a sympathetic listener. Therefore, although Mark feels some fear about revealing his past experiences with homelessness, he feels that Sean is ready to hear about them and to respond compassionately.

Be Sure the Amount and Type of Disclosure Are Appropriate

Although there are a few exceptions to this rule, the amount and type of disclosure should match the perceived intimacy level of the relationship. On a first date, it's probably unwise to tell all your insecurities and past indiscretions. Early in your relational life, you and your partner should share talk time. You don't want to dominate the conversation with long self-revelations. You should pace your disclosures so that they roughly match the developing intimacy of your relationship.

Estimate the Effect of the Disclosure on Your Relationship

Think about how the disclosure might affect the relationship. For example, Jake asks himself if telling Rochelle about his growing interest in her will actually cause the end of their friendship. Ellie considers whether telling Marc about her trouble with commitment in the past will hurt or intensify their relationship. Of course, you can never know for sure what the specific effects a disclosure will have, but making well-founded assessments of effects is an important skill to develop.

Because self-disclosure is a very well-researched communication behavior and because researchers' thoughts about it are challenged by the current explosion of social media use, we had to cover a great deal of ground in this chapter. We defined self-disclosure as the process of telling another something personal about yourself that they'd not easily discover any other way. We explored the components of our basic definition (process, intentionality, risk, trust, and subjectivity), and offered the Johari Window as a model to illustrate both our self-awareness and self-disclosures. We reviewed reasons researchers advance for choosing to either reveal or conceal information. And, we examined several factors affecting self-disclosure: individual difference, relational patterns, culture, sex and sex role,

and channel, specifically online disclosures. We discussed four norms of self-disclosure (it occurs in few interactions; in close relationships between two people, it's reciprocal and incremental). The chapter profiled two theories, CPM and Social Penetration Theory, that help explain what happens when we self-disclose (or choose not to). Finally, we offered a skill set for effective self-disclosure.

As you interact in your current interpersonal relationships as well as develop new ones, we hope you see many applications for the material in this chapter about self-disclosing. It is a behavior that can enhance initial encounters as well as deepen subsequent ones, but it requires skill and understanding to use it judiciously.

/// COMMUNICATION ASSESSMENT TEST (CAT): DEGREE OF SELF-DISCLOSURE IN A RELATIONSHIP

Choose a specific person to use as you answer these questions: mother, father, male friend, female friend, or romantic partner. You may redo the questionnaire for each of these relationships if you wish. You are to read each item on the questionnaire, and then indicate beside it the extent that you have talked about that item to the person you chose—that is, the extent to which you have made yourself known to that person. Use the following rating scale to describe the extent that you have talked about each item:

0: Have told the other person nothing about this aspect of me

1: Have talked in general terms about this. The other person has only a general idea about this aspect of me.

2: Have talked in full and complete detail about this item to the other person. They know me fully in this respect and could describe me accurately.

X: Have lied or misrepresented myself to the other person so that they have a false picture of me

Attitudes and Opinions

_____1. What I think and feel about religion; my personal religious views

_____2. My personal opinions and feelings about other religious groups than my own

_____3. My views on communism

_____4. My views on the present government—the president, government policies, etc.

_____5. My views on racial groups other than my own

_____6. My personal views on drinking

_____7. My personal views on sexual morality—how I feel that people ought to behave in sexual matters

_____8. Things I regard as desirable for a woman to be

_____9. The things I regard as desirable for a man to be

_____10. My feelings about how parents ought to deal with children

Tastes and Interests

_____1. My favorite foods, the ways I like food prepared, and my food dislikes

_____2. My favorite beverages, and the ones I don't like

_____3. My likes and dislikes in music

_____4. My favorite reading matter

_____5. The kinds of movies and TV shows that are my favorites

_____6. My tastes in clothing

_____7. The style of house, and the kinds of furnishings that I like best

_____8. The kind of party, or social gathering that I like best, and the kind that would bore me, or that I wouldn't enjoy

_____9. My favorite ways of spending spare time

_____10. What I would appreciate most for a present

Work (or Studies)

_____1. What I find to be the worst pressures and strains in my work

_____2. What I find to be the most boring and least enjoyable aspects of my work

_____3. What I enjoy most, and get the most satisfaction from, in my present work

_____4. What I feel are _my_ shortcomings and handicaps that prevent me from working as I'd like to, or that prevent me from getting further ahead in my work

_____5. What I feel are my special strong points and qualifications for my work

_____6. How I feel that my work is appreciated by others (e.g., boss, coworkers, teacher, partner)

_____7. My ambitions and goals in my work

_____8. My feelings about the rewards that I get for my work

_____9. How I feel about the choice of career/major that I have made—whether or not I'm satisfied with it

_____10. How I really feel about the people that I work for, or work with

Money

_____1. How much money I make at my work, or get as an allowance

_____2. Whether or not I owe money; if so, _how much_

_____3. Whom I owe money to at present or whom I have borrowed from in the past

_____4. Whether or not I have savings, and the amount

_____5. Whether or not others owe me money, the amount, and who owes it to me

_____6. Whether or not I gamble; if so, the way I gamble and the extent of it

_____7. All of my present sources of income—wages, fees, allowance, dividends, etc.

_____8. My total financial worth, including property, savings, bonds, insurance, etc.

_____9. My most pressing need for money right now, e.g., outstanding bills, some major purchase that is desired or needed

_____10. How I budget my money—the proportion that goes to necessities, luxuries, etc.

Personality

_____1. The aspects of my personality that I dislike, worry about, that I regard as a handicap to me

_____2. What feelings, if any, that I have trouble expressing or controlling

_____3. The facts of my present sex life—including knowledge of how I get sexual gratification, any problems that I might have, with whom I have relations, if anybody

_____4. Whether or not I feel that I am attractive to others; my problems, if any, about getting favorable sexual attention from others

_____5. Things in the past or present that I feel ashamed and guilty about

_____6. The kind of things that just make me furious

_____7. What it takes to get me feeling really depressed

_____8. What it takes to get me really worried, anxious, and afraid

_____9. What it takes to hurt my feelings deeply

_____10. The kinds of things that make me especially proud of myself, elated, full of self-esteem or self-respect

Body

_____1. My feelings about the appearance of my face— things I like and don't like

_____2. How I wish I looked: my ideals for overall appearance

_____3. My feelings about different parts of my body: legs, weight, hips, ankles, etc.

_____4. Any problems and worries that I have had with my appearance in the past

_____5. Whether or not I now have any health problems

_____6. Whether or not I have any long-range worries about my health

_____7. My past record of illness and treatment

_____8. Whether or not I make special efforts to keep fit and healthy

_____9. My current weight

_____10. My feelings about my sexual adequacy

Scoring: for each category, total the numbers, counting X as 0. Then add all the totals together for an overall total.

For each category:

0–6 = low self-disclosure in that area

7–13 = moderate self-disclosure in that area

14–20 = high self-disclosure in that area

For overall total: 0–40 = low self-disclosure overall

41–80 = moderate self-disclosure overall

81–120 = high self-disclosure overall

Source: Modified from the work of Sidney M. Jourard and Paul Lasakow.

/// KEY TERMS

self-disclosure   223

public information   224

private information   225

history   228

story   228

Johari Window   229

open self   230

hidden self   230

blind self   230

unknown self   230

catharsis   231

capitalization   232

co-rumination   237

androgynous   241

dyadic effect   246

reciprocity   246

Communication Privacy Management Theory (CPM)   247

Social Penetration Theory   248

breadth   249

depth   249

/// KEY QUESTIONS FOR APPLICATION

1. *CQ/CultureQuest*: Explore the following claim: "No two cultures look at self-disclosure the same way. When we think about self-disclosure only from a Western perspective, we'll always be wrong in our conclusions about the behavior." Do you agree or disagree? Defend your views.

2. *TQ/TechQuest*: Explore the following claim: "Social media apps make self-disclosing a lot easier to do than face-to-face settings." Do you agree or disagree? Defend your views.

3. Defend or refute our statement that self-disclosure is a process. What does it really mean to say it's a process? Explain your answer.

4. Can you add to our list of reasons to reveal or conceal personal information in a relationship? Give some specifics.

5. Which theory (CPM or Social Penetration Theory) do you think offers the clearest picture of self-disclosure? Explain your answer with specific examples relating to the theory of your choice.

6. Explain the norm of reciprocity. How do you think it works in self-disclosures? Does it have so many exceptions that it's not really worth calling it a norm? Explain your answer with specifics.

$SAGE edge™

Access practice quizzes, eFlashcards, video, and multimedia at **edge.sagepub.com/west**.

Visit **edge.sagepub.com/west** to help you accomplish your coursework goals in an easy-to-use learning environment.

CHAPTER 9

COMMUNICATING CONFLICT

LEARNING OUTCOMES

After studying this chapter, you will be able to

9–1 Understand the complexities of conflict

9–2 Detail communication patterns and styles of conflict

9–3 Identify the destructive and constructive sides of conflict

9–4 Describe the explanatory process model of interpersonal conflict

9–5 Identify the relationship between power and conflict

9–6 Employ skills for communicating during conflict that afford increased satisfaction in interpersonal interactions

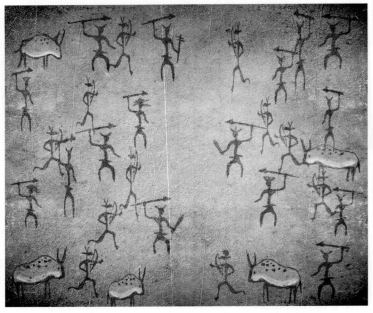

iStock.com/lolloj

Master the content at
edge.sagepub.com/west

$SAGE edge™

Most people think of conflict as an unpleasant experience, and, in fact, some conflicts can have negative impacts on emotional and physical health. Yet, it's impossible to interact with others without sometimes experiencing conflict; conflict is an unavoidable part of life. Conflicts are common in interpersonal communication because we're all unique, and differences between people are what prompt conflict. Not all differences cause conflict, however. Sometimes, people recognize differences between them that don't matter enough to cause conflict. For example, let's say that Lauryn really likes Kesha, and her cousin, Naomi, can't stand Kesha. If Lauryn and Naomi don't live together, don't go to concerts together, and don't talk about music when they see each other, this difference probably won't cause a conflict between them.

How much conflict arises from people's differences also depends on what stage they're in in their relationship. When people first meet, they usually focus on their similarities, thus reducing opportunities for conflict. Part of the fun of getting to know someone is discovering the things you have in common. However, later in the relationship, you may notice and discuss differences.

IPC Praxis

Think back to the first time you met someone you later became good friends with or dated. How do your early encounters with this person compare to your later interactions? When did you start engaging in conflict with this person? What does that tell you about conflict in interpersonal relationships?

Another factor influencing conflict between people has to do with the type of relationship they share. In some relationships, people notice differences relatively quickly because the nature of the relationship implies differing interests, concerns, and bases of power. For instance, in a relationship between a worker, Carlos, and his boss, Manuel, their job titles indicate that despite the fact that they work for the same company, they'll have differing perspectives. Manuel's job as boss makes him responsible for maximizing productivity and minimizing expense. This goal may run counter to Carlos's needs and desires as an employee. Furthermore, the power relationship between the two is not equal. Manuel has the power to punish or reward Carlos in ways that aren't reciprocal. These inherent differences make workplace friendships or romances tricky (although not impossible) to negotiate. Parent–child and teacher–student are other types of relationships in which intrinsic differences between the roles played offer ripe arenas for difference and, thus, conflict. Some people suggest that relationships between people of different cultures or even relationships between men and women maximize differences and, thus, provide opportunities for more conflicts than do relationships between more similar people.

In short, unless you only talk to people who are just like you, you never develop a relationship beyond its initial stages; or unless you're able to avoid any discussions about areas of difference with another, conflict in interpersonal communication is inevitable. But, you can control how you deal with conflicts. You can implement skills that will influence how the conflict proceeds and how it affects your relationship. Before we learn about how to manage conflict, we'll first define the term, examining its complexities, including common myths that people hold about interpersonal conflict; types of conflict people engage in; and factors that exert an influence on the experience of conflict.

 IPC Voice: Jacob

I'll never forget the first time my boyfriend and I discovered we disagreed on something. When we first got together, it was like perfection. I'd never met anyone who just "got me" like he did. We talked for hours and spent so much time together watching TV, playing basketball, cooking dinner, and going to plays. We liked all the same things—it was great. Then we started to plan our first vacation together. That was a disaster. He wanted to camp and I absolutely hate camping. That was the end of the honeymoon, for sure. We got over it, but it was a lot more fun when we just got along so effortlessly.

9–1 DEFINING CONFLICT

We've all experienced conflict, but often it comes as a surprise. We're left scratching our heads, wondering what happened. Knowing how to define conflict won't stop us from experiencing it, but it can be the first step in helping us manage it better. **Interpersonal conflict** is commonly defined as interaction between interdependent people who believe that they have incompatible goals and expect interference from each other in achieving those goals.[1] The key parts of this definition include the following:

- interaction
- interdependence
- perception or beliefs
- incompatible goals

We'll discuss each one of these terms individually, to help clarify the meaning of conflict.

Interaction

Here, **interaction** means that conflicts are created and sustained through verbal and nonverbal communication. Some conflicts involve yelling, crying, swearing, and screaming. Other conflicts consist of icy silences, cold shoulders, frowns, and withdrawal. It's also the case that conflicts may be expressed in a calm, unemotional manner; our definition is not limited to emotionally intense discussions. However, no matter whether people are yelling or ignoring each other, remember that our definition specifies that conflict is interaction *between* people. In other words, if Cate is talking to James the same way she always does, even though she's angry with him, they aren't engaging in conflict by our definition. They enter into conflict only when she says or does something that shows how she feels, and James responds.

Because this text is focused on explaining interpersonal communication, we emphasize the expression of conflict through verbal and nonverbal cues. However, this focus doesn't mean that we're not interested in what people are thinking during conflicts. Our emphasis here is on how our thoughts influence what we say; for students of communication, interaction is in the foreground, and cognition is in the background, but the two work together, each affecting the other.

Several studies examine the relationship between thoughts and communication behaviors in marital conflict. In one, the researchers asked 118 married couples to discuss a current issue that caused conflict for them, and then to watch videotapes of their own discussion. This method allowed the researchers to find out how the couples thought about their conflict communication. The study found that in severe conflicts especially, husbands and wives tended to construct individual accounts that didn't agree with their partner's account. Thus, as wives watched the tapes and recalled what they were thinking, they generated a very different picture from what their husbands thought about the same tape. The researchers commented that selective perception is a central dynamic in conflict interactions; people's differing thought patterns seemed to affect the ways they conducted the conflict.[2]

Interdependence

Interdependence means that the people involved in the conflict are in some type of a relationship together that requires them to rely on one another. Parties must feel some degree of interdependence to experience conflict. If you are completely independent of another person, then generally a conflict won't arise. The person simply isn't important enough to you to bother engaging in conflict with them.

Let's say that Lola meets Justin at a party. Justin doesn't interest Lola much, and Lola finds herself disagreeing with his loudly stated views. Justin is talking about a recent case on campus where a woman has accused a star student basketball player of date rape. Justin proclaims that the accuser was probably asking for it because the campus paper had reported that she was drunk at the time of the alleged attack. Lola listens for a while, getting a little agitated because she totally disagrees with Justin. She decides to talk to someone else and politely excuses herself. On the other hand, if Lola and Justin were good friends, they may find that their different opinions on this case will lead to conflict. It wouldn't be so easy for Lola to just walk away from a good friend with whom she disagrees.

Interdependence brings up one of the striking ironies of conflict. Although people's need for others is a basic, fundamental human desire, people rank conflicts with others one of the most critical stressors they experience. Our connection to others provides us both pleasure and pain, both the joy of feeling understood and the unhappiness when we disagree and engage in conflict. When Jeff thinks of his happiest moments, he usually thinks of the times he has spent with his best friend, Ray. However, Jeff's worst time is also associated with Ray. Ray had thought that Jeff was spreading a rumor about him, and talking to others about something he'd told Jeff in confidence. Ray had been furious, and didn't speak to Jeff for a week, unless it was to yell and accuse him of betrayal. Nothing Jeff said seemed to have any effect, and he had felt a lot of pain and anxiety because he thought that their friendship was over. Finally, Ray started to listen to Jeff and they talked through the issue. Ray saw that Jeff wasn't guilty of betraying his trust, he apologized, and they were able to resume their friendship. Jeff found it surprising that being around the same friend could sometimes be so much fun and other times feel like torture.

▶ IPC Around Us

iStock.com/PeopleImages

The holidays often become a fertile breeding ground for family conflict, according to Olga Khazan.[3] Khazan explains that families fight for many reasons when they get together to celebrate. Two conflict starters that she discusses at length are what she calls "small differences" and "social allergens." First, she points to Freud's theory called "the narcissism of the small difference." As Khazan states, it's the small differences between people who are otherwise quite similar that can cause great aggravation and lead to conflict. She offers that this may be the case because we focus more on the differences between ourselves and our family members than we do on our similarities. So, if you and your sister look a lot alike and have many of the same hobbies, but she votes Democratic and you vote Republican, Khazan predicts a political conflict over the holiday dinner.

Khazan calls the other reason for family conflicts "social allergens." Social allergens refer to those little annoying habits that people have that tend to drive you wild when you're exposed to them over time. When your uncle has the habit of clearing his throat excessively or your brother always uses the phrase "to be sure" before giving his opinion about something, annoyance may build up as you listen. These cumulative annoyances are especially difficult when families are under the same roof and increasingly interdependent.

Khazan suggests some methods for dealing with these two conflict starters, including reframing them so you can regard them as positives rather than negatives. She notes, for instance, that rather than asking yourself how it's possible that you can be related to such idiots, you could instead marvel that such diversity could come from the same gene pool.

Reflection: Have you noticed any small differences or social allergens precipitating conflicts within your family? If so, how have you tried to manage the conflicts?

Perception

Perception, as we discussed in Chapter 3, refers to the psychological process involved in sensing meaning. The definition we provided for conflict states that conflict exists when interdependent people *think* that they have incompatible goals. For example, Carmen wants to go on a family vacation to Florida. She misunderstands a statement that her husband, Dave, makes and jumps to the conclusion that he disagrees with her preferred vacation destination. Even though Carmen and Dave really agree on where to take their vacation, if Carmen believes they disagree, they'll probably experience conflict. This conflict will persist until Carmen and Dave realize that their goals really are similar.

Of course, the opposite situation may occur as well: Ana and Bonnie believe that they both hold the same opinion about their boss, Dawn, so they do not engage in any conflict on the topic. In fact, however, Ana holds a much more positive opinion of Dawn than Bonnie does, but because they don't talk about Dawn much, they don't realize they disagree and thus, they don't get into arguments about Dawn.

Some researchers emphasize the importance of perception to the conflict process when they apply a competence model to interpersonal conflict. Communication competency suggests that people judge themselves and their conversational partners based on how well they communicate and how successful they are in reaching their conversational goals. A study examining conflict between nurses used this model. The study found that professional competence was a key cause of the nurses' workplace conflicts. The researchers discovered that when nurses believed another nurse questioned their competence, conflicts ensued. In addition, nurses reported that workplace conflict was common when they thought that another nurse was incompetent at the job.[4]

Incompatible Goals

The definition of conflict specifies that friction results when people's goals differ (as in "I want to study, but Jordan wants me to go to a party with him") at the same time that they think others stand in the way of the achievement of personal goals (as in "I want to get promoted at work, but my supervisor wants me to stay in her department"). This feature of the definition implies that conflict is goal oriented. For instance, imagine two sisters, Karla and Meredith, who spend a lot of time together. One Sunday, Karla wants to go to the beach, and her sister wants to stay home and have a barbeque. Because Karla's goal isn't compatible with what Meredith wants, they will engage in conflict if they are dependent on one another to accomplish their goals. If Karla needs Meredith to drive her to the beach and Meredith needs Karla to start the barbeque, or even if they simply just want to be together for the day, they are interdependent and have incompatible goals, which will likely cause conflict between them, according to our definition.

 **IPC Praxis**

Think about a recent conflict you have had with someone—a friend, coworker, or romantic partner. Can you identify these four elements (interaction, interdependence, perception, and incompatible goals) in your recollected conflict? Be specific about how each of the four parts of our definition was (or wasn't) present in the conflict. What does this application tell you about conflict?

Myths About Conflict and Communication

Another way to understand what conflict is consists of examining what it is not. So, we turn our attention to false beliefs, or myths, about the nature of interpersonal conflict. As we've stated previously, conflict is a normal part of life, but many people find it unpleasant. Perhaps as a result, people talk a great deal about conflict, and this tends to generate myths about it. We'll discuss three very common (but mistaken) beliefs about the relationship between conflict and communication:

- Conflict is just miscommunication.
- All conflict can be resolved through good communication.
- It's always best to talk through conflicts.

Myth 1: Conflict is just miscommunication.

Many people believe that all conflict results from miscommunication or unclear communication, and this may be the case for some conflicts. However, it's possible to communicate perfectly clearly to others, and still disagree. For instance, if Tim wants to go to Harvard and his parents tell him they do not want him to go to school so far away from home, Tim and his parents may continue to argue about this topic even though they've all clearly communicated their positions and they understand each other perfectly. The problem in this case is not that they misunderstand each other; rather, they disagree about whose goal is more important and, possibly, who has the power in their relationship to make such a decision.

Myth 2: All conflict can be resolved through good communication.

The corollary to the myth of miscommunication is the notion that all conflicts can be resolved through good communication. This myth tells us that if we master a certain set of skills for managing conflict, we can resolve all of our conflicts. Although we offer a set of skills later in this chapter, we recognize that some conflicts persist, and partners may have to agree to disagree on some things. For example, no amount of good communication practices will convince Harry to vote for an independent candidate even though his friend James tries to persuade him that the independent candidate in the current election advocates better policies than does either the Republican or the Democrat. Harry simply states that voting for an independent is just the same as not voting and he won't ever consider doing that. If Harry won't listen, it doesn't matter how good a communicator James is; they won't resolve their conflict.

Myth 3: It is always best to talk through conflicts.

Underlying the first two myths is the idea that it's always best to talk about conflicts. People often believe that they need to communicate more to reach a mutually satisfying solution to their conflicts. And it's certainly true that people derive many benefits from talking through issues that bother them. However, this myth obscures the benefits that might come from avoiding certain topics rather than talking about them in great detail. Sometimes continuing to talk about a point of disagreement just exaggerates it and prolongs the conflict. Some arguments are not that important, and if you ignore them, they really will go away. For instance, when

Mel broke the rain gauge in their backyard, Tina was angry. However, because she realized that it was just a $20 item and that getting into a big discussion about it wouldn't be productive for their relationship, she didn't say anything. Within a day or two, Tina had completely forgotten the incident and was no longer angry.

Although we acknowledge that many people subscribe to these myths about conflict, it's important to realize they aren't accurate. Not all conflicts are based on misunderstandings, are resolvable, or are best dealt with by talking. Remember that communication is an important part of managing interpersonal conflict, but conflict management isn't only about communicating well.

Types of Conflict

Now that we have a basic working definition of conflict, we'll discuss six conflict types: image, content, value, relational, meta-, and serial conflicts. Understanding these different types helps us gain a better sense of conflict communication.

Image Conflicts

Image conflicts concern differences in how the participants view issues of self-image. For example, if Annika considers herself to be a competent adult, she may engage in conflict with her mother when her mother offers suggestions about how to manage her career. Annika may feel that her mother isn't respecting her as an adult and, as such, is challenging Annika's image of herself. Sometimes image conflicts result from a problem of misperception; Annika may believe her mother still thinks of her as a child, but really her mother accepts Annika as an adult. An image conflict, however, is especially difficult when two different images are, in fact, in play. If Annika's mother does still view Annika as a child, then they actually do have two competing images. A similar problem exists when a parent pushes a child to grow up faster than the child feels comfortable doing. In that case, the parent views the child as an adult, whereas the child may still see herself or himself as a child. Sometimes, image conflicts may masquerade as another type of conflict, but at the core of an image conflict is a disagreement about self-definition.

Content Conflicts

Content conflicts are often called "substantive" because they revolve around the substance of a specific issue. Interdependent people fight about myriad topics. Maeve calls her Internet provider to complain about the service, and the service provider tells her there's no evidence to support her complaint. Nanette likes a tree on her property line, but her neighbor thinks its roots are responsible for cracking his driveway. Matt hates to bowl, and his best friend, Drew, loves bowling. Ginna wants to spend some of their savings on a vacation, and her husband, Sean, thinks that would be a waste of money. Penny thinks that the data for her work group's presentation should be rechecked, and the other members of the group think they've been checked sufficiently. Lou believes that even though he works part time, he should be respected as a member of the company and allowed a say in company policies; however, the full-time workers don't want the part-timers involved in those matters. Although all of these examples involve topics of disagreement, some of these content conflicts have undertones of the other types of conflicts within them.

Video 9.1

Content conflicts can focus on public issues, such as those that are often the subject of political or community debate.

Some researchers believe that content conflicts can either focus on **public issues**, meaning issues outside the relationship, or involve **private issues** that relate more closely to the relationship, and in this way resemble the relational conflict type we'll discuss later. For instance, when Stan and Frank disagree about whether the United States should have zero tolerance when it comes to immigrants who enter the country illegally, they're debating a public issue. When Stan complains that Frank has no time to hang out with him anymore because he is always spending time with his new girlfriend, they are tackling a private issue. Not surprisingly, research finds that people enjoy arguments about public issues more than conflicts about private issues.

Value Conflicts

Value conflicts are conflicts focused specifically on questions of right and wrong. For instance, the neighbors we mentioned previously who are arguing about the tree on their property line may be having a values conflict if they are discussing it in terms of ecosystems and environmental protection. When people disagree about gun control, marriage equality, U.S. immigration laws, or the Affordable Care Act (Obamacare), they are often engaging in value conflicts because opinions on these topics largely depend on competing value judgments made by the participants. For example, arguments about gun control often hinge on the value placed on risks to human life compared to the value placed on the freedom to bear arms.

Relational Conflicts

Relational conflicts focus on issues concerning the relationship between two people. When Rachel and Taylor argue about how much Taylor respects Rachel's opinions, they are having a relational conflict. Couples who argue about how much they should tell their in-laws about their financial situation, compared to how much they should keep private, are engaging in relational conflict. Our previous example of Ginna and Sean's fight about whether or not to spend savings on a vacation could be classified as a relational conflict if it centers on how they make decisions in their relationship. The disagreement would be a values conflict if it underscores a difference in how the two value money. Figure 9.1 presents a

Figure 9.1 /// Overlap in Types of Conflicts

Conflict Dialogue

Andre: "It's a real shame that all these states are legalizing medical marijuana. People will abuse the system and get prescriptions even if there's nothing wrong with them. Drugs are illegal for a reason!"

Michael: "I really thought I knew you, Andre, but that just blew me away. Alcohol and tobacco are legal, and they're much more harmful than marijuana. With proper regulation, marijuana can be a beneficial treatment for a number of illnesses."

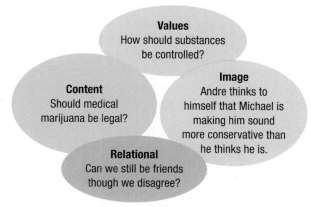

dialogue and an image showing how these four conflict types overlap within a single conflict dialogue. Even though the types cannot be completely separated, being able to identify what kind of conflict you're having is useful in helping you decide how to manage it.

Meta-Conflicts

Meta-conflicts are conflicts about the way you conduct conflict. Anytime people engage in any type of conflict, they may also be concerned about *how* they're conducting the conflict. If Jennifer and Dominic argue repeatedly, they may also reflect on their conflict process, and this reflection may lead to meta-conflicts. A meta-conflict might sound like the following:

Jennifer: "Honestly, Dom, it's impossible to talk to you. All you do is interrupt me!"

Dominic: "Well, Jen, if you would get to the point when you talk, I wouldn't have to interrupt to get a word in edgewise. You go on so long, I never have a chance to speak unless I do interrupt."

Jennifer: "That is completely untrue. I don't talk that much. It might seem like it because whatever I want to say gets interrupted, so I have to start over so often."

Dominic:	"Oh, right, you're going to blame me because you hog the conversation all the time."
Jennifer:	"I give up, Dominic. Talking to you is a no-win situation—I'm over it."

Meta-conflicts can happen at any time, but they are especially likely in long-term relationships when partners have had many chances to engage in conflict and to notice the ways the other communicates in disagreements.

Serial Conflicts

Serial conflict is a sixth conflict type, but it differs from the other five types because it doesn't refer to the subject or the underlying focus of the conflict. Instead, it refers to the timeframe for the conflict. Up to this point, we've been talking about conflicts as discrete episodes, with specific starting points ("I'm so sick of you using up all the hot water every morning") and specific ending points ("Okay, okay, I'll take a quicker shower"). Serial conflicts are those that recur over time in people's everyday lives, without a resolution ("Last week you said you'd take a quicker shower, but you aren't doing that. It's the same thing over and over." "Well, you're always on my case! We've argued about the hot water for months. Leave me alone about the stupid shower, already").

Researchers find that these serial conflicts tell us a lot about relational communication. In relationships with a long history (such as dating, marriage, or families), partners are likely to have unsettled issues that come up repeatedly whether they want them to or not. Some researchers tried to figure out what factors sustain serial arguments in relationships. They found that factors such as whether the participants believe the conflict is resolvable, as well as their perceptions of the intensity of the conflict, affect how likely it is to recur (those conflicts perceived as irresolvable and very intense seem to be the ones that turn into serial arguments).[5] Some research suggests that serial conflicts persist when people rehearse interactions in their minds prior to engaging in them. When people go through this rehearsal, they mentally establish the argument, making it difficult to deviate from past interactions.[6] To read short dialogues illustrating each of these six conflict types see Table 9.1.

Table 9.1 /// Types of Conflict	
Image Conflict	
Marlee:	"Mom, why do you still treat me like a child? I'm 22 years old!"
Mom:	"Marlee, you are always going to be my little girl."
Marlee:	"That's ridiculous, Mom. You have to let me grow up."
Content Conflict	
Jaylen:	"Tony, I don't think that New York has the largest state population in the United States. I'm pretty sure I read that it was California."
Tony:	"No, it's New York."
Jaylen:	"Well, Google it."

Value Conflict	
Elyise:	"Travis, I can't believe we're so close to getting married, and I am just finding out that you don't want to have kids! To me, that's what marriage is all about."
Travis:	"Are you kidding? I never believed that marriage is all about having kids. What about love, companionship, and fun? Aren't those the things that marriage is all about?"
Relational Conflict	
Angela:	"Regina, I know this sounds funny, but I feel kinda left out when you and I are together with Justine. We used to be best friends, and now it seems like you don't even want to be around me if you have the chance to hang out with her."
Regina:	"That's not exactly true, Angela."
Angela:	"It sure feels that way to me."
Regina:	"I know I've been spending a lot of time with Justine, but that's just because we have the same major and are in a lot of classes together. You and I have developed different interests."
Meta-conflict	
Laura:	"I'm tired of hearing you take that tone with me!"
Adrianne:	"What are you talking about?"
Laura:	"You just did it now—you sound so patronizing whenever we disagree about anything. It sounds like you think you're so superior."
Adrianne:	"That is totally not true. I don't think that at all."
Laura:	"Well, it sounds like you do."
Serial Conflict	
Fran:	"It's time for us to clean out the attic."
Marcus:	"You are so bossy about the house."
Fran:	"What are you talking about, Marcus? I just said let's clean the attic! Every time I suggest cleaning, you say I'm bossy. That's not fair."
Marcus:	"Yeah, but every time I complain, you start crying unfair."
Fran:	"Here we go again. I'm sick of this same old fight!"

 **IPC Praxis**

As you think about your own behavior in conflicts, how helpful is it to try to figure out the type of conflict you're having? If you think it might be helpful to you, explain how. Give some specifics about how knowing that you're having an image conflict, for example, might help you deal with it better than not being able to type the conflict.

Factors Influencing Interpersonal Conflict

In this section, we broaden our understanding of conflict by briefly discussing two factors that affect conflict interaction: sex or sex role and culture. Although we review them separately, they most often act together to affect conflicts. For example, a German American woman and a Chinese American man who both work at a small software company may have a disagreement over how to invest their limited research and development budget. As they discuss their different approaches to the budget, cultural and gendered messages about how to conduct conflict influence this particular conflict between them. For instance, some gendered prescriptions suggest that women should be harmonizers and conflict avoidant, and some cultural messages suggest that Asians should be the same. In order to understand conflict, it's important to remember that all conflicts take place between people who are gendered and who come from a specific cultural background.

Sex and Sex Role

When we talk about *sex,* we are referring to the biological categories that divide people into two groups: women and men. When we talk about *sex role,* we are referring to cultural socialization, not biological sex. Sometimes people call the behaviors that society prescribes for women and men *gender.* Men and women are not inherently different in their orientations to conflict or in their conflict behaviors; rather, they have been taught a set of responsibilities and norms that affect their conflict interactions. Furthermore, not all men or all women are socialized to the same degree. Thus, we may see great variety in how women and men enact gendered social norms.

Because in the United States women are taught to be keepers of relational life and men are socialized to pay attention to public life, women often want to talk about relationship issues, and men do not. This imbalance itself may cause conflict within relationships. For example, when Moira tells Jack that she wants to talk about their relationship, Jack may perceive her statement as an indication that their relationship is in trouble and, as a result, try to avoid the conversation. Moira may not have intended to imply that she wanted to discuss specific problems; she just wanted to connect with Jack about the topic of their life together. And one study found that men identified more hurtful messages in conflict than women did (although the difference was not statistically significant). The researchers

Research is unclear as to how much sex affects conflict behaviors. It's probably the case that sex role stereotypes indicate more differences than actually exist when men and women engage in conflict.

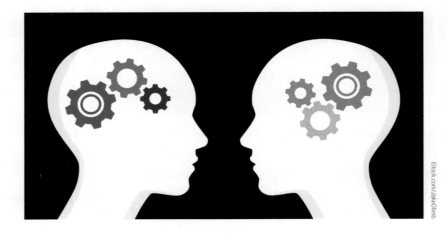

iStock.com/JakeOlimb

suggested that this finding might be due to men perceiving physiological arousal more bothersome than women do.[7]

Some research suggests that women are more collaborative and men are more competitive in conflict interactions.[8] However, other studies call this generalization into question. One study examining college students found that women were more likely than men to report that they used both cooperative and competitive conflict strategies.[9] Another study found that women and men in romantic relationships did not differ in their use of competition as a conflict strategy.[10] Some researchers found that women were more collaborative in conflicts with women friends, but not with romantic partners, thus suggesting that context interacts with gender in terms of how conflict is conducted.[11] And, it's probably the case that men's and women's conflict behavior is contingent on other variables as well—the duration of the relationship, for instance—in interaction with sex, rather than simply their sex alone.[12]

As we mentioned at the beginning of this section, it's important to note that all communication behaviors, including conflict, are influenced by several factors at the same time. Researchers have talked about *intersectionality*, which means that people behave as they do because of a variety of factors that intersect in their identity, such as age, race, and sex. We in the field of communication, for instance, are just beginning to examine how sex and conflict interact when the participants don't identify with either of the two categories, women and men, that are commonly believed to divide people.

Culture

As we have discussed throughout this text, we live in a diverse world where technology, travel, business practices, and so forth increasingly link us with people who are culturally different from ourselves. Differing cultural practices and norms may put us in conflict with one another. In 2018, the U.S. Bureau of Labor Statistics released a report stating that in 2017, there were 27.4 million foreign-born persons in the U.S. labor force, comprising 17.1 percent of the total. It's reasonable to believe that the percentage may continue to grow. So, even without traveling, U.S. workers undoubtedly will come into contact with people from cultures other than their own. Given this situation, it is crucial that we understand how culture impacts conflict interactions.

When Yaguang moved to the United States from China to begin graduate school, he was amazed and distressed to see how much the U.S. students criticized each other and engaged in conflict about a variety of issues. He found their behaviors threatening and unpleasant. Some evidence exists that conflict should be viewed as a culturally distinct behavior. In a study examining Japanese and U.S. college students, researchers found that students in the United States used conflict as a motivation to change their own behaviors significantly more than did the students in Japan. The researchers explained this finding by noting that Asian culture prompts more sensitivity to information about weaknesses, and that Asians have high levels of fear about hearing criticism. They go on to state that "viewing conflict as a cultural behavior helps explain why disputes over seemingly similar issues can be handled so dissimilarly in different cultures" (p. 148).[13]

All people wish to be respected and shown approval, but the ways in which respect and approval are expressed often differ from culture to culture. Even the meaning of the word *conflict* may differ across cultures. For instance, for the French, the term means warlike opposition. The negative connotations of conflict are extremely strong for the French. For the Chinese, the meaning of the word *conflict* involves intense struggle and fighting. Not surprisingly, Chinese people report that they don't like conflict, which they consider disruptive to the harmoniousness of interpersonal relationships. Although the value of harmony predominates in Chinese culture, conflict style differences do exist within the culture. One study found that modern-day Chinese families seem to endorse conversation and conflict rather than simple conformity to preserve harmony. It may be the case that the Chinese are being influenced by Western values and losing some of their traditional approaches to conflict.[14]

People from the United States may not enjoy conflict either, but they define the word more broadly than the French or the Chinese do, allowing for more possible responses to the interaction itself. Some other cultures may have even more positive responses to conflict than the United States does. For example, the Spanish word for conflict, *conflicto,* looks quite similar to the English word. But in Spanish, *conflicto* doesn't have very many negative connotations, and many Latinx cultures consider conflict an interesting exercise, allowing for dramatic flair that is enjoyable, which is different from most English speakers' connotations.

Culture affects our conduct of interpersonal conflict in myriad ways. A person whose primary orientation is toward individualism might come into conflict with a person whose primary orientation is toward collectivism because of their different values. An individualistic orientation leads to a concern with one's own image (self-face), whereas a collectivistic orientation leads to a concern for the other person's image (other-face). The individualist wishes to resolve a conflict so that the solution is equitable or fair. The collectivist wishes to resolve a conflict so that the solution benefits the community. The two people will have opposing communication behaviors (e.g., competition vs. avoidance) during conflict, probably leading to an escalation of conflict and misunderstanding.

One study examined the impact of high- and low-context cultures on conflict styles. In Chapter 2, we stated that people in high-context cultures reveal most of what they mean through contextual cues in the environment and embodied nonverbally by a person, thus relying less on direct verbal expression. In low-context cultures, the opposite approach exists, and people depend on verbal clarity to make meaning known. The United States is an example of a low-context culture, and Thailand is an example of a high-context culture. The study found, as expected, that people in high-context cultures did choose avoiding and obliging conflict more than those in low-context cultures; people in low-context cultures preferred the dominating conflict style more than those in high-context cultures did.[15]

Some research examines conflict in interracial couples beginning with the premise that their racial differences will be the catalyst for more conflict than same-race couples experience. Two studies found that this was not the case. There was actually no difference in the conflict patterns reported by couples in same-race and interracial couples.[16]

9–2 COMMUNICATION PATTERNS AND STYLES IN CONFLICT

Long-term relational partners often notice that their communication behaviors form repeating patterns. Although these patterns are sometimes negative and the participants wish to break out of them, they generally find it difficult to do so. Other times, the patterns are more productive. Additionally, sometimes individuals develop habitual responses to conflict; researchers call these conflict styles. In this section, we review four conflict patterns—three negative and one positive:

- symmetrical escalation
- symmetrical withdrawal
- pursuit–withdrawal and withdrawal–pursuit
- symmetrical negotiation

We conclude this section by discussing five common styles people use in response to conflict situations:

- competing
- accommodating
- collaborating
- compromising
- avoiding

Conflict Patterns

We'll first review the three negative patterns that researchers commonly describe, and then we'll discuss the one positive pattern.

Symmetrical Escalation

Symmetrical escalation exists when each partner chooses to increase the intensity of the conflict. When Mike yells at Sally and she yells back at him, they begin the symmetrical escalation pattern. If Mike then advances on Sally with a menacing look, she might slap his face. Each partner matches the other's escalating fight behaviors. Sometimes this pattern is called "fight–fight."

This pattern cannot go on indefinitely. Because the amount of escalation that is possible is limited, and because the intensity in the conflict is negative, this pattern is a futile one for communicators.

Symmetrical Withdrawal

Symmetrical withdrawal means that when conflict occurs, neither partner is willing to confront the other. Thus, one person's move away is reciprocated by the other's move away. For example, if Jolene stops speaking to Marianne because she feels she did all the work for their joint presentation in their organizational communication class, and Marianne responds in kind, they both withdraw from their relationship. This pattern, like symmetrical escalation, spells the end of the relationship if it's carried to its logical conclusion. If both partners move away from each other when conflict happens, they will soon be so far apart that they may have difficulty reuniting.

Pursuit–Withdrawal and Withdrawal–Pursuit

The previous two patterns are symmetrical, meaning that the partners mirror each other (or each behaves in the same way as the other). So, if Mike yells, Sally does too. When Jolene stops talking to Marianne, Marianne stops talking to Jolene. The **pursuit–withdrawal** and **withdrawal–pursuit** patterns are asymmetrical. This means that the behavior of one partner is the opposite of the other's behavior. In the pursuit–withdrawal pattern, when one partner presses for a discussion about a source of conflict, the other partner withdraws. For example, Pam tells her son Nicky that they have to talk about his staying out so late on school nights, and Nicky disappears into his room and shuts the door. Withdrawal–pursuit is just the opposite. In this pattern, a partner's withdrawal prompts the other's pursuit. When Anthony retreats to the attic to work on a project and Missy runs up to the attic several times to try to get him to continue arguing about buying a new car, they are exhibiting withdrawal–pursuit.

These patterns are extremely unsatisfying to the participants; they have the quality of a dog chasing its tail. Gregory Bateson referred to these types of conflicts as *schismogenesis*: both partners do what they wish the other would do for them, and both are rebuffed. Missy wants Anthony to come talk to her about their conflict, so she pursues him. Anthony wants to avoid talking about it, so he withdraws. Anthony's withdrawal spurs Missy to advance more, which in turn causes Anthony to withdraw further.

In a study investigating the pursuit–withdrawal pattern in conflicts between parents and children, researchers found that the young adults in their sample reported a high degree of stress related to this pattern. This was the case regardless of whether the young adult was the pursuer and the parent withdrew or vice versa. The researchers suggest that pursuing and withdrawing are both control strategies, and because parents usually win arguments with their children as a result of the power differential, children subsequently feel stress and frustration. Additionally, the researchers believe that this conflict pattern may cause children to feel hopeless about ever satisfying their own goals, which results in stress.[17]

Symmetrical Negotiation

Symmetrical negotiation is the one positive pattern on our list. In this pattern, each partner mirrors the other's negotiating behaviors. They listen to each other and reflect back what they have heard. They offer suggestions for dealing with the conflict and are willing to talk as much or as little as necessary to come to a mutually satisfying resolution.

People in relationships don't use only one of these patterns exclusively to communicate. Even satisfied couples may use a negative pattern, but they are likely to break out of it and get back to discussing the problem in a more positive manner fairly quickly, using techniques we discuss at the end of the chapter.

Conflict Styles

The pattern information we just reviewed focuses on the dynamic interplay *between* the participants participating in a conflict. Researchers have also been interested in the habitual ways a single individual copes with conflict when it occurs. They've called this approach conflict styles. Do you think you have a consistent style when you find yourself engaged in conflict? One of the most common listing of conflict styles is based on crossing a person's concern for themselves in the conflict with their concern for their partner. Figure 9.2 shows how combining these two concerns produces five conflict styles.[18] These five styles include

Video 9.2

1. **Competing:** a style resulting from a high concern for self and a low concern for the other

2. **Accommodating**: a style resulting from a high concern for the other and a low concern for self

3. **Collaborating:** a style resulting from a high concern for both self and the other

4. **Compromising:** a style resulting from a moderate concern for both self and the other

5. **Avoiding:** a style resulting from a low concern for both self and the other

Each style has its pros and cons. The collaborating style tends to solve problems in ways that maximize the chances that the best result is provided for all involved. The pluses of a collaborating style include creating mutual trust, maintaining positive relationships, and building commitment. However, it's time consuming and it takes a lot of energy to collaborate with another during conflict. The competing style offers an authoritarian approach ("my way or the highway") and it may develop hostility in the person who doesn't achieve their goals. However, the competing style tends to resolve a conflict quickly. The avoiding style is nonconfrontational and won't escalate conflicts. But, it results in unresolved problems that usually will reappear later. The accommodating style is relationship focused, so the person with this style will generally give in to preserve relational harmony. However, over time someone using this style may become resentful because the relationship will begin to appear one-sided. The compromising style takes a middle-ground approach that can be useful when the conflict addresses complex issues without simple solutions. Both parties are afforded equal power in a compromise. Yet, compromises usually leave both parties somewhat unsatisfied, and it's possible that the compromise solution isn't as effective as one of the other choices might have been.

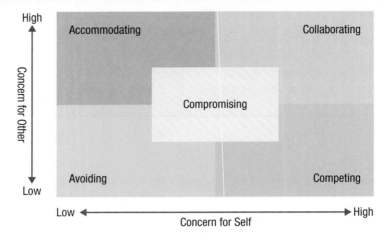

Figure 9.2 /// Five Conflict Styles

Two researchers have labeled three additional styles based on emotional aspects and strategy in a conflict:

- **emotional:** a style that relies on emotional responses to cope with conflict
- **neglect:** a coping response that's passive-aggressive
- **the third-party style:** asking for help from someone outside the conflict[19]

Do you recognize yourself in any of these styles? Examining styles offers us some insight about how conflict operates in a relationship, but it's useful to acknowledge that most people switch their styles around depending on their partner, the situation, and a variety of other issues. At the end of the chapter, you can take the CAT to try to identify your preferred style(s).

Now that we've reviewed negative and positive patterns of communicating during conflict, and examined some of the conflict styles people utilize, we'll turn our attention to negative and positive outcomes of conflict: the destructive and constructive sides to interpersonal conflict.

9–3 THE DESTRUCTIVE AND CONSTRUCTIVE SIDES OF INTERPERSONAL CONFLICT

As we stated at the beginning of the chapter, conflicts between people are inevitable and inescapable. Therefore, we engage in conflict frequently. Sometimes we feel better about ourselves and others after a conflict, while other times we may feel more upset and frustrated than we did before the conflict began. We may emerge from a conflict with a friend having a stronger sense of our friendship; we may leave a conflict with our boss feeling diminished and impotent. Often, the key to the outcome is found in the way the conflict is managed. We'll now discuss ways that conflict communication can be negative and destructive for people individually and for their relationships with others. Later, we'll talk about the more constructive aspects of conflict communication.

Destructive Aspects of Interpersonal Conflict

There is a strong association between children who are exposed to a lot of family conflict and a host of negative psychological consequences in adulthood such as depression, anger, anxiety, and so forth. Furthermore, when children experience a lot of conflict in their family, they are likely to become desensitized to verbal aggression, which may result in them becoming verbally aggressive themselves as adults. When conflict is constant and not well managed, negative consequences ensue. Here we discuss two: bullying and violence.

Bullying

Western scholars have traditionally defined **bullying** by noting three specific criteria: A bully seeks to inflict *intentional harm* through *repeated unwanted actions* (verbal or physical) directed toward an individual who is of *lesser power* (e.g., physical, emotional, financial) than the bully.[20] However, there are situations where bullying occurs that provide exceptions to this definition. Occasionally bullying is just a one-time offense; bullying may not need to actually be repeated if the victim fears that it will be. Once three students cornered Jonah after school, pushed him around and called him names because they suspected he was gay. If Jonah believes they might do so again, that's enough to call the one episode bullying.

Also, sometimes bullies don't attack one individual, but instead focus on a group, such as women or members of co-cultures, sometimes called *bias bullying*. In some ways, the #MeToo movement begun in 2017 is a response to bias bullying. Finally, some have argued that bullying may not need an uneven power dynamic because it can occur between peers of the same age or social class, coworkers of the same standing, or individuals of the same sex. So, bullying is a rather expansive behavior and it occurs frequently.

By some estimates, 15% of any given population in a school or workplace has been involved in bullying, as either the bully or the victim. Others cite higher numbers, especially with reference to cyberbullying (or bullying behavior online). According to some statistics, over half of all adolescents in the United States have been bullied online, and about the same number have engaged in bullying behaviors online.[21] The National Education Association reports that 6 out of 10 American teens witness bullying daily in schools.[22] Bullying is immensely crucial in the lives of not only the victims, but also the bullies and their respective communities. When a person is the victim of bullying, the consequences can be severe. Victims are more likely to express sadness, depression, thoughts of suicide, and suicide attempts than those who have not been bullied. When a person has been a bully, they also can have severe repercussions, and may suffer guilt and depression for many years. In communities where bullying exists, the social fabric is torn, leaving everyone in a poorer condition than is optimal. If a school has a bullying problem, the whole school suffers the negative consequences even though not everyone is a perpetrator or a victim.

Violence can be psychological as well as physical, as demonstrated by cyberbullying behavior.

AP Photo/Patti Blake

Communication behaviors characteristic of bullying include isolating or ignoring, nitpicking or excessively criticizing, humiliating, and even physically abusing someone. Some research indicates that a big problem for those who are bullied at work involves convincing others to believe them. This research offers suggestions for getting others to listen to and believe accounts of bullying including speaking rationally but expressing appropriate emotion; telling a plausible story with consistent, relevant, specific details; emphasizing your own competence; and showing consideration for others' perspectives.[23]

Violence and Aggression

Violence within interpersonal relationships is distressingly common in the United States; FBI statistics show that 35% of the women killed in the United States in 2012, whose murderers were known, died at the hands of a husband or a boyfriend. Furthermore, in 2012, for those murders where the circumstances of the crime were known, over 40% occurred during conflicts. Acts of violence are common between couples. Used when conflicts get out of hand, these behaviors—which include minor acts of violence such as pushing and shoving—might affect as many as 50% of couples in the United States.[24] In addition, it is estimated that 1 in 4 children will be exposed in some way to violence in their family before they are 18 years old.[25]

Violence in relationships begins early. In one study of over 5,000 sixth graders, 42% reported being the victim of some type of violence from their boyfriend or girlfriend. Twenty-nine percent of the sixth graders reported that they had been perpetrators of teen dating violence.[26]

Violence and aggression may be seen as conflict going to extremes, occurring when one person imposes their will on someone else through verbal and nonverbal acts geared to hurt or cause suffering. Violence and aggression can be psychological (as when parents belittle their children) or physical (as when someone is hit or battered). These two types may often be seen together. Someone who's verbally aggressive may also be physically abusive. Because these two are related, teaching more constructive forms of conflict management to reduce verbal aggression could also reduce physical abuse.

In the communication discipline, most of the research on violence has focused on the family. Family violence ranges from child abuse to spousal abuse to sibling abuse to elder abuse to incest. Some research examines how families can reconcile after violence. In this line of research, reconciliation doesn't mean excusing the violence or forgetting it happened but instead means focusing on forgiveness and moving forward. Other research shows that mothers who have been victims of intimate partner violence believe that they can stop the cycle of violence through effective, open communication with their children.[27]

While violence and aggression are significant social problems, these topics are beyond the scope of this text, and we won't discuss them more extensively here. Interpersonal conflict can be managed without resorting to violence and aggression, and it may even have positive outcomes. We now turn to those and discuss conflict's constructive side.

Constructive Aspects of Interpersonal Conflict

As we have previously discussed, relationships of any depth cannot exist without conflict. Furthermore, there are many positives to engaging in conflict with a relational partner. Managing conflict with sensitivity leads to positive evaluations of communication competence. In addition, dealing productively with conflict in romantic relationships promotes positive feelings, and contributes to each partner feeling understood. The following benefits can come from conflict that's handled constructively: getting feelings out in the open and increasing knowledge of one another, promoting feelings of confidence in relationships that survive conflicts, promoting genuine human contact, increasing the intimacy of a relationship, maximizing the chances of making a good decision, and shaking a relationship out of a rut. Although all conflict doesn't automatically produce positive outcomes for relationships, the possibility almost always exists.

Additionally, it may be the case that it's not the presence of conflict per se that's an issue in relationships. For instance, if Ella and Larry fight an average of 5 times a week while Grace and Steven argue 10 times a week, it is still possible that Grace and Steven are happy in their relationship. In fact, they could be happier than Ella and Larry. If during Grace and Steven's arguments they have a **positive interaction ratio** (i.e., they say more nice things to each other than negative things), they could be more satisfied in their relationship than Ella and Larry, who fight less but have a **negative interaction ratio** (i.e., they're more negative than positive in their encounters).

This line of thinking began with psychologist John Gottman's work examining positive-to-negative ratios in marriage. Gottman claims that five positive comments to one negative is the *magic ratio,* supporting this claim with substantial research data from couples in his Seattle lab. He and his colleagues predicted with 94% accuracy whether 700 newlywed couples would stay together or divorce based on whether or not they exhibited the magic ratio during conflict encounters.[28]

9–4 EXPLAINING CONFLICT

In this section, we review one model that helps us sort us out the complex phenomenon of conflict by diagramming its component parts. The Explanatory Process Model is useful in helping us think about the nature and the process of interpersonal conflict. And, this should help us become better communicators in conflict.

The Explanatory Process Model

The **Explanatory Process Model**[29] pictures conflict as a process that occurs in the following episodes: distal context, proximal context, conflict interaction, proximal outcomes, and distal outcomes. In this section, we discuss each of these episodes in turn. Figure 9.3 illustrates how the episodes fit together to make up the conflict process.

Conflict begins with a **distal context**, or the background that frames the specific conflict. The distal context sets the stage for conflict and contains the history between the two parties and the areas of disagreement they have discussed in the past. For example, when Ryan and Geoff became roommates, they had a history going back to the second grade. Geoff knows that Ryan is messier than he is and that Ryan doesn't care about his physical surroundings nearly as much as he does. In addition, Geoff knows that Ryan is quiet, and less inclined to enjoy conflict the way Geoff does. They had talked about how they would deal with these differences before moving in together. All of this background information forms the distal context.

The second episode in this model is the **proximal context**, which refers to the rules, emotions, and beliefs of the individuals involved in the conflict. If Ryan and Geoff set some rules about how to conduct conflict when it arises (e.g., no yelling, or no complaining behind the other's back), those rules will become part of the proximal context. Geoff's goal to keep the apartment clean and Ryan's goal not to fuss about his living space also comprise the proximal context. The proximal context combines with the distal context, creating a background for any overt conflict Geoff and Ryan may have.

The next episode is **conflict interaction**. This occurs when the differences between the partners become a problem and one or both people begin to address the issue. For instance, Geoff tells Ryan he has to start picking up the stuff he leaves lying out in the common spaces of the apartment, and Ryan responds by saying that he knows it's bothering Geoff, and he feels bad about that, but he's tired of trying to

Figure 9.3 /// The Explanatory Process Model

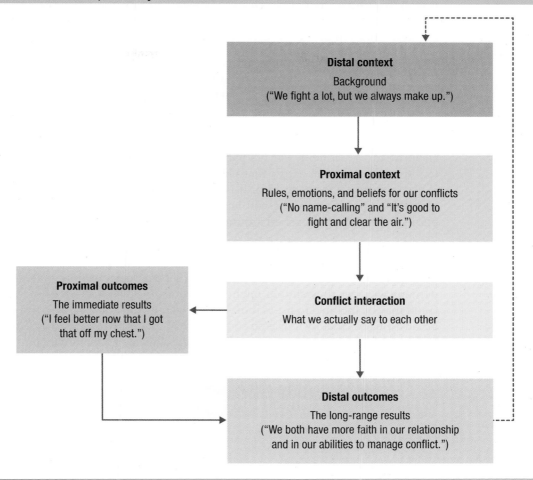

live in a "magazine-ready" apartment. This episode includes the messages Ryan and Geoff exchange and the patterns of their communication as they talk about the problem in their apartment.

The next episode is **proximal outcomes**, or the immediate results after the conflict interaction. For instance, Ryan and Geoff might decide that they don't want to be roommates any longer because they can't come up with a plan to clean the apartment that satisfies them both. Or they might get sick of arguing about it and ignore the problem for a while, until Geoff can't stand the mess anymore, and the conflict begins again. Or they might decide that Ryan will pay for a cleaning person to come in once a month.

Finally, this model shows that conflicts are never completely over. The proximal outcomes affect the **distal outcomes**, which include the residue of having engaged in the conflict and the feelings that both the participants have about their interaction. For instance, if they've decided that Ryan will hire a cleaning person, Geoff and Ryan might feel proud that they came up with a great idea that pleases them both—Geoff is glad that he gets to live in a clean apartment, and Ryan is relieved that he doesn't have to change lifelong habits. Alternatively, Ryan could feel a little resentful about the solution. Even though he agreed to do it, he might feel that it's unfair that he has to pay a monthly fee beyond the rent just to keep Geoff happy.

In addition to the parties' responses to the solution, they both have feelings about the ways they interacted during the conflict. Geoff, for example, might congratulate himself for not losing his temper and confronting Ryan before building up too much resentment. Geoff might also feel grateful to Ryan for listening to his point of view and empathizing even though Ryan can't see the point of thoroughly cleaning the apartment. For his part, Ryan might think he did a great job of listening and might feel happy that Geoff explained his position in such a way that it began to make sense to him. It is also possible that both men could feel a bit resentful about the way the conflict interaction unfolded. One or both of them might feel that he got pushed around by the other.

As we see in Figure 9.3, the distal outcomes feed into the distal context for the next conflict. For instance, if Geoff feels grateful to Ryan for his behavior during the conflict about cleaning the apartment, that will set the stage for how a later conflict—perhaps whether they should pitch in together to buy a flat-screen TV—unfolds. Geoff may be inclined to listen more carefully to Ryan's point of view in this conflict because he feels that Ryan was so cooperative in their previous conflict. Thus, we see in this model how conflicts affect relationships and shape relational life.

Theory-Into-Practice (TIP)

Explanatory Process Model

Think of a conflict that you have had with a roommate or any friend at school. Briefly describe the conflict, and then map the conflict onto the parts of this model: distal context, proximal context, conflict interaction, proximal outcomes, and distal outcomes. Explain what formed the distal context for the conflict, the proximal context, and so forth. In what ways does this model help you understand the conflict?

9–5 THE RELATIONSHIP OF CONFLICT TO POWER

Video 9.3

Power can be defined as the ability to control the behavior of another. In conflict situations, power often influences the outcome as well as the process of the interaction. Power has relevance in all communication encounters; even simple conversations used to exchange demographic or superficial information may reflect power issues between the partners. For instance, if one person asks a lot of questions (Where are you from? What's your major? and so forth), while the other person provides the answers, that could indicate a power imbalance between the two. Whether or not you agree that *all* communication rests on power differentials, it is true that conflict communication utilizes power in a variety of ways. The following sections briefly discuss how people use power, as well as some sex differences in power.

Using Power

Researchers[30] discuss four ways that people use power in conflict interactions: direct application, direct and virtual use, indirect application, and hidden use. See Table 9.2 for a brief summary of these ways of using power.

Direct application of power in a conflict situation involves using any resources at your disposal to compel the other to comply, regardless of their desires. When Marla spanks her 2-year-old son, Jerry, and sends him to his room, she is using direct application of power. Related to this use, a second way that people use power, **direct and virtual use of power**, involves communicating the *potential* use of direct application. The use of threats and promises are good illustrations of this way of using power. For example, when Dr. Moore says that he will fail Lorna in his Introduction to Communication class unless she rewrites a paper to his satisfaction, he is exercising a threat. When Dr. Seltzer promises the students in his communication theory class that they will all receive "A"s if they complete all the written work on time, he is offering a promise. Threats and promises are two sides of the same coin.

The **indirect application of power** concerns employing power without making its employment explicit. For instance, if Jaylen has heard his boss, Pamela, mention that she likes to be copied on all office memos, and he follows that practice even though it's not an official office policy, Pamela has used indirect application of power. One example of the indirect application of power is the relational message. When people send **relational messages**, they define the relationship (and implicitly state that they have the power to do this). For instance, when Tim tells Sue how much he gave up so they could move to Ohio to be near her parents, he sends a message that in their relationship Sue is indebted to him. Of course, partners may accept or contest the implicit message. If Sue agrees that Tim has done her an enormous favor at some cost to himself, she accepts his relationship definition and his power. If she argues with him that he really wanted to move, too, or that he didn't give up that much, they will conflict over the balance of power in their relationship.

Most of the time we think of power as the ability to talk someone else into complying with what we want, but in the case of **hidden use of power** (also called *unobtrusive power*), we don't have to say a word. For example, if Sam doesn't bring up a topic for discussion because he knows his friend Dale won't agree with him, Dale exercises hidden power. And when Liz complies with her mother's wishes for a big, lavish wedding, although she and her fiancé really want a small, more conservative ceremony, Liz succumbs to her mother's hidden power. Liz doesn't even

Table 9.2 /// Types of Power

Method	Definition
Direct application	Using any means to get your way
Direct and virtual use	Using threats and promises to communicate the potential use of direct application
Indirect application	Using an implicit approach
Hidden use of power	Having the other follow your wishes without having to say anything

Gender stereotypes in the United States affect conflict, power, and decision-making processes.

broach the subject, and she and her mother do not argue about it; Liz just lets her mother be in charge without talking about it.

Throughout this discussion, we adopt a relational perspective on power. In other words, we see power, like conflict, as a process that is co-constructed by relational partners. Thus, although one partner may try to utilize direct application of power or any of the other power modes we have discussed, the power loop is not closed until the other partner responds. For instance, when Marla spanks her son, Jerry, and sends him to his room, she checks in on him later to find that Jerry has thrown all his toys on the floor and ripped all the pages out of his books. Thus, Marla's direct application of power is not met with compliance; rather, it encounters resistance in the form of an exercise of direct power on Jerry's part.

Sex Differences

Sex role stereotypes in the United States suggest that husbands have more power in decision making than their wives. But one study[31] suggests that sex differences do not operate in stereotypical ways in marital decision making. In fact, wives exhibited more power in a decision-making exercise than their husbands did. Power was measured both by the verbal and nonverbal behaviors of the spouses and also by the results (i.e., who "gave in" to whom). The researchers found that wives talked more than their husbands, and husbands accepted their wives' opinions and followed their lead in the study. In discussing the study, the lead author commented that perhaps a healthy marriage is one where men accept their wives' influence.

It's also possible that men and women tend to mirror one another's communication of power. In other words, men and women are not significantly different in how they express power verbally and nonverbally; what one did—such as interrupt—the other did as well. This relates to our discussion of conflict patterns. When power (or conflict) is wielded symmetrically, then both partners, regardless of sex, will behave the same way.

💬 IPC Voice: Faye

It's interesting to think back on how my mom and dad conducted conflict. I think I learned a lot from them. They definitely were a little different in how they approached conflict—my mom liked to talk and my dad liked to yell—but they both held equal power as far as I could tell. We seemed to do things my mom's way about half the time and my dad's way the other half. They listened to each other, though, and it worked out great for them—they've been married 30 years.

9–6 SKILL SET FOR EFFECTIVE CONFLICT MANAGEMENT

In the following section, we discuss five specific techniques for conflict management that demonstrate a high concern for both self and the other in a conflict. See Table 9.3 for a list of the skills.

Lighten Up and Reframe

Lightening up refers to your ability to stay cool-headed when others get "hot." Techniques that can help you do this include staying in the present and acknowledging that you have heard what your relational partner just said. Maintain eye contact and nod to show that you heard your partner's contribution. You can say, "I understand you have a concern"; or you can reframe, a skill we've mentioned in previous chapters, by changing something that has a negative connotation to something with a more positive connotation. Rather than becoming annoyed because a friend has a different political view than yours, you can reframe your differences to see them as interesting opportunities for discussion. Finally, lightening up might involve your asking permission to state your views: "May I tell you my perspective?" Keep your nonverbal communication genuine—avoid sarcasm.

Presume Goodwill and Express Goodwill

Go into each conflict interaction believing that you and your partner both want to come to a constructive resolution. Build rapport by focusing on the areas where you do agree. Reach out to your partner and expect that your partner will do the same for you. While you are engaging in conflict, tell your partner the things about them that you respect. Keep it real, but mix in praise with your complaints.

Ask Questions

Focus on the other. After you both have had a chance to speak, ask your partner if they have anything further to add. Reflect back what you have heard and ask if you understood it correctly. Ask, "What would make this situation better in your opinion?" "What would you like to see happen now?" "How can I understand your position better?" "What do I seem to be missing?"

Table 9.3 /// Skill Set for Effective Conflict Management
a. Lighten up and reframe.
b. Presume goodwill and express goodwill.
c. Ask questions.
d. Apply listening skills.
e. Practice cultural sensitivity.
f. Your skill suggestion

Law Enforcement Officers and Conflict Management Skills

AP Photo/David Goldman

Law enforcement professionals have demanding jobs that require many varied skills. According to the Career Profiles website, interpersonal skills such as handling conflict well are equally important to the more obvious physical and tactical skills we usually associate with the job of law enforcement. It's important that those in the law enforcement professions cultivate some of the same skills we've discussed in this chapter. Although they deal with criminals, they also deal with the general public, and so can benefit by expressing and expecting goodwill. In doing this, they demonstrate their commitment to helping others. The Career Profiles website suggests that law enforcement professionals want to resolve issues without having to resort to physical confrontations. In the current climate in the United States, where law enforcement officers have been prosecuted for killing unarmed black men, conflict management skills are essential to law enforcement professionals. The material on the website notes that the number one asset any law enforcement professional should have is effective verbal communication. Additionally, law enforcement professionals need to develop cultural sensitivity in order to manage conflicts with those from a variety of cultures different from their own.

Reflection: *Think about the career that you want to pursue after college. How would an understanding of the principles in this chapter be helpful in that career? Be as specific as possible.*

Apply Listening Skills

It's difficult to manage conflict effectively unless we spend time listening to the other person. Remember to practice all of the behaviors associated with effective listening we discussed in Chapter 6, including looking at the other person, focusing on the words, and allowing the full story to unfold. In conflict situations, listening to another person is more than just hearing the words spoken; it's a way to show them that resolving the conflict is important to you, and that the relationship between the two of you is valuable in your life.

Practice Cultural Sensitivity

Be mindful, and tune in to your own culture's norms and assumptions first before evaluating others. Slow down your judgments of others; suspend your evaluations until you have had a chance to engage in an internal dialogue. Ask yourself questions such as these: "Am I respectful of the different cultural background of the other person?" "Am I using my own cultural lens to understand what is being said and misunderstanding how their cultural lens directs their thinking?" "What types of strategies am I using to make sure that I don't inadvertently evaluate the person rather than the message?" These are just a few of the questions to ask as you consider the cultural backgrounds of others. Think about the material we discussed in Chapter 2 to help you understand how cultural differences can come into play in a conflict situation.

/// CHAPTER WRAP-UP

Conflict in interpersonal communication is a very well researched behavior. It was one of the first places researchers began their work in the new field of interpersonal communication. In this chapter, we balanced some of the more classic work on communication patterns and styles in conflict with newer ideas about bullying and violence. We examined the complex definition for conflict by exploring its four key components: interaction, interdependence, perception, and incompatible goals. We further expanded the definition by exposing three myths about conflict, reviewing six conflict types, and examining two influences on conflict behavior (sex/sex role stereotypes and culture).

We also discussed the research on conflict patterns and conflict styles and offered one explanation for conflict in interpersonal relationships: the Explanatory Process Model. We looked at the destructive as well as the constructive outcomes from conflict and concluded with a skill set that can be helpful in approaching conflict situations.

Conflict plays a substantial role in our interpersonal relationships, and it's important that we understand it and attempt to manage it well so its constructive outcomes are enhanced and its destructive outcomes are less likely to occur.

/// COMMUNICATION ASSESSMENT TEST (CAT): ASSESSING YOUR CONFLICT STYLE

Each statement below provides a strategy for dealing with a conflict. Rate each statement on a scale of 1 to 4 indicating how likely you are to use this strategy in general.

1 = rarely, 2 = sometimes, 3 = often, 4 = always

Be sure to answer the questions indicating how you *would* behave rather than how you think you *should* behave.

_____1. I explore issues with others so as to find solutions that meet everyone's needs.

_____2. I try to negotiate and adopt a give-and-take approach to problem situations.

_____3. I try to meet the expectations of others.

_____4. I argue my case and insist on the merits of my point of view.

_____5. I gather as much information as I can and keep the lines of communication open.

_____6. I usually say very little and try to leave as soon as possible.

_____7. I try to see both sides. What do I need? What does the other person need? What are the issues involved?

_____8. I prefer to compromise and just move on.

_____9. I approach it as a challenge and I enjoy the battle of wits that usually follows.

_____10. I feel uncomfortable and anxious.

_____11. I try to accommodate the wishes of my friends and family.

_____12. I figure out what needs to be done and I'm usually right.

_____13. To break deadlocks, I meet people halfway.

_____14. I give in to keep the peace.

_____15. I avoid hard feelings and just keep my opinions with others to myself.

Scoring the Styles Assessment

Three questions relate to each of the five styles. To find your most preferred style, total the points for the questions listed for each style below. The one with the highest score indicates your most commonly used style. The one with the lowest score indicates your least preferred style. You may find your style to be a blend of styles.

Style Corresponding Statements:

Collaborating: questions 1 + 5 + 7 = _____

Competing: questions 4 + 9 + 12 = _____

Avoiding: questions 6 + 10 + 15 = _____

Accommodating: questions 3 + 11 + 14 = _____

Compromising: questions 2 + 8 + 13 = _____

Source: Reginald (Reg) Adkins, PhD, Elemental Truths (http://elementaltruths.blogspot.com/2006/11/conflict-management-quiz.html).

/// KEY TERMS

/// KEY QUESTIONS FOR APPLICATION

1. **_CQ/CultureQuest_**: Explore the following claim: "Cultural beliefs and practices make conflict very different across cultures. It's extremely difficult to engage in conflict with someone of another culture; this makes intercultural relationships a challenge." Do you agree or disagree? Defend your views.

2. **_TQ/TechQuest_**: Explore the following claim: "Cyberbullying only happens because of the channel. If we didn't conduct so much of our lives online, bullying would be vastly reduced." Do you agree or disagree? Defend your views.

3. How well do you think the Explanatory Process Model explains conflict as you've experienced it? Be specific in your answer and give some examples.

4. What other influences do you think are important to consider in a conflict situation besides the participants' sex or sex role socialization and culture? Give some specific examples to support your answer.

5. Do you agree with the constructive aspects we suggest that conflict can have? Give some instances where you thought conflict had a constructive effect on a relationship.

6. Do you agree with the skills we listed for managing conflict effectively? Why or why not? Give some examples of when you used a particular skill and describe the outcome. Give an example of a successful outcome when you didn't use the skills we listed.

Access practice quizzes, eFlashcards, video, and multimedia at **edge.sagepub.com/west**.

Visit **edge.sagepub.com/west** to help you accomplish your coursework goals in an easy-to-use learning environment.

CHAPTER 10

COMMUNICATING IN CLOSE RELATIONSHIPS

LEARNING OUTCOMES

After studying this chapter, you will be able to

10–1 Develop a definition of close relationships

10–2 Detail the ways that we talk and think about close relationships

10–3 Explain the influences impacting close relationships

10–4 Discuss stage model approaches to relationship development

10–5 Understand explanations for communication in close relationships

10–6 Demonstrate a variety of skills and techniques to enhance and maintain your communication in close relationships

iStock.com/Zoran Zeremski

Master the content at
edge.sagepub.com/west

$SAGE edge™

Our close relationships mean a great deal to us. For one thing, they help satisfy our need for connection. Abraham Maslow's[1] famous hierarchy of needs (see Figure 10.1), which ranks people's needs in order of importance, places social needs (such as love, inclusion, and connection) in the third ranking, immediately after physical and safety needs. Satisfying social needs constitutes an enduring human occupation. A 2013 survey of 4,000 people in various age groups showed that the most important factor for quality of life for those ages 60 and older was strong relationships with friends and family. In addition, for both seniors as well as adults ages 18 to 59, family and friends were critically important and were how respondents defined community.[2]

The following theories/models are discussed in this chapter:

Social Information Processing Theory

Systems Theory

Relational Dialectic Theory

Social Exchange Theory

Knapp's Stage Model of Relationship Development

And, we know that communication is central to relationships. We use communication to begin, maintain, and terminate relationships, and when we're happy or dissatisfied with our relationships, it's often because of the quality of communication we're experiencing in them. We think of communication as both an indicator of our closeness with another person ("You're the only one I'd tell this to") and a means for developing a sense of closeness ("I feel

Figure 10.1 /// Maslow's Hierarchy of Needs

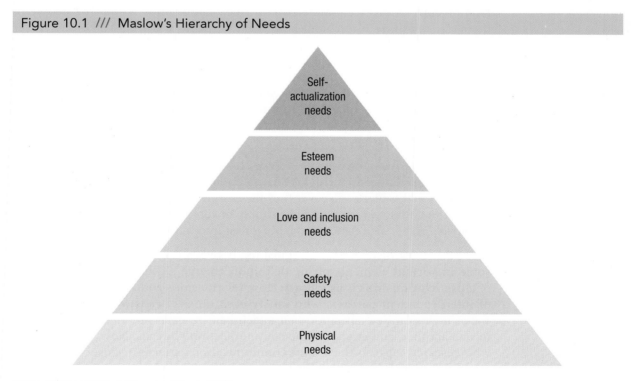

Source: Based on Maslow's Hierarchy of Needs (1943).

so much closer to you now that we've talked about this"). Ironically, intimate partners and family members tend to talk to each other with less consideration than they accord friends and less intimate partners.[3] Researchers suggest this is because in developed, intimate relationships people feel confident that the connection will endure even if they communicate less than optimally to one another. We aren't that confident with less intimate relationships so we have to speak more politely in them.

As we've introduced the topic of this chapter, we've been speaking as though everyone has the same understanding of a *close relationship*. Although we do have intuitive definitions for close relationships because they are such an important and ubiquitous part of our lives, we still need to establish a common definition to frame our approach in this chapter. Here we'll map out the foundations of close relationships, and detail theoretical thinking about how people communicate in close relationships generally. In Chapter 11, we'll specifically apply this information to friendships, family relationships, and relationships with romantic partners.

10–1 UNDERSTANDING CLOSE RELATIONSHIPS

One reason why it's difficult to define a close relationship is that we experience many kinds of relationships in our lives. Some relationships are **role relationships**, meaning that the partners are interdependent while accomplishing a specific task. The server and customer at a restaurant, for instance, have a role relationship. One key characteristic of role relationships is that the people in them are relatively interchangeable. That is, while you might like one server better than another, you can still eat in a restaurant as long as *someone* is the server—anyone could fill the role, and the relationship still exists. Role relationships may be fleeting and your interdependence doesn't endure. When Jane wanted to buy a condo, she hired a realtor, Laura, who specialized in condo sales. Over the 2 months it took Jane to find the perfect place, she and Laura talked frequently, and were very friendly. But after Jane settled in her new place, they no longer saw one another.

Role and close relationships can overlap, however. For instance, as an employee, Jon has a role relationship with his boss, Malcolm. But over time, they begin to talk about personal subjects, discover they have similar senses of humor, and come to feel that the other person could not simply be replaced with a new boss or a new employee. Their role relationship has evolved into a close relationship.

From this brief discussion distinguishing between role and close relationships, some important elements of the definition emerge. To be clear, our definition of **close relationships** is as follows: close relationships endure over time, consist of interdependent partners who satisfy each other's needs for connection and social inclusion, feel an emotional attachment to each other, are irreplaceable to one another, and enact unique communication patterns. Now, we'll examine what research suggests the unique communication patterns in close relationships are like. Research finds the following seven characteristics of communication in close relationships:

- **The content of the interactions contains variety and depth:** What do people talk about and do together? Robert and Nelson have a close relationship if they hang out together frequently, engage in conversations beyond the superficial, and discuss a variety of topics in some depth.

- **There's a diversity of interactions:** How many different experiences do people share? Melanie and Lori are close if they go to the movies together, play together on the basketball team, study together, and spend time talking with one another about their futures and their jobs.

- **The interactions contain affection and conflict:** How do the partners talk to one another? Most people agree that affectionate communication is extremely important in close relationships. Affection can be expressed directly ("You're my best friend," "I love you") or indirectly (through giving support, compliments, or planning future activities together). As we discussed in Chapter 9, conflict is also an inevitable part of close relationships. People who speak affectionately to one another but also sometimes get into heated arguments probably have a close relationship.

- **The interactions are intimate:** How much do the partners self-disclose? Is their conversation characterized by a private language that identifies them as part of a unique, closed circle? What nonverbal behaviors do they exhibit? For example, Carla and Kevin share their problems with one another. They also call one another private nicknames based on elementary school experiences. Carla is "Tootsie" because Tootsie Rolls were her favorite candy, and Kevin is "Slurps" because he was famous for slurping his milk in the cafeteria. They always hug one another hello and take walks together arm in arm. Their willingness to self-disclose, create a private language, share activities and nonverbal behaviors all create intimacy and mark their relationship as close, compared to their more casual acquaintances.

- **The partners perceive the interactions to be intimate:** How do the partners see each other and talk about their relationship? Kelly and Ray are in a close relationship because they perceive each other in a similar fashion and feel understood by each other. They share a perception that their relationship is a close one, and their communication reflects this, as they both describe their friendship in similar terms and talk about each other using the same relationship label: BFFs.

- **The interactions reflect commitment:** Does each partner feel the other is committed to the relationship? Chase and Cal have a close relationship because they speak openly about how devoted they are to one another. They participated in a marriage ceremony where they publicly declared their commitment to each other.

- **The interactions express satisfaction:** How closely do the partners' interactions fit their ideal? Camille and Pat have a close relationship because they frequently say that they couldn't want a better sister than each other. They each praise the other and talk about how fulfilling their relationship is.[4]

Personal Trainers' and Clients' Relationships

iStock.com/michaeljung

One career that offers the possibility of changing a role relationship into a close one is personal training. Even if the trainer and the client do not become close friends, it is necessary for the trainer to establish themself as someone who is compatible with the client as well as experienced in training skills. As a result, it's important for trainers to be skilled in many of the same things that people find beneficial in their friendships. The Aerobics and Fitness Association of America discusses personality traits and communication skills on its website before addressing the certifications needed to become a personal trainer. The AFAA website suggests that being a good listener and having a nurturing approach to others are critical skills for succeeding in the profession.

Reflection: Have you ever experienced a role relationship that turned into a close one? What were the circumstances that accompanied this evolution? How did the communication behaviors the two of you exhibited change as the relationship changed? Do you think the workplace is an appropriate place for friendships? Why or why not?

10–2 THINKING AND TALKING ABOUT CLOSE RELATIONSHIPS

We can understand more about close relationships when we explore how people think and talk about them. Close relationships are represented in several ways that shed light on what they mean to people. In an effort to illustrate how that process works, we'll explore close relationships as cultural performances, as cognitive constructs, and as linguistic constructions.

Relationships as Cultural Performances

Close relationships are seen as cultural performances when they are defined by ongoing public and private exchanges. These exchanges include myriad communication practices enacted in private conversations, and public rituals such as weddings and commitment ceremonies as well as public discourse by politicians and others indicating what marriages, families, and other relationships should be like and what values should define them. Thus, relationships are both defined by and enacted in the culture that surrounds them.

From this perspective, we would say that Brea and Tal have a close relationship because they do things that people in close relationships do. They had a wedding and publicly vowed that they were in a close relationship, labeled marriage. They go to parties together, own a home together, make budgets, take out loans, and have a joint checking account. In other words, they are performing a close relationship according to U.S. cultural and social rules.

 ## IPC Voice: McKenna

As a lesbian in 2018, I'm still frustrated by the limits that are put on my performance of my romantic relationships. Yes, marriage equality passed, but if you're gay, you aren't allowed to get a baker of your choice to prepare your wedding cake. My cisgender friends have no problem holding hands or kissing their significant others in public, but my girlfriend and I have to be careful. Some places it'll be OK, but other places, definitely no. It's just painful and I think many people think it's a problem we've solved. Believe me, it's still a problem.

Relationships as Cognitive Constructs

Some research examines the notion of relationship scripts, which are cognitive structures containing a pattern for the key events we expect to occur in a relationship.[5] This concept is similar to the notion of relational schema discussed in prior chapters. In the United States, there are both *narrow* scripts (what should happen on a first date) and *broad* scripts (how a friendship should progress).

Relationship scripts, such as what should happen in a dating relationship, are useful because they allow us to process information about a relationship quickly and efficiently, help us know how to behave in certain situations, and make us feel comfortable when our scripts and our lived experiences match.

Relationship scripts serve several functions for people: They serve as cognitive shortcuts, allowing us to process information about the relationship efficiently and rapidly; they help guide behavior, making it easier for us to know what to do in certain relational situations; and they enhance satisfaction when there's a match between the script and a person's actual experience of a close relationship.

We also frame close relationships as cognitive constructs when we define them as when partners share mental images of the relationship. Mental images of relationships occur on two levels. At a basic level, people are simply aware of each other and the fact that they're in a relationship with one another. The second level is more complex. On this level, several things happen in a specific order:

1. The communication between the partners becomes patterned, and each partner can imagine with some predictive accuracy what the other will say or do in different situations.

2. The partners perceive a past, present, and future together. They're able to bring the past forward into the present and future by holding a mental image of what the partner has done in the past and generalizing it to the present or the future ("When we went skiing last winter, she liked it, so she'll probably want to go again this year"). This can be called "carrying the relationship with you," and it happens whenever people imagine what a relational partner's reaction to something might be.

3. People label their relationship ("This is my best friend," "This is my daughter," or "This is my girlfriend"). In the following section, we address the question of language and close relationships in more detail.

Relationships as Linguistic Constructions

Language influences our sense of close relationships. Giving a relationship a label (friendship, love, etc.) helps us feel "in relationship" to another. Yet, as we discussed in Chapter 4 when addressing lexical gaps, some relationships don't have convenient labels. What do you call your father's second wife, her children by her first marriage, your brother's former wife, or a person you're dating when both of you are in your 50s? What do children of gay parents call their two mothers or fathers? Language has not always kept pace with the relationships we live in now.[6]

Another way that relationships exist in language is through figurative language. Figurative language—specifically, metaphors and similes—helps us understand relationships by comparing them to other phenomena. In such linguistic comparisons, the qualities of the phenomenon to which a relationship is linked shed light on the qualities of the relationship itself. Dana understands her relationship with her mother better when she is able to come up with a comparison for it, like a Mama Bear defending her cub.

In addition to offering a vocabulary for understanding our relationships, figurative language also *shapes* our understanding of them. Using a metaphor highlights some elements of the relationship while downplaying other elements. For example, the metaphor of relationship-as-dance emphasizes the coordination and enjoyment elements of a relationship while it downplays the conflicts, struggles, and missteps. Table 10.1 lists common relational metaphors.

Table 10.1 /// Common Metaphors Used to Describe Close Relationships	
Nature	Thunderstorm Volcano Sunny day Meadow with flowers Tree with deep roots
Machines	Well-oiled machine Leaky boat Merry-go-round Roller coaster Broken record
Food	Stew Gooey cake with ice cream TV dinner Milkshake Tossed salad
Clothing	Ripped sweater Comfortable old shoes Tie that's choking me Pair of pants with an elastic waist Party outfit

Researchers argue that metaphors influence our thinking and communication.[7] For instance, if Ben and Leslie picture their marriage as a "well-oiled machine," they may adopt communication behaviors that focus on efficiency ("keeping the wheels turning") and functioning ("We don't want a breakdown in communication") at the expense of emotional communication. If Melody and Kim picture their relationship as volcanic, their communication behaviors will probably highlight conflict and emotion ("If we don't talk about this, I'll just explode").

 **IPC Praxis**

Think about some close relationships you have. Do any of these metaphors ring true in describing them? If yes, explain how the metaphor tells you something about the relationship and the communication within it. If no, is there another comparison you can make that does illuminate the relationship and your communication behaviors in it?

10–3 INFLUENCES ON CLOSE RELATIONSHIPS

Like all the topics in this book, close relationships are affected by many influences. In this section we'll detail four factors that exert influence on interpersonal communication in close relationships. These include attraction, culture, gender and sex, and electronic media. Attraction influences both the inception and the continuance of close relationships, as well as how partners express themselves to one another.

Cultural practices and beliefs influence how people think they should talk and act in a close relationship. Gender and sex have an impact on how people enact roles in close relationships. Finally, social media sites offer new ways for close relationships to form and endure, and for the partners to communicate with one another.

Attraction

Video 10.1

Attraction, especially what is known as short-term attraction, initiates relationships. **Short-term attraction**, a judgment of relationship potential, propels us into beginning a relationship with someone. **Long-term attraction**, which makes us want to continue a relationship over time, sustains and maintains relationships. Sometimes the things that attract you to someone in the short term may be the same things that turn you off in the long term. For example, Maggie may have initially struck up a friendship with Anita because she saw Anita as outgoing and friendly. However, later in their relationship, Maggie may come to see Anita's outgoing ways as egocentric and childish. She may wonder why Anita never seems to reflect on anything and always has to be with a lot of people. Anita's outgoing personality may begin to seem negative to Maggie as the relationship grows.

Both types of attraction are based on several elements, such as

- physical attractiveness
- charisma
- physical closeness (or proximity)
- similarity
- complementary needs
- reciprocation

People are attracted to others who fit their cultural ideal of attractiveness, but they are more likely to initiate relationships with others who tend to match their own level of attractiveness, which is known as the *matching hypothesis*.[8] In other words, we feel more comfortable talking with people who are about as physically attractive as we see ourselves to be. We also like people who are confident and exude charisma. In addition, it's more likely that we'll be attracted to those who are in physical proximity to us than to those who are more distant, because, at least before the advent of social media, it's difficult to enter the initiating stage with someone who is far away.

We are also motivated to initiate conversations with those who share some of our own attributes, values, and opinions. A study investigating why people are attracted to one another found that a "likes-attract" rule was much stronger than an "opposites-attract" rule for heterosexual couples in Western cultures.[9] Yet, too much similarity can be boring, so we may seek a partner with some attributes that complement ours as well. For example, if Chris is quiet and Glenn is talkative, they may want to initiate a friendship because Chris's listening behavior is a good complement for Glenn's tendency to hold forth at length. Finally, we are attracted to others who seem attracted to us, or who reciprocate our interest. For instance, when Renny smiles at Natalie at a party and she doesn't smile back, Renny may not go any further with the relationship.

Culture

As we have discussed throughout this book, cultural norms, values, and expectations shape us in important ways. Thus, it should come as no surprise that culture plays a role in how we define close relationships and how we communicate within them. For example, traditional Hawaiian culture is fundamentally collectivistic, which affects how Hawaiians define family (or ʻohana). For traditional Hawaiians, ʻohana is extended and expanded; it consists of the immediate family (people with blood and marital ties), those who have been adopted into the family (a common practice), and spiritual ancestors. Hawaiian culture reflects values similar to the Latinx concept of *familism,* which focuses on an extended family that includes aunts, uncles, cousins, and dear friends. The African value of *collectivism* is also similar but emphasizes relationships among the entire race or community, as reflected in the proverb "It takes a village to raise a child."

Even within cultures, attitudes about close relationships may vary over time. One researcher studied people's scripts for arranged marriages and love marriages in a small village in India. Arranged marriages were the dominant type of marriage in the past, but now love marriages are more common. The study found that respondents thought the ideal marriage was a hybrid of the two types. Respondents' scripts for the ideal marriage reflected changing cultural beliefs and customs.[10]

Some researchers examine **relational culture**, a term that describes the partners' shared understandings, roles, and rituals that are unique to their relationship. Elaine and Sophia define their friendship by doing things together such as shopping, walking their dogs, and sitting and talking at the coffee shop. They have special rituals for ordering their coffee and private jokes about their dogs. Through their activities and their shared jokes and rituals, Elaine and Sophia create their own relational culture that is unique and differs from the culture established by other friends. Just as a larger culture would, relational cultures affect people's expectations and assessments of relationships.

 **IPC Around Us**

Olga Khazan[11] writes about differences in how women and men approach close relationships, and what that might mean for online dating sites. Khazan cites research showing that although women and men said they wanted different things from mates (men ranked good looks as their top priority, while women ranked money first), there was no difference in the type of mates women and men actually chose in a speed-dating exercise. Further, what participants in the study said they wanted in a partner didn't correlate with what they ended up saying they liked about the people they met at the speed-dating event. The researchers believe that this was the case because when people are on dating sites or at speed-dating functions, they compare the different people they meet or the different profiles they read against each other. But, when they actually meet one person and try to make a relationship decision, they're just judging that person alone, and asking if that person is right for them. When you focus on comparing people against each other it's easy to look at qualities like income and physical appearance. But, those ultimately don't turn out to be the most

(Continued)

(Continued)

iStock.com/skynesher

important qualities to people. Things like compatibility, rapport, and sense of humor are more important to both men and women. And, those qualities are harder for dating sites to quantify on their surveys. Overall, Khazan concludes that even though apps like Tinder can help both men and women increase their pool of possible mates, they cannot really determine who will be compatible mates. That's still up to individuals.

Reflection: *Do you think men and women look for different things when they search for a relationship partner? Why or why not? How do you think meeting someone online impacts your answer? How does it impact women's and men's behaviors?*

Gender and Sex

As we've discussed throughout this book, differences between men and women permeate our understanding of interpersonal communication. Close relationships provide another context in which sex differences (or perceived differences) have an impact. We take the perspective that differences between the sexes are learned—in other words, that cultural instructions guide girls to behave in ways that society has deemed feminine and teach boys to engage in what are considered masculine behaviors. Furthermore, our notions of sex and gender are somewhat fluid and can change over time.

This perspective does not deny that biological sex as well as learned gendered behaviors and values make a difference in our definitions of close relationships. In fact, one study indicates that biological differences between men and women, like responses to stress and propensity to depression, may affect how people think about close relationships.[12] However, despite some evidence of biological explanations, many studies reinforce the notion that gendered behaviors are learned. One study examined narratives that men and women told about relationships and found that despite a strong cultural push for gender equity, the stories actually contributed to inequity. Both men and women told stories about men behaving badly in relationships, but men blamed their bad behavior on immaturity and women chalked up their bad experiences to the normal life lessons they needed to learn on the way to adulthood.[13]

Although women and men differ in what they have learned about, what they expect from, and what they experience within close relationships, popular writers and reality shows often take our cultural interest in sex differences to an extreme. They construct some differences where none really exist, overestimate the differences that do appear, and fail to talk about the cultural context framing these differences.

Further, relatively little research examines gay or lesbian couples' relationships or romantic relationships between any gender-nonconforming people. Some research suggests that same-sex couples may be more successful in relationships than heterosexual couples. The explanation for this has to do with smaller gender role differences and perhaps more power equality between the partners.[14]

Electronic Media

Communication between and among individuals is forever changed because of technology. Electronic media, like social networking sites, have provided important channels for conducting interpersonal relationships as well as communicating about them. Online dating sites are the fastest growing way for unmarried heterosexual people to meet one another. Unquestionably, social network sites have had an impact on how users approach close relationships. Yet, research suggests that the impact is a complex one. Some researchers suggest that online dating is a good idea, because it is an improvement on the random quality of traditional dating. These researchers mean that during the traditional dating stage, people tend to "stumble" onto others at a social gathering. You might find yourself in the right place at the right time and meet the right person. Or, you might not. Regardless, this way of meeting people involves a lot of luck.

However, developing an online relationship is not as random; online dating offers a number of advantages compared to traditional dating:

- Many people online are available and seeking companionship.

- Before you exchange personal information, you have the power to secure a profile of the other person.

- You know something about how the other person thinks and writes.

- You know how to contact them.

- You have the chance to exchange e-mails and talk on the phone without ever revealing your identity.

- You can do all of this for less than what it might cost for a typical first date, such as dinner at a moderately priced restaurant.[15]

Other research finds both upsides and downsides to relationships online. One study found that Facebook has dramatically changed the way people acquire information about potential romantic partners (because they can learn so much about the person without ever interacting with them), and Facebook has introduced a new category for romantic relationships: FBO (Facebook Official). But this study also found that people felt Facebook could be detrimental to romantic relationships, and respondents in the study stated that they preferred to meet potential romantic partners offline.[16]

Another study found that college students reported a sequence for new media use in developing relationships. Respondents said that they used Facebook in the early stages of relational development. Later they moved to instant messaging and then to cell phones as the relationship matured. Respondents noted that they used the medium that most matched their goals for the relationship at the time. The authors found some sex differences in that generally women were more explicit about this sequence than were men.[17]

One theory detailing the ways that people communicate online is Social Information Processing Theory (SIP).[18] As discussed previously in the text, SIP alleges that online relationships may be just as close and important to partners as offline ones. Joseph Walther, the theorist who created SIP, talks about the notion that online communication may be **hyperpersonal**, or overly intense and intimate, because participants have the ability to strategically present themselves, highlighting their positive qualities. Furthermore, as people receive information online about others, they "fill in the blanks" to make attributions about the other. This often results in overattributing similarities and a positivity bias. Additionally, online communication is often asynchronous, meaning that the communicators are not required to be online at the same time. This asynchronous nature allows for editing, retracting, and polishing messages so they are of high quality, and again, provide a positive impression. Finally, the feedback online often contributes to the positive, intimate, or hyperpersonal nature of online communication and relationships. When people receive highly edited messages and images of another online, they may begin to idealize that person, who then responds to that idealization and a cycle begins. In this manner, SIP predicts that relationships conducted online may become intimate rather quickly, and may intensify much faster than offline relationships. When, or if, partners meet offline, however, there may be disappointment.

One study examined the combined influences of gender and electronic dating sites on initiating close relationships. In this study, the researchers used data from over 14,000 men and women who posted profiles on an online dating site. They found that, online, the assertions of the matching hypothesis that we discussed earlier didn't seem to hold. Instead, posters (both male and female) opted for the most attractive partner in their initial request, regardless of how they judged their own level of attractiveness. The researchers suggested that this result might be a function of the hyperpersonal nature of online communication that we just reviewed. In addition, the study found that some conventions from 1950s dating protocols still seemed to govern women's and men's behaviors online. Women in this study made four times fewer initial contacts than did men, and seemed to be waiting to be asked. This was the case despite the facts that the women users were educated and living in a progressive urban area, and women who initiated dates had significantly better odds of success than women who waited to be contacted. The researchers comment that inequality between the sexes may be maintained and reproduced when women hang back and wait for men to make the first move.[19]

Do you agree with the hyperpersonal perspective? Have you ever had the experience of developing a relationship online that became personal really quickly? Do you think it was because you and your partner were able to present your best selves forward to the other as SIP says? Explain your answer with some specific examples.

10–4 DEVELOPING INTERPERSONAL RELATIONSHIPS THROUGH STAGES

Stage models of relational development are concerned with how relationships develop (primarily offline) and how communication changes as we deepen or weaken our relational ties with another. Perhaps the best known stage model was originated by Mark Knapp in 1978. Knapp's model answers the following questions: "Are there regular and systematic patterns of communication that suggest stages on the road to a more intimate relationship? Are there similar patterns and stages that characterize the deterioration of relationships?" (p. 36).[20] The model provides five stages of coming together and five stages of coming apart. See Table 10.2 for a summary of the model.

Table 10.2 /// Knapp's Model of Relationship Development

Coming Together Stages	Sample Communication
Initiating	"Hi, how are you?"
Experimenting	"Do you like water polo?"
Intensifying	"Let's take a vacation together this summer. We can play water polo!"
Integrating	"You are the best friend I could ever have! I know we're on the same team!"
Bonding	"Let's wear our team shirts to the party. I want everyone to know we're on the same team!"
Coming Apart Stages	**Sample Communication**
Differentiating	"I am surprised that you supported a Republican. I am a long-time Democrat."
Circumscribing	"Maybe we'd be better off if we didn't talk about politics."
Stagnating	"Wow, I could have predicted you'd say that!"
Avoiding	"I have too much homework to meet you for coffee."
Terminating	"I don't think we should hang out together anymore. It's just not fun now."

Knapp and his colleagues argue that the model is useful for all kinds of relationships because it provides for relationships that end after only a couple of stages as well as relationships that don't move beyond an early stage. The model also provides for relationships that move back and forth between stages or skip stages. In addition, it explains the movement of friendships as well as romantic relationships.

Some people have criticized stage models for presenting a linear picture of relationship development. These critics note that a linear picture doesn't provide an accurate representation of relationships that "cycle" or go back and forth between episodes of breaking up and renewal. Furthermore, critics note that relational development doesn't happen neatly in stages and that Knapp's model doesn't clarify what happens when one partner moves to a new stage and the other doesn't. For example, stage models can't show us what happens when one partner wants to terminate the relationship while the other resists.

Stage models simplify a complicated process. Each stage may contain some behavior from other, earlier stages, and people sometimes slide back and forth between stages as they interact in their relationship. When Liam and Alexandra met, they didn't like each other. They initiated a relationship, but it quickly terminated once they began talking and found they had nothing much in common. Four years later, they found themselves working at the same company and they began their relationship again, this time with better results because they agreed about a lot of things surrounding work. But then Alexandra took another job, and she and Liam again discovered that without the job in common, they had little to talk about. So, they ended their relationship again, although this time Liam was more disappointed and tried to engage Alexandra in activities that would keep them in relationship. Alexandra usually rebuffed these efforts.

Critics of stage models would argue that the model doesn't help us understand Liam and Alexandra's relationship. Knapp might respond that even though Liam and Alexandra didn't go through all the stages, the model still explained some of what they did experience. Stage models give us a snapshot of the process of relationship development, but they don't tell the entire story. In the following sections, we briefly discuss each of the stages in the Knapp Model. As you read about these stages, keep in mind the criticisms of stage models.

Initiating

This stage is where a relationship begins. In the **initiating stage**, two people notice one another and indicate to each other that they are interested in making contact: "I notice you, and I think you're noticing me, too. Let's talk and see where it goes." Initiation depends on attraction, which as we've previously mentioned, can be either short term or long term.

Some of our relationships stay in the initiating stage. You may see the same person often in a place that you frequent, such as a supermarket, bookstore, or coffee shop. Each time you see this person, you might exchange smiles and pleasantries. You may have short, ritualized conversations about the weather or other topics but never move on to any of the other stages in the model. Thus, you could have a long-term relationship that never moves out of the initiating stage.

Experimenting

In the second stage, the **experimenting stage**, people become acquainted with one another. They ask a lot of questions to discover areas of commonality. They engage in **small talk**—interactions that are relaxed, pleasant, uncritical, and casual. Through small talk, people learn about one another, reduce their uncertainties, find topics that they might wish to spend more time discussing, "test the waters" to see if they want to develop the relationship further, and maintain a sense of community.

Many of our relationships stay in the experimenting stage. We may have many friends whom we know through small talk but not at a deeper level. If you see a friend in the coffee shop and go beyond "Hi, can you believe how cold it is today?" to small talk (including gossip about mutual friends, comments about sports teams, low-level observations about your job), then you have deepened the relationship some, but you still have kept it at a low level of commitment. Furthermore, even people in close relationships spend time in this stage, perhaps in an effort to understand their partner more, to pass the time, or to avoid uncomfortable feelings stirred up by a more intense conversation.

Intensifying

The **intensifying stage** begins to move the relationship to a closeness not seen in the previous stages. Intensifying refers to deepening intimacy in the relationship. During this stage, partners self-disclose, forms of address become more informal, and people may use nicknames or terms of endearment to address one another ("I miss you, Boomer"; "Hi, honey.") Relational partners begin to speak of a "we" or "us," as in "We like to go to basketball games" or "It'll be nice for us to get a break from studying and go for a walk."

In this stage, people begin to develop their own language based on private symbols for past experiences or knowledge of each other's habits, desires, and beliefs. For instance, Missy and her mother still say "hmmm" to each other, because that's

Westend61/Getty Images

When relationships reach the intensifying stage, partners develop their own language based on private symbols, and sometimes they don't need to talk at all in order to express themselves to each other.

what Missy said when she was little to mean "I want more." And Neil says, "It's just like walking on a rocky path" when he wants Trudy to do something, because when they first became friends, he made her take a walk along a path scattered with rocks when Trudy wanted to go the movies instead.

In addition, this stage is marked by more direct statements of commitment—"I have never had a better friend than you" or "I am so happy being with you." Often these statements are met with reciprocal comments—"Me neither" or "Same here." In intensifying, the partners become more sophisticated nonverbally. They are able to read each other's nonverbal cues accurately, may replace some verbalizations with a touch, and may mirror one another's nonverbal cues—how they stand, gesture, dress, and so forth may become more similar. One way Louisa intensified her friendship with Tricia was to stop dressing like her old friends did, and to start wearing clothes and makeup that mirrored Tricia's style.

Integrating

Video 10.2

The fourth stage, the **integrating stage**, represents the two people forming a clear identity as a couple. Their couple identity is often acknowledged by the pair's social circles; they cultivate friends together and are treated as a unit by their friends. They are invited to places together, and when information is shared with one partner, it's assumed that the information will be passed on to the other. When children tell something to one parent, unless they ask for the information to be kept confidential, they'll assume the other parent will find out the information too.

Sometimes the partners designate common property. They may pick a song to be "our song," open a joint bank account, buy a dog together, or move into an apartment together. In our case as authors of this book, coauthoring a series of books together has created a couple identity for us in our professional lives. We are often referred to together, and if people ask one of us to do something (such as make a presentation at a convention), they usually assume that the other will come along as well.

Bonding

The final stage in the coming together part of the model is the **bonding stage**, which refers to a public commitment of the relationship. Bonding is easier in some types of relationships than in others. For romantic couples, the marriage ceremony is a traditional bonding ritual. Having a bonding ritual provides a certain social sanction for the relationship, which may explain in part why gay and lesbian couples fought to gain the legal right to marry in the United States. There are bonding ceremonies for other relationships as well. Examples include commitment ceremonies, naming ceremonies for new babies to welcome them to the family, and initiation ceremonies to welcome new "sisters" or "brothers" to sororities and fraternities.

Differentiating

The first stage in the coming apart section of the model is the **differentiating stage**. This refers to highlighting the individuality of the partners. This is unlike the coming together stages, which featured the partners' similarities. The most dramatic episodes of differentiating involve conflict, as we discussed in Chapter 9. However, people can differentiate without engaging in conflict. For example, the following seemingly inconsequential comment exemplifies differentiation: "Oh, you like that sweater? I never would have thought you'd wear sweaters with Christmas trees on them. I guess our taste in clothes is more different than I thought."

People switch from "we" to "I" in this stage and talk more about themselves as individuals than as part of a couple. According to the model, this stage is the beginning of the relationship's unraveling process. However, we know that relationships oscillate between differentiation and some of the coming together stages, such as intensifying. No two people can remain in a coming together stage such as intensifying, integrating, or bonding without experiencing some differentiating.

Circumscribing

The next stage, the **circumscribing stage**, refers to restraining communication behaviors so that fewer topics are raised (for fear of conflict) and more issues are out of bounds. The couple interacts less. This stage is characterized by silences and comments such as "I don't want to talk about that anymore," "Let's not go there," and "It's none of your business." Again, all relationships may experience some taboo topics or behaviors that are typical of circumscribing. But when relationships enter the circumscribing stage (in other words, if the biggest proportion of their communication is of this type), that's a sign of a decaying relationship. If measures aren't taken to repair the situation—sitting down and talking about why there's a problem, going to counseling, taking a vacation, or some other remedy— the model shows that people will probably enter the next stage.

Stagnating

The third stage of coming apart, the **stagnating stage**, consists of extending circumscribing so much that the partners virtually no longer talk to each other. They express that there's no use in talking because they already know what the other will say. "There's no point in bringing this up—I know she won't like the idea" is a common theme during this stage. People feel "stuck," and their communication is draining, awkward, stylized, and unsatisfying.

Each partner may engage in **imagined conversations**,[21] where one partner plays the parts of both partners in a mental rehearsal of the negative communication that characterizes coming apart.

Me:	"I want to go on a vacation."
Me in Role of Partner:	"Well, I'm too busy to go with you. And we shouldn't spend any money right now."
Me:	"You never want to do anything fun and you're always complaining about money."
Me in Role of Partner:	"That may be true, but you're irresponsible with money, and you won't stick to a budget!"

After this rehearsal, people usually decide that it's not worth the effort to engage in the conversation for real.

Avoiding

If a relationship stagnates for too long, the partners may decide that the relationship is unpleasant. As a result, they move to the **avoiding stage**, a stage where partners try to stay out of the same physical environment. Partners make excuses for why they can't see one another ("Sorry, I have too much work to go out tonight" or "I'll be busy all week" or "I've got to go home for the weekend.") They may vary their habits so that they do not run into their partner as they used to. For example, if people used to meet at a particular restaurant or a certain spot on campus, they change their routines and no longer stop by these places.

Sometimes it isn't possible to physically avoid a partner. If a couple is married and unable to afford two residences, or if siblings still live in their parents' home, it's difficult for the partners to be completely separate. In such cases, partners in the avoiding stage simply ignore one another or make a tacit agreement to segregate their living quarters as much as possible. For example, the married couple may sleep in separate rooms, and the siblings may come into the den at different times of day. When partners in the avoiding stage accidentally run into one another, they will turn away without speaking.

Terminating

The **terminating stage** comes after the relational partners have decided, either jointly or individually, to part permanently. Terminating refers to the process of ending a relationship. Some relationships enter terminating almost immediately. You meet someone at a party, go through initiating and experimenting, and then decide you don't want to see them anymore, so you move to terminating. Other relationships go through all or most of the stages before terminating. Some relationships endure in one stage or another and never go through terminating. And other relationships go through terminating and then begin again (people remarry and estranged friends and family members reunite). Furthermore, some relationships terminate in one form and then begin again in a redefined way. When Sam and Virginia got divorced, they ended their relationship as married partners. However, because they have two children, they redefined their relationship and became friends.

The communication during the terminating stage can be simple ("We have to end this") or complicated (involving lots of discussion and even the intervention of third parties such as counselors, mediators, and attorneys). It may happen suddenly or drag out over a long time. It can be accomplished with a lot of talk that reflects on the life of the relationship and the reasons for terminating it, or it can be accomplished with relatively little or no discussion between the partners.

IPC Praxis

Think about a past relationship of yours that has now ended. Can you map that relationship on the stages of Knapp's model? How descriptive of your relationship is the model? How useful is it to employ this model in terms of understanding your relational communication?

10–5 EXPLAINING COMMUNICATION IN CLOSE RELATIONSHIPS

A stage model gives us a description of what communication behaviors characterize the evolution of a relationship, but it doesn't really explain why these behaviors occur. Given the importance of communication in close relationships, it's understandable that researchers have provided many theories to explain it. In fact, trying to explain communication in our relationships is something everyone spends a lot of time doing. Most people frequently wonder why their relationships develop the way they do, and why some communication behaviors help relationships, while others make things worse. In this section, we review the basic tenets of three major theories—Systems Theory, Relational Dialectics Theory, and Social Exchange Theory—that help us understand communication in close relationships.

Systems Theory

Systems Theory[22] compares relationships to living systems (such as cells or the body), which have six important properties:

1. Wholeness
2. Interdependence
3. Hierarchy
4. Boundaries or openness
5. Calibration or feedback
6. Equifinality

Systems researchers find that understanding how each of these six properties operates allows them to understand how communication in relationships works. We'll now consider each of the properties in turn.

Wholeness

Wholeness means that you can't understand a system by taking it apart and understanding each of its parts in isolation from one another. Wholeness indicates that knowing Ahmed and Ernie separately is not the same as knowing about the relationship between Ahmed and Ernie. The relationship between people is like a third entity that extends beyond each of the people individually. If you think of a specific relationship that you are in, the concept of wholeness becomes quite clear. The way you act and communicate in that relationship is probably different from the way you act and communicate in other relationships. The other person's reactions, contributions, and perceptions of you make a difference in how you behave, and vice versa. Furthermore, the way you perceive the relationship between the two of you matters. If you are longtime friends with someone, you don't have to explain things to that person the same way you might to someone who is a newer friend of yours. Wholeness tells us that just because Karen knows Cara and Susie individually doesn't mean she knows them *in relationship* to each other.

Interdependence

Interdependence builds on the notion of wholeness by asserting that members of systems depend on each other and are affected by one another. If Derek's sister, Dina, is injured in a car accident, of course that changes Dina's life. But, interdependence says that Derek's life is also affected because of his relationship with Dina. When you talk to the people in your close relationships, you monitor their behavior and respond to it—you are affected by their shifts in mood and tone, and your communication shifts accordingly. When Ariel comes home upset after work, her partner, Meg, has to pause whatever she's been doing or feeling to attend to Ariel's mood. It wouldn't work to ignore Ariel and pretend she's not upset, so what has happened in Ariel's day affects Meg because they're interdependent.

Hierarchy

Hierarchy states that these shifts and accommodations we're making don't exist in a vacuum. Derek's relationship with his sister, Dina, is embedded in the larger system of his family, which consists of his mother and four siblings (all of the members of which are interdependent), and his family is embedded in the larger system of his extended family, his neighborhood, his culture, and so forth. Lower level systems are called **subsystems**, and higher levels systems are called **suprasystems**. Derek and his sister form a subsystem of his immediate family. Derek's neighborhood is a suprasystem around his family (see Figure 10.2).

Figure 10.2 /// Hierarchy as a Systems Principle

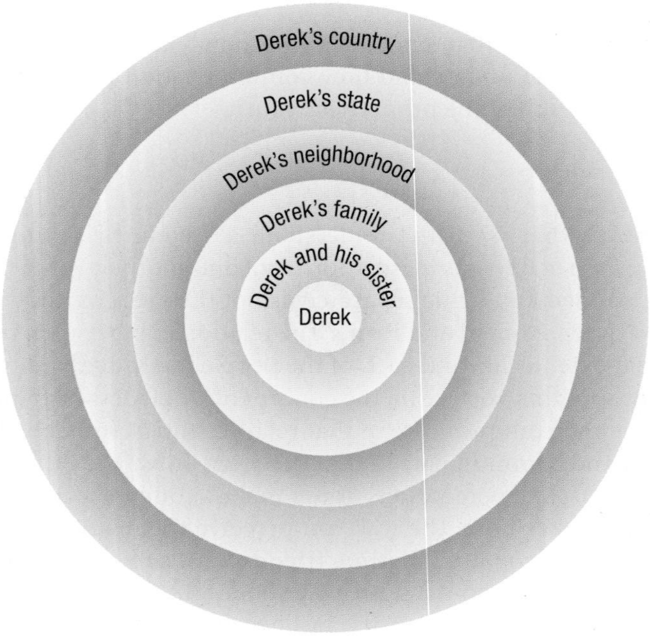

Derek's country
Derek's state
Derek's neighborhood
Derek's family
Derek and his sister
Derek

Boundaries/Openness

Boundaries or openness refers to the fact that subsystems and suprasystems exist because we create boundaries around each separate system, making it distinct from others (i.e., Derek and Dina, the family as a whole). However, human systems are inherently open, and information passes through these boundaries. Therefore, some researchers call this element "openness," and some call it "boundaries." For example, Marsha and Hal are best friends who have a very close relationship, and they tell each other things that they don't tell other people. This closeness forms the boundary around their relationship. Yet, if Marsha confides something to Hal that he finds disturbing, such as that she is abusing drugs or feeling suicidal, Hal might ask members of his family or other friends for help. In so doing, Hal would expand the boundaries of their subsystem. Boundaries exist to keep information in the subsystem, but they also act to keep some information out of the subsystem. For instance, if Teri's mother doesn't like Teri's boyfriend, Ron, Teri might work to keep that information out of the subsystem that she and Ron create.

Calibration

Calibration centers on how systems set their rules, check on themselves, and self-correct. For example, Maggie and her grandmother have a close relationship, and the two of them form a subsystem of Maggie's extended family. When Maggie was 10, she and her grandmother calibrated their system by setting a weekly lunch date. As Maggie got older, she found it harder to meet her grandmother every Saturday for lunch because she wanted to do more activities with her friends. She expressed this to her grandmother, and they **recalibrated** (or reset the rules of their system) by changing their lunch date to once a month. When systems experience such a change, it's a result of **positive feedback** (or feedback that produces change). But, if Maggie's grandmother looked crestfallen at the idea of losing their weekly lunch date, and Maggie just decided to make the time, then the rules for the system are not changed, and the feedback is judged as **negative feedback** (or feedback that maintains the status quo).

Equifinality

Equifinality means the ability to achieve the same goals (or ends) by a variety of means. For instance, you may have some friends with whom you spend a lot of time and other friends with whom you spend less time. Some of your friends may be people you play tennis with, and others may be those you like to go to movies with. Each of these friendships may be close, but you become close (and maintain your closeness) in different ways. Equifinality is often used to explain how a variety of families with very different ways of interacting may all be happy (i.e., there is no one way to be a happy family).

Table 10.3 illustrates how each of the six properties of Systems Theory relates to communication behaviors. Systems Theory doesn't explain all communication with our relational partners; it isn't specific enough to give us answers to questions such as why some couples argue more than others or why some communication in friendships is more satisfying than others. However, it does give us an overall impression of how relationships work and how communication behaviors function within relationships.

Table 10.3 /// System's Properties and Communication Outcomes

Property	Communication Outcome
Wholeness	The Thompson family is considered outgoing and funny. Ella Thompson is quiet and shy.
Interdependence	Lydia expresses unhappiness at work after her friend, Bethany, is transferred to another department. Lydia's communication has to change as a result of Bethany's changing situation.
Hierarchy	Jake talks to his son, Marcus, much more than he speaks to his other children. Jake and Marcus form a subsystem within the larger family system.
Boundaries or openness	Frieda tells a secret to her sister, Laya, and trusts her not to tell the rest of the family.
Calibration or feedback	Hap tells Miles that they can't play basketball every Wednesday because he needs to spend more time with his son. Miles agrees to change their playing times to every other week.
Equifinality	Laura and Roy are happily married, and they tell each other everything. Nadine and Bob are happily married, and they keep many things private and don't confide in each other that much.

 IPC Praxis

Think about a relationship you have. How useful do you find the six properties of Systems Theory in understanding that relationship and the role of communication in it? Give some specific examples to justify calling the theory helpful or not helpful.

Relational Dialectics Theory

A different explanation for communication in close relationships comes from Relational Dialectics Theory.[23] **Relational Dialectics Theory (RDT)** explains relational life as consisting of tensions resulting from people's desire to have two conflicting things at the same time, and it addresses how we deal with the tensions raised by this conflict. For instance, RDT assumes that we all want to have *both* privacy *and* the comfort that comes from being known by others, even though these two things seem like polar opposites. According to RDT, the core of relational life consists of partners engaging in a search for seemingly incompatible goals. Partners engage in this search so they can have *both/and* rather than *either/or* in their relationships.

Research suggests that the most common tensions in close relationships are those between autonomy and connection, openness and protection, and novelty and predictability. The contradiction in an **autonomy and connection dialectic** centers on our desire to be independent or autonomous while simultaneously wanting to feel a connection with our partner. This tension is apparent when Donna

iStock.com/laflor

Close relationships are characterized by both a desire for connection and a desire for autonomy.

Video 10.3

wants her friendship with Jessie to be really close, but at the same time she wants to be an independent individual, and it bugs her when their other friends talk about the two of them like they were one person. When we have an **openness and protection dialectic**, we want to self-disclose our innermost secrets to a friend, but we also want to keep quiet to protect ourselves from the chance that our friend will use the information against us somehow. This tension surfaces when Mika agonizes about telling Claire that he feels inadequate at work. Mika wants Claire's empathy, but he's a little afraid she might think less of him if she knew how he feels. The tension in a **novelty and predictability dialectic** manifests in our simultaneous desires for excitement and stability. Malcolm feels bored with the everyday routines he's established in his relationship with Brandon, but he also feels comforted and reassured by them. It's scary to leave familiar routines, even when you might find them tedious. These three basic contradictions or dialectics are all seen as dynamic. This means that the interplay between the two opposites permeates the life of a relationship and is never fully resolved.

In addition to these, some other dialectics are found specifically in friendships, including the following:

- judgment and acceptance
- affection and instrumentality
- public and private
- ideal and real

The tension caused by the **judgment and acceptance dialectic** involves criticizing a friend as opposed to accepting them. People are often torn between offering (unwanted) advice and just accepting a friend's behavior. If Maria has a friend, Josh, who is dating someone Maria thinks is wrong for him, should she offer her opinion or simply accept Josh's choice? Most people want both things simultaneously; they want to be able to make and hear judgments, but they also want unconditional acceptance. The **affection and instrumentality dialectic** poses a tension between framing your friendship with someone as an end in itself (affection) or seeing it as a means to another end (instrumentality). This dialectic suggests that in close friendships, people want to both just enjoy their friends and get some help from them. For example, if Tony often gets a ride to work from his close friend, Michael, then that friendship serves an instrumental function. But Tony values the friendship for affectionate reasons as well, such as the fun he and Michael have talking to each other on the way to work.

All the tensions we've discussed so far are considered **internal dialectics** because they focus on how the partners communicate with one another. The next two are **external dialectics** because they have to do with how people negotiate the more public aspects of their relationship. The **public and private dialectic** specifically centers on how much of the relationship is demonstrated in public and what parts are kept private. Some emblems of friendship are fine for public consumption (such as the fact that Kelly and Amy both like horror movies and they have a few rituals around how they watch them—they have to have popcorn and Pepsi, and the room has to be completely dark), while other things (such as the silly nicknames they have for one another) might be kept just between them. Some friendships, especially in adolescence, are kept more private. Ted, the football team captain at Metropolitan High School, doesn't always share publicly that he's friends with Paul, a computer geek. In private, Ted and Paul get along well, but neither especially wants to publicize their friendship.

Finally, the **ideal and real dialectic** reveals the tension between an idealized vision of a relationship and the real relationships we have. We may carry images in our heads of how self-sacrificing, other-oriented, and altruistic friends should be. We get these mental images in large part from popular culture: TV shows, buddy movies, books, and magazines that show examples of friendships. Although Georgia recognizes that these idealized images of friendship are fantasies, she can't help feeling some tension when her best friend, Ada, goes on a ski trip, even though Georgia can't make it. Georgia had hoped that Ada would refuse to go without her. Table 10.4 presents a summary of the dialectic tensions we've discussed.

Table 10.4 /// Summary of Dialectic Tensions	
Most Common Internal Relational Dialectics	
Autonomy and connection	
Openness and protection	
Novelty and predictability	
Additional Internal Dialectics Found in Friendships	
Judgment and acceptance	
Affection and instrumentality	
External Dialectics	
Public and private	
Ideal and real	

RDT says that to reduce the tension arising from our competing desires, we use several coping strategies including cyclic alternation, segmentation, selection, and integration.[24] We explain each of these strategies below:

- **Cyclic alternation** helps communicators handle tension by featuring the oppositions at alternating times. If Eileen discloses a great deal with her mother when she is in high school and then keeps much more information private from her mother when she goes to college, she is engaging in cyclic alternation. By sometimes being open and other times keeping silent, cyclic alternation allows Eileen to satisfy both goals in her relationship with her mom.

- **Segmentation** allows people to isolate separate arenas for enacting each of the oppositions. For example, if Mac works in a business with his father, Nathan, they may not disclose to one another at work but do so when they are together in a family setting.

- **Selection** means that you choose one of the opposites and ignore your need for the other. Rosie might decide that disclosing to her friend, Wendy, isn't working. Wendy often fails to be empathic and has occasionally told something that Rosie told her in confidence to another friend. Rosie can use selection and simply stop disclosing to Wendy altogether, making their relationship less open but also less stressful.

Integration takes one of the following three forms:

- **Neutralizing**, which involves compromising between the two oppositions. If Mira and her sister Reva have been arguing because Reva feels that Mira is leaving her out of her life and not telling her anything, then Mira might decide to use neutralizing with Reva. Mira would then disclose a moderate amount to her—maybe telling Reva a little less than Reva wants to hear but a little more than she would normally tell her. The strategy of neutralizing copes with the tension by creating a happy medium.

- **Disqualifying**, which allows people to cope with tensions by exempting certain issues from the general pattern. Paris might make some topics, such as her love life, off limits for disclosure with her mom but otherwise engage in a lot of self-disclosure with her. This coping strategy creates taboo topics, or issues that are out of bounds for discussion. Most relationships contain topics that are not talked about by unspoken mutual consent. Many families avoid discussing sex and money. Even when couples engage in the most intimate of sexual behaviors, they may not talk about sex to each other. Disqualifying provides for a lot of disclosure on topics other than those considered taboo.

- **Reframing**, which refers to rethinking the opposition. In doing so, people redefine the tension. For instance, couples may say that they actually feel closer to each other if they don't tell each other everything. Reframing is illustrated in a couple's belief that if they keep some secrets, that makes what they do tell each other more significant. You'll notice that this is a specialized definition of reframing and it differs from how we've used the term in other chapters.

Theory-Into-Practice (TIP)

Relational Dialectics Theory

Can you give an example of a dialectic tension that operates (or operated) in one of your relationships? How do you use any of the above coping strategies as a method for dealing with the dialectic tensions that exist in your close relationships? Give some examples from your own experiences in interpersonal communication encounters when you used one of the strategies.

Like Systems Theory, RDT is rather general. Although it provides a framework for understanding how people struggle with oppositions in relationships and helps us understand some communication behaviors as strategies for dealing with these tensions, it doesn't clearly predict which strategies people will use, nor does it tell us why some relationships are more stressed than others by these tensions. However, RDT is a good starting place for revealing some of the undercurrents that guide communication in close relationships.

Social Exchange Theory

Social Exchange Theory[25] (SET) comes from a different line of thinking than Systems Theory and RDT. Rather than providing a large framework for understanding communication in close relationships, SET is more specific and points us more directly toward testable predictions about it. First, SET makes three basic assumptions about human nature:

1. People are motivated by rewards and wish to avoid costs.

2. People are rational.

3. People evaluate costs and rewards differently.

For example, according to the first assumption, social exchange theorists believe that Jennifer and Laurie each want to do things that they find rewarding (such as going to the movies together) and that neither wants to do things that seem like punishment (e.g., Jennifer wouldn't want to do Laurie's laundry). The next assumption clarifies the first by asserting that people are thinking rationally most of the time, enabling them to calculate accurately what are the costs and rewards of any given relationship. People keep mental balance sheets about relational activities (e.g., "I had to spend two hours helping Dan with his economics homework, and he repaid me by buying my lunch yesterday").

Finally, according to the third assumption of SET, what is costly for one person might seem rewarding for another. For example, Malcolm finds babysitting for his cousin a drag. But Meg majored in early childhood education and doesn't have a chance to spend time with children, so she welcomes the opportunity to babysit for her cousin. Furthermore, both people in a relationship may see their costs and rewards differently. Hillary thinks that the fact that her parents don't like Patrick is a huge cost to their relationship, but Patrick isn't concerned about parental approval, so he ranks the cost much lower.

As you can see by these assumptions, the heart of social exchange thinking lies in two concepts: costs and rewards. **Costs** are those things in relational life that people judge as negative. Examples include having to do favors for friends, listening to Uncle Al's boring stories at family gatherings, or baby-sitting for a bratty younger cousin. **Rewards** are those parts of being in a relationship that are pleasurable to people. Examples include having your partner listen to your problems and offer empathy, sharing favorite activities with a friend, and laughing about private jokes with your brother. SET asserts that people are motivated to maximize their rewards while minimizing their costs and predicts that when costs exceed rewards, people will leave the relationship.

Yet, we can all think of examples of people who stay in relationships that seem, at least to outsiders, to be very costly. Abusive relationships (either physically or verbally), relationships where one person seems to have to do all the work, relationships where one person is wealthy and always pays for her poorer friend when they do expensive activities all provide examples of situations where it looks like the costs outweigh the rewards for at least one member of the relationship. SET explains these relationships with two other concepts: comparison level and comparison level for alternatives.

Comparison level consists of a person's expectations for a given relationship. People learn from a variety of sources—such as the media, their families, and their past experiences—what to expect from relationships. Your comparison level might tell you that friendship is a relationship in which you should expect to give and take in equal proportions, whereas love relationships require more giving than taking. SET predicts that people will be satisfied in relationships where the actual relationship matches or exceeds their comparison level.

Comparison level for alternatives refers to comparing the costs and rewards of a current relationship to the possibility of doing better in a different relationship. For example, Melanie calculates that she has more costs than rewards in her relationship with her husband, Erik. However, she still might stay with Erik if she also calculates that her chances of doing better without him, either by finding a better relationship or being alone, are poor. Some researchers have used this theory to explain why some women stay in abusive relationships.

 **IPC Praxis**

Using a specific relationship, divide a piece of paper in half and on one half list the costs of that relationship and on the other list the rewards. As you look at your lists, what does SET predict about the future of the relationship? How do comparison level and comparison level for alternatives factor into the prediction?

10-6 SKILL SET FOR COMMUNICATING IN CLOSE RELATIONSHIPS

This section presents several ways to improve communication in close relationships. As we've emphasized, communicating with people in close relationships is the source of both our greatest pleasure and greatest grief, so people are usually motivated to improve their communication with important relational partners. Because many factors affect relationship development, we are necessarily broad in offering these suggestions. We divide the skills by how they help to begin, maintain, and repair relationships. See Table 10.5 for a list of skills to begin a relationship.

Table 10.5 /// Skill Set for Beginning a Relationship		
a. Network or find out information from a third party.		
b. Offer or make yourself accessible.		
c. Approach or actually go up to another.		
d. Sustain the conversation with questions.		
e. Seek affinity with another.		
f. Your skill suggestion		

Communication Skills for Beginning Relationships

Beginning a relationship requires a fair amount of skill, although you may not think about developing these skills. Most people meet new people fairly frequently, and they don't consciously think about how they go about striking up conversations and cultivating new friends. Some research suggests the following skills are needed to initiate relationships:

- **Networking**: finding out information about the person from a third party. Easing into a relationship with the help of a third person means that you're behaving efficiently and in a socially acceptable fashion.

- **Offering**: putting yourself in a good position for another to approach you. If you sit near a person you'd like to get to know better, or walk along the same route as they do, you're putting physical proximity to work for you.

- **Approaching**: actually going up to a person or smiling in that person's direction to give a signal that you would like to initiate contact. Approaching allows the relationship to begin, with both parties involved in some interaction.

- **Sustaining**: behaving in a way that keeps the initial conversation going. Asking appropriate questions is a way to employ sustaining.

- **Affinity seeking**: emphasizing the commonalities you think you share with the other person. Sometimes affinity seeking goes hand in hand with asking appropriate questions; you first ask questions to determine areas of common interest or experience and then you comment on them. "Do you like reality shows?" "No kidding? I'm a big fan, too." According to research, people use a variety of affinity-seeking strategies to get others to like them. See Table 10.6 for a summary of these strategies.[26]

Table 10.6 /// Affinity-Seeking Strategies

1.	Altruism	Help the other person and offer to do things for them.
2.	Assume control	Take a leadership position.
3.	Assume equality	Don't show off. Treat the other as an equal.
4.	Comfort	Act at ease.
5.	Concede control	Allow the other to be in charge.
6.	Conversational rules	Follow the cultural norms for a conversation.
7.	Dynamism	Project excitement and enthusiasm.
8.	Elicit disclosure	Ask questions and encourage the other to talk.
9.	Inclusion	Include the other in activities and conversations.
10.	Facilitate enjoyment	Make time together enjoyable.
11.	Closeness	Indicate that the two of you have a close relationship.
12.	Listening	Lean in, listen intently, and respond appropriately.
13.	Nonverbal immediacy	Display good eye contact, appropriate touching, and so forth.
14.	Openness	Disclose appropriate personal information.
15.	Optimism	Display cheerfulness and positivity.
16.	Personal autonomy	Project independence.
17.	Physical attraction	Try to look good.
18.	Present self as interesting	Highlight past accomplishments and things of interest about yourself.
19.	Reward association	Offer favors and remind the other about past favors.
20.	Confirmation	Flatter the other.
21.	Inclusion	Spend time with the other.
22.	Sensitivity	Display empathy appropriately.
23.	Similarities	Point out things you have in common.
24.	Support	Be encouraging of the other and avoid criticism.
25.	Trustworthiness	Be dependable and sincere.

Communication Skills for Maintaining Relationships

Some people focus all their attention on beginning a relationship, thinking that after they have a friend, a boyfriend, or a girlfriend, they've achieved their goal. They fail to realize that close relationships need attention, and some amount of work, to keep them functioning. Of course, close relationships aren't all work, or we wouldn't enjoy them so much. But if you ignore your closest relationships, they'll begin to falter and perhaps deteriorate. **Preventative maintenance** involves both partners paying attention to the relationship even when it's not experiencing trouble. See Table 10.7 for a list of relational maintenance skills.

Table 10.7 /// Skill Set for Relational Maintenance

a. Offer assurances. ("I am committed to our relationship.")

b. Express openness. ("Here's how I feel about our relationship.")

c. Reflect positivity. ("You did such a great job on that!")

d. Share tasks. ("If you'll clean the bathroom, I'll do the kitchen.")

e. Activate your social networks. ("Why don't you ask your sister to come to the movies with us?")

f. Express support. ("I want to help. Tell me what you'd like me to do.")

g. Your skill suggestion

 IPC Voice: Axel

I agree it's a great idea to pay attention to a relationship before it gets into trouble. When I was dating my first serious girlfriend, I didn't know about that though, and the relationship got into trouble so bad that we couldn't fix it. Later when I met my current girlfriend, Grace, I knew better. We do a weekly check-in and that helps us with our problems before they get too big to deal with.

We'll discuss the skill expressing support in a bit more detail. A supportive communication climate, which encourages relational growth and maintenance, is conducive to maintaining relationships. However, supportive climates do not happen by chance; skillful communication is necessary to build this type of climate. The overall guidelines for developing supportive climates for communication are as follows:

- Make *descriptive* rather than evaluative comments. ("You have interrupted me twice" rather than "You are the rudest person!")

- Speak in *provisional* ways rather than in an absolute manner. ("I'm not sure, but I think that's the case" rather than "That's the only possible way it can be.")

- Be more *spontaneous* than strategic. ("Let's go on a picnic today—it's so beautiful out!" rather than "Let's plan a picnic for next week.")

- Strive for a *problem orientation* rather than a control orientation. ("How can we solve this so we're both happy?" rather than "You need to do it this way in order for things to work well between us.")

- Provide *empathy* instead of neutrality to your partner. ("I can tell that you're upset. Do you want to talk to me about it?" rather than simply waiting for your partner to come to you with a problem.)

- Establish *equality* between partners rather than superiority of one over the other. ("What do you think? I really want to know your opinion" rather than "Here's what I think and we're done talking about this!")[27]

Communication Skills for Repairing Relationships

As we've discussed throughout this chapter, having close relationships is critically important to people. However, some communication in close relationships can be unhealthy or toxic. In close relationships, people can betray, deceive, and say hurtful things to each other. Researchers call these negative behaviors **relational transgressions**. When people in close relationships experience a relational transgression, they have to decide whether to repair or terminate the relationship. If they decide not to terminate the relationship, they must engage in the difficult task of **corrective maintenance or repair**. Repair skills are more difficult to implement than maintenance skills because repair involves correcting a problem, whereas maintenance is simply aimed at keeping things moving in a positive direction. We briefly discuss two repair skills: meta-communication and apology. See Table 10.8 for a list of repair skills.

Table 10.8 /// Skill Set for Relational Repair
a. Engage in effective meta-communication.
b. Utilize sincere apologies.
c. Your skill suggestion

Meta-communication means communicating about communication. If communication is the problem in the relationship, the partners need to address how to improve their communication. For example, if Caitlin tells her friend Alonzo that she doesn't like it when he raises his voice to her, she is engaging in meta-communication. Alonzo might respond that he raises his voice when he gets excited. Caitlin can then tell him that she interprets it as anger. After the two define the problem through meta-communication, they can work on figuring out how to repair the problem.

Apologies have several parts: an expression of remorse, a promise not to repeat the transgression, an acknowledgment of fault, a promise to make it up to the victim, and a request for forgiveness. Sometimes apologies are accompanied by **accounts**, or explanations for the transgression. Accounts may include justifications ("It's really not as bad as you think—look at it from my perspective") and excuses ("I couldn't help being late—my boss gave me a huge project just as I was leaving"). As an example of how apologies can help repair relationships, consider Kelli and Ella. The two had been really close friends all through high school. They had kept in touch after graduation, even though they had moved to opposite ends of the country. For several years, they exchanged Christmas cards, and they even saw each other from time to time. Each time they met, it was as if they had just been together, and they talked and talked, catching up with each other's lives. However,

Rawdon Wyatt/Alamy Stock Photo

The ability to communicate sincere apologies is a critical skill for repairing relationships.

one year, Kelli sent Ella her usual Christmas card, and Ella didn't respond. After a couple of years, Kelli stopped sending the cards, and the two ceased contact.

Then out of the blue, Ella called and apologized, providing an account of her behavior. She told Kelli that problems she had been having with her family had demanded all her concentration. She said she just hadn't had the energy for keeping up with any of her long-distance friendships. Kelli felt a lot better when she heard Ella's explanation, and the two were able to resume their friendship. Apologies are not always successful, but they are one way that relational partners strive to repair their relationship after a transgression, and they often help.

/// CHAPTER WRAP-UP

In this chapter, we've taken on a huge topic: close relationships. We've given you an overview that you can apply to Chapter 11's discussion of specific relationships (like family and friends). We offered a definition of close relationships and investigated how people may talk and think about them. Then we considered how all those things are affected by attraction, culture, gender and sex, and electronic media. We examined a stage model approach to close relationships and then discussed three different theoretical frameworks that explain communication in close relationships. We provided a list of skills that are useful in beginning, maintaining, and repairing relationships.

As you think about all the material in this text, you can see how communication and close relationships are intertwined. As long as we're communicating with another, we're in relationship with them. And communication propels us through a variety of stages in relationship development.

/// COMMUNICATION ASSESSMENT TEST (CAT): ASSESSING YOUR RELATIONSHIP HEALTH

Mark Yes or No to the following statements based on your assessment of how your significant other behaves toward you.

The person I'm with

_____1. Is very supportive of things that I do

_____2. Encourages me to try new things

_____3. Likes to listen when I have something on my mind

_____4. Understands that I have my own life too

_____5. Is not liked very well by my friends

_____6. Says I'm too involved in different activities

_____7. Texts me or calls me all the time

_____8. Thinks I spend too much time trying to look nice

_____9. Gets extremely jealous or possessive

_____10. Accuses me of flirting or cheating

_____11. Constantly checks up on me or makes me check in

_____12. Controls what I wear or how I look

_____13. Tries to control what I do and who I see

_____14. Tries to keep me from seeing or talking to my family and friends

_____15. Has big mood swings, getting angry and yelling at me one minute but being sweet and apologetic the next

_____16. Makes me feel nervous or like I'm "walking on eggshells"

_____17. Puts me down, calls me names, or criticizes me

_____18. Makes me feel like I can't do anything right or blames me for problems

_____19. Makes me feel like no one else would want me

_____20. Threatens to hurt me, my friends, or family

_____21. Threatens to hurt themselves because of me

22. Threatens to destroy my things (phone, clothes, laptop, car, etc.)

23. Grabs, pushes, shoves, chokes, punches, slaps, holds me down, throws things, or hurts me in some way

24. Breaks or throws things to intimidate me

25. Yells, screams, or humiliates me in front of other people

26. Pressures or forces me into having sex or going farther than I want to

Scoring:

Give yourself 1 point for every NO to statements 1–4; 1 point for every YES to statements 5–8; and 5 points for every YES to statements 9–26. Total your score.

Interpreting your score:

0 = your relationship is on a pretty healthy track. Keep it up!

1–2 = you might be noticing a couple of things in your relationship that you don't like, but that's not necessarily a warning sign. You may want to talk with your partner about these things.

3–4 = you may be seeing some warning signs of an unhealthy relationship. Don't ignore these red flags. You and your partner may want to seek some outside help to deal with these issues.

5+ = you are definitely seeing warning signs of an unhealthy relationship. Remember, the most important thing is your safety. Consider making a safety plan and definitely consult a counselor or other professional so you don't have to deal with this alone.

Source: Adapted from loveisrespect.org./National Domestic Violence Hotline

/// KEY TERMS

1. **CQ/CultureQuest:** Explore the following claim: "People from cultures that do not embrace the notion of romantic love tend to have stronger marriages than those from cultures who do expect romance in marriage." Do you agree or disagree? Defend your views.

2. **TQ/TechQuest:** Explore the following claim: "Relationships formed online are just as strong and enduring as relationships formed face-to-face." Do you agree or disagree? Defend your views.

3. Which theory, Systems, Relational Dialectics, or Social Exchange, do you think explains communication in relationships the best? Give examples to illustrate your position.

4. Describe relationship scripts. How do you think they work in practice? Do you think you have scripts for the relationships you are in now? Where did these scripts come from?

5. Do you agree that language sometimes fails to label the various forms of relational life that we experience? Give some examples (beyond the ones mentioned in the chapter) of important relationships you experience or know about that don't have a good name. Can you come up with a name for these relationships?

6. What do you think makes a good apology after a relational transgression? Are there things that can tear a relationship so severely that nothing can be done to mend it? Give some specific examples.

Access practice quizzes, eFlashcards, video, and multimedia at **edge.sagepub.com/west**.

Visit **edge.sagepub.com/west** to help you accomplish your coursework goals in an easy-to-use learning environment.

CHAPTER 11

COMMUNICATING WITH FAMILIES, FRIENDS, AND ROMANTIC PARTNERS

LEARNING OUTCOMES

After studying this chapter, you will be able to

11–1 Identify and describe the types of family configurations in the United States

11–2 Explain the various stages of childhood and adult friendships

11–3 Articulate the dimensionality of romantic relationships

11–4 Employ skills that help to improve communication in families, close friendships, and romantic relationships

iStock.com/monkeybusinessimages

Master the content at
edge.sagepub.com/west

$SAGE edge™

The enduring value of our close relationships cannot be disputed. Throughout this book, we have underscored the importance of fostering long-term, satisfying close relationships with others. In Chapter 10, you learned the various theoretical and practical foundations that frame these relationships. By now, we're sure you know that our interpersonal communication with others can provide us ample opportunities to make our relationships more or less compelling and valuable to us.

And yet, many times our relationships are messy. People are unpredictable and we can't confidently project what will happen to us or the influences of others upon us. Challenges exist, including those, for instance, related to finances, housing, child care, fidelity, time management, and jealousy, making relational life very tough for many. And yet, we persevere because relationships are important and we find ourselves among people who care for us and who help us grow. These types of connections are the focus of this chapter.

Of all the interpersonal relationships in which we engage, three types figure prominently in the lives of most people: family, friends, and romantic partners. Although we understand that each of these relational types are discrete and unique in many ways, it's also true that each overlap in some significant ways. For example, some married couples refer to each other as a "best friend." In addition, close friends can, at times, turn into romantic partners, with various levels of relationship satisfaction. Or, consider the fact that some family members view other family members as close friends.

> **The following theories/models are discussed in this chapter:**
>
> Selman's Stages of Childhood Friendships
>
> Rawlins's Stages of Adult Friendship Development
>
> Triangular Theory of Love

💬 IPC Voice: Brandon

Okay, you want to talk about family! I always thought that mine was the craziest with the weirdest people (try coming to my family reunions each June!). But, as I talk with my buddies, they all tell me that they have crazy families too! In my family, we all yell to get our points heard. There's name-calling and people interrupt all the time—you know, the stuff that our book tells us NOT to do! But, one time, I was in trouble with a speeding ticket and my dad got me out of the ticket and my sister didn't hassle me at all. . . . I guess they're not all that crazy.

Despite this overlapping, each of the three close relationship types we're about to explore has distinct characteristics and expectations. And, to be sure, it's also true that while each may resemble the other, it's the interpersonal communication that exists within each relationship that creates the uniqueness we're about to discuss.

Among the many relational types we find ourselves in and the ones we noted above, we wish to focus on family, friends, and romantic relationships. (Complete the CAT on Relational Quality for an indication of how your relationships function in your lives.) We've been introduced to these types most prominently through media. Historically, for instance, over the years television shows have been instrumental in communicating various examples of (1) family life (e.g., *All in the Family* in the 1970s to *Black-ish* today), (2) friends (e.g., *Friends* in 1994 to *Lovesick* today), and (3) romantic relationships (e.g., *I Love Lucy* in 1951 to *Sister Wives* today). Using this television vantage point, you can quickly see that these three relationship types can vary tremendously. And, outside of a Hollywood set, this variation continues. Let's begin our discussion with the sort of relationship that remains as one of the most vexing of all groups in a person's life: family.

IPC Praxis

Suppose you were invited to develop your own television series featuring a television family. What would the show look like? What kind of family situations and interpersonal dilemmas would you have in your pilot episode? How are they communicative in nature?

11–1 FAMILY RELATIONSHIPS

Families are unique close relationships for many reasons. First, family ties can be voluntary or involuntary. Some families consist of people who come together of their own free will, such as married partners, communes, or **intentional families** who band together by choice rather than by blood relationships. But many family members have relationships with others they did not choose, such as parents, grandparents, cousins, siblings, and so forth, which form different relationships within this family type (e.g., sibling/grandparent, husband/mother-in-law).

Families are also distinctive because for many members, the close relationship is lifelong. Some research[1] indicates that even though Western families expect children to leave the nest as they reach adulthood, continuity of relationships with family members is just as important as increasing autonomy. In fact, if you have a sibling, it's likely that your sibling experience will be the longest lasting relationship you have in your life.[2] Finally, unlike friendship or dating relationships, family is typically a close relationship that receives social, cultural, and legal sanctions through, for example, marriage, adoption, and inheritance. Let's address "family" a bit further so you can see its relevancy, function, and possibilities in your interpersonal relationships. We begin by defining the family, discussing some interpersonal communication practices in the family, and identifying various family types. Further, although we have sustained a commitment to cultural inclusion throughout this text, we necessarily limit the following discussion to family life in the United States.

Elsewhere, we have discussed the difficulties with defining family.[3] We noted that interpreting the term *family* could be problematic because of all of the different incarnations existing. Further, we posited that "defining family often is a problem that bedevils policy makers, laypeople, and scholars alike."[4] That is, we have multiple family types (e.g., single parent, multigenerational) that we know through research, and we also know that there are various options and choices (e.g., reproductive technologies, adoption) that influence the interpretation of family. Furthermore, family types exist that are not universally known and, of course, there are family types yet to be realized, given the influence of culture, technology, gender, sexual identity, among others.

There is some debate in the family communication literature concerning how to define a family. Some researchers advocate a very narrow definition of family as a "socially, legally, and genetically oriented relationship."[5] Others, however, argue for allowing functions such as communication to define the family.[6] In other words, if a group of people function like a family by sharing affection and resources, and refer to themselves as a family, then they are a family. Still others[7] advance an expansive definition of family that includes the notion of choice; if you choose a person to be considered a family member, then that person is recognized as such. We refer to this as **voluntary kin**, or individuals who feel like family but who are not related either by blood or law. So, for example, when he was a teenager, after telling his father that he wanted to explore gender reassignment, 15-year-old Tony was kicked out of his house. In the two years subsequent to his father's directive, Tony became close to one of his "street friends," Amber. In fact, Amber allowed him to stay with her in a place she shared and the two became quite close. Today, if we were to ask Tony who he would identify as a family member, according to an expansive view of family, he would mention Amber. In all likelihood, he would not mention his father, despite the DNA connecting the two.

IPC Praxis

What's your view about the notion of a "voluntary" family? Do you believe that to define a family, members have to share the same DNA? Or, can we define others as members of our family? How will your interpretation affect government policy? Explain with examples.

We believe in a more inclusive, communication-based definition. We contend that it's valuable for us, as we try to understand what a family is, to be vigilant in addressing the diversity that characterizes much family life.

Families are created through interpersonal communication. To illustrate why we embrace this position, we provide you with two examples of how communication influences family life. One interpersonal communication practice that has been examined as unique to families is storytelling. **Family stories** are those bits of narrative about family members and activities that are told and retold and that have been seen as a way for members to construct a sense of family identity and meaning.[8] Some researchers argue that families don't just tell stories, but that storytelling is a way of creating a family.[9] So, when Marie brings her new friend, Danielle, home to meet her parents, for example, the stories that are told to Danielle are a way to bring the family alive for her and to integrate Danielle into the family.

Family stories can be pleasurable and entertaining as well as difficult to listen to. The stories can sometimes serve as cautionary tales about family members who went astray in some way. Consider Blake as he recalls hearing the story about his great-uncle Thomas, who lost the family fortune by gambling. Blake always got the impression that the story was told repeatedly to warn his generation to keep working hard and avoid developing bad habits. Or, consider the family stories that may not be as clear or coherent as other stories. For example, stories handed down by African Americans regarding slavery are often incomplete. Because slavery tore families apart, it's sometimes difficult to find connected, linked stories regarding family life. In fact, African American families have a rich history, but not every African American family knows much about their history because the family lineage has been disrupted and, in some cases, destroyed.[10]

A second important family interpersonal communication practice is the **ritual**, or a repeated patterned communication event in a family's life. Rituals can take three forms: everyday interactions (e.g., the Gilbert family members always say a prayer together before going to bed), traditions (e.g., Rollie and Elizabeth mark their anniversary each year by eating dinner at McDonald's because that's where they met each other), and celebrations (e.g., Ben and Rachel eat Thanksgiving dinner with their children and their neighbors). Celebrations differ from traditions because they involve holidays that are shared throughout a culture as opposed to traditions, which are practices that evolve in a specific family. Still, both celebrations and holidays involve the back and forth nature of conversations, and each provides for enhanced intimacy as well as enhanced conflict. We will talk a bit further about these interpersonal possibilities later in the chapter.

Now that you have a general understanding of what family is and a few interpersonal communication practices, let's move deeper into recognizing current family life. First, most of us are born into a **family-of-origin**. This is the family in which we have been raised and this family is usually important in establishing our values and our worldviews. The family-of-origin is also instrumental to our interpersonal communication style. That is, the family in which we were raised can be—and often is—responsible, directly or indirectly, for how we communicate

Most of us are born into a family-of-origin while still being unaware of our ancestry.

with others today. Certainly, as we grow older, we develop and nurture effective interpersonal communication patterns and skills—otherwise, why would you be in this course? Still, we also need to acknowledge that our parents, siblings, grandparents, and other family members likely have (had) an extraordinary influence upon our interpersonal skills today.

Understanding our family-of-origin helps us to realize one family foundation. Yet, recognizing family types widens our understanding of different families. We now touch a bit on different family configurations that are found around us. As we examine each, keep in mind that even if we had 100 pages to write on this subject, we could never capture every family type! In fact, we present you with a group of family types that are representative and not meant to be exhaustive. So, let's discuss the definition, roles, rules, and patterns of interpersonal communication in four very different family types: nuclear family, gay and lesbian family, multigenerational family, and single-parent family (see Table 11.1). Please note that some family arrangements may overlap with the other (e.g., a single dad, his daughter, and her grandfather living together). Further, over the years, one type may morph into another. There is clearly no longer one dominant form. Still, we offer the following category system rooted in the research on U.S. families.

Video 11.1

Nuclear families are named this way, in part, because the "nucleus," or center, was the core where others would gravitate. In this case, it was the father and mother who served as the family's "center." In a sense, a nuclear family was the original foundation of family life, and all the remaining family types coalesced or diverted from this configuration. Nuclear families can be categorized in two ways. First, the **traditional nuclear family** is composed of a married couple living with their biological children, with a husband/father providing financial support (e.g., "breadwinner") to the family and the wife/mother providing domestic support, cleaning, cooking, and so forth. The **contemporary nuclear family** is a modernized version of the nuclear family and can include two situations: a stay-at-home dad with a mom working outside of the home and a dual-career couple that includes both father and mother working outside the home and both providing primary care to their children. The U.S. Census Bureau reports that around 22% of households are defined as nuclear (their definition of *nuclear* includes the more traditional view

Table 11.1 /// Primary Family Types in the United States

Type	Definition
I. Nuclear	Married couple living with their biological children
A. Traditional	Father/husband is financial provider Mother/wife is responsible for domestic duties
B. Contemporary	Stay-at-home father with mother working outside the home Dual-career couple working outside the home, both providing care for their children
II. Gay and Lesbian	Same-sex intimate couple caring for at least one child
III. Multigenerational	A number of generations living together, including parents, children, grandparents, aunts, uncles, etc.
IV. Single Parent	One adult serving as the primary parent to at least one child

of this family type).[11] Furthermore, the upswing of stay-at-home dads (SAHDs) cannot be ignored. There are 1.9 million SAHDs compared with 10.4 million stay-at-home moms.[12] Clearly, SAHDs are growing in number, but they still comprise a very small group compared to stay-at-home moms.

Interpersonal communication within nuclear families can be both comfortable and defensive. For instance, in a traditional family arrangement, because both the husband and wife understand and embrace traditional gender roles,[13] interpersonal communication conflict is generally limited. Yet, some internal conflict may exist as this family arrangement bumps up against some external forces, namely the macro-culture. That is, consider the challenge that Maria Venegas experiences as she helps out at the annual Christmas pageant at school. Because she is a stay-at-home mom, Maria did not have to have permission to leave work or take a vacation day. This situation caused other mothers who work outside the home to feel rather envious, causing Maria to avoid talking about her family arrangement.

Interpersonal communication challenges occur with the contemporary traditional family. Why? Stay-at-home dads may experience some intrapersonal conflict between their domestic style and the Westernized cultural expectations of men serving as the primary financial provider; in fact, many cultures around the globe have a pretty limited view of men's roles in the home. The U.S. recession of 2008–2012, however, stimulated more of this family arrangement as men were either laid off or terminated during company downsizing. In addition, despite the growing numbers of SAHDs, role conflict may occur as men perceive themselves as less effective than stay-at-home moms.[14]

When two people of the same sex maintain an intimate relationship and care for at least one child, they are part of a **gay- and lesbian-headed family**. Although this family type has existed for decades, in 2004, the year that the Massachusetts Supreme Judicial Court declared it unconstitutional to deny gay men and lesbians the right to marry, the cultural tides of support turned. Although this family configuration enjoys much more support than it did even a decade ago, the United

Marriage equality has ushered in millions of new same-sex family configurations.

States is far from universal in its embrace. The U.S. Supreme Court "approved" marriage equality in 2015, and despite other countries subsequently approving same-sex marriage since that time (e.g., Colombia, Germany, Malta), many states have worked to "undo" the implications of this bond by invoking religion and morality exemptions.

Research notes that 4.5% of U.S. adults are gay, lesbian, bisexual, or transgender.[15] Furthermore, there are an estimated 605,000 same-sex spousal couple households in the United States,[16] although, like other reporting, it's not always clear whether individuals are willing or accurate in reporting the presence of children. Regardless, the exponential growth in this family type cannot be ignored and has supplied communication researchers with some information.

What do we know about the interpersonal communication within families with gay fathers and lesbian mothers? First, the "coming out" process of gay fathers is often different than mothers[17] (see Chapter 8 for more information on self-disclosure). Perhaps because both gay fathers and lesbian mothers continue to feel that they are targets of homophobia, this family type experiences unique challenges unlike other family types. Furthermore, "legitimacy challenges" are experienced, including direct attacks, discriminating silence, and legal discrimination that serve to undercut the dignity of this family configuration. All of these life events likely undermine the interpersonal communication taking place in any family. Yet, researchers[18] note that there is much resilience in this family type, resulting in interpersonal communication and parenting skills that are typically supportive, nonjudgmental, and functional. Further, lesbian moms typically employ rituals to communicate their family form to others, from the subtle (walking in the park) to the overt (marriage ceremony).[19] In addition, same-sex couples, overall, managed their tasks in a democratic and egalitarian manner, regardless of whether it was a lesbian mom or gay dad.[20]

Many people belong to families where several generations live under the same roof. Multigenerational families are considered to be extended families, meaning that they "extend" from the nuclear arrangement we talked about earlier. Mutigenerational families include multiple generations living together, including parents and children, as well as other relatives such as aunts, uncles, and grandparents. This family type has become more commonplace for a few reasons. First, economic reasons have forced unexpected family dynamics, including college students returning home after their degree because they could not find a job (called "boomerang kids"). Second, economic and demographic factors, coupled with the fact that people are living longer, have resulted in aging relatives living with families under the same roof. Third, because of the influx of immigrants over the past several decades, and despite shortsighted efforts to curtail their legitimacy, multigenerational households have soared. Children, in particular, have altered the multigenerational immigrant home, accounting for about 75% of the growth of the child population.[21]

The Pew Research Center[22] reports that nearly 64 million people, or about 20% of the population, live in a multigenerational household. The U.S. Census Bureau[23] reports that by 2050, about 100 million U.S. citizens will be over the age of 65, resulting in a significant uptick in the numbers of this family type. Furthermore, as alluded to earlier, nearly 1 of every 3 adults have moved in and live with a parent[24] (prompting new forms of family communication), and the growth of this household type will continue.

Multigenerational families, as we have noted, who experience the addition of older family members will be especially affected by this newly formed family configuration. Grandparents, in particular, can influence the interpersonal communication within the family. One researcher,[25] for instance, claims that the grandparent–grandchild relationship can be a safe place where confidences are kept and family histories are learned. This relationship can be a great deal more free than the parent–child relationship. Communication among family members with grandparents may be problematic, however, if a grandparent is around every day—all day—causing expectations to be placed on them (e.g., laundry, dishes). In fact, in what some may view as an interesting twist with respect to babysitting, aging grandparents may necessitate adult children to care for them The **sandwich generation**, or the generation of people who simultaneously cares for its (aging) parents and their own children, will become even more prominent in multigenerational households, creating a bit of role confusion.

Thus far, we've addressed nuclear families, gay- and lesbian-headed families, and multigenerational families. One additional family type is the **single-parent family**. Images of single parents have evolved over the years. Presentations of single parents were usually relegated to single mothers, most of whom were created as a result of divorce and allegations that, for whatever reason, the mother "did something wrong." Today, we have a myriad of images related to single-parent families, which comprise one adult serving as the primary parent to at least one child. Although it's true that some still hold an antiquated image of this family type, and some even believe that the number of single parents is "alarming," both Western and Eastern cultures have come a long way. Portraits of single parents include both men and women who are capable of quality parenting.

IPC Careers

Family Life and Child Protective Specialists

iStock.com/ViktoriiaNovokhatska

Nearly all families have a child or children. In fact, in many family configurations, children are instrumental to a family's dynamic. The communication in a single-parent family, nuclear family, multigenerational family, among others, is impacted by the presence of children, and children can be sources of pride, stress, conflict, and joy in many families. A child welfare specialist works to keep children in safe, supportive, and violence-free home environments. These child-centered professionals are busy people. They are responsible for a multitude of tasks that ensure that children are given the best protection and support structures. In addition to managing caseloads that relate to children in various family situations, the child welfare specialist also is often required to understand a number of different difficult issues, including poverty, unemployment, substance abuse, illness, and other factors that impact the child's well-being. Each of these topics requires skills in interpersonal communication and also a sensitivity to multiple populations, including those that are the most vulnerable.

Reflection: *Given the many types of families that exist and that are still on the horizon and yet to be identified, what general pieces of relational advice would you give to a child welfare specialist as they consider the home, school, and other environments where we'd find the child?*

Demographically, about 11.9 million single-parent households exist in the United States, comprising nearly 30% of all households in the country. Yes, this is a large percentage of all family types, and single parents have more than tripled as a share of all U.S. households since 1960. Breaking down the numbers a bit further shows that 17% of single parents are men, with 9% raising three or more children; there are 2.7 million single fathers and nearly 10.3 million single mothers.[26]

Day-to-day interpersonal communication in single-parent households (i.e., a parent residing with a child who is less than age 18) is somewhat unique. Consider the reasons that a single-parent household may exist: death, divorce, choice, among others. Think about Victoria, for example, who as a single mom must not only deal with the untimely death of her husband but also the economic and communicative challenges of parenting three children under the age of 11. Or, imagine the interpersonal communication in a family with Robby, who was awarded joint custody of his 14-year-old, Isabella. And think about the different discourses taking place in a family with Julien, who, at the age of 35, successfully adopted twin 8-year-old sisters from Russia. Each of these affords opportunities for various interpersonal struggles and triumphs.

In addition, the parent–child relationship in single-parent families is complicated by the dynamics contained within each family. For instance, suppose a single parent decided to date. What sort of communication might exist between the dating partner and the parent? Or, how is co-parenting done in divorced families? Some research shows that a "good divorce" is possible and that cooperative co-parenting can result in close relationships.[27] Also, if a single parent adopted a child, how might that parent address a child's request to meet her biological parents? Each of these scenarios, and so many others, require a template of interpersonal communication skills. We will address a skill set later in the chapter that we believe would assist this, and other family types.

11–2 CLOSE FRIENDSHIPS

In a first of its kind, the *State of Friendship in America* report[28] presented a national snapshot of friendships in the United States. The report identifies several conclusions related to close friends. Five are of particular relevance:

- Most people are not fully satisfied with the state of their friendships. Seniors (age 70 and over), Millennials, and Generation Yers (ages 16–34) are more likely to say they're extremely satisfied than are Generation Xers (ages 35–49).

- People who say they have close friends report more happiness and more fulfillment in life than those without close friends.

- Women report more close friends, but they are no happier than men in their close friendships.

- Social media is fairly *in*significant in long-term close friendships. In fact, there is no relationship between the number of Facebook friends and a person's satisfaction with their friends.

- Individuals who observe weekly religious services, who are ideologically conservative, and who reside in an urban center report the highest levels of satisfaction in their friendships.

The report concludes by noting that friendship runs deep and requires us to toss out our stereotypes and predispositions to friendship formation. And, unlike most family relationships, friendship is clearly voluntary.

For our purposes, we adopt the following view of friendship: **Friendship** is a significant close relationship of choice that exists over a period of time between individuals who provide social support and who share various commonalities (e.g., time together). Still, despite this expansive view, friendship continues to be a slippery concept because the term has been tossed around in popular culture with a multitude of meanings. You will recall in Chapter 4 that language can be problematic. When you hear the word *friend,* a number of difficulties can arise because of the various uses of the term. People use the word in ways that don't foster emotional closeness or social support. For instance, politicians refer to their political enemies as "friends" (e.g., "I will not yield the floor to my good friend because he has already wasted our time"). And, of course, today we have "Facebook friends," and these are often people we've never met but whom we're comfortable labeling a "friend." We take friendships for granted, yet we rarely understand their importance in our lives. Scholars have summed up this "take-for-granted" rationale by stating, "Friendships receive no ceremonial celebration; no legal, political, religious, or other institutional support."[29]

In this chapter, we are focused on **authentic friends**—those individuals whom we identify as close friends, with whom we share our personal feelings, and whom we hold in high esteem. Because there are no formal ceremonies to sanction friendships or any legal bonds to make dissolving them difficult, friendships are often amorphous, making it a somewhat fragile close relationship. Friends may be sacrificed for family in the belief that family relationships are more primary.

For instance, Maggie had to exclude her best friend, Leah, from her son's wedding rehearsal because only family members were invited. Friends may also come and go based on situational factors. Randi, for example, found it hard to stay friends with Marlene after she got married and moved to California while Randi remained single in Chicago. She wanted to stay friends with Marlene, but the long distance and their different circumstances doomed the friendship.

Although we have a wide variety of differences in perceptions and experiences with friends, the truth is that we believe that our close friends need to possess certain qualities. So, let's now discuss the expectations we hold of a friend. We close our conversation about friendships by taking a lifespan approach to understanding friendships.

 IPC Around Us

iStock.com/LDProd

Friendships at work are inevitable. Today, more and more businesses have coworkers who also define themselves as friends.[30] The work–life dividing line is disappearing, bringing with it new friendships that even a few years ago were unimaginable. Today's workplace requires people to work in teams and spend long hours together. Some people believe that friendships at work have business advantages, including increased productivity and employee retention. Further, workers indicate that they have higher job satisfaction if they are able to cultivate friendships with their coworkers. In the end, there must be a cultural framework in place that accommodates the development and maintenance of friendships. It's a "win-win" scenario for both employee and company.

Reflection: Years ago, it was taboo for friendships to develop in the workplace. Today, the lines are not so clear, and many workplaces—particularly start-ups—encourage workplace friendships. Other companies, however, frown upon it, believing that inappropriate events taking place outside of the workplace may influence what takes place in the workplace. Discuss how you feel about the entire situation, commenting on both the challenges and possibilities.

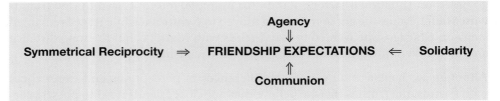

Figure 11.1 /// Friendship Expectations

Agency
⇓
Symmetrical Reciprocity ⇒ FRIENDSHIP EXPECTATIONS ⇐ Solidarity
⇑
Communion

A close friend provides us both tangible and intangible support. Whether we are asking to borrow a truck so we can move to another apartment or hugging after we receive devastating news about the death of a family member, we have come to rely on this close relationship in many ways. Embedded in this reliance are expectations; we wish for our close friends to possess certain attributes and behave in ways that we expect. One scholar[31] argues that expectations play a major role in establishing, maintaining, and terminating friendships. We will explore four expectations or highly valued qualities we have of friendships: symmetrical reciprocity, communion, solidarity, and agency (see Figure 11.1).

First, **symmetrical reciprocity** includes a number of factors, including trust, loyalty, and genuineness. When symmetrical reciprocity exists, both members of the friendship strategically choose to enact behaviors that keep friendship alive. Symmetrical reciprocity is highly valued by both women and men, and that without qualities such as these bonding behaviors, a close friendship wouldn't exist.

A second friendship expectation is called **communion**. Communion includes self-disclosure, empathy, loyalty, and emotional availability. Communion is connection, meaning that two friends are trying to unite in some way. Two elements are essential in communion, trust and intimacy, and both qualities are especially important for women in their same-sex friendships. Communion has often been undertaken in stressful times. In particular, this research concludes that because women value intimacy more than men, from an evolutionary perspective, females have conditioned to form allegiances during tough times.

Video 11.2

Solidarity, a third expectation of friendship, refers to sharing mutual activities and companionship. To understand solidarity, think of the times that you and a close friend go out for coffee, meet at a social event, or just chill together. These are all elements of a solidarity dimension. Time spent together is what promotes and sustains friendship solidarity. Research indicates that both males and females perceive solidarity to be an essential ingredient in a close friendship.

IPC Praxis

Does it make a difference whether or not we have "best friends," or is that an overused phrase these days? Has social media influenced your impressions of what constitutes a "best" friend? If so, how? If not, describe how platforms such as Facebook can affect our views of a best friend.

Agency is a fourth expectation in close friendships. Agency expectations arise when close friends are perceived as vehicles from whom benefits can be derived. Think of agency this way: In what ways can I benefit from the resources and talents of my close friend? Agency includes such factors as wealth, attractiveness, intellect, popularity or status, and physical abilities. An agency expectation is not suggesting that we exploit our close friends. Rather, we (and they) find various qualities that can come in handy should we be in need of them. Agency is more profound than, say, simply borrowing $10 from a close friend. Agency is the expectation that a friend would be available and able to lend the money to you. With respect to women and men, it's been found that males hold higher agency expectations than females.

The four expectations—symmetrical reciprocity, communion, solidarity, and agency—are essential attributes that others would like their close friends to possess. Yet, many others exist, including expectations of compatibility, ego reinforcement, a sense of humor, and a good personality. What others can you identify that have facilitated a close bond with your friends?

We continue our conversation about friendship by asking you to consider the following: As a 5-year-old, Anthony loved to play house. His mom set up a tent in the basement and he and his neighbor, Meghan, also a 5-year-old, would play "mom and dad." Anthony loved to "cook the meals" while Meghan loved to "plant flowers around the house."

Flash-forward a decade. While Anthony and Meghan still live next door to each other, they have taken drastically different friendship routes. Anthony is a soccer player at school and at times mixes with some other boys who, on occasion, smoke cigarettes. He's a "gamer" and loves to hang out with his three close friends, Evan, Jessie, and Terry. Meghan, however, goes to the mall with her best friend, Alicia, and the two often sit in the food court, texting other friends and, although less than two feet from each other, text each other.

Now, as both Anthony and Meghan turn 21, they find themselves in different colleges and both have "abandoned" their friends from a few years ago. Anthony still talks to his mother every week, but Meghan has a rather tense relationship with her parents. Both have started new friendships, and both were also a bit overwhelmed by all the demands that college required.

As they both approach 35, Anthony and Meghan are fully employed in jobs that they both really like. Anthony's closest friend is his work colleague, and the two friends are both married and both have children. Meghan's college roommate, Stephanie, remains her closest friend, and although Meghan is not married, she and her friend reside in the same city and socialize quite a bit. The two also are tennis partners and they belong to a team that meets every other week.

Turning 50 saw the two childhood friends reflecting on their close friends. While Meghan remains single, she is still close friends with Stephanie. Anthony's friends have expanded beyond his work colleagues, and he is busy with his children and spends much more time with his wife than his close friends. Yet, he makes time for Eric, a neighbor whom he has lived next to for 11 years. They two hang out in the garage a lot, talking about sports, food, and their favorite TV reality show. They FaceTime each other quite a bit as well when they're both traveling. It was during this time that Anthony and Meghan reconnected at their high school reunion. They were quite excited to meet up after so many years and exchanged e-mail addresses.

This extended illustration points to a significant conclusion: Close friendship is a lifespan experience. We are not inoculated from the ebbs and flows that go along with being a close friend to someone, and others experience the same relational ups and downs with us. And, this friendship *journey* can be a thrilling, frustrating, and unpredictable one! As the following two approaches explain, friendships between people typically fall along particular life markers. We start friendships a few years after we're born, and like Anthony and Meghan, these friendships undergo quite a bit and continue in unforeseen ways. In this section of the chapter, we provide you two templates to understand friendship across the lifespan. As usual, keep in mind that cultural variations to friendship exist, and that no uniform, overarching model will capture these cultural differences. Nonetheless, we begin with a model representing the childhood of many.

Selman's Model of Childhood Friendship

Our friendships that we establish and maintain (and lose) as children may appear to be unimportant, but they are instrumental as a foundation for our future friends. Children are considered to be "friendship philosphers"[32] insofar as they have the capacity to determine the ethical, moral, emotional, and cognitive dimensions of being a friend. The following comprise Selman's Stages of Childhood Friendship (see Table 11.2) and should be understood as influenced by age.[33] A bit later, we explore friendship in adulthood.

Between the ages of 3 and 7, we engage in **momentary playmateship**, which we can identify as Stage 0. A friendship occurs because this person lives in close proximity. The friendship is clearly on a physical level since it relies upon children who are conveniently located near each other to play together.

Table 11.2 /// Stages of Childhood Friendship
Stage 0: Momentary Playmateship (Ages 3–7) *Description:* Proximity defines the friendship and friends are valued because of their possessions. *Perspective:* "I want that!"
Stage 1: One-Way Assistance (Ages 4–9) *Description:* Arrogance and egocentrism exists because children are incapable of being other-centered. *Perspective:* "What's in it for me?"
Stage 2: Two-Way, Fair-Weather Cooperation (Ages 6–12) *Description:* Children begin to have self-reflection and conversational turn-taking. *Perspective:* "What do you think?"
Stage 3: Caring and Sharing (Ages 8–15) *Description:* Mutuality begins to set in and children take an objective view of the friendship. *Perspective:* "Let me see if I can help you."
Stage 4: Mature Friendship (Ages 15 and up) *Description:* More complex friendships are established because of interdependency and autonomy. *Perspective:* "We're trusting friends."

Interestingly, however, at this level, young children have instincts about how friendships develop and conflicts are resolved. One researcher[34] asserts that this level is similar to the claim "I want it my way" because children usually fight over such things as toys or space.

The level of **one-way assistance** occurs between the ages of 4 and 9. Stage 1 includes children who show arrogance and egocentrism because they are incapable of adopting an other-centeredness in their friendship ("I like her because she lets me play with her toys"). Friends at this stage are "close" because they are perceived as performing tasks that the "self" wants accomplished. The name of this stage says it all: It's all about getting and receiving. This stage asks the question "What's in it for me?"

When children are between the ages of roughly 6 to 12, they start to become newly aware of what an interpersonal relationship is. They begin being concerned with fairness and reciprocity and embrace turn taking in conversations. This second stage, called **two-way, fair-weather cooperation**, includes children understanding that friendship includes two people sharing (e.g., "two-way"), but if the exchange does not include something pleasant for them, they will exit the friendship (e.g., "fair-weather"). At this level, children invent secret clubs which involve a lot of rules and procedures. Yet, like the fleeting friendships at this level, the clubs don't last long.

Stage 3 begins the process of self-disclosure (see Chapter 8) between children and usually occurs between the ages of 8 and 15. This level includes early developments of "best friends," since there are many confidences shared between the two friends. This **caring and sharing** level also finds children reflecting on the value of intimacy and the notion of mutuality. Children begin to find a transactional friendship as having lasting importance, and particularly in the early teen years, children are able to adopt an objective perspective of the friendship. Still, some jealousy and possessiveness may enter this stage and cause some unexpected conflict. This conflict, however, does not mean the end of the relationship, but merely an opportunity to adjust to the relational intimacy.

Stage 4 is the **mature friendship** and occurs from ages 12 and up. These friendships are rather stable, given the age group, and a sense of interdependence and autonomy begins to foster between the friends. Close friends at the mature friendship level accept the fact that they each have external relationships with others, and yet each will still rely on the other for social support. Close friends at this stage grow as they begin to understand the complexity of emotions and feelings related to being a friend.

Each of these stages, while unique, is not consistently distinct when we're talking about children. That is, some kids may be influenced by, say, family size in their friendship development. Others may have a certain family structure that will affect how their friends are formed. And, still others may be less comfortable or competent in their communication skills in establishing a friendship. Finally, regardless whether children develop close friendships in stages, researchers state that they will gain quite a bit through their friendships, including heightened self-esteem, an increased ability to cope with challenges, improved skills in decision-making and problem-solving, and healthier levels of empathy.

Friendship qualities typically change over our lifetimes.

Rawlins Model of Adult Friendship Development

Like children, adult friendships follow a path. However, we don't want you to think that adult friendship models are finite and stage restricted. As we all know, friendships are often filled with surprises, especially in adulthood as we try to balance and negotiate a number of issues, including children, marriage, aging, death, birth, college, among many others. Furthermore, we are quick to point out that cultural background influences friendship formation, and these cultural variations need to be acknowledged as you review the following. So, let's look at a practical approach to close friendship development that focuses on adults as conceptualized by Rawlins.[35] As you consider this model, keep in mind how you might map out the stages in a close friendship of yours (see Table 11.3).

Table 11.3 /// Stages of Adult Friendship Development

Stage 1: Role-Limited Interaction ("Let's check this person out.")
Perceptions and Behaviors: We stick with cultural rules and civility practices for talking to another person; we rely on the exchange of basic demographic information; we are cautious about opening ourselves up to another.

Stage 2: Friendly Relations ("Do we have shared interests?")
Perceptions and Behaviors: We begin to engage in small talk and are less guarded about what we say to another; we assess the possibility of a long-term relationship; we place more focus on commonalities with the other person.

Stage 3: Moving Toward Friendship ("I think this may be the one.")
Perceptions and Behaviors: Increased self-disclosure occurs; we begin to move toward identifying the other as a close friend; we invite the other person to locations; if it's an Internet friendship, we agree to meet face to face.

Stage 4: Nascent Friendship ("Let's work on making this a great friendship.")
Perceptions and Behaviors: Communication patterns and routines set in; friends develop rules for conversations and the time they spend together.

Stage 5: Stabilized Friendship ("What time should we get to their birthday party?")
Perceptions and Behaviors: We begin to trust the other person more than ever; there is a common belief that this is an enduring friendship; close friends and social circles merge; there are few "my" or "his" or "her" and more "our" and "we."

(Stage X) Waning Friendship ("Wow, what happened to us?")
Perceptions and Behaviors: Friendship intimacy bonds begin to decay; friends spend less and less time together, and the marker "best friend" is no longer used; friendship can be "repaired and saved" and trust can be rebuilt, prompting the relationship to move to a previous stage of development.

When we rely on polite conversations, engage in a fixed view of gender and cultural roles, and employ discourse clichés, we are part of the first stage of adult friendships: **role-limited interaction**. When meeting someone, we stick with our social expectations and guidelines because the relationship is new to us. Our preliminary conversations are marked by what we call basic demographic and foundational information (e.g., "Where are you from?"; "What's your major?"; "You come here often?"). Those who meet on Tinder or on a similar website, too, may start with standard, less vulnerable communication before meeting. Although this cliché level of dialogue may seem unimportant, it allows for both to assess how similar or dissimilar they are. Here, a "friendship foundation" is laid for future meetings and interpersonal communication.

IPC Praxis

Many people establish their friendships online. Do you believe that the coming together of a friendship online differs from those we establish face to face? Why or why not? Use examples.

The second stage, **friendly relations**, is characterized by friends checking each other out and becoming less guarded about what they say. The small talk that depicted role-limited interaction has now shifted in terms of its content and risk level. We are more inclined to discuss something to figure out if we have something in common with the other person. At the friendly relations stage, we try to determine whether or not this early relationship has enough substance to become more long term. In other words, we're trying to figure out the possibilities of this relationship.

Moving toward friendship, the third stage, is concerned with even more personal disclosures to the other. This stage can be an experimental stage of sorts. That is, both friends begin to cautiously move toward identifying the other as a close friend, unsure of whether the vulnerability of disclosure will turn out poorly. It's likely that we may invite the other to locations so that both of you have the opportunity to spend time together. For instance, you may ask a classmate to study together for a midterm or ask a coworker to lunch. If you met over the Internet, you may decide to meet up in person to put a face to the words the two of you have shared.

The fourth stage is called **nascent friendship**, meaning that friendships start to blossom and build. During this stage, both friends agree to spend time together that would widen their activities and communication together. Patterns begin to emerge. Also, routine sets in. For example, we may go to Starbucks every Sunday evening or watch a college game every Saturday during football season. We will also likely hang out more in less strategic and more spontaneous ways, suggesting that high levels of security and belongingness needs are being met. During this stage, friends begin to develop rules for their conversations and time together. The rules are co-constructed. This stage sees the inevitable emergence of a very close friend.

A great deal of trust typifies those close friends who enter a **stabilized friendship**. Learning how to trust and how to be trustworthy is an essential component of a stabilized friendship. During this stage, friendship partners admit that they are close and their emotional bond suggests this is an enduring friendship. Those in the stabilized stage recognize that the friendship is primary and that if conflict ensues, they will have some relational rules that provide them ways to manage or resolve the conflict. Stabilized friendships witness close friends merging social circles; there are few "my" or "his" or "her" friends, but rather "our" friends. This integration necessitates an appreciation for the other's friendship values.

Interestingly, despite the model's focus on friendship formation and development, friends may also drift apart and, for various reasons, decouple. This is called a **waning friendship**. Intimacy bonds become broken, time spent together is reduced, and identifying the other as a "best friend" now seems so removed. Why does this happen? Well, for various reasons, whether it's related to a job, family, health, school, boredom, or new interests or activities, people may not sustain their close friendships. Both face-to-face and virtual relationships decay and breakups (via texting or social media) exist. Sometimes, it's beyond the control of the two people: Graduation happens, one person needs to move to take care of a sick relative, as well as other events that are usually outside the control of friends. Other times, however, a violation of trust may have occurred or another person may now occupy your time. These are clearly choices that are (or were) in the control of the close friend. So, waning may take place slowly or it may be abrupt, depending on the reasons for deterioration.

Waning may also prompt attitudinal and behavioral change. If both friends recognize that the relationship is important and wish to rebuild trust and compatibility, the waning stage may not last long. Depending on the severity of the waning period, the friendship may be able to stabilize.

These proposed stages are not intended to capture all of our adult friendships, but rather present an evolutionary approach to how close friends develop their relationships. We have friendships that fall under each stage, and in many cases, we may remain at a stage for years. Still, this approach identifies a process by which friends grow, and marks the kinds of communication that indicate each stage.

As we've learned so far, friendships, then, are close relationships in which interpersonal communication plays a vital role—either in friendship escalation or in its deescalation. Friends communicate social support, solidarity, and positive affect as well as engage in other daily interactions that can intensify feelings of connection. But not all communication in friendship is positive. As we allude to throughout this book, some communication behaviors may be toxic; what was once a close friendship can become a relationship to dissolve.

What happens when a friendship becomes much more intimate than we expected? In Western cultures, these may turn into romantic relationships. It is this close relationship that we now wish to examine to provide you further understanding of the diversity of close relationships in our lives.

11–3 ROMANTIC RELATIONSHIPS

Romance is often viewed as necessary and essential in lifelong relationships with others. As we begin our discussion about romantic relationships, think about

Figure 11.2 /// Sternberg's Triangular Theory of Love

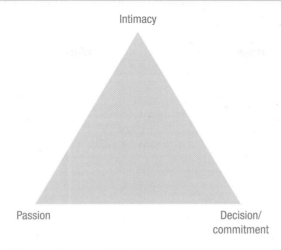

your, well, romantic notions of the word *romantic*. We've all seen and listened to the nostalgic messages about being romantic, often depicted by a candlelight dinner, roses, chocolates, tender touches and kisses, walking on a summer night on a beach, and so forth. Now think about the reality in most romantic relationships: paying bills, being exhausted, handling physical challenges, working long hours, shuttling children, and so forth. These two images of romance are not incompatible; rather, they are reflective of the complexity and vastness of what takes place in our romantic relationships.

Early conceptions of romantic relationships focused on mating and creating a family. These days, however, most of us will agree that this option is rather limited. People establish and maintain romantic relationships for various purposes, and numerous qualities of romantic relationships exist. And, given the diversity in the population, it's nearly impossible to develop one universal model of what constitutes romance. Therefore, we wish to elaborate on one of the primary and crucial foundations of romance: love. We will close this section by providing representative research on romantic relationships. The word *love* is one of those terms that people think they understand but have a tough time defining. We frequently use the term in ways that do not always reflect its value and importance ("I love this picture of a goat!"). Loving romantic relationships, however, reflect unique communication patterns, patterns that differentiate these relationships from, say, your friends or family.

Video 11.3

The dimensionality of love has been discussed through the **Triangular Theory of Love**.[36] This theory contends that love can be understood by examining three components, or dimensions that, together, form the vertices of a triangle (see Figure 11.2): intimacy, passion, and commitment.

When a romantic relationship has closeness, connectedness, and bonding, it has **intimacy**. These qualities each play an essential role in love over and above other qualities. While we don't wish to reiterate this component of the triangle in too much detail, a few points merit attention as they relate to the triangle. Ten elements are included in this vertex on the triangle:

- Desire to promote the welfare of the loved one
- Experiencing happiness with the loved one
- Holding the loved one in high regard
- Being able to count on the loved one in times of need
- Having mutual understanding with the loved one
- Sharing oneself and one's possessions with the loved one
- Receiving emotional support from the loved one
- Giving emotional support to the loved one
- Communicating intimately with the loved one
- Valuing the loved one

It's not necessary to experience all of these in order to experience intimacy. Rather, there is a "feeling" by one or both romantic partners that love is present; the couple may experience a small number of these to feel love. Or, maybe many are practiced at the right time. For instance, when Erika's dog died, Zack stayed with her for three days, holding her and letting her cry. Which of the preceding 10 qualities are represented in this example?

 IPC Praxis

Over your lifetime, you have been introduced to variations of the word *love.* As a child, you were likely loved by a parent or guardian. As you became an adult, you may have been loved by a romantic partner. As you get older, you may find yourself in love with someone. Or, you may find yourself loving a family member much more than you did, say, when you were an adolescent. Discuss such an evolution of your experiences with how love has become manifest in your life.

The component of **passion** refers to those drives that lead to desires, such as self-esteem, nurturance, affiliation, and sexual fulfillment. When people think of the word *passion,* they often think about it in sexual ways. Yet, while that is part of this dimension, other arousals also exist that demonstrate passion in a relationship. Think about the times where you strongly, but sensitively, expressed your opinion on an issue, such as whether you believe in cohabitating before marriage or waiting until marriage before living together. As long as the passion is undertaken with civility and other-centeredness, this passion may demonstrate to another person that you have a relational spark and that you are willing to defend your perceptions.

A symbiotic relationship exists between passion and intimacy. Relationship intimacy may be a function of the person's need for passion. And, conversely, passion may prompt intimacy. So, a romantic relationship may be passionate at first, and this passion fuels the intimacy that eventually characterizes all close romantic relationships.

A third element in the Triangular Theory of Love is **commitment,** which is the likelihood to which a person will stick with another person. This vertex includes two aspects: **short-term commitment,** which is the decision to love a certain person, and **long-term commitment,** which is the decision to maintain that love. Commitment can also refer to a decision that a person didn't make, such as those in arranged marriages. Most often, though, decisions precede commitment. Further, conflict may ensue because of different perceptions of commitment. That is, two people may interpret their commitments differently and may not always be able to work out these disagreements. Imagine, for instance, the challenge that Ezra feels after seven years of marriage to Henry. Although he professed commitment during the marriage ceremony, he now feels differently about the relationship. Ezra is committed and loves his husband, but he has had a change of heart with respect to the long-term nature of the marriage. Such a perceptual change occurs quite frequently in marriages across the country.[37]

 Theory-Into-Practice (TIP)

Triangular Theory of Love

The three primary elements of the Triangular Theory of Love are intimacy, passion, and commitment. Each is ever-present in most romantic relationships. Yet, can you experience, or have you ever experienced, a relationship whereby one or two of these are not present? Is it even possible? Or, can one or two (or all three) evolve slowly in a relationship? How is each component maintained?

So, what does this theory have to say about the sorts of romantic relationships we find ourselves in? First, let's reiterate that these are not always distinct qualities; they are related. This means that you can simultaneously experience two or three qualities or you can experience one without the other. Second, think of these triangular elements as foundations of love. They each (along with other qualities we talk about throughout the text) provide an important relational "structure" that is needed to form a loving, lasting relationship with another. Third, sometimes, intimacy starts and stops in our romantic partnerships. The theory suggests that there is an intimacy pendulum of sorts, swinging back and forth and supplying the excitement that keeps relationships exciting.

In this section thus far, we've given you a sense of a valuable theoretical model related to the development and maintenance of romantic relationships. The Triangular Theory of Love elaborates on one of the most significant components in romance: love. Let's now briefly talk about some research related to romantic relationships to illustrate the complexity and diversity in this area of study.

Saying "I Love You"

One area that has received frequent research attention relates to expressions of romantic affection. A pioneering study[38] looked at the phrase "I love you" and questioned who—men or women—was more likely to confess this first to the other. Researchers asked the following question of heterosexual couples who had been together for an average of 84 months: "Who is most likely to express romantic commitment first in a relationship?" Contrary to popular conception, men expressed love first in a romantic relationship (70% of couples agreed to this). In fact, men first thought about expressing their love an average of six weeks before their female partners. What has been your experience with this phrase in your romantic relationships? Do you think same-sex partners are impacted by this research?

Additional research on romantic relationships has been both diverse and expansive. Much of this research is framed around relational scripts, a topic we addressed in Chapter 10. For our purposes here, think of *relational scripts* as mental stories we have about how people are to behave and the various roles they play in our various relationships. For instance, although we know that couples break up and divorce, relational scripts suggest that romantic partners, in particular, will experience a relationship termination in a way that is usually different from, say, a close friend.

As we already know, regardless of whether we're studying a same-sex or mixed-sex relationship, relational scripts function prominently. And, some research suggests that individual scripts for communicating in romantic relationships, in particular, can vary widely. For example, one group of researchers[39] found that an individual's love style—passionate, stable, playful, other-centered, logical, or obsessive—made a difference in three communication practices during three stages of a relationship: (1) opening lines for picking up someone as a potential partner, (2) intensification strategies for moving a relationship along to greater intimacy, and (3) secret tests for checking on the state of a developing relationship. For example, if Manny believes that love is playful, he'll use cute, flippant (and trite) pick-up lines like "God must be a thief. He stole the stars from the skies and put them in your eyes" to initiate a relationship, sexual intimacy to intensify it, and indirect secret tests like joking and hinting to check the state of a romance. See Table 11.4 for people's perceptions of "love."

The "signs" of romance differ from one person to another and from culture to culture.

Other researchers[40] found that how secure a person is affects how he or she communicates to maintain romantic relationships. People who are more secure tend to use more positive or prosocial behaviors. For example, if Amina is a confident person who's not anxious about relationships, she'll be likely to try to maintain her relationship with Jerome by saying, "I love you," touching Jerome affectionately, complimenting him, and being open in her conversations with him. A different group of researchers[41] made a similar finding that married people who are uncertain about their marriages tend to interpret conversations pessimistically, whereas those who are more confident in their marriages draw more favorable conclusions.

One type of romantic relationship that has received recent research attention is the long-distance relationship (LDR), which is, as we know, a couple who continues to maintain a romantic relationship while separated geographically. While it would seem that being apart would strain LDRs, some research has found that LDRs persevere in profound ways. For example, in a study on romantic relationships following wartime deployment, couples indicated that it was challenging to relearn how to be interdependent (again) and that there was an ongoing renegotiation of roles.[42] Furthermore, the researchers found that during deployment, the couples relied on others for social support; once reunited, they gradually shifted back to relying on romantic partners

Table 11.4 /// People's Notions of Love

Addiction	Strong anxious attachment; clinging behavior; anxiety at thought of losing partner
Art	Love of partner for physical attractiveness; importance to person of partner's always looking good
Business	Relationships as business propositions; money is power
Cookbook	Doing things a certain way (recipe) results in relationship being more likely to work out.
Fantasy	To be saved by a knight in shining armor, or marry a princess and live happily ever after
Game	Love as a game or sport
Horror	Relationships become interesting when you terrorize or are terrorized by your partner.
Mystery	Love is a mystery and you shouldn't let too much of yourself be known.
Police	You've got to keep close tabs on your partner to make sure he or she "toes the line."
Science	Love can be understood, analyzed, and dissected, just like any other natural phenomenon.
Sewing	Love is whatever you make it.
Theatre	Love is scripted, with predictable acts, scenes, and lines.
War	Love is a series of battles in a devastating but continuing war.

Source: Sternberg (2013, p. 99).

for their social support. Following a tour of duty, a reunion was somewhat emotionally volatile because couples found it tough to return to some "normalcy."

In addition to military couples, some interpersonal communication research focuses on gay and lesbian couples as well as multiracial couples.[43] Although many communication issues are the same across all romantic relationships, couples that are same-sex and multiracial must also contend with bouts of discrimination and identity. In both gay/lesbian and multiracial relationships, the partners are aware of social disapproval. Like those who are transgender or in relationships with transgender individuals, alienation from friends and family members can be daunting. These individuals are required to consider social and historical forces concerning race and sexual identity in ways that other couples do not. The couples also may have to preempt this discrimination. So, for example, Danica (an African American woman) may tell her partner, Brad (a white man), that they need to be alert when they're visiting his hometown because many of the people there have little, if any, experiences with a person of color. Brad may respond with some strategies they can use to manage any racist comments they might hear on the visit.

If you are in a romantic relationship now, chances are you're trying to make it work. Yet, we understand that like the relationships with our family members and friends, no matter how hard we try, unforeseen events will occur. As we know, we cannot control the future. To help you in this area, we close our chapter with some suggestions of how to sustain quality interpersonal relationships with a family member, close friend, or romantic partner.

11–4 SKILL SET FOR IMPROVING YOUR INTERPERSONAL COMMUNICATION WITH FAMILY MEMBERS, CLOSE FRIENDS, AND ROMANTIC PARTNERS

In Chapter 10, we incorporated a myriad of strategies to consider as you initiate, maintain, and repair your relationships. In this chapter, although many of the skills we previously identified are relevant to consider in this chapter, we believe that taken together, there are several efforts to put in motion as you communicate with your family, (close) friends, and romantic partners. Of course, as you reflect on many of the skills we've already identified throughout this book (e.g., listening, nonverbal effectiveness, cultural awareness), you will

Table 11.5 /// Skill Set for Improving Interpersonal Communication With Family Members, Close Friends, and Romantic Partners
a. Take time to C.A.R.E.
b. Recognize your history together.
c. Find ways to keep your relationship "alive."
d. Ensure equity when possible.
e. Your skill suggestion

soon see that much of what we've presented already can be applied to a number of your interpersonal relationships. Nonetheless, let's outline four different skills (see Table 11.5), and along the way, we will include examples from the three relational types we discussed in this chapter.

Take Time to C.A.R.E.

To suggest that we should care about another person may seem a bit far removed when you have arguments or heated discussions with, say, a spouse who won't clean up after himself. Still, as we think about this suggestion and its roots in an ethical system we discussed in Chapter 1, we need to be diligent in this connection.

We think that C.A.R.E. (*Constantly Assess the Relationship Excellence*) can take many forms. We demonstrate care/C.A.R.E. by practicing some of the skills of empathy and other-centeredness, behaviors we addressed a few times in this text. Caring also includes the willingness to be mindful of the relationship's value to you. Consider a family relationship. It's easy to lose sight of a family member's value if we are mad at her because of her words or insensitive remarks. Think about, for instance, 45-year-old Shannon's experience with Mary, her 50-year-old sister. As the two discussed what to do with their aging mother, a lot of very tense back-and-forth ensued. One dialogue especially stood out:

Mary: "You have no idea what it's like because you chose not to have kids! It's killing her to know that she has to leave this house! If you weren't so wrapped up in your little life and worrying about your Caribbean vacations, you'd know that this is tough for her."

Shannon: "Um. Yeah . . . I'm going to listen to someone who has secretly written checks from Mom's account to pay for your teeth whitening? I don't think so!"

Clearly, the two are in a difficult conflict, and although they have been quite close over the years, the stress related to their mother's fragility has obviously wreaked havoc on this family relationship. We would suggest that the two take time to extend caring qualities to each other. Families, in particular, are prone to lapses in care because they're of the "take-for-granted" quality that we addressed earlier. In most cases, we believe we know what makes our family members tick. Yet, especially in challenging times, retaining an ethic of care should remain paramount.

Recognize Your History Together

Caring is best accompanied by an understanding of the relation's past. Staying aware of relational history is a valued skill to practice in our relationships with family members, close friends, and romantic partners. The time and co-created experiences help to establish a foundation as the relationship evolves, and this foundation will be instrumental to draw upon for future reference. For example, think about your closest friend. Now, think about what the two of you have gone through. There may have been late night conversations about boyfriends, endless dialogues over coffee about careers, frequent episodes of shared anxieties about finances, among many other situations that have bonded the two of you. This relational history should not be discarded as the friendship moves to higher levels of intimacy. As we know from Chapter 8, self-disclosure is essential in relationship-building. We also know that reciprocal self-disclosure is essential to relational growth.

Our times with a close friend serve to facilitate a long-term cooperative relationship. Recall that friendship generally goes through various stages in our life-span. Furthermore, consider, too, that throughout our lives, we will cultivate friendships with people from all cultural backgrounds. Particularly as adults, we need to be cognizant of our relationship development and all the various factors that contributed to its importance.

Find Ways to Keep the Relationship "Alive"

The fundamental assumption sustained throughout this chapter is that our family, close friendships, and romantic relationships are central in our lives. Still, it's likely that you find yourself in **relationship ruts**, or patterns of relational behavior that become dull and unproductive. Romantic relationships sometimes become lackluster and fall prey to rituals that undercut the vibrancy of the relationship. We already know that connection is closer to intimacy than disconnection. So, when there is "routinized intimacy," habitual arguments about petty issues (e.g., "Why do you keep leaving the freezer door open?!"), an absence of affection, or a job that takes priority over your relational partner, a rut is setting in.

What helps us to avoid relationship ruts? First, practice random acts of romance. This includes doing things that have been missing for years, such as having a "date night," a weekend getaway, or providing "love notes" in unexpected places (e.g., next to your partner's toothbrush). Even everyday actions can be repackaged to avoid ruts. Stale and boring do not have to replace new and exciting. Think about greeting your partner at the door with a prolonged hug or kiss, rather than a "hello." Or, consider getting a romantic card and placing it between the screen and keyboard of your partner's laptop. You might even leave a sexy note on the bathroom mirror as a reminder of the passion that was once present.

Although we have focused on romantic relationships, all interpersonal relationships can use some spice! We should confront any relational rut head on and talk openly with the other person. Together, two people will be able to resolve an unwelcomed stale relationship productively.

Ensure Equity When Possible

In its basic form, equity is fairness. And, equity comes in many forms, including emotional, financial, physical, as well as other dimensions of a relationship. Today, more than ever, couples and families are demanding that they live in equitable relationships. Spouses share domestic duties. Children collaborate with their parents. Close friends return phone calls and contribute equally to a costly night out.

Despite these overtures of relational justice, we still find ourselves in relationships that are very imbalanced. Although husbands may be doing more around the house, for instance, a gendered division of household labor continues, with women often leaving the workplace and returning home, only to have another round of tasks to accomplish. Imbalances occur, too, with dating couples. One who discloses more personal information without the other reciprocating can be distressing and cause a partner to feel guilty or angry.

Family members, close friends, and romantic partners need to keep in mind that caring about the other requires communication that is equitable and just. No matter how good a relationship is, in order for it to survive the various challenges, individuals need to be equal. When interpersonal desires and needs conflict, both people in the relationship need to work toward ensuring an outcome.

 IPC Voice: Jessie

My wife and I have been married 2.5 years to be precise! We have very close friends and we all seem to get along pretty well—except when margaritas are involved! But, I do have some issues with her family. Her mom still thinks that I "stole" her "little girl," as if I could.

/// CHAPTER WRAP-UP

We spent considerable time in this chapter linking up three critical people in our lives: family members, close friends, and romantic partners. We recognize that we tackled a lot in this review, and yet, we also know that your other college courses are usually available for you to consider if you're further interested in these relationship types. In this chapter, we identified various family types, and explained representative communication within different family configurations. Next, we explored the notion of close friends, articulating various friendship typologies (*Stages of Childhood Friendship, Stages of Adult Friendship Development*) that we find in research. In addition to family and friends, we presented information on those romantic relationships in which we find ourselves. We introduced the Triangular Theory of Love and detailed the various angles and interpretations of *love*. Finally, we closed the chapter with a skill set that can be applied to all three relational contexts.

We close this book with the most appropriate overview of the three most important relationships we sustain throughout our lives. We know we've only touched the surface and could never capture the complexity, rewards, and challenges characterizing families, close friendships, and romantic partners. Still, it's our hope that as you digest the contents of this book, you will see that so much of the information can be readily applied to nearly every relationship you have—even those you've cultivated online. In the end, every relationship experiences various levels of intimacy. The responsibility for an action plan falls on both partners to ensure the relationship's vitality for years to come.

/// COMMUNICATION ASSESSMENT TEST (CAT): RELATIONSHIP QUALITY INVENTORY

Think about your closest family member, friend, or romantic partner. As you consider the relationship overall, complete the following inventory. After you complete it, return to it and reflect on those responses that you feel deserve more attention. Come back to this CAT frequently to see if you need to add or delete issues, once they've been addressed. Try not to share this with others since these are your private perceptions and reflections.

1. On a scale of 1–5, how satisfied are you in this relationship? (1—not at all; 5—very much so)

2. What areas of the relationship are sources of satisfaction for you?

   a. What have you done or said to prompt the satisfaction?

   b. What has the other person done or said to prompt the satisfaction?

3. What areas of the relationship are dissatisfying for you?

   a. What have you done or said to prompt the dissatisfaction?

   b. What has the other person done or said to prompt the dissatisfaction?

4. Identify three of the most important relationship qualities that are nonnegotiable in your eyes.

   a. Are any or all of these three in your current relationship?

   b. Which of these qualities, if any, need to be addressed in your relationship?

5. Are there issues on the horizon that you feel need to be dealt with today? If so, what are they? If not, why not?

6. Explain how you're going to go about making sure that your close relationships are maintained?

/// KEY TERMS

/// KEY QUESTIONS FOR APPLICATION

1. *CQ/CultureQuest:* Explore the following claim: "Failing to acknowledge how culture affects our family, friends, and romantic partners usually can be perilous." Do you agree or disagree? Defend your view with examples.

2. *TQ/TechQuest:* Explore the following claim: "Developing and maintaining relationships online are only for the bold and persistent." Do you agree or disagree? Defend your view with examples.

3. It is often said that relational support is disappearing in the United States. Some scholars believe that we are now living in a time where caring for someone else and helping them when necessary is fading away. Do you subscribe to this interpretation? Why or why not?

4. Have you ever had, or do you currently have, any voluntary kin? What has been your experience, if any, with this family dynamic?

5. Earlier in the chapter, we acknowledged that with many people, their spouses serve three purposes: family member, closest friend, and romantic partner. Do you believe that is a lot of responsibility for one person to shoulder? Why or why not?

6. After reading this chapter, if you had an opportunity to speak to preteens and offer them advice about relationships in college, what three suggestions would you make?

Access practice quizzes, eFlashcards, video, and multimedia at **edge.sagepub.com/west**.

Visit **edge.sagepub.com/west** to help you accomplish your coursework goals in an easy-to-use learning environment.

abstract. Referents that cannot be detected through your senses.

accounts. Explanations for transgressions.

acculturation. The process that occurs when a person learns, adapts to, and adopts the appropriate behaviors and rules of a host culture.

action-centered listening style. A listening style associated with listeners who want messages to be highly organized, concise, and error free.

active listening. When you suspend your own responses while listening to another and simply concentrate on them. When it's your turn to speak, you try to reflect back what you heard them tell you.

activity. Whether an emotion implies action or passivity.

actual self. Attributes of an individual.

affection and instrumentality dialectic. A dialectic found in friendships that poses a tension between framing your friendship with someone as an end in itself (affection) or seeing it as a means to another end (instrumentality).

affinity seeking. Emphasizing the commonalities you think you share with the other person.

agency. An expectation in friendship that arises when close friends perceive each other as possible resources and benefits.

ambushing. Listening carefully to a message and then using the information later to attack the sender.

American Sign Language (ASL). A visual rather than auditory form of communication that is composed of precise hand shapes and movements.

androgynous. A person who embodies both masculine and feminine traits.

apologies. Statements containing an expression of remorse, a promise not to repeat the transgression, an acknowledgment of fault, a promise to make it up to the victim, and a request for forgiveness.

approaching. Actually going up to a person or smiling in that person's direction to give a signal that you would like to initiate contact.

attending and selecting stage. The first stage of the perception process requiring us to use our visual, auditory, tactile, and olfactory senses to respond to stimuli in our interpersonal environment.

authentic friends. Those individuals whom we identify as close friends and whom we hold in high esteem.

autonomy and connection dialectic. A primary dialectic that centers on our desire to be independent or autonomous while simultaneously wanting to feel a connection with our partner.

avoiding stage. Stage 4 of Knapp's Coming Apart Model, it's when partners try to stay out of the same physical environment.

blind self. A quadrant of the Johari Window that encompasses information that others know about you, although you are unaware of this information.

body artifacts. Items we wear that are part of our physical appearance and that have the potential to communicate, such as clothing, religious symbols, military medals, body piercings, and tattoos.

body orientation. The extent to which we turn our legs, shoulders, and head toward or away from a communicator.

bonding stage. Stage 5 of Knapp's Coming Together Model, it's when the partners make a public commitment to the relationship.

boundaries or openness. A systems principle stating that we create boundaries around each separate system, making it distinct from others but information passes through these boundaries.

breadth. Surface information across multiple topics.

bullying. When someone seeks to inflict *intentional harm* through *repeated unwanted actions* (verbal or physical)

directed toward an individual who is of *lesser power* (e.g., physical, emotional, financial).

calibration. A system principle focusing on how systems set their rules, check on themselves, and self-correct.

capitalization. People enjoy good news more when they are able to share it with others.

caring and sharing. A stage in childhood friendship (ages 8–15) in which children reflect on the value of intimacy and the notion of mutuality.

categorical imperative. An ethical system, based on the work of philosopher Immanuel Kant, advancing the notion that individuals follow moral absolutes. The underlying tenet in this ethical system suggests that we should act as an example to others.

catharsis. A therapeutic release of tensions and negative emotion through disclosing.

central executive. A component of Working Memory Theory that acts as a conduit for the flow of information within a cognitive system.

channel. A pathway through which a message is sent.

chronemics. The study of a person's perception and use of time.

chunking. Placing pieces of information into manageable and retrievable sets.

circumscribing stage. Stage 2 of Knapp's Coming Apart Model, it's when the partners restrain their communication behaviors so that fewer topics are raised (for fear of conflict) and more issues are out of bounds

citing gestures. Gestures that acknowledge another's feedback in a conversation.

close relationships. Relationships that endure over time, consist of interdependent partners who satisfy each other's needs for connection and social inclusion that feel an emotional attachment to each other, are irreplaceable to one another, and enact unique communication patterns.

co-culture. A culture within a culture.

codability. The number of words in a language it takes to express a thought.

collectivism. A cultural mindset that emphasizes the group and its norms, values, and beliefs over the self.

commitment. A component of the Triangular Theory of Love that relates to the likelihood of an individual sticking with another individual.

communicating emotionally. When the emotion itself is a part of the way the message is delivered.

communication. The cocreation and interpretation of meaning.

Communication Accommodation Theory (CAT). A theory explaining how two speakers of different backgrounds (based on age, culture, sex, or other differences) may adjust their style of speaking relative to each other.

communication apprehension (CA). A fear or anxiety pertaining to the communication process.

communication models. Visual, simplified representations of complex relationships in the communication process.

Communication Privacy Management Theory (CPM). A theory explaining how and why people decide to reveal or conceal private information.

communion. An expectation in friendship whereby two friends are trying to unite in a compatible way.

community. The common understandings among people who are committed to coexisting.

comparison level. A person's expectations for a given relationship.

comparison level for alternatives. Comparing the costs and rewards of a current relationship to the possibility of doing better in a different relationship.

concrete. Referents that you are able to detect with one of your senses. Concrete referents are those that you can see, smell, taste, touch, or hear.

confirmation. The acknowledgment, validation, and support of another person.

conflict interaction. The third episode of the Explanatory Process Model, it occurs when the differences between the partners become a problem and one or both people begin to address the issue.

connotative meaning. People's personal and subjective experience with a verbal symbol.

contemporary nuclear family. A modernized version of the nuclear family with two variations: (1) stay-at-home dad with the mom working outside the home and (2) a dual-career couple that includes both parents working outside the home, and both providing primary child care.

content conflicts. Type of conflict revolving around the substance of a specific issue.

content level. The verbal and nonverbal information contained in a message that indicates the topic of the message.

content-centered listening style. A listening style associated with listeners who focus on the facts and details of a message.

context. The environment in which a message is sent.

Context Orientation Theory. The theory that meaning is derived from either the setting of the message or the words of a message and that cultures can vary in the extent to which message meaning is made explicit or implicit.

converge. A process described in Communication Accommodation Theory involving making one's speech style similar to another's.

conversational narcissism. Engaging in an extreme amount of self-focusing during a conversation to the ultimate exclusion of another person.

corrective maintenance or repair. Skills applied to correct a relational problem.

co-rumination The behavior related to when adolescents exchange disclosures about their problems with friends.

costs. Those things in relational life that people judge as negative.

cultural context. The cultural environment in which communication occurs; refers to the rules, roles, norms, and patterns of communication that are unique to a particular culture.

cultural empathy. The learned ability to accurately understand the experiences of people from diverse cultures and to convey that understanding responsively.

cultural imperialism. The process and practice whereby individuals, companies, and/or the media impose their way of thinking and behaving upon another culture.

Cultural Variability Theory. A theory that describes the four value dimensions (uncertainty avoidance, distribution of power, masculinity–femininity, individualism–collectivism) that offer information regarding the value differences in a particular culture.

culture. The shared, personal, and learned life experiences of a group of individuals who have a common set of values, norms, and traditions.

culture clash. A conflict over cultural expectations and experiences.

cyclic alternation. A strategy for dealing with dialectic tensions by featuring the oppositions at alternating times.

decoding. Developing an understanding of the speaker's meaning based on hearing language.

defensive listening. Viewing innocent comments as personal attacks or hostile criticisms.

delivery gestures. Gestures that signal shared understanding between communicators in a conversation.

denotative meaning. The literal, conventional meaning that most people in a culture have agreed to be the meaning of a symbol. Denotation is the type of meaning found in a dictionary definition.

depth. Information within any given topic that goes beyond the superficial.

dialogue enhancers. Supporting statements, such as "I see" or "I'm listening," that indicate we are involved in a message.

differentiating stage. Stage 1 of Knapp's Coming Apart Model, it's when the partners highlight their differences and individuality.

direct and virtual use of power. Involves communicating the *potential* use of direct application of power.

direct application of power. Involves using any resources at your disposal to compel the other to comply, regardless of their desires.

disconfirmation. Occurs when someone feels ignored and disregarded. Disconfirmation makes people feel that you don't see them—that they are unimportant.

disqualifying. A strategy for dealing with dialectic tensions that allows people to cope with tensions by exempting certain issues from the general pattern.

distal context. The first episode of the Explanatory Process Model, it forms the background that frames a specific conflict.

distal outcomes. The fifth episode of the Explanatory Process Model, it includes the residue of having engaged in the conflict and the feelings that both the participants have about their interaction. The distal outcomes feed into the distal context for the next conflict the partners have.

diverge. A process described in Communication Accommodation Theory involving speaking in a way that highlights the differences between two people's speaking styles.

dualism. A way of thinking that constructs polar opposite categories to encompass the totality of a thing, prompting us to think about the thing in an either/or fashion.

dyadic effect. The tendency for us to return another's self-disclosure with one that matches it in level of intimacy.

emojis. Graphical emoticons.

emoticons. Icons that can be typed on the keyboard to express emotion.

emotion. The feelings we have within ourselves and related to our relationships with others.

emotional afterglow. When your mood brightens when you're around someone who expresses positive feelings.

emotional communication. Talking about the experience of emotion to someone else.

emotional contagion. The process of transferring emotion from one person to another.

emotional effects. How emotional experience impacts communication behavior.

emotional experience. The intrapersonal aspect of feeling emotion.

emotional expression. The combination of communicating emotionally (e.g., yelling) and emotional communication (e.g., telling someone how you feel) that we consider in this text.

empathy. The process of identifying with or attempting to experience the thoughts, beliefs, and actions of another.

encoding. Putting our thoughts into meaningful language.

enculturation. The process that occurs when a person—either consciously or unconsciously—learns to identify with a particular culture and a culture's thinking, way of relating, and worldview.

equifinality. A systems principle stating that systems have the ability to achieve the same goals (or ends) by a variety of means.

equivocation. A type of ambiguity involving choosing your words carefully to give a listener a false impression without actually lying.

ethic of care. An ethical system, based on the concepts of Carol Gilligan, that is concerned with the connections among people and the moral consequences of decisions.

ethics. The perceived rightness or wrongness of an action or behavior.

ethnocentrism. The process of judging another culture using the standards of one's own culture.

euphemisms. A kind of equivocation using milder or less direct words substituted for other words that are more blunt or negative.

Expectancy Violations Theory (EVT). A theory stating that we expect other people to maintain a certain distance from us in their conversations with us.

experimenting stage. Stage 2 of Knapp's Coming Together Model, it's when people become acquainted by gathering information about one another.

Explanatory Process Model. An explanation of conflict as a process that occurs in sequential episodes.

external dialectics. Tensions that occur because of how partners negotiate the more public aspects of their relationship.

external feedback. The feedback we receive from other people.

face. The image of the self we choose to present to others in our interpersonal encounters.

facework. The set of coordinated behaviors that help us either reinforce or threaten our competence.

Facts. A piece of information that is verifiable by direct observation.

family stories. Pieces of narrative about family members and activities that are told and retold.

family-of-origin. The family into which we are all born.

feedback. A verbal or nonverbal response to a message.

feeling rules. The rules a culture develops to instruct people in expressing their own emotion and reacting when others express emotion; these rules may change over time.

feminine cultures. Cultures that emphasize characteristics stereotypically associated with feminine people, such as sexual equality, nurturance, quality of life, supportiveness, affection, and a compassion for the less fortunate.

field of experience. The influence of a person's culture, past experiences, personal history, and heredity on the communication process.

four Rs of listening. The four components of the listening process: receiving, responding, recalling, and rating.

friendly relations. The second stage in adult friendship development characterized by friends checking each other out and becoming less guarded about what they say.

friendship. A significant close relationship of choice that exists over a period of time between individuals who provide social support and who share various commonalities.

gap fillers. Listeners who think that they can correctly guess the rest of the story a speaker is telling and don't need the speaker to continue.

gay- and lesbian-headed family. Two people of the same sex who maintain an intimate relationship and who serve as parents to at least one child.

gender. The learned behaviors a culture associates with being a male or female, generally referred to as masculinity or femininity.

gender role socialization. The process by which women and men learn the gender roles appropriate to their sex. This process affects the way the sexes perceive the world.

gender schema. A mental framework we use to process and categorize beliefs, ideas, and events as either masculine or feminine in order to understand and organize our world.

general. A word with the fewest restrictions in terms of possible referents.

generic he. The rule in English grammar, dating from 1553, requiring the masculine pronoun *he* to function generically when the subject of the sentence is not known to be a woman or man.

global village. The concept that all societies, regardless of size, are connected in some way. The term also can be used to describe how communication technology ties the world into one political, economic, social, and cultural system.

golden mean An ethical system, articulated by Aristotle, proposing that a person's moral virtue stands between two vices, with the middle, or the mean, being the foundation for a rational society.

grammar. Refers to the set of rules in a specific language dictating how words should be organized.

halo effect. The result of matching like qualities with each other to create an overall perception of someone or something.

haptics. The study of how we communicate through touch.

hearing. The physical process of letting in audible stimuli without focusing on the stimuli.

hidden self. A quadrant of the Johari Window that contains the information that you are aware of but have chosen not to disclose.

hidden use of power. Controlling another without saying a word.

hierarchy. A systems principle stating that smaller systems are embedded in larger systems.

high-context cultures. Cultures in which there is a high degree of similarity among members and in which the meaning of a message is drawn primarily from its context, such as one's surroundings, rather than from words.

historical context. A type of context in which messages are understood in relationship to previously sent messages.

history. Information that sounds personal to a listener but is relatively easy for a speaker to tell.

homophobia. An irrational fear and/or anxiety of gay men or lesbians.

hyperpersonal. A quality of online relationships resulting from participants' ability to strategically present themselves, highlighting their positive qualities.

ideal and real dialectic. An external dialect revealing the tension between an idealized vision of the relationship and the real relationship that one has.

ideal self. Attributes an individual ideally possesses.

identity management. A notion that explains the manner in which you handle your "self" in various circumstances; it includes competency, identity, and face.

identity marker. An electronic extension of who someone is (e.g., screen name).

idiom. A word or a phrase that has an understood meaning within a culture, but that meaning doesn't come from exact translation.

image conflicts. A type of conflict focused on differences in the way the participants see one or both of their images.

imagined conversations. When one partner plays the parts of both partners in a mental rehearsal of the communication they expect their partners will exhibit.

I-messages. A way to own; messages that begin with "I think/feel/believe . . ."

implicit personality approach. We rely on a set of a few characteristics to draw inferences about others and use these inferences as the basis of our communication with them.

impression management. A component of Social Information Processing Theory; the unconscious or strategic effort to influence another's perceptions.

indexing. Acknowledging the time frame of your judgments of others and yourself.

indirect application of power. Concerns employing power without making its employment explicit.

individualism. A cultural mindset that emphasizes self-concept and personal achievement and that prefers competition over cooperation, the individual over the group, and the private over the public.

Inferences. Conclusions derived from a fact, but they do not reflect direct observation or experience.

in-group. A group to which a person feels he or she belongs.

initiating stage. Stage 1 of Knapp's Coming Together Model; it's when two people notice one another and indicate to each other that they are interested in making contact.

integrating stage. Stage 4 of Knapp's Coming Together Model, it's when the partners form a clear identity as a couple.

intensifying stage. Stage 3 of Knapp's Coming Together Model, it's when the relationship deepens in intimacy.

intensity. How strongly an emotion is felt.

intentional families. Family members who band together by choice rather than by blood relationships.

Interactional Model of Communication. A characterization of communication as a two-way process in which a message is sent from sender to receiver and from receiver to sender.

intercultural communication apprehension. A fear or anxiety pertaining to communication with people from different cultural backgrounds.

intercultural communication. Communication between and among individuals and groups from different cultural backgrounds.

interdependence. A systems principle that says members of systems depend on each other and are affected by one another.

internal dialectics. Tensions that occur because of how the partners communicate with one another.

internal feedback. The feedback we give ourselves when we assess our own communication.

interpersonal communication. The process of message transaction between two people to create and sustain shared meaning.

interpersonal conflict. The interaction of interdependent people who perceive incompatible goals and interference from each other in achieving those goals.

interpreting stage. The third stage of the perception process, in which we assign meaning to what we perceive.

intimacy. A component of the Triangular Theory of Love that encompasses giving and receiving emotional support, holding a loved one in high regard, and so forth.

intimate distance. The distance that extends about 18 inches around each of us that is normally reserved for people with whom we are close, such as close friends, romantic partners, and family members.

Johari Window. A model providing a pictorial representation of the extent to which you are "known" to yourself and to others.

judgment and acceptance dialectic. A dialectic found in friendships that involves the competing desires of criticizing a friend and accepting them.

kinesics. The study of a person's body movement and its effect on the communication process.

language. Consists of both verbal symbols and grammar; it enables us to engage in meaning making with others.

lexical gaps. Experiences and ideas that aren't named in a language.

Linear Model of Communication. A characterization of communication as a one-way process that transmits a message from a sender to a receiver.

Linguistic Determinism. Sometimes called the "strong form" of the Sapir-Whorf hypothesis, it refers to the notion that without a word in your language for a thing/idea, you cannot perceive that thing/idea.

Linguistic Relativity. Sometimes called the "weak form" of the Sapir-Whorf hypothesis, it refers to the notion that while language doesn't completely determine your thinking, it strongly influences it.

listening. The dynamic, transactional process of receiving, responding, recalling, and rating to stimuli, messages, or both.

listening gap. The time difference between our mental ability to interpret words and the speed at which they arrive at our brain.

listening style. A predominant and preferred approach to listening to the messages we hear.

long-term attraction. An attraction that makes us want to continue a relationship over time and sustains and maintains relationships.

long-term commitment. The decision to maintain love with another person.

long-term memory. Memory storage over an extended period of time. Theoretically, the capacity of LTM is unlimited and indefinite and it can range from a few minutes to a lifetime.

low-context culture. A culture in which there is a high degree of difference among members and in which the meaning of a message must be explicitly related, usually in words.

man-linked words. Words—such as *chairman, salesman, repairman, mailman,* and *mankind*—that include the word *man* but are supposed to operate generically to include women as well.

masculine culture. A culture that emphasizes characteristics stereotypically associated with masculine people, such as achievement, competitiveness, strength, and material success.

mature friendship. A stage in childhood friendship (ages 12 and up) in which a sense of interdependence and autonomy begin to foster between friends.

meaning. What communicators create together through the use of verbal and nonverbal messages.

memorizing stage. The fifth stage of the perception process entailing storing information for later retrieval.

message exchange. The transaction of verbal and nonverbal messages being sent simultaneously between two people.

message overload. The result when senders receive more messages than they can process.

meta-communication. Communicating about communication.

meta-conflicts. A type of conflict centering on the way you conduct conflict.

meta-emotion. Emotion about emotion.

microaggressions. The insults, indignities, and denigrating messages delivered to marginalized communities.

mindful. Having the ability to engage our senses so that we are observant and aware of our surroundings.

mindful listening. Listening that requires us to be engaged with another person—the words, the behaviors, and the environment.

mixed message. The incompatibility that occurs when our nonverbal messages are not congruent with our verbal messages.

momentary playmateship. A stage in childhood friendship (ages 3–7) in which children play together because they are conveniently located near each other.

moving toward friendship. The third stage in adult friendship development whereby friends begin to move cautiously toward more personal disclosures and more time spent together.

multigenerational families. Extended family members (children, parents, grandparents, etc.) living under the same roof.

Muted Group Theory. A theory explaining what happens to people whose experiences are not well represented by the verbal symbols in their language.

nascent friendship. The fourth stage in adult friendship development whereby friends begin to widen their activities together; communication patterns and routines begin to emerge.

negative contagion. A verbal ritual where each person's negative comment is matched by the following speaker's negative comment.

negative face. Our desire that others refrain from imposing their will on us, respect our individuality and our

uniqueness, and avoid interfering with our actions or beliefs.

negative feedback. In Systems Theory, feedback that maintains the status quo.

negative halo. The result of grouping negative qualities (e.g., unintelligent, rude, and temperamental) together.

negative interaction ratio. Couples who say more negative than positive things to one another.

networking. Finding out information about a person from a third party.

neutralizing. A strategy for dealing with dialectic tensions that involves compromising between the two oppositions.

noise. Anything that interferes with accurate transmission or reception of a message. *See also* physical noise, physiological noise, psychological noise, and semantic noise.

nonjudgmental feedback. Feedback that describes another's behavior and then explains how that behavior made us feel.

nonverbal communication. All behaviors—other than spoken words—that communicate messages and that have shared meaning between people.

novelty and predictability dialectic. A primary dialectic that manifests in our simultaneous desires for excitement and stability.

nuclear families. The original foundation of family life in the United States.

offering. Putting yourself in a good position for another to approach you.

one-way assistance. A stage in childhood friendship (ages 4–9) in which children show arrogance and egocentrism because they are incapable of being other-centered.

open self. A quadrant of the Johari Window that includes all the information about you that you know and have shared with others through disclosures.

openness and protection dialectic. A primary dialectic that focuses on our desire to self-disclose our innermost secrets to a friend, while also wanting to keep quiet to protect ourselves from the chance that our friend will somehow use the information against us.

organizing stage. The second stage of the perception process in which we place what are often a number of confusing pieces of information into an understandable, accessible, and orderly arrangement.

ought self. Attributes an individual should possess.

Out-groups. Groups to which a person feels they do not belong.

outsourcing. A practice in which a nation sends work and workers to a different country because doing so is cost-efficient.

owning. The skill of verbally taking responsibility for your feelings.

paralanguage. The study of a person's employment of voice. Also called vocalics. Nonverbal behaviors that include pitch, rate, volume, inflection, tempo, and pronunciation as well as the use of vocal distractors and silence.

paraphrasing. Restating the essence of a sender's message in our own words.

passion. A component of the Triangular Theory of Love that refers to those drives leading to desires such as nurturance, affiliation, and sexual fulfillment.

people-centered listening style. A listening style associated with concern for other people's feelings or emotions.

perception. The process of using our senses to understand and respond to stimuli. The perception process occurs in four stages: attending and selecting, organizing, interpreting, and retrieving.

personal distance. Ranging from 18 inches to 4 feet, the space most people use during conversations.

personal space. The distance we put between ourselves and others.

perspective taking. Acknowledging the viewpoints of those with whom you interact.

phatic communication. Idiomatic communication used for interpersonal contact only.

physical characteristics. Aspects of physical appearance, such as body size, skin color, hair color and style, facial hair, and facial features.

physical context. The tangible environment in which communication occurs.

physical environment. The setting in which our behavior takes place.

physical noise. External disturbances that interrupt the meaning between a sender and receiver.

physiological noise. Interference in message reception because of physical, biological, or chemical functions of the body.

polarization. When people utilize the either/or aspect of the English language and use words that cast topics in extremes.

positive face. Our desire to be liked by significant people in our lives and have them confirm our beliefs, respect our abilities, and value what we value.

positive feedback. In Systems Theory, feedback that produces change.

positive halo. The result of placing positive qualities (e.g., warm, sensitive, and intelligent) together.

positive interaction ratio. Couples who say more nice things to each other than negative things.

power. The ability to control the behavior of another.

power distance. How a culture perceives and distributes power.

preventative maintenance. When both partners pay attention to the relationship even when it's not experiencing trouble.

private information. Consists of the assessments—both good and bad—that we make about ourselves. It also includes our personal values and interests, fears, and concerns.

private issues. Issues that relate to a relationship (how much time two people spend together, how two people talk to one another, and so forth).

process. When used to describe interpersonal communication, an ongoing, unending, vibrant activity that always changes.

proxemics. The study of how people use, manipulate, and identify their personal space.

proximal context. The second episode of the Explanatory Process Model, it refers to the rules, emotions, and beliefs of the individuals involved in the conflict.

proximal outcomes. The fourth episode of the Explanatory Process Model, it consists of immediate results after the conflict interaction.

pseudolisten. To pretend to listen by nodding our heads, looking at the speaker, smiling at the appropriate times, or practicing other kinds of attention feigning.

psychological noise. The biases or prejudices of a sender or receiver that interrupts the meaning of a message.

public and private dialectic. An external dialectic centering on how much of the friendship is demonstrated in public and what parts are kept private.

public distance. The space of 12 feet or more that is closely associated with a speaker and audience.

public information. Facts that we make part of our public image—the parts of ourselves that we present to others.

public issues. Issues outside a relationship (politics, the climate, and so forth).

pursuit–withdrawal. A conflict pattern when one partner presses for a discussion about the source of conflict and the other partner withdraws.

rapport talk. The type of communication women typically use to establish and build relationships with others.

rating. Evaluating or assessing a message.

recalibrated. When a system resets its rules.

recalling. Understanding a message, storing it for future encounters, and remembering it later.

receiver. The intended target of a message.

receiving. The verbal and nonverbal acknowledgment of a message.

reciprocity. The process of responding to something with something else similar.

referents. The thing the word represents.

reframing. Rethinking the opposition and redefining the tension so it no longer is a tension. (Chapter 10)

reframing. The ability to change the frame surrounding a situation and put it in a more productive light. (Chapter 7)

reification. The tendency to respond to words, or labels for things, rather than the things themselves.

relational conflicts. A type of conflict concerning the relationship between two people.

relational culture. The partners' shared understandings, roles, and rituals that are unique to their relationship.

Relational Dialectics Theory (RDT). Explains that in our relationships we want to have conflicting, seemingly incompatible, things and we try to deal with the tensions raised by this conflict.

relational history. The prior relationship experiences that two people share.

relational messages. Messages that define a relationship.

relational rules. Negotiable rules that indicate what two relational partners expect and allow when they talk to each other.

relational schema. A mental framework or memory structure that we rely on to understand experience and to guide our future behavior in relationships.

relational transgressions. When people in close relationships betray, deceive, and say hurtful things to each other.

relational uniqueness. The ways in which the particular relationship of two relational partners stands apart from other relationships they experience.

relational uppers. People who support and trust us as we improve our self-concept.

relationship level. The information contained in a message that indicates how the sender wants the receiver to interpret the message.

relationship ruts. Patterns of relationship behavior that become dull and unproductive.

report talk. The type of communication men typically use to command attention, reaffirm status, and win arguments.

responding. Providing observable feedback to a sender's message.

retrieving stage. The fourth stage of the perception process in which we recall information stored in our memories.

rewards. Those parts of being in a relationship that are pleasurable to people.

ritual. A repeated patterned communication event.

role relationships. Partners are interdependent while accomplishing a specific task.

role-limited interaction. A stage of adult friendship development whereby we adhere to social expectations and cultural guidelines for conversation.

rules. A prescribed guide that indicates what behavior is obligated, preferred, or prohibited in certain contexts.

sandwich generation. A generation of people who simultaneously take care of their (aging) parents and their own children.

second-guess. To question the assumptions underlying a message.

seeking gestures. Gestures that request agreement or clarification from a sender during a conversation.

segmentation. A strategy for dealing with dialectic tensions by allowing people to isolate separate arenas for using each of the poles of the dialectic tension.

selection. A strategy for dealing with dialectic tensions by choosing one of the opposites and ignoring your need for the other.

selective listening. Responding to some parts of a message and rejecting others.

selective perception. Directing our attention to certain stimuli while ignoring other stimuli.

selective retention. Recalling information that agrees with our perceptions and selectively forgetting information that does not.

self-actualization. The process of gaining information about ourselves in an effort to tap our full potential, our spontaneity, and our talents, and to cultivate our strengths and eliminate our shortcomings.

self-awareness. Our understanding of who we are.

self-concept. A relatively stable set of perceptions we hold of ourselves.

self-disclosure. The process of intentionally telling another person somewhat significant personal information that they would have trouble finding out without being told.

self-esteem. An evaluation of who we perceive ourselves to be.

self-fulfilling prophecies. Predictions or expectations about our future behavior that are likely to come true because we believe them and thus act in ways that make them come true.

self-monitoring. Actively thinking about and controlling our public behaviors and actions.

self-worth. How we feel about our talents, abilities, knowledge, expertise, and appearance.

semantic derogation. The use of one term with a positive connotation and its supposed parallel term with a negative connotation (e.g., *master* and *mistress*).

semantic noise. Occurs when senders and receivers apply different meanings to the same message; may take the form of jargon, technical language, and other words and phrases that are familiar to the sender but that are not understood by the receiver.

Semiotics Theory. A theory that examines the study of symbols in relation to their form and content.

sender. The source of a message.

serial conflict. A type of conflict that recurs over time in people's everyday lives without a resolution.

sex. The biological makeup of an individual (male or female).

sexist language. Language that is demeaning to one sex.

short-term attraction. A judgment of relationship potential that propels us into beginning a relationship with someone.

short-term commitment. The decision to love a certain person.

short-term memory. Memory that is stored sequentially, meaning that something is linked up to a previously recognized memory.

silent listening. Listening that requires individuals to listen without words to another person.

single-parent family. Families that consist of one adult serving as a parent and at least one child.

small talk. Interactions that are relaxed, pleasant, uncritical, and casual.

social distance. Ranging from 4 to 12 feet, the spatial zone usually reserved for professional or formal interpersonal encounters.

social-emotional context. The relational and emotional environment in which communication occurs.

social identity. The part of one's self that is based on membership in a particular group.

Social Information Processing (SIP) Theory. Our online relationships typically demonstrate the same sort of intimacy as those we have developed f2f. SIP Theory underscores the fact that people who work to establish online relationships usually take longer periods of time to develop than traditional f2f relationships.

Social Penetration Theory. A theory proposing that people, like onions, have many layers. A person's layers correspond to all the information about them, ranging from the most obvious to the most personal.

solidarity. An expectation in friendship that includes a sharing of mutual activities and the companionship of friends.

specialized others. Individuals who remain central in our lives.

specific. A word with a restricted number of possible referents.

speech communities. Groups who share norms about how to speak; what words to use; and when, where, and why to speak.

stabilized friendship. The fifth stage in adult friendship development whereby close friends merge social circles, establish emotional bonds, and begin to appreciate the others' values on friendship.

stagnating stage. Stage 3 of Knapp's Coming Apart Model, it's when the partners no longer talk much.

static evaluation. When words conceal change; when we speak and respond to people today the same way we did many years ago.

stereotypes. Fixed mental images of a particular group; communicating with an individual as if they were a member of that group.

stereotyping. Categorizing individuals according to a fixed impression, whether positive or negative, of an entire group to which they belong.

story. Story, or true self-disclosure, exists when the teller *feels* the risk they are taking in telling the information.

strategic ambiguity. The lack of clarity people use intentionally when they do not want others to completely understand their intentions.

subsystems. Smaller, lower level systems.

suprasystems. Larger, higher level systems.

sustaining. Behaving in a way that keeps the initial conversation going.

Symbolic Interactionism Theory. The theory suggesting that our understanding of ourselves and of the world is shaped by our interactions with those around us.

symbols. Arbitrary labels or representations (such as words) for feelings, concepts, objects, or events.

symmetrical escalation. A conflict pattern when each partner chooses to increase the intensity of the conflict.

symmetrical negotiation. A conflict pattern where each partner mirrors the other's negotiating behaviors.

symmetrical reciprocity. An expectation in friendship that occurs when both members of the friendship strategically choose to enact behaviors that sustain friendship.

symmetrical withdrawal. A conflict pattern when one person's move away is reciprocated by the other's move away.

Systems Theory. The theory underscoring the complex interrelationships existing between and among phenomena. One element of the system necessarily affects and influences other elements of a system.

talkaholics. A compulsive talker who hogs the conversational stage and monopolizes encounters.

terminating stage. Stage 5 of Knapp's Coming Apart Model, it's when the relational partners have decided, either jointly or individually, to part permanently.

territorial markers. Items or objects that humans use to mark their territories, such as a newspaper set on a table in a coffee shop.

territoriality. The sense of ownership of space that remains fixed.

time-centered listening style. A listening style associated with listeners who want messages to be presented succinctly.

traditional nuclear family. A married couple living with their biological children, with the husband/father as the financial provider and the wife/mother as the domestic provider.

Transactional Model of Communication. A characterization of communication as the reciprocal sending and receiving of messages. In a transactional encounter, the sender and receiver do not simply send meaning from one to the other and then back again; rather, they build shared meaning through simultaneous sending and receiving.

Triangular Theory of Love. A theoretical perspective of love that includes three components: intimacy, passion, and commitment.

turn gestures. Gestures that indicate another person can speak or that are used to request to speak in a conversation.

Two-Culture Theory. An explanation for differences in women's and men's verbal codes based on conceptualizing the two sexes as two separate cultures.

two-way, fair-weather cooperation. A stage in childhood friendship (ages 6–12) in which children understand

friendship as reciprocal, but if the friendship is unpleasant, they will exit the relationship.

uncertainty avoidance. A cultural mind-set that indicates how tolerant (or intolerant) a culture is of uncertainty and change.

unknown self. A quadrant of the Johari Window that consists of the information about you that neither you nor others are aware of.

valence. Whether an emotion reflects a positive or negative feeling.

value conflicts. A type of conflict focused specifically on questions of right and wrong.

verbal symbols. The words or the vocabulary that make up a language.

vocal characterizers. Nonverbal behaviors such as crying, laughing, groaning, muttering, whispering, and whining.

vocal distractors. The "ums" and "ers" used in conversation.

vocal qualities. Nonverbal behaviors such as pitch, rate, volume, inflection, tempo, and pronunciation.

voluntary kin. Individuals who feel like family but who we're not related to by blood or law.

waning friendship. The stage in an adult friendship development that includes friends drifting apart for various reasons (e.g., job, health, school, boredom).

wholeness. A systems principle meaning that you can't understand a system by taking it apart and understanding each of its parts in isolation from one another.

withdrawal–pursuit. A conflict pattern where a partner's withdrawal prompts the other's pursuit.

Working Memory Theory. A theory stating that we can pay attention to several stimuli and simultaneously store stimuli for future reference.

worldview. A personal framework to view the events surrounding us.

/// NOTES

/// CHAPTER 1

1. Richmond, V. P., Wrench, J., & McCroskey, J. C. (2012). *Communication apprehension avoidance and effectiveness*. Boston, MA: Pearson.
2. Neuliep, J. W. (2017). *Intercultural communication: A contextual approach*. Thousand Oaks, CA: Sage.
   Neuliep, J. W. (2017). Intercultural communication apprehension. *The International Encyclopedia of Intercultural Communication*, 1–5.
3. Craig, R. T. (2003). *Discursive origins of a communication discipline*. Paper presented at the annual meeting of the National Communication Association, Miami, FL.
4. Friedrich, G. W., & Boileau, D. M. (1999). The communication discipline. In A. L. Vangelisti, J. A. Daly, & G. W. Friedrich (Eds.), *Teaching communication: Theory, research and methods* (2nd ed., pp. 3–13). Mahwah, NJ: Erlbaum.
   Simonson, P., Peck, J., Craig, R. T., & Jackson, J. P. (2013). The history of communication history. In P. Simonson, J. Peck, R. T. Craig, & J. P. Jackson (Eds.), *The handbook of communication history* (pp. 13–57). New York, NY: Routledge.
   Gehrke, P. J., & Keith, W. M. (Eds.). (2014). *A century of communication studies: The unfinished conversation*. New York, NY: Routledge.
5. Galvin, K. M. (2006). Diversity's impact on defining the family: Discourse-dependence and identity. In L. H. Turner & R. West (Eds.), *The family communication sourcebook* (pp. 3–19). Thousand Oaks, CA: Sage.
6. Hanna, A., & Walther, J. B. (2013). What perceptions do people form after viewing Facebook profiles? In K. Schultz & A. K. Goodboy (Eds.), *Introduction to communication studies: Translating scholarship into meaningful practice* (pp. 11–17). Dubuque, IA: Kendall/Hunt.
7. Walther, J. B., & Jang, J.-W. (2012). Communication processes in participatory web sites. *Journal of Computer-Mediated Communication, 18*, 2–15. doi: 10.1111/j.1083-6101.2012.01592.x

8. Walther, J. B., Van Der Heide, B., Ramirez, A., Jr., Burgoon, J. K., & Pena, J. (2014). Interpersonal and hyperpersonal aspects of computer-mediated communication. In S. S. Sundar (Ed.), *The handbook of psychology and communication technology* (pp. 3–22). West Sussex, England: Wiley-Blackwell.
8. https://www.reddit.com/r/funny/comments/5z84d9/1960s_vs_today/
9. Duck, S. W., & Wood, J. T. (1995). For better, for worse, for richer, for poorer: The rough and smooth of relationships. In S. Duck & J. T. Wood (Eds.), *Confronting relationship challenges* (pp. 1–21). Thousand Oaks, CA: Sage.
10. Shannon, C. E., & Weaver, W. (1949). *The mathematical theory of communication*. Urbana: University of Illinois Press.
11. Liu, S., Volcic, Z., & Gallois, C. (2014). *Introducing intercultural communication: Global cultures and contexts*. Thousand Oaks, CA: Sage.
12. Anderson, R., & Ross, V. (2002). *Questions of communication: A practical introduction to theory*. New York, NY: St. Martin's Press.
13. Schramm, W. L. (1954). *The process and effects of mass communication*. Urbana: University of Illinois Press.
14. Barnlund, D. C. (1970). A transactional model of communication. In K. K. Sereno & C. D. Mortensen (Eds.), *Foundations of communication theory* (pp. 83–102). New York, NY: Harper & Row.
   Watzlawick, P., Beavin, J., & Jackson, D. D. (1967). *Pragmatics of human communication*. New York, NY: Norton.
15. Wood, J. T. (1998). *But I thought you meant . . . misunderstandings in human communication*. Mountain View, CA: Mayfield.
16. Sumner, E. M., & Ramirez, A., Jr. (2017). Social information processing theory and hyperpersonal perspective. In P. Rössler, C. A. Hoffner, & L. van Zoonen (Eds.), *The international encyclopedia of media effects* (pp. 1–11). Chichester, England: Wiley-Blackwell.
17. Miller, G. R., & Steinberg, M. (1975). *Between people: A new analysis of interpersonal communication*. Chicago, IL: Science Research Associates.

18. Shimanoff, S. B. (1980). *Communication rules: Theory and research*. Beverly Hills, CA: Sage.
19. https://www.onetonline.org/
20. Watzlawick, P., Beavin, J., & Jackson, D. D. (1967). *Pragmatics of human communication*. New York, NY: Norton.
21. Barthes, R. (1994). *The semiotic challenge*. Berkeley: University of California Press.
22. Craig, R. T. (2007). Pragmatism in the field of communication theory. *Communication Theory, 17*, 125–145.
23. Shimanoff, S. B. *Communication rules: Theory and research,* 1980.
24. Tompkins, P. S., & Anderson, K. E. (2015). *Practicing communication ethics: Development, discernment, and decision-making*. New York, NY: Routledge.
25. Cupach, W. R., & Spitzberg, B. H. (2014). *The dark side of relationship pursuit: From attraction to obsession and stalking*. New York, NY: Routledge.
26. Roper Poll. (1999). *How Americans communicate*. Washington, DC: National Communication Association.
27. https://qz.com/823918/how-doctors-give-patients-bad-news/
28. Johannesen, R. L., Valde, K. S., & Whedbee, K. E. (2007). *Ethics in human communication* (6th ed.). Lake Zurich, IL: Waveland Press.
29. https://news.gallup.com/poll/224639/nurses-keep-healthy-lead-honest-ethical-profession.aspx
30. Kant, I. (1785). *The groundwork for the metaphysics of morals*. Peterborough, Ontario, Canada: Broadview Press.
   Thompson, M. L. (2013). *Imagination in Kant's critical philosophy*. New York, NY: Walter de Gruyter.
31. https://www.forbes.com/2010/01/19/knauss-clorox-ethics-leadership-citizenship-ethics.html#778e758b7279
32. Gensler, H. J. (2013). *Ethics and the golden rule*. New York, NY: Routledge.
33. Gilligan, C. (1982). *In a different voice: Psychological theory and women's development*. Cambridge, MA: Harvard University Press.

/// CHAPTER 2

1. Abu-Hamda, B., Soliman, A., Babekr, A., & Bellaj, T. (2017). Emotional expression and culture: Implications from nine Arab countries. *European Psychiatry, 41,* S230.

2. Yen, H. (2017). *Census: Whites no longer a majority in US by 2043.* Retrieved from http://nbclatino.com/2012/12/12/census-whites-no-longer-a-majority-in-us-by-2043/

3. Samovar, L. E., Porter, R. E., & McDaniel, E. R. (2017). (Eds.). *Intercultural communication: A reader* (9th ed.). Boston, MA: Cengage.

4. Asante, M. K., Miike, Y., & Yin, J. (Eds.). (2013). *The global intercultural communication reader.* New York, NY: Routledge.

5. Sorrells, K. (2015). *Intercultural communication: Globalization and social justice.* Thousand Oaks, CA: Sage.

6. Hall, B. J. (2005). *Among cultures: The challenge of communication.* Fort Worth, TX: Harcourt.

7. Peters, F. (2016). Fostering mixed race children. In F. Peters, *Fostering mixed race children* (pp. 7–21). London, England: Palgrave Macmillan.

8. Orbe, M. P. (1998). *Constructing co-cultural theory: An explication of co-culture, power, and communication.* Thousand Oaks, CA: Sage; Orbe, M. P., & Roberts, T. L. (2012). Co-cultural theorizing: Foundations, applications, and extensions. *Howard Journal of Communications, 23,* 293–311.

9. Fernandez, R. M., & Greenberg, J. (2013). Race, identity, hiring, and statistical discrimination. In S. McDonald (Ed.), *Networks, work, and inequality* (pp. 81–102). Bradford, England: Emerald Group. Midtbøen, A. H. (2014). The invisible second generation? Statistical discrimination and immigrant stereotypes in employment processes in Norway. *Journal of Ethnic and Migration Studies, 40*(10), 1657–1675.

10. Evans, R. (2013, October 16). Culture clashes provide benefits in the long run. *Construction News.* Retrieved from http://www.cnplus.co.uk/opinion/editors-comment/culture-clashes-provide-benefits-in-the-long-run/8654365.article#.U2EBD41OU5s

11. Jonas, M. (2007, August 5). The downside of diversity. *Boston Globe,* D2, D4.

12. Lamble, L. (2018, April). *With 250 babies born each minute, how many people can the Earth sustain?* Retrieved from https://www.theguardian.com/global-development/2018/apr/23/population-how-many-people-can-the-earth-sustain-lucy-lamble

13. Worldometers. (n.d.). *7 Continents.* Retrieved from http://www.worldometers.info/geography/7-continents/

14. Martinez, R. (2000, July 16). The next chapter: America's next great revolution in race relations is already underway. *New York Times Magazine,* 11–12.

15. Engstrom, D. (2017). *Hispanics in the United States: An agenda for the twenty-first century.* New York, NY: Routledge.

16. Chishti, M., & Bergeron, C. (2012, December 18). *Deferred action program revives debate over driver's licenses for unauthorized immigrants.* Retrieved from https://www.migrationpolicy.org/article/deferred-action-program-revives-debate-over-driver%E2%80%99s-licenses-unauthorized-immigrants

17. Capps, R., Bachmeier, J. D., Fix, M., & Van Hook, J. (2013, May). *A demographic, socioeconomic, and health coverage profile of the unauthorized immigrants in the United States* (Issue Brief No. 5). Washington, DC: Migration Policy Institute. Retrieved from http://migrationpolicy.org/research/demographic-socioeconomic-and-health-coverage-profile-unauthorized-immigrants-united-states

18. Hall, E. T. (1959). *The silent language.* New York, NY: Doubleday.

19. Haug, J. (2013). *The diversity movement: Defeating itself, destroying society.* Retrieved from http://www.americanthinker.com/2013/01/the_diversity_movement_defeating_itself_destroying_society.html

20. Hathaway, G. (2013, May 3). *Diversity then and now.* Retrieved from https://www.insidehighered.com/advice/2013/05/03/essay-evolving-role-diversity-director

21. Martin, J., & Nakayama, T. (2018). *Experiencing intercultural communication: An introduction* (6th ed.). New York, NY: McGraw-Hill.

22. https://woca.afs.org/afs-announcements/b/icl-blog/posts/understanding-culture-using-metaphors

23. McLuhan, M. (1964). *Understanding media: The extensions of man.* New York, NY: McGraw-Hill.

24. https://www.indexmundi.com/g/r.aspx?c=us&v=85

25. Palmer, K. S. (2002, October 10). Cultures clash in workplaces. *USA Today,* 13A.

26. Withnall, A. (2016, June 8). *Global Peace Index 2016: There are now only 10 countries in the world that are actually free from conflict.* Retrieved from https://www.independent.co.uk/news/world/politics/global-peace-index-2016-there-are-now-only-10-countries-in-the-world-that-are-not-at-war-a7069816.html

27. Buber, M. (1970). *I and thou* (W. Kaufmann, Trans.). New York, NY: Scribner.

28. Mashru, R. (2012). *It's a girl! The three deadliest words in the world.* Retrieved from https://www.ippf.org/blogs/its-girl-three-deadliest-words-world

29. Yang, S. (2013, November 15). China easing one-child policy amid elderly boom. *USA Today.* Retrieved from http://www.usatoday.com/story/news/world/2013/11/15/china-one-child-policy/3570593/

30. Hofstede, G. (1980). *Culture's consequences.* Beverly Hills, CA: Sage; Hofstede, G. (1984). The cultural relativity of the quality of life concept. *Academy of Management Review, 9,* 389–398; Hofstede, G. (2001). *Culture's consequences: Comparing values, behaviors, institutions, and organizations across nations.* Thousand Oaks, CA: Sage; Hofstede, G. (2003). *Geert Hofstede cultural dimensions.* Retrieved from http://www.geert-hofstede.com/

31. Singh, S. P. (2018). A study of caste system, family life and values In ancient India. *International Journal of Scientific Research in Science and Technology, 4,* 910–914.

32. Carrasquillo, H. (1997). Puerto Rican families in America. In M. K. DeGenova (Ed.), *Families in cultural context: Strengths and challenges in diversity* (pp. 155–172). Mountain View, CA: Mayfield.

33. Hall, E. T., & Hall, M. R. (1990). *Understanding cultural differences.* Yarmouth, ME: Intercultural Press.

34. Martinez-Carter, K. (2013, June 19). What does 'American' actually mean? Retrieved from https://www.theatlantic.com/national/archive/2013/06/what-does-american-actually-mean/276999/

35. Lippman, W. (1922). *Public opinion.* New York, NY: MacMillan.

/// CHAPTER 3

1. Taheri, M. (2013). *Human worldview.* Toronto, Canada: Interuniversal Press.

2. Scatolini, F. L., Zani, K. P., & Pfeifer, L. I. (2017). The influence of epilepsy on children's perception of self-concept. *Epilepsy & Behavior, 69,* 75–79.

3. Bowling, A. (2007). Aspirations for older age in the 21st century: What is successful aging?. *The International*

Journal of Aging and Human Development, 64(3), 263–297.

4. Langer, E. (1989). *Mindfulness*. Reading, MA: Addison-Wesley

5. Kabat-Zinn, J. (2018). *Falling awake: How to practice mindfulness in everyday life*. New York, NY: Hachette Books.

6. Germino, B. B., Mishel, M. H., Crandell, J., Porter, L., Blyler, D., Jenerette, C., & Gil, K. (2012). Outcomes of an uncertainty management intervention in younger African American and Caucasian breast cancer survivors, *Oncology Nursing Forum*, 1–11.

7. Cowan, N. (2016). *Working memory capacity: Classic edition*. New York, NY: Routledge.

8. Hamer, A. (2018, February 12). Your short-term memory can only hold 7-items (but you can use this trick). Retrieved from https://curiosity.com/topics/your-short-term-memory-can-only-hold-7-items-but-you-can-use-this-trick-curiosity/

9. Grossman, T. (2013). The early development of processing emotions in face and voice. In P. Belin, S. Campanella, & T. Ethofer (Eds.), *Integrating face and voice in person perception* (pp. 95–116). New York, NY: Springer.

10. Hamilton, W. L. (2004, July 5). For Bantu refugees, hard-won American dreams. *New York Times*, A1, A14.

11. Bizumic, B. (2014). Who coined the concept of ethnocentrism? A brief report. *Journal of Social and Political Psychology, 2*.

12. Hashem, M. (2015). The power of Wastah in Lebanese speech. In A. Gonzalez, & V. Chen (Eds.), *Our voices: Essays in culture, ethnicity, and communication* (pp. 187–194). New York, NY: Oxford University Press.

13. Miller, J. B., Plant, E. A., & Hanke, E. (1993). Girls' and boys' views of body type. In C. Berryman-Fink, D. Ballard-Reisch, & L. H. Newman (Eds.), *Communication and sex-role socialization* (pp. 49–58). New York, NY: Garland.

14. Franzoi, S. L., & Klaiber, J. R. (2007). Body use and reference group impact. *Sex Roles, 55*, 205–214.

15. Bem, S. (1993). *The lenses of gender: Transforming the debate on sexual inequality*. New Haven, CT: Yale University Press.

16. Zak, D. (2013, November 19). "Selfie"-reliance: The word of the year is the story of our individualism. *Washington Post*. Retrieved from http://www.washingtonpost.com

17. MacNeil, L., Driscoll, A., & Hunt, A. N. (2015). What's in a name: Exposing gender bias in student ratings of teaching. *Innovative Higher Education, 40*(4), 291–303. doi: 10.1007/s10755-014-9313-4

18. Phua, J., Jin, S. V., & Kim, J. J. (2017). Gratifications of using Facebook, Twitter, Instagram, or Snapchat to follow brands: The moderating effect of social comparison, trust, tie strength, and network homophily on brand identification, brand engagement, brand commitment, and membership intention. *Telematics and Informatics, 34*(1), 412–424.

19. Mead, G. H. (1934). *Mind, self and society: From the standpoint of a social behaviorist*. Chicago, IL: University of Chicago Press.

20. Graham, E. E. (1997). Turning points and commitments in post-divorce relationships. *Communication Monographs, 64*, 350–368; Graham, E. E. (2003). Dialectic contradictions in postmarital relationships. *Journal of Family Communication, 4*, 193–214.

21. Yadegaran, J. (2013, December 11). Are selfies good or bad for our self-esteem? *San Jose Mercury News*. Retrieved from http://www.mercurynews.com/ci_24696982/are-selfies-good-or-bad-our-self-esteem

22. Wang, R., Yang, F., & Haigh, M. M. (2017). Let me take a selfie: exploring the psychological effects of posting and viewing selfies and groupies on social media. *Telematics and Informatics, 34*(4), 274–283.

23. Cupach, W. R., & Imahori, T. T. (1993). Identity management theory communication competence in intercultural episodes and relationships. In R. L. Wiseman & J. Koester (Eds.), *Intercultural communication competence* (pp. 112–131). Newbury Park, CA: Sage.

24. Chen, G. M. (2013). Losing *face* on social media: Threats to *positive face* lead to an indirect effect on retaliatory aggression through negative affect. *Communication Research, 42*, 819–838.

25. Snyder, M. (1979). Self-monitoring processes. In L. Berkowitz (Ed.), *Advances in experimental social psychology* (pp. 86–131). New York, NY: Academic Press.

26. Döring, N. (2002). Personal home pages on the Web: A review of research. *Journal of computer-mediated communication, 7*(3). Retrieved from https://onlinelibrary.wiley.com/doi/full/10.1111/j.1083-6101.2002.tb00152.x

27. Taubner, H., Hallén, M., & Wengelin, Å. (2017). Signs of aphasia: Online identity and stigma management in post-stroke aphasia. *Cyberpsychology: Journal of Psychosocial Research on Cyberspace, 11*(1).

28. Walther, J. B. (1992). Interpersonal effects in computer-mediated interactions. *Communication Research, 19*, 52–90; Walther, J. B. (2011). Theories of computer-mediated communication and interpersonal relations. In M. L. Knapp & J. A. Daly (Eds.), *The handbook of interpersonal communication* (pp. 443–479). Thousand Oaks, CA: Sage; Walther, J. B. (2012). Interaction through technological lenses: Computer-mediated communication and language. *Journal of Language and Social Psychology, 31*, 397–414.

29. Gibbs, J. L., Ellison, N. B., & Heino, R. D. (2006). Self-presentation in online personals: The role of anticipated future interaction, self-disclosure, and perceived success in Internet dating. *Communication Research, 33*, 152–177.

/// CHAPTER 4

1. Dunbar, R. (1998). *Grooming, gossip, and the evolution of language*. Cambridge, MA: Harvard University Press.

2. Giles, H. (2008). Communication accommodation theory. In L. A. Baxter & D. O. Braithwaite (Eds.), *Engaging theories in interpersonal communication* (pp. 161–174). Thousand Oaks, CA: Sage.

3. Ogden, C. K., & Richards, I. A. (1923). *The meaning of meaning*. London, England: Kegan Paul, Trench, & Trubner.

4. Chozick, A. (May 11, 2015). *As middle class fades, so does use of term on campaign trail*. Retrieved from https://www.nytimes.com/2015/05/12/us/politics/as-middle-class-fades-so-does-use-of-term-on-campaign-trail.html

5. Gay & Lesbian Alliance Against Defamation (GLAAD). (2013). *GLAAD media reference guide—Transgender glossary of terms*. Retrieved from http://www.glaad.org/reference/transgender

6. Kitzinger, C. (2000). How to resist an idiom. *Research on Language and Social Interaction, 33*, 121–154.

7. Merriam-Webster Online Dictionary. (2018). Retrieved from http://www.merriam-webster.com/

8. Floyd, S., Rossi, G., Baranova, J., Blythe, J., Dingemanse, M., Kendrick, K. H., . . . & Enfield, N. J. (2018). Universals and cultural diversity in the expression of gratitude. *The Royal Society Open Science*. doi: 10.1098/rsos.180391

9. Shuter, R., & Turner, L. H. (1997). African American and European American women in the workplace: Perceptions of conflict communication. *Management Communication Quarterly, 11*, 74–96.

10. Linguistic Society of America. (1997, January). *LSA resolution on the Oakland "Ebonics" issue*. Retrieved from http://www.linguistlist.org/topics/ebonics/lsa-ebonics.html

11. Craig, H. K., Kolenic, G. E., & Hensel, S. L. (2014). African American English-speaking students: A longitudinal examination of style shifting from kindergarten through second grade. *Journal of Speech, Language, and Hearing Research, 57*, 143–157.

12. Jones, S. C. T., Neblett, E. W., Gaskin, A. L., & Lee, D. B. (2015). Assessing the African American child and adolescent: Special considerations and assessment of behavioral disorders. In L. T. Benuto & B. D. Leany (Eds.), *Guide to psychological assessment with African Americans* (pp. 105–120). New York, NY: Springer.

13. Peterson, B. (2013, October 19). Baseball, shaper of language: Why linguists love America's favorite pastime. *Boston Globe*. Retrieved from https://www.bostonglobe.com/opinion/2013/10/19/baseball-shaper-language-baseball-shaper-language/r0zg0H6rmsYPraJcaecqXK/story.html

14. Hoijer, H. (1994). The Sapir-Whorf hypothesis. In L. A. Samovar & R. E. Porter (Eds.), *Intercultural communication: A reader* (pp. 194–201). Belmont, CA: Wadsworth.

15. Radiolab. (2012). *Why isn't the sky blue?* Retrieved from http://www.radiolab.org/story/211213-sky-isnt-blue/

16. Seay, E. (2004, February 11). Lost city, lost languages. *Princeton Alumni Weekly, 17*, 43.

17. Barner, D., Inagaki, S., & Li, P. (2009). Language, thought, and real nouns. *Cognition, 111*, 329–344.

18. Maltz, D. J., & Borker, R. A. (1982). A cultural approach to male-female miscommunication. In J. J. Gumpertz (Ed.), *Language and social identity* (pp. 196–216). Cambridge, England: Cambridge University Press.

19. Canary, D. J., & Hause, K. S. (1993). Is there any reason to research sex differences in communication? *Communication Quarterly, 41*, 129–144.

20. Lytle, R. (2011, June 13). *How slang affects students in the classroom*. Retrieved from http://www.usnews.com/education/high-schools/articles/2011/06/13/how-slang-affects-students-in-the-classroom

21. Gould, M. (2017). *Transcending generations*. Collegeville, MN: Liturgical Press.

22. Porten-Cheé, P., & Eilders, C. (2015). Spiral of silence online: How online communication affects opinion climate perception and opinion expression regarding the climate change debate. *Studies in Communication Sciences, 15*, 143–150.

23. Schwartz, H. A., Eichstaedt, J. C., Kern, M. L., Dziurzynski, L., Ramones, S. M., Agrawal, M., . . . & Ungar, L. H. (2013). Personality, gender, and age in the language of social media: The open vocabulary approach. *PLoS ONE 8*, e73791. Retrieved from http://journals.plos.org/plosone/article?id=10.1371/journal.pone.0073791. doi:10.1371/journal.pone.0073791

24. Engeln-Maddox, R., Salk, R. H., & Miller, S. A. (2012). Assessing women's negative commentary on their own bodies: A psychometric investigation of the negative body talk scale. *Psychology of Women Quarterly, 36*, 162–178.

25. Kramarae, C. (1981). *Women and men speaking*. Rowley, MA: Newbury House.

26. Carter, B. (2013, November 15). *MSNBC suspends Alec Baldwin and his talk show*. Retrieved from https://www.nytimes.com/2013/11/16/business/media/msnbc-suspends-baldwin-and-show.html

27. Quann, J. (2017, May 17). *UN "deeply concerned" over use of homophobic language*. Retrieved from https://www.newstalk.com/UN-deeply-concerned-over-use-of-homophobic-language

/// CHAPTER 5

1. Burgoon, J. K., Buller, D. B., & Woodall, W. G. (1996). *Nonverbal communication: The unspoken dialogue*. New York, NY: McGraw-Hill.

2. Moore, N., Hickson, M., & Stacks, D. (2009). *Nonverbal communication: Studies and application*. New York, NY: Oxford University Press.

3. Mehrabian, A., & Ferris, S. R. (1967). Inference of attitudes from nonverbal communication in two channels. *Journal of Consulting Psychology, 21*, 248–252.

4. Matsumoto, D., Frank, M. G., & Hwang, H. (2013). *Nonverbal communication: Science and applications*. Thousand Oaks, CA: Sage.

5. Botha, J. E. (1996). Exploring gesture and nonverbal communication in the Bible and the ancient world: some initial observations. *Neotestamentica*, 1–19.

6. Andersen, P. (2008). *Nonverbal communication: Forms and functions*. Long Grove, IL: Waveland Press.

7. Giles, H., & Le Poire, B. A. (2006). Introduction: The ubiquity and social meaningfulness of nonverbal communication. In V. L. Manusov & M. L. Patterson (Eds.), *Handbook of nonverbal communication* (pp. xv–xxvii). Thousand Oaks, CA: Sage.

8. Grossberg, B. (2017). *Asperger's and adulthood*. Berkeley, CA: Althea Press.

9. Knapp, M. L., Hall, J. A., & Horgan, T. (2014). *Nonverbal communication in human interaction*. Boston, MA: Cengage.

10. Burgoon, J. K., Guerrero, L. K., & Floyd, K. (2016). *Nonverbal communication*. New York, NY: Routledge.

11. Burgoon, J. K., Buller, D. B., & Woodall, W. G. (1996). *Nonverbal communication: The unspoken dialogue*. New York, NY: McGraw-Hill.

12. Corballis, M. C. (2011). *The recursive mind*. Princeton, NJ: Princeton University Press.

13. Bavelas, J. B. (1994). Gestures as part of speech: Methodological implications. *Research on Language and Social Interaction, 27*, 201–222.

14. Johnson, K. K., Lennon, S. J., Mun, J. M., & Choi, D. (2015). Fashion/clothing research: An analysis of three journals. *Journal of Fashion Marketing and Management, 19(1)*, 41–55.

15. Rebell, B. (2015, July 28). Tattoos may be taboo for U.S. millennials seeking to dress for success. Retrieved from https://www.reuters.com/article/us-column-rebell-tattoos-idUSKCN0Q21NU20150728

16. Knapp, M. L., Hall, J. A., & Horgan, T. (2014). *Nonverbal communication in human interaction*. Boston, MA: Cengage.

17. Williams, R. B. (2011, August 6). Why we pay more attention to beautiful people. Wired for Success blog, *Psychology Today*. Retrieved from http://www.psychologytoday.com

18. Akst, D. (2016, August 26). *Yes, students do learn more from attractive teachers*. Retrieved from https://www.wsj.com/articles/yes-students-do-learn-more-from-attractive-teachers-1472223974

19. Jones, D. (2004, January 9). Women trump the men in first episode. *USA Today*, 3B.

20. Sharma, S., & Chakravarthy, B. K. (2013). How people view abstract art: An eye

movement study to assess information processing and viewing strategy. In A. Chakrabarti & R. V. Prakash (Eds.), *IcoRD'13 Global Product Development: Lecture notes in mechanical engineering* (pp. 477–487). New York, NY: Springer.

21. Stevenson, S. (2012). There's magic in your smile: How smiling affects your brain. *Psychology Today*. Retrieved from http://www.psychologytoday.com/blog/cutting-edge-leadership/201206/there-s-magic-in-your-smile

22. Gueguen, N., & De Gail, M. (2003). The effect of smiling on helping behavior: Smiling and good Samaritan behavior. *Communication Reports, 16*, 133–140.

23. Griffin, C. L. (2018). *Invitation to public speaking*. Boston, MA: Wadsworth.

24. Benjamin, B., & Werner, R. (2004). Touch in the Western world. *Massage Therapy Journal, 43*, 28–32.

25. Morris, D. (2002). *Peoplewatching: The Desmond Morris guide to body language*. New York, NY: Vintage Books.

26. Crane, D. R., Dollahite, D. C., Griffin, W., & Taylor, V. L. (1987). Diagnosing relationships with spatial distance: An empirical test of a clinical principle. *Journal of Marital and Family Therapy, 13*(3), 307–310.

27. Hall, E. T. (1963). A system for the notation of proxemic behavior. *American Anthropologist, 65*(5), 1003–1026.

28. Burgoon, J. K. (2009). Expectancy violations theory. In S. W. Littlejohn & K. Foss (Eds.), *Encyclopedia of communication theory* (pp. 367–369). Thousand Oaks, CA: Sage.

29. Burgoon, J. K., Buller, D. B., & Woodall, W. G. (1996). *Nonverbal communication: The unspoken dialogue*. New York, NY: McGraw-Hill.

30. Shovlin, C. (2015). *Your true colors: A practical guide to color psychology*. CreateSpace Independent Publishing Platform.

31. Roethlisberger, F. L., & Dickson, W. (1939). *Management and the worker*. New York, NY: Wiley.

32. Samovar, L. E., Porter, R. E., & McDaniel, E. R. (2014). (Eds.). *Intercultural communication: A reader* (14th ed.). Boston, MA: Cengage.

33. Gestures across cultures. (2013). Retrieved from https://www.thesociologicalcinema.com/videos/gestures-across-cultures#.W0TaYthKjw4

34. Richmond, Y., & Gestrin, P. (2009). *Into Africa: A guide to Sub-Saharan culture and diversity*. Boston, MA: Nicholas Brealey.

35. Hall, E. T., & Hall, M. R. (1990). *Understanding cultural differences*. Yarmouth, ME: Intercultural Press.

36. Field, T. (1999). American adolescents touch each other less and are more aggressive toward their peers as compared with French adolescents. *Adolescence, 34*, 753–759.

37. Kagitçibasi, Ç. (2017). *Family, self, and human development across cultures: Theory and applications*. New York, NY: Routledge.

38. Ekman, P. (1973). Cross-cultural studies of facial expressions. In P. Ekman (Ed.), *Darwin and facial expressions* (pp. 169–229). New York, NY: Academic Press.

39. Bauerlein, M. (2009). *The dumbest generation: How the digital age stupefies young Americans and jeopardizes our future (or, don't trust anyone under 30)*. London, England: Penguin Books.

40. Green, M. (2012). The human side of a mediated life: How mediated communication is affecting relationships and nonverbal literacy. Unpublished manuscript, California Polytechnic State University, San Luis Obispo.

/// CHAPTER 6

1. Jones, D., & Hodson, P. (Eds.). (2017). *Unlocking speaking and listening*. New York, NY: Routledge.

2. Pilgrim, D. (2017). *Key concepts in mental health*. Thousand Oaks, CA: Sage.

3. Ferrari, B. (2012). *Power listening: The most critical business skill of all*. New York, NY: Penguin Books.

4. Baddeley, A. (2012). Working memory: Theories, models, and controversy. *Annual Reviews of Psychology, 63*, 1–29.

5. Mackay, H. (2011, June 23). *Listen if you want to learn*. Retrieved from http://www.harveymackay.com/listen-if-you-want-to-learn/

6. Wolvin, A. D. (2010). Introduction: Perspectives on listening in the 21st century. In A. D. Wolvin (Ed.), *Listening and human communication in the 21st century* (pp. 1–4). Oxford, England: Wiley-Blackwell. doi: 10.1002/9781444314908.fmatter

7. Wolvin, A. D., & Coakley, C. G. (1996). *Listening*. Madison, WI: Brown & Benchmark.

8. King, G., Baxter, D., Rosenbaum, P., Zwaigenbaum, & Bates, A. (2009). Belief systems of families of children with autism spectrum disorders or Down syndrome. *Focus on Autism and other Developmental Disabilities, 24*, 50–64; Hendrick, B. (2010, September 27). Mindfulness meditation vs. multiple sclerosis: Mindfulness meditation helps multiple sclerosis patients, *researchers say*. Retrieved from http://www.webmd.com/multiple-sclerosis/news/20100927/mindfulness-meditation-vs-multiple-sclerosis

9. Bostrom, R. N. (1990). *Listening behavior: Measurement and application*. New York, NY: Guilford Press.

10. Bostrom, R. N., & Waldhart, E. S. (1988). Memory models in the measurement of listening. *Communication Education, 37*, 1–12.

11. Tine, M. (2013). Working memory differences between children living in rural and urban poverty. *Journal of Cognition and Development, 24*, 599–613. doi: 10.1080/15248372.2013.797906

12. Brownell, J. (2012). *Listening: Attitudes, principles, and skills*. Boston, MA: Pearson.

13. Gearhart, C. C., Denham, J. P., & Bodie, G. D. (2014). Listening as a goal-directed activity. *Western Journal of Communication, 78*(5), 668–684.

14. Grognet, A., & Van Duzer, C. (2002). *Listening skills in the workplace*. Denver, CO: Spring Institute for International Studies.

15. Carnevale, A. P., & Smith, N. (2013). Workplace basics: The skills employees need and employers want. *Human Resource Development, 16*, 491–501. doi: 10.1080/13678868.2013.821267

16. Purdy, M. (2004). *Listen up, move up*. Retrieved from https://www.monster.com/career-advice/article?q=move+up+listen+up

17. Simpson, L. (2003). Get around resistance and win over the other side. *Harvard Management Communication Letter*, 3–5.

18. Bentley, S. C. (2000). Listening in the 21st century. *International Journal of Listening, 14*, 129–142.

19. Lumley, M., & Wilkinson, J. (2014). *Developing employability for business*. Oxford, England: Oxford University Press.

20. Meldrum, H. (2011). The listening practices of exemplary physicians. *International Journal of Listening, 25*, 145–160.

21. Donaghue, E. (2007, July 25). Communication now part of the cure. *USA Today*, D1; Kee, J. W., Khoo, H. S., Lim, I., & Koh, M. Y. (2018). Communication skills in patient–doctor interactions: Learning from patient complaints. *Health Professions Education, 4*(2), 97–106.

22. Hubbard, P. (2017). Technologies for teaching and learning L2 listening. In C. A. Chapelle, & S. Sauro (Eds.), *The handbook of technology and second language teaching and learning* (93–106). Hoboken, NJ: Wiley.

23. Davies, H., & Christensen, P. (2018). Sharing spaces: Children and young people negotiating intimate relationships and privacy in the family home. *Families, Intergenerationality, and Peer Group Relations*, 27–49; Turner, L. H., & West, R. (2018). *Perspectives of family communication*. New York, NY: McGraw-Hill.

24. Worthington, D. L., & Fitch-Hauser, M. (2012). *Listening: Processes, functions, and competency*. Boston, MA: Allyn & Bacon.

25. Nichols, R. G. (1948). Factors in listening comprehension. *Communications Monographs*, 15(2), 154–163.

26. Nelson, L. (2014, April 28). *More students are learning sign language than Chinese*. Retrieved from https://www.vox.com/2014/4/28/5654468/the-incredible-rise-of-american-sign-language

27. Chui, M., Manyika, J., Bughin, J., Dobbs, R., Roxburgh, C., Sarrazin, H., . . . Westergren, M. (2012, July). *The social economy: Unlocking value and productivity through social technologies*. Retrieved from https://www.mckinsey.com/industries/high-tech/our-insights/the-social-economy

28. National Governor's Association. (2013, May 14). *STEM Hatch-Klobuchar-Coons Amendment*. Retrieved from https://www.nga.org/cms/center/issues/education/stem

29. Knapp, M. L., Hall, J. A., & Horgan, T. (2014). *Nonverbal communication in human interaction*. Boston, MA: Cengage/Wadsworth; Leit, L. (2015). Narcissism and communication in marriage. In C. R. Berger, M. E. Roloff, S. R. Wilson, J. P. Dillard, J. Caughlin, & D. Solomon (Eds.), *The international encyclopedia of interpersonal communication* (pp. 1–6). Hoboken, NJ: Wiley-Blackwell.

30. Johnson, E. N., Kuhn, J. R., Apostolou, B. A., & Hassell, J. M. (2013). Auditor perceptions of client narcissism as a fraud attitude risk factor. *AUDITING: A Journal of Practice & Theory, 32*, 203–219.

31. Bell, S., Berg, T., & Morse, S. (2016). *Rich pictures: Encouraging resilient communities*. New York, NY: Routledge.

32. Johnston, M. K., Weaver, J. B., Watson, K. W., & Barker, L. B. (2000). Listening styles: Biological or psychological differences? *International Journal of Listening, 14*, 32–46.

33. Sargent, S. L., Weaver, J. B., III, & Kiewitz, C. (1997). Correlates between communication apprehension and listening style preferences. *Communication Research Reports, 14*, 74–78; Watson, K. W., & Barker, L. L. (1995). *Winning by listening around*. Tega Cay, SC: SPECTRA.

34. Campbell, A., Carrick, L., & Elliott, R. (2013). A hierarchy of personal agency for people with life-limiting illness. *American Journal of Hospice and Palliative Medicine, 30*, 2–9.

35. Lewis, R. D. (1999). *When cultures collide: Managing successfully across cultures*. London, England: Brealey; London School of International Communication. (2017, March 22). *Active listening as an essential intercultural skill*. Retrieved from https://www.londonschool.com/lsic/resources/blog/active-listening-essential-intercultural-skill/

36. Carbaugh, D. (1999). "Just listen": "Listening" and landscape among the Blackfeet. *Western Journal of Communication, 63*, 250–270.

37. Zohoori, A. (2013). A cross-cultural comparison of the HURIER listening profile among Iranian and U.S. students. *International Journal of Listening, 27*, 50–60.

38. Women's Media. (2017, January 3). *Gal interrupted, why men interrupt women and how to avert this in the workplace*. Retrieved from https://www.forbes.com/sites/womensmedia/2017/01/03/gal-interrupted-why-men-interrupt-women-and-how-to-avert-this-in-the-workplace/

39. Tannen, D. (2001). *Talking from 9 to 5: Women and men at work*. New York, NY: HarperCollins.

40. Shellenbarger, S. (2013, October 15). Teens are still developing empathy skills: Vital social skill ebbs and flows in adolescent boys; how to cultivate sensitivity. Work & Family, *Wall Street Journal*. Retrieved from https://www.wsj.com/articles/teens-are-still-developing-empathy-skills-1381876015

41. Weger, H., Jr., Castle Bell, G., Minei, E. M., & Robinson, M. C. (2014). The relative effectiveness of active listening in initial interactions. *International Journal of Listening, 28*(1), 13–31.

/// CHAPTER 7

1. Russell, J. A. (1978). Evidence of convergent validity of the dimensions of affect. *Journal of Personality and Social Psychology, 36*, 1152–1168; Russell, J. A. (1980). A circumplex model of affect. *Journal of Personality and Social Psychology, 39*, 1161–1178; Russell, J. A. (1983). Pancultural aspects of the human conceptual organization of emotions. *Journal of Personality and Social Psychology, 45*, 1281–1288.

2. Plutchik, R. (1984). Emotions: A general psychoevolutionary theory. In K. R. Scherer & P. Ekman (Eds.), *Approaches to emotion* (pp. 197–219). Hillsdale, NJ: Erlbaum.

3. Ury, W. (2010, November). *The walk from "no" to "yes."* Retrieved from http://www.ted.com/talks/william_ury.html

4. Barrett, L. F. (2017). *How emotions are made: The secret life of the brain*. Boston, MA: Mariner Books.

5. Yoo, J., & Miyamoto, Y. (2018). Cultural fit of emotions and health implications: A psychosocial resources model. *Social and Personality Psychology Compass, 12, 2*, https://doi.org/10.1111/spc3.12372

6. Pressman, S. D., Gallagher, M. D., & Lopez, S. (2013). Is the emotion-health connection a "first-world problem"? *Psychological Science, 24*, 544–549.

7. Hochschild, A. R. (1983). *The managed heart: Commercialization of human feeling*. Berkeley: University of California Press.

8. Gerth, H., & Mills, C. W. (1964). *Character and social structure: The psychology of social institutions*. New York, NY: Harcourt, Brace & World.

9. Goleman, D. (2006). *Social intelligence: The new science of human relationships*. New York, NY: Bantam.

10. Leggitt, J. S., & Gibbs, R. W. (2000). Emotional reactions to verbal irony. *Discourse Processes, 29*, 1–24.

11. Planalp, S. (1999). *Communicating emotion: Social, moral, and cultural processes*. Cambridge, England: Cambridge University Press.

12. Miller, K. I. (2007). Compassionate communication in the workplace: Exploring processes of noticing, connecting, and responding. *Journal of Applied Communication Research, 35*, 223–245.

13. Gottman, J. M., Katz, L. F., & Hooven, C. (1997). *Meta-emotion: How families communicate emotionally*. Mahwah, NJ: Erlbaum.

14. Kayyal, M. H., & Russell, J. A. (2013). Language and emotion: Certain English–Arabic translations are not equivalent. *Journal of Language and Social Psychology, 32*, 261–271.

15. Planalp, S., & Fitness, J. (1999). Thinking/feeling about social and personal relationships. *Journal of Social and Personal Relationships, 16*, 731–750.

16. Seiter, J. S., & Bruschke, J. (2007). Deception and emotion: The effects of motivation, relationship type, and sex on expected feelings of guilt and shame following acts of deception in United States and Chinese samples. *Communication Studies, 58,* 1–16.

17. Fischer, A. H. (2000). Preface. In A. H. Fischer (Ed.), *Gender and emotion: Social psychological perspectives* (pp. ix–x). Cambridge, England: Cambridge University Press.

18. MacArthur, H. J., & Shields, S. A. (2015). There's no crying in baseball: Or is there? Male athletes, tears, and masculinity in North America. *Emotion Review, 7,* 39–46.

19. Hall, J. A., Carter, J. D., & Horgan, T. G. (2000). Gender differences in nonverbal communication of emotion. In A. H. Fischer (Ed.), *Gender and emotion: Social psychological perspectives* (pp. 97–117). Cambridge, England: Cambridge University Press.

20. Dickson, F. C., & Walker, K. L. (2001). The expression of emotion in later-life married men. *Qualitative Research Reports in Communication, 2,* 66–71.

21. Stearns, P. N. (1994). *American cool.* New York, NY: New York University Press.

22. Rourke, L., Anderson, T., Garrison, D. R., & Archer, W. (2001). Assessing social presence in asynchronous text-based computer conferencing. *Journal of Distance Education, 14,* 50–71.

23. Turkle, S. (2015, March 5). *Face-to-face friendships involve real emotions.* Retrieved from https://www.nytimes.com/roomfordebate/2015/03/05/real-relationships-in-a-digital-world/only-face-to-face-friendships-involve-real-emotions

24. Markle, A. (2015, March 5). *Increased social support, even online, is beneficial.* Retrieved from https://www.nytimes.com/roomfordebate/2015/03/05/real-relationships-in-a-digital-world/only-face-to-face-friendships-involve-real-emotions

25. Rodríguez-Hidalgo, C., Tan, E. S. H., & Verlegh, P. W. J. (2017). Expressing emotions in blogs. *Computers in Human Behavior, 73,* 638–649.

26. Waterloo, S. F., Baumgartner, S. E., Peter, J., & Valenburg, P. M. (2018). Norms of online expressions of emotion: Comparing Facebook, Twitter, Instagram, and WhatsApp. *New Media & Society, 20*(5), 1813–1831.

27. Schuman, R. (2017, December 13). How 2017 became all about the schadenfreude of watching powerful men get served. *Quartz.* Retrieved from https://qz.com/1154544/2017-was-our-year-of-schadenfreude/

28. Spiegel, D., & Kimerling, R. (2001). Group psychotherapy for women with breast cancer: Relationships among social support, emotional expression, and survival. In C. D. Ryff & B. H. Singer (Eds.), *Emotion, social relationships, and health* (pp. 97–123). New York, NY: Oxford University Press.

29. Holder, M. D, Love, A. B., & Timoney, L. R. (2015). The poor subjective well-being associated with alexithymia is mediated by romantic relationships. *Journal of Happiness Studies, 16,* 117–133.

30. Cherwin, K. A. (2011, July 25). *Using emotional intelligence to teach.* Retrieved from https://www.higheredjobs.com/Articles/articleDisplay.cfm?ID=285

/// CHAPTER 8

1. Song, H., Kim, J., & Park, N. (2018). I know my professor: Teacher self-disclosure in online education and a mediating role of social presence. Advance online publication. *International Journal of Human-Computer Interaction.* doi: 10.1080/10447318.2018.1455126

2. Sprecher, S., & Hendricks, S. S. (2004). Self-disclosure in intimate relationships: Association with individual and relationship characteristics over time. *Journal of Social and Clinical Psychology, 23*(6), 857–877.

3. Dindia, K. (1998). Going into and coming out of the closet: The dialectics of stigma disclosure. In B. M. Montgomery & L. A. Baxter (Eds.), *Dialectical approaches to studying personal relationships* (pp. 83–108). Mahwah, NJ: Erlbaum.

4. Brown, R. D., & Weigel, D. J. (2018). Exploring a contextual model of sexual self-disclosure and sexual satisfaction. *The Journal of Sex Research, 55*(2), 202–213.

5. Hamid, P. N. (2000). Self-disclosure and occupational stress in Chinese professionals. *Psychological Reports, 87,* 1075–1082.

6. Woods, S., Lambert, N., Brown, P., Fincham, & May, R. (2015). "I'm so excited for you!" How an enthusiastic responding intervention enhances close relationships. *Journal of Social and Personal Relationships, 32,* 24–40.

7. Pennebaker, J. W., Barger, S. D., & Tiebout, J. (1989). Trauma and health among Holocaust survivors. *Psychosomatic Medicine, 51,* 577–589.

8. Osborn, P., Berg, C. A., Hughes, A. E., Pham, P., & Wiebe, D. J. (2013). What Mom and Dad don't know CAN hurt you: Adolescent disclosure to and secrecy from parents about type 1 diabetes. *Journal of Pediatric Psychology, 38*(2), 141–150.

9. Cole, S. W., Kemeny, M. E., Taylor, S. E., Visscher, B. R., & Fahey, J. L. (1996). Accelerated course of human immunodeficiency virus infection in gay men who conceal their homosexual identity. *Psychosomatic Medicine, 58,* 219–231.

10. Tardy, C. H. (2000). Self-disclosure and health: Revisiting Sidney Jourard's hypothesis. In S. Petronio (Ed.), *Balancing the secrets of private disclosures* (pp. 111–122). Mahwah, NJ: Erlbaum.

11. Sprecher, S., & Treger, S. (2015). The benefits of turn-taking reciprocal self-disclosure in get-acquainted interactions. *Personal Relationships, 22*(3), 460–475; Sprecher, S., Treger, S., Wondra, J. D., Hilaire, N., & Wallpe, K. (2013). Taking turns: Reciprocal self-disclosure promotes liking in initial interactions. *Journal of Experimental Social Psychology, 49*(5), 860–866.

12. Ijams, K., & Miller, L. D. (2000). Perceptions of dream-disclosure: An exploratory study. *Communication Studies, 51,* 135–148.

13. Derlega, V. J., Metts, S., Petronio, S., & Margulis, S. T. (1993). *Self-disclosure.* Newbury Park, CA: Sage.

14. Stone, L. B., & Gibb, B. E. (2015). Brief report: Preliminary evidence that co-rumination fosters adolescents' depression risk by increasing rumination. *Journal of Adolescence, 38,* 1–4.

15. Sprecher, S., & Hendricks, S. S. (2004). Self-disclosure in intimate relationships: Association with individual and relationship characteristics over time. *Journal of Social and Clinical Psychology, 23*(6), 857–877.

16. Hastings, S. O. (2000). "Egocasting" in the avoidance of disclosure: An intercultural perspective. In S. Petronio (Ed.), *Balancing the secrets of private disclosures* (pp. 235–248). Mahwah, NJ: Erlbaum.

17. Barkowiak, A., & Cao, M. (2018, June 22). Coming out to my parents in China by video. *The New York Times.* Retrieved from https://www.nytimes.com/2018/06/22/lens/coming-out-video-china.html

18. Quek, K. M.-T., & Fitzpatrick, J. (2013). Cultural values, self-disclosure, and conflict tactics as predictors of marital

satisfaction among Singaporean husbands and wives. *Family Journal, 21,* 208–216.

19. Schwartz, A. L., Galliher, R. V., & Rodríguez, M. M. D. (2011). Self-disclosure in Latinos' intercultural and intracultural friendships and acquaintanceships: Links with collectivism, ethnic identity, and acculturation. *Cultural Diversity and Ethnic Minority Psychology, 17,* 116–121.

20. Sheldon, P. (2013). Examining gender differences in self-disclosure on Facebook versus face-to-face. *Journal of Social Media in Society, 2,* 88–104.

21. Waldman, K. (2013, December 9). Society tells men that friendship is girly. Men respond by not having any friends. *Slate.* Retrieved from http://www.slate .com/blogs/xx_factor/2013/12/09/white_ heterosexual_men_can_t_have_friends_ gender_norms_are_to_ blame

22. Dindia, K., & Allen, M. (1992). Sex-differences in self-disclosure: A meta-analysis. *Psychological Bulletin, 112,* 106–124; Mathews, A., Derlega, V. J., & Morrow, J. (2006). What is highly personal information and how is it related to self-disclosure decision-making? The perspective of college students. *Communication Research Reports, 23,* 85–92.

23. Davis, K. (2012). Friendship 2.0: Adolescents' experiences of belonging and self-disclosure online. *Journal of Adolescence, 35,* 1527–1536.

24. Mesch, G. S. (2012). Is online trust and trust in social institutions associated with online disclosure of identifiable information online? *Computers in Human Behavior, 28*(4), 1471–1477.

25. Hollenbaugh, E. E., & Everett, M. K. (2013). The effects of anonymity on self-disclosure in blogs: An application of the online disinhibition effect. *Journal of Computer-Mediated Communication, 18,* 283–302.

26. Moors, R., & Webber, R. (2013). The dance of disclosure: Online self-disclosure of sexual assault. *Qualitative Social Work, 12,* 799–815.

27. Pan, W., Feng, B., & Wingate, V.S. (2017). What you say is what you get: How self-disclosure in support seeking affects language use in support provision in online support forums. *Journal of Language and Social Psychology, 37*(1), 3–27; Bazarova, N. N., & Choi, Y. H. (2014). Self-disclosure in social media: Extending the functional approach to disclosure motivations and characteristics on social network sites. *Journal of Communication, 64*(4), 635–657; Tait, S., & Jeske, D. (2015) Hello stranger! Trust and self-disclosure effects on online information sharing. *International Journal of Cyber Behavior, Psychology and Learning, 5*(1), 42–55; Levontin, L., & Yom-Tov, E. (2017). Negative self-disclosure on the web: The role of guilt relief. *Frontiers in Psychology.* Retrieved from https:// www.frontiersin.org/articles/10.3389/ fpsyg.2017.01068/full

28. Dell'Antonia, K. (2013, November 21). *A stillbirth's living silver linings* [Blog post]. Retrieved from https://parenting.blogs. nytimes.com/2013/11/21/a-stillbirths-living-silver-linings/

29. Petronio, S. (2002). *Boundaries of privacy: Dialectics of disclosure.* Albany: SUNY Press.

30. Petronio, S. (2010). Communication privacy management theory: What do we know about family privacy regulation? *Journal of Family Theory & Review, 2,* 175–196.

31. Altman, I., & Taylor, D. (1973). *Social penetration: The development of interpersonal relationships.* New York, NY: Holt, Rinehart & Winston.

32. Helens-Hart, R. (2017). Females' (non) disclosure of minority sexual identities in the workplace from a communication privacy management perspective. *Communication Studies, 68*(5), 607–623.

/// CHAPTER 9

1. Folger, J. P., Poole, M. S., & Stutman, R. K. (2018). *Working through conflict: Strategies for relationships, groups, and organizations,* (8th ed.). New York, NY: Routledge.

2. Sillars, A. L., Roberts, L., Leonard, K. E., & Dun, T. (2000). Cognition during marital conflict: The relationship of thought and talk. *Journal of Social and Personal Relationships, 17,* 479–502.

3. Khazan, O. (2013, December 23). Why families fight during holidays: A time for good food, comfort, joy, and . . . "you could be so pretty if you only lost a little weight." *The Atlantic.* Retrieved from http://www.theatlantic.com/health/ archive/2013/12/why-families-fight-during-holidays/282584/

4. Wright, R. R., Mohr, C. D., & Sinclair, R. R. (2014). Conflict on the treatment floor: An investigation of interpersonal conflict experienced by nurses. *Journal of Research in Nursing, 19,* 26–37.

5. Carr, K., Schrodt, P., & Ledbetter, A. M. (2012). Rumination, conflict intensity, and perceived resolvability as predictors of motivation and likelihood of continuing serial arguments. *Western Journal of Communication, 76,* 480–502.

6. Honeycutt, J. M. (2010). Forgive but don't forget: Correlates of rumination about conflict. In J. M. Honeycutt (Ed.), *Imagine that: Studies in imagined interaction* (pp. 17–29). Cresskill, NJ: Hampton Press.

7. Young, S. L., Bippus, A. M., & Dunbar, N. E. (2015). Comparing romantic partners' perceptions of hurtful communication during conflict conversations. *Southern Communication Journal, 80,* 39–54.

8. Keener, E., Strough, J., & DiDonato, L. (2012). Gender differences and similarities in strategies for managing conflict with friends and romantic partners. *Sex Roles, 67,* 83–97.

9. Rudawsky, D. J., Lundgren, D. C., & Grasha, A. F. (1999). Competitive and collaborative responses to negative feedback. *International Journal of Conflict Management, 10,* 172–190.

10. Messman, S. J., & Mikesell, R. L. (2000). Competition and interpersonal conflict in dating relationships. *Communication Reports, 13,* 21–34.

11. Keener, E. et al., Gender differences and similarities in strategies for managing conflict with friends and romantic partners, 2012.

12. Gayle, B. M., Preiss, R. W., & Allen, M. (2014). Where are we now? A meta-analytic review of sex difference expectations for conflict management strategy selection. In N. A. Burrell, M. Allen, B. M. Gayle, & R. W. Preiss (Eds.), *Managing interpersonal conflict: Advances through meta-analysis* (pp. 226–247). New York, NY: Routledge.

13. Kim, E. J., Yamaguchi, A., Kim, M.-S., & Miyahara, A. (2015). Effects of taking conflict personally on conflict management styles across cultures. *Personality and Individual Differences, 72,* 143–149.

14. Zhang, Q. (2007). Family communication patterns and conflict styles in Chinese parent-child relationships. *Communication Quarterly, 55,* 113–128.

15. Croucher, S. M., Bruno, A., McGrath, P., Adams, C., McGahan, C., Suits, A., & Huckins, A. (2012). Conflict styles and high-low context cultures: A cross-cultural extension. *Communication Research Reports, 29,* 64–73.

16. Troy, A. B., Lewis-Smith, J., & Laurenceau, J.-P. (2006). Interracial and intraracial romantic relationships: The

search for differences in satisfaction, conflict, and attachment style. *Journal of Social and Personal Relationship, 23,* 65–80.

17. Reznik, R. M., Miller, C. W., Roloff, M. E., & Gaze, C. M. (2015). The impact of demand/withdraw patterns on health in emerging adults' serial arguments with parents. *Communication Research Reports, 32,* 35–44.

18. Blake, R. R., & Mouton, J. S. (1964). *The managerial grid: Key orientations for achieving production through people.* Houston, TX: Gulf.

19. Ting-Toomey, S., & Oetzel, J.G. (2001). *Managing intercultural conflict effectively.* Thousand Oaks, CA: Sage.

20. West, R., & Turner, L. H. (2019). Coming to terms with bullying: A communication perspective. In R. West & C. Beck (Eds.), *Routledge handbook of communication and bullying* (pp. 3–12). New York, NY: Routledge.

21. Bullying Statistics. (2014). *Cyberbullying statistics.* Retrieved from http://www.bullyingstatistics.org/content/cyber-bullying-statistics.html

22. Daily Herald (Provo, UT). (2013, May 19). *Scared in school: Bullying statistics.* Retrieved from http://www.heraldextra.com/news/local/education/precollegiate/scared-in-school-bullying-statistics/article_74844177-1669-5ef5-9609-2c7234e92987.html

23. Tracy, S. J., Alberts, J. K., & Rivera, K. D. (2007, January 31). *How to bust the office bully* (Report # 0701, The Project for Wellness and Work-Life, The Hugh Downs School of Human Communication). Retrieved from https://www.sarahjtracy.com/wp-content/uploads/2015/11/howtobusttheofficebully1.pdf

24. Olson, L. N. (2002). Compliance gaining strategies of individuals experiencing "common couple violence." *Qualitative Research Reports in Communication, 3,* 7–14; Olson, L. N. (2008). Relational control-motivated aggression: A theoretical framework for identifying various types of violent couples. In D. D. Cahn (Ed.), *Family violence: Communication processes* (pp. 27–47). Thousand Oaks, CA: Sage.

25. Insetta, E. R., Akers, A. Y., Miller, E., Yonas, M. A., Burke, J. G., Hintz, L., & Chang, J. C. (2015). Intimate partner violence victims as mothers: Their messages and strategies for communicating with children to break the cycle of violence. *Journal of Interpersonal Violence, 30,* 703–724.

26. Simon, T. R., Miller, S., Gorman-Smith, D., Orpinas, P., & Sullivan, T. (2010). Physical dating violence norms and behavior among sixth-grade students in four US sites. *The Journal of Early Adolescence, 30,* 395–409.

27. Insetta, E. R. et al., Intimate partner violence victims as mothers: Their messages and strategies for communicating with children to break the cycle of violence, 2015.

28. Gottman, J. M., & DeClaire, J. (2001). *The relationship cure.* New York, NY: Three Rivers Press; Benson, K. (2017, October 4). *The magic relationship ratio, according to science.* Retrieved from https://www.gottman.com/blog/the-magic-relationship-ratio-according-science/

29. Cupach, W. R., & Canary, D. G. (2000). *Competence in interpersonal conflict.* Prospect Heights, IL: Waveland Press.

30. Folger, J. P. et al., *Working through conflict: Strategies for relationships, groups, and organizations,* 2018.

31. Vogel, D. L., Murphy, M. J., Werner-Wilson, R. J., Cutrona, C. E., & Seeman, J. (2007). Sex differences in the use of demand and withdraw behavior in marriage: Examining the social structure hypothesis. *Journal of Counseling Psychology, 54,* 165–177.

/// CHAPTER 10

1. Maslow, A. H. (1968). *Toward a psychology of being.* New York, NY: Van Nostrand Reinhold.

2. National Council on Aging. (2013, July). *The United States of Aging Survey 2013.* Retrieved from http://www.ncoa.org/assets/files/pdf/united-states-of-aging/2013-survey/USA13-Full-Report.pdf

3. Lannutti, P. J. (2013). Same-sex marriage and privacy management: Examining couples' communication with family members. *Journal of Family Communication, 13,* 60–75.

4. Hinde, R. A. (1995). A suggested structure for a science of relationships. *Personal Relationships, 2,* 1–15.

5. Patterson, G. E., Ward, D. B., & Brown, T. B. (2013). Relationship scripts: How young women develop and maintain same-sex romantic relationships. *Journal of GLBT Family Studies, 9,* 179–201.

6. Nelson, M. K. (2014). Whither fictive kin? Or, what's in a name? *Journal of Family Issues, 35,* 201–222.

7. Lakoff, G. (2013). Neural social science. In D. D. Franks & J. H. Turner (Eds.), *Handbook of neurosociology* (pp. 9–25). Amsterdam, The Netherlands: Springer;

Lakoff, G., & Johnson, M. (1980). *Metaphors we live by.* Chicago, IL: University of Chicago Press.

8. Carter, P. J., & Gibbs, R. J. (2013). *Using horrific body and avatar creation as an extension of the Proteus effect.* Retrieved from http://eprints.hud.ac.uk; Cash, T. F., & Derlega, V. J. (1978). The matching hypothesis: Physical attractiveness among same-sexed friends. *Personality and Social Psychology Bulletin, 4,* 240–243.

9. Johnson, M. D. (2016). *Great myths of intimate relationships: Dating, sex, and marriage.* New York, NY: Wiley; Montoya, R. M., & Horton, R. S. (2013). A meta-analytic investigation of the processes underlying the similarity-attraction effect. *Journal of Social and Personal Relationships, 30*(1), 64–94.

10. Allendorf, K. (2013). Schemas of marital change: From arranged marriages to eloping for love. *Journal of Marriage and Family, 75,* 453–469.

11. Khazan, O. (2013, December 11). A psychologist's guide to online dating: Can we predict romantic prospects just from looking at a face? *The Atlantic.* Retrieved from http://www.theatlantic.com/health/archive/2013/12/a-psychologists-guide-to-online-dating/282225/

12. Nolen-Hoeksema, S., Gilbert, K., & Hilt, L. (2015). Rumination and self-regulation in adolescence. In G. Oettingen & P. Gollwitzer (Eds.), *Self-regulation in adolescence* (The Jacobs Foundation Series on Adolescence, pp. 311–331). Cambridge, England: Cambridge University Press. doi:10.1017/CBO9781139565790.015

13. Dalessandro, C., & Wilkins, A. C. (2017). Blinded by love: Women, men, and gendered age in relationships stories. *Gender & Society, 31*(1), 96–118.

14. Hartwell, E. E., Serovich, J. M., Reed, S. J., Boisvert, D., & Falbo, T. (2017). A systematic review of gay, lesbian, and bisexual research samples in couple and family therapy journals. *Journal of Marital and Family Therapy, 43*(3), 482–501.

15. Silverstein, J., & Lasky, M. (2004). *Online dating for dummies.* Indianapolis, IN: Wiley.

16. Fox, J., Warber, K. M., & Makstaller, D. C. (2013). The role of Facebook in romantic relationship development: An exploration of Knapp's relational stage model. *Journal of Social and Personal Relationships, 30,* 771–794.

17. Yang, C., Brown, B. B., & Braun, M. T. (2014). From Facebook to cell calls: Layers of electronic intimacy in college students' interpersonal relationships. *New Media & Society, 16,* 5–23.

18. Walther, J. B. (1996). Computer-mediated communication: Impersonal, interpersonal, and hyperpersonal interaction. *Communication Research*, *23*, 3–43; Walther, J. B. (2011). Theories of computer-mediated communication and interpersonal relations. In M. L. Knapp & J. A. Daly (Eds.), *The handbook of interpersonal communication* (pp. 443–479). Thousand Oaks, CA: Sage.

19. Kreager, D. A., Cavanagh, S. E., Yen, J., & Yu, M. (2014). Where have all the good men gone? Gendered interactions in online dating. *Journal of Marriage and Family, 76*, 387–410.

20. Knapp, M. L., & Vangelisti, A. L. (2000). *Interpersonal communication and human relationships*. Boston, MA: Allyn & Bacon.

21. Bodie, G. D., Honeycutt, J. M., & Vickery, A. J. (2013). An analysis of the correspondence between imagined interaction attributes and functions. *Human Communication Research*, *39*, 157–183; Honeycutt, J. M. (2003). *Imagined interactions*. Cresskill, NJ: Hampton Press.

22. Yoshimura, C. G., & Galvin, K. M.(2018). General systems theory: A compelling view of family life. In D. O. Braithwaite, E. A. Suter, & K. Floyd (Eds.), *Engaging theories in family communication: Multiple perspectives* (2nd ed., pp. 164–174). New York, NY: Routledge; von Bertalanffy, L. (1968). *General system theory*. New York, NY: Braziller.

23. Baxter, L. A. (2011). *Voicing relationships: A dialogic perspective*. Thousand Oaks, CA: Sage; Suter, E. A., & Seurer, L. M. (2018). Relational dialectics theory: Realizing the dialogic potential of family communication. In D. O. Braithwaite, E. A. Suter, & K. Floyd (Eds.), *Engaging theories in family communication: Multiple perspectives* (2nd ed., pp. 244–254). New York, NY: Routledge.

24. Baxter, L. A. (1988). A dialectical perspective on communication strategies in relationship development. In S. Duck (Ed.), *A handbook of personal relationships* (pp. 257–273). New York, NY: Wiley; Baxter, *Voicing relationships*, 2011.

25. Roloff, M. E. (1981). *Interpersonal communication: The social exchange approach*. Beverly Hills, CA: Sage.

26. Bell, R. A., & Daly, J. A. (1984). The affinity-seeking function of communication. *Communication Monographs*, *51*, 91–115.

27. Gibb, J. (1961). Defensive communication. *Journal of Communication*, *11*, 141–148; Gibb, J. (1964). Climate for trust formation. In Bradford, J. Gibb, & K. Benne (Eds.), *T-group theory and laboratory method* (pp. 279–309). New York, NY: Wiley; Gibb, J. (1970). Sensitivity training as a medium for personal growth and improved interpersonal relationships. *Interpersonal Development*, *1*, 6–31.

/// CHAPTER 11

1. Serewicz, M. C. M., Dickson, F. C., Morrison, J. H. T. A., & Poole, L. L. (2007). Family privacy orientation, relational maintenance, and family satisfaction in young adults' family relationships. *Journal of Family Communication*, *7*, 123–142.

2. Kreppner, K., & Lerner, R. M. (2013). *Family systems and lifespan development*. Hillsdale, NJ: Erlbaum.

3. Turner, L. H., & West, R. (2015). The challenge of defining "family." In L. H. Turner & R. West (Eds.), *The SAGE handbook of family communication* (pp. 10–25). Thousand Oaks, CA: Sage.

4. Turner & West, The challenge of defining "family," 2015.

5. Floyd, K., Mikkelson, A. C., & Judd, J. (2006). Defining the family through relationships. In L. H. Turner & R. West (Eds.), *The family communication sourcebook* (pp. 21–39). Thousand Oaks, CA: Sage.

6. Galvin, K. M. (2006). Diversity's impact on defining the family: Discourse-dependence and identity. In L. H. Turner & R. West (Eds.), *The family communication sourcebook* (pp. 3–19). Thousand Oaks, CA: Sage.

7. Turner & West, The challenge of defining "family," 2015.

8. Kellas, J. K., & Kranstuber-Horstman, H. (2015). Communicated narrative sense-making: Understanding family narratives, storytelling, and the construction of meaning through a communicative lens. In L. H. Turner & R. West (Eds.), *The SAGE handbook of family communication* (pp. 76–90). Thousand Oaks, CA: Sage.

9. Langellier, K. M., & Peterson, E. E. (2006). Narrative performance theory: Telling stories, doing family. In D. O. Braithwaite & L. A. Baxter (Eds.), *Engaging theories in family communication* (pp. 99–114). Thousand Oaks, CA: Sage.

10. Thomas, P. M. (2013, October). *Researching African American family history*. Harrisonburg, VA: Coming to the Table, Eastern Mennonite University. Retrieved from http://comingtothetable. org /wp-content/uploads/2013/10/07-Researching_African_American_Family_ History.pdf

11. Schulte, B. (2014, September 4). *Unlike in the 1950s, there is no 'typical' U.S. family today*. Retrieved from https:// www.washingtonpost.com/news/local/ wp/2014/09/04/for-the-first-time-since-the-1950s-there-is-no-typical-u-s-family/?utm_term=.6feb894792f0

12. Cohn, D., Livingston, G., & Wang, W. (2014, April 8). *After decades of decline, a rise in stay-at-home mothers*. Retrieved from http://www.pewsocialtrends .org/2014/04/08/after-decades-of-decline-a-rise-in-stay-at-home-mothers/

13. Fitzpatrick, M. A. (1988). *Between husbands and wives: Communication in marriage*. Thousand Oaks, CA: Sage; Ivy, D. K. (2012). *GenderSpeak: Personal effectiveness in gender communication* (5th ed.). Boston, MA: Pearson.

14. Chen, V. (2013, December 9). When stay-at-home husbands are embarrassing to their wives. *Time*. Retrieved from http://ideas.time.com/2013/12/09 / the-househusbands-of-wall-street/

15. Newport, F. (2018, May 22). In U.S., estimate of LGBT population rises to 4.5%. Retrieved from https://news. gallup.com/poll/234863/estimate-lgbt-population-rises.aspx

16. U.S. Census Bureau. (2013). Frequently asked questions about same-sex couple households. Retrieved from https:// www2.census.gov/topics/families/same-sex-couples/faq/sscplfactsheet-final.pdf

17. West, R., & Turner, L. H. (1995). Communication in lesbian and gay families: Building a descriptive base. In T. J. Socha & G. Stamp (Eds.), *Parents, children, and communication: Frontiers of theory and research* (pp. 147–169). Mahwah, NJ: Erlbaum.

18. Suter, E. A. (2015). Communication in gay and lesbian families. In L. H. Turner & R. West (Eds.), *The SAGE handbook of family communication* (pp. 235–247). Thousand Oaks, CA: Sage.

19. Oswald, R. F. (2003). A member of the wedding? Heterosexism and family ritual. *Journal of Lesbian Studies*, *7*(2), 107–131; Oswald, R. F. (2014). *Lesbian rites: Symbolic acts and the power of community*. New York, NY: Routledge.

20. Goldberg, A. E., Smith, J. Z., & Perry-Jenkins, M. (2012). The division of labor in lesbian, gay, and heterosexual new adoptive parents. *Journal of Marriage and Family*, *74*(4), 812–828.

21. Landale, N. S., Thomas, K. J., & Van Hook, J. (2011). The living arrangement of children in immigrant families. *The Future of Children*, *21*, 43–70.

22. Cohn, D., & Passel, J. S. (2018, April 5). *A record 64 million Americans live in multigenerational households*. Retrieved from http://www.pewresearch.org/fact-tank/2018/04/05/a-record-64-million-americans-live-in-multigenerational-households/

23. U.S. Census Bureau. (2011). *Older Americans month*. Retrieved from http://www.census.gov/ newsroom/releases/archives/facts_for_features_special_editions/cb08-ff14.html

24. Fry, R. (2018, May 24). *For first time in modern era, living with parents edges out other living arrangements for 18- to 34-year-olds*. Retrieved from http://www.pewsocialtrends.org/2016/05/24/for-first-time-in-modern-era-living-with-parents-edges-out-other-living-arrangements-for-18-to-34-year-olds/

25. Harwood, J. (2004). Relational, role, and social identity as expressed in grandparents' personal web sites. *Communication Studies, 55*, 300–318. doi: 10.1080/10510970409388621

26. U.S. Census Bureau. (2017, June 8). Facts for features: Father's Day: June 18, 2017. Retrieved from https://www.census.gov/newsroom/facts-for-features/2017/cb17-ff12-fathers-day.html; U.S. Census Bureau. (2017, May 12). Facts for features: Mother's Day: May 14, 2017. Retrieved fromhttps://www.census.gov/newsroom/facts-for-features/2017/cb17-ff09-mothers-day.html

27. Ahrons, C. R. (2011). Divorce: An unscheduled family transition. In M. McGoldrick, B. Carter, & N. Garcia Preto (Eds.), *The expanded family life cycle: Individual, family, and social perspectives* (pp. 292–306). Boston, MA: Allyn & Bacon.

28. Styles, R. (2013, September 29). Looking for love? Try the office! *Daily Mail* (UK). Retrieved from http://www.dailymail.co.uk/femail/article-2437181/Relationships-begin-workplace-likely-result-marriage-new-study-reveals.html

29. DeFrancisco, V. P., & Palczewski, C. (2014). *Gender in communication: A critical introduction* (2nd ed.). Thousand Oaks, CA: Sage.

30. Clark, D. (2013). *Debunking the "no friends at work" rule: Why friend-friendly workplaces are the future*. Retrieved from http://dorieclark.com/debunking-the-no-friends-at-work-rule-why-friend-friendly-workplaces-are-the-future/

31. Hall, J. A. (2011). Sex differences in friendship expectations: A meta-analysis. *Journal of Social and Personal Relationships, 28*, 723–747.

32. Selman, R. (1981). The child as friendship philosopher. In S. Asher & J. M. Gottman (Eds.), *The development of children's friendships* (pp. 242–272). New York, NY: Cambridge University Press.

33. Curtis-Tweed, P. (2011). Selman's stages of friendship development. In S. Goldstein & J. Neglieri (Eds.), *Encyclopedia of child behavior and development* (pp. 1327–1328). New York, NY: Springer.

34. Kennedy-Moore, E. (2012). *Children's growing friendships*. Retrieved from http://www.psychologytoday.com/blog/growing-friendships/201202/childrens-growing-friendships

35. Rawlins, W. K. (1992, 2008). *Friendship matters: Communication, dialectics, and the life course*. New York, NY: Aldine de Gruyter.

36. Sternberg, R. J. (1998). *Cupid's arrow*. New York, NY: Cambridge University Press; Sternberg, R. J. (2006). *Cognitive psychology*. Belmont, CA: Thomson/Wadsworth.

37. Abela, A., Walker, J., & Pryor, J. (2013). *Marriage and divorce in the Western world*. Oxford, England: Wiley-Blackwell.

38. Ackerman, J. M., Griskevicius, V., & Li, N. (2011). Let's get serious: Communicating commitment in romantic relationships. *Journal of Personality and Social Psychology, 100*, 1079–1094.

39. Levine, T. R., Aune, K. S., & Park, H. S. (2006). Love styles and communication in relationships: Partner preferences, initiation, and intensification. *Communication Quarterly, 54*, 465–486.

40. Bachman, G. F., & Guerrero, L. K. (2006). Relational quality and communicative responses following hurtful events in dating relationships: An expectancy violations analysis. *Journal of Social and Personal Relationships, 23*, 943–963.

41. Knobloch, L. K., Miller, L. E., Bond, B. J., & Mannone, S. E. (2007). Relational uncertainty and message processing in marriage. *Communication Monographs, 74*, 154–180.

42. Knobloch, L. K., & Theiss, J. A. (2014). Relational turbulence with military couples during reintegration following deployment. In S. M. Wadsworth & D. Riggs (Eds.), *Military deployment and its consequences for families* (pp. 37–60). New York, NY: Springer.

43. Suter, E. A. (2015). Communication in gay and lesbian families. In L. H. Turner & R. West (Eds.), *The SAGE handbook of family communication* (pp. 235–247). Thousand Oaks, CA: Sage; Thompson, J., & Collier, M. J. (2006). Toward contingent understandings of intersecting identifications among selected U.S. interracial couples: Integrating interpretive and critical views. *Communication Quarterly, 54*, 487–507; Levine, T. R., Aune, K. S., & Park, H. S. (2006). Love styles and communication in relationships: Partner preferences, initiation, and intensification. *Communication Quarterly, 54*, 465–486.